SHOP PRICE
£45.00

ENGLISH DRY-BODIED
STONEWARE

Wedgwood and Contemporary Manufacturers 1774 to 1830

ENGLISH DRY-BODIED
STONEWARE

Wedgwood and Contemporary Manufacturers 1774 to 1830

Diana Edwards and Rodney Hampson

ANTIQUE COLLECTORS' CLUB

ISBN 1 85149 288 7

British Library Cataloguing-in-Publication Data
A catalogue record for this book is available from the British Library

FRONTISPIECE: *Tripod vase*, solid blue jasper with white jasper reliefs, 11¼ inches high, c. 1791–92. (Beeson
Collection of Wedgwood, Birmingham Museum of Art, Alabama.) See also Colour Plate 20a, page 21.
TITLE-PAGE: *Teapot*, red stoneware following on Yixing prototypes, with black basalt relief and Fo lion finial,
5 inches high, c. 1805. (Coles collection, photograph by Bill Coles.) See also Colour Plate 59, page 40.

Printed in England
by the Antique Collectors' Club Ltd., Woodbridge, Suffolk IP12 1DS
on Consort Royal Era Satin from Donside Mill, Aberdeen, Scotland

Antique Collectors' Club

THE ANTIQUE COLLECTORS' CLUB was formed in 1966 and quickly grew to a five figure membership spread throughout the world. It publishes the only independently run monthly antiques magazine, *Antique Collecting*, which caters for those collectors who are interested in widening their knowledge of antiques, both by greater awareness of quality and by discussion of the factors which influence the price that is likely to be asked. The Antique Collectors' Club pioneered the provision of information on prices for collectors and the magazine still leads in the provision of detailed articles on a variety of subjects.

It was in response to the enormous demand for information on 'what to pay' that the price guide series was introduced in 1968 with the first edition of *The Price Guide to Antique Furniture* (completely revised 1978 and 1989), a book which broke new ground by illustrating the more common types of antique furniture, the sort that collectors could buy in shops and at auctions rather than the rare museum pieces which had previously been used (and still to a large extent are used) to make up the limited amount of illustrations in books published by commercial publishers. Many other price guides have followed, all copiously illustrated, and greatly appreciated by collectors for the valuable information they contain, quite apart from prices. The Price Guide Series heralded the publication of many standard works of reference on art and antiques. *The Dictionary of British Art* (now in six volumes), *The Pictorial Dictionary of British 19th Century Furniture Design*, *Oak Furniture* and *Early English Clocks* were followed by many deeply researched reference works such as *The Directory of Gold and Silversmiths*, providing new information. Many of these books are now accepted as the standard work of reference on their subject.

The Antique Collectors' Club has widened its list to include books on gardens and architecture. All the Club's publications are available through bookshops world wide and a full catalogue of all these titles is available free of charge from the addresses below.

Club membership, open to all collectors, costs little. Members receive free of charge *Antique Collecting*, the Club's magazine (published ten times a year), which contains well-illustrated articles dealing with the practical aspects of collecting not normally dealt with by magazines. Prices, features of value, investment potential, fakes and forgeries are all given prominence in the magazine.

Among other facilities available to members are private buying and selling facilities and the opportunity to meet other collectors at their local antique collectors' club. There are over eighty in Britain and more than a dozen overseas. Members may also buy the Club's publications at special pre-publication prices.

As its motto implies, the Club is an organisation designed to help collectors get the most out of their hobby: it is informal and friendly and gives enormous enjoyment to all concerned.

For Collectors — By Collectors — About Collecting

ANTIQUE COLLECTORS' CLUB
5 Church Street, Woodbridge Suffolk IP12 1DS, UK
Tel: 01394 385501 Fax: 01394 384434
or
Market Street Industrial Park, Wappingers' Falls, NY 12590, USA
Tel: 914 297 0003 Fax: 914 297 0068

To Gaye Blake Roberts

Other books by Diana Edwards:
*Tea and Sympathy: Post Revolutionary Ceramics in
the Stamford Historical Society*
The Castleford Pottery 1790-1821
Neale Pottery and Porcelain
Black Basalt

Other books by Rodney Hampson:
Longton Potters 1700-1865
Churchill China: Great British Potters since 1795

Contents

Acknowledgements

THE authors are grateful to the many individuals and to the institutions which they represent for access to materials, to collections and for the generosity typical of those who share a common enthusiasm. Two museum curators were particularly helpful in allowing access to the collections of their respective museums, making it possible to illustrate many of the shapes found in the sales records. Robin Emmerson who spent days away from his work while making it possible to photograph at both the Lady Lever Art Gallery and at the Liverpool Museum and who, in addition, shared much of his vast knowledge on Wedgwood, and Pam Wood, who was equally helpful at the Nottingham Museum. To the following we also owe thanks: Mrs P.J. Adams, John Adeney, David Barker, Sandra Bernaus, Martin Blake, Mr and Mrs Harold Blakey, The Revd and Mrs Henry Burgin, Helen Burton, Miranda Goodby, Deborah Skinner and the other staff of the City Museum and Art Gallery, Stoke-on-Trent, Mark Clark, Bill Coles, Howard Coutts, Diana Darlington, Aileen Dawson, Ulysses Dietz, Roger Edmundson, Gordon Elliott, Geoffrey Fisk, Hazel Forsyth, Adela Goodall, Lindsay Grigsby, the staff of the Hanley Reference Library, Pat Halfpenny, Jonathan Horne, Mollie Hosking, Ray A. Howard, Peter Hyland, Harwood Johnson, William R. Johnston, Pam Judkins, Dr Peter Kaellgren, Dr Alvin Kanter, Mrs Samuel Laver, Lorraine Lloyd-Davies, Terry Lockett and the late Isabel Lockett, John Mallet, William Mangana, Rose Meldrum, Lynn Miller, Dr David Pendergast, Claude D. Pike, Martin Phillips, Dr and Mrs Victor Polikoff, Roger Pomfret, Dr A.J.N.W. Prag, Helen Proctor, Rosalind and Martin Pulver, Alison and the late Kenneth Quinn, Gaye Blake Roberts and fellow Trustees of the Wedgwood Museum for permission to quote from the Wedgwood papers on deposit at Keele University, Peter Roden, Janine Skerry, the staff of the Stafford Record Office, Warren and Susan Spencer, Jane Standen, Edward Streator, Olive Talbot, Gail Trexsel, Jill Turnbull, Mr and Mrs Henry Weldon, J. Tracy Wiggin, and Mrs David Zeitlin.

Finally we thank our spouses, Francis and Eileen, for their patience, tolerance and wise advice, during the writing of the book.

The publication of this book was made possible by a
generous grant from Ceramica-Stiftung, Basel, Switzerland.

Preface

THIS is the first monograph[1] on the subject of English-type dry-bodied Stoneware. Although scores of books have been written on Wedgwood for nearly a century and a half, until recently the interest in the other manufacturers operating in the Wedgwood *métier* has been minimal. Therefore, the importance of this volume is concentrated in two areas. The existence of a large number of records of Wedgwood sales from the London retail establishment at Greek Street in Soho, dating from 1774 to 1794 and hitherto unexplored, document the day by day sales which provide insight into the introduction of bodies, shapes and decoration and often indicate the buyer. The ramifications are obvious and provide, in addition to much clearer guidelines for dating, a great deal of information about the material cultural history of the late eighteenth century both in England and abroad. These daily sales accounts frequently indicate vase and other vessel shapes by number and when coordinated with a copy of the *Wedgwood Shape Book Number 1*[2] they will make it possible, for the first time, to identify the exact vessel purchased, when, how often and by whom.

The second area in which the book breaks ground is in historical data contributed by Rodney Hampson on the other manufacturers. These manufacturers, often underestimated, were frequently serious Wedgwood competitors and their wares are illustrated here, in many cases, also for the first time.

We have sought to limit our original research to the above two areas while providing an overview of the dry-bodied stoneware manufacture in England from 1670 to 1830. After 1830, the industry moved substantially away from its roots into new and more complicated hybrid bodies and into forms which related either to the Victorian aesthetic, or in the case of much of the Wedgwood output, reiterated the old themes providing reprises which have been adequately covered in other books.

Additionally, it seems appropriate to note that owing to the recent concerns about spurious manufacture of Wedgwood items we have sought to include only those pieces with impeccable Wedgwood provenances. Thus, the major museums are the primary sources: Lady Lever Art Gallery comprising the Lord Leverhulme collection purchased in 1905 in its entirety from the collection of Lord Tweedmouth (1820-1894), Liverpool Museum with the majority of the pieces illustrated here from the collection of Joseph Mayer (1803-1886) accessioned in 1882 (accession numbers include the letter 'M'), Nottingham Museum from the Felix Joseph (1840-1892) collection bequeathed in 1892, the collection given by Sir Richard and Mr George Tangye to the Birmingham Museum in 1885 and that of Jesse Haworth (1835-1920) given to the University of Manchester in 1912. Other inclusions have been carefully scrutinised in the light of the current information on fakes.[3]

Finally, the unmarked and unidentified stonewares have not been addressed in any detail. The large, unmarked 'spur-handled' group is discussed under 'Mist' and, with the exception of a considerable body of unidentified fine white stonewares of the so-called felspathic variety, there is not any other large body of unidentified dry-bodied ware. And of the felspathic varieties there is very little to say if these wares are not marked. Therefore, the examples included in the photographs have been left to speak for themselves. Likewise for the few Continental factory inclusions. The examples are not meant to be inclusive of the whole range of dry-bodied stonewares produced on the Continent or in Asia, but merely as illustrations of those wares produced in the English manner by Continental manufacturers.

Diana Edwards

ADDENDUM

Authors' note – late addition

The caneware milk jug shown below is the first example discovered to date outside one in the Schreiber collection at the Victoria and Albert Museum. (See also page 121)

Hot Milk Jug and Cover, *caneware with blue enamel. Unmarked, attributed to Edmund John Birch from marked examples in basalt and in caneware in the Schreiber collection (Sch.II.569) at the Victoria and Albert Museum, 4¾ inches high, c. 1800. (Grigsby Collection.)*

CORRIGENDA

1. Page 186. The final sentence is incomplete and should read: A large bust of Voltaire (Fig. 317) speaks to the variety and quality emanating from a factory which always spoke in its own voice and *métier.*

2. Page 206. Fig. 360 – height of teapot is 5⅜ inches, not as shown.

3. Page 208. Figs. 355, 356, 357 and 358 have been renumbered and are now 361, 362, 363 and 364 respectively.

Introduction

IF a single instance is of use in framing a theory it might be said that English dry-bodied stoneware revolutionized the ceramic world. Initially it was basalt, that black stoneware which sculpted as well as threw a beautiful pot, tempting the potter to emulate Greek vases, and mould likenesses of gods and goddesses. Pre-eminently suited to take neoclassicism beyond architecture into the domestic situation, basalt walked hand in hand with an era which demanded innovations. As one potter who understood all of this, Josiah Wedgwood made way for himself and others in adding exuberant dimensions to the basalt *métier* : caneware, jasper, fine stoneware (including Turner's 1780s cream stoneware and the other coloured bodies) and ultimately another tangential body, felspathic stoneware of the Castleford variety, joined forces to augment an already established ethos in architecture, embellishing both homes and country houses, and continental venues ordinary and palatial.

An English innovation, the essential Englishness of the dry-body has remained intact and preserved today though a few continental manufacturers included small productions of basalt and jasper in their own factories. The immediate success of each new manifestation of the dry or unglazed body, particularly jasper, justified the time and expense of the introduction which radically changed the thrust of the ceramic industry, diverting it from a cottage industry, aimed exclusively at tea and table wares, to one where sophisticated ornamental wares were sought after by English and European nobility and gentry alike.

Colour Plates

Colour Plate 1
Teapot, *glazed red earthenware slip-cast in hexagonal shape with oval panels of crude figures in low relief. Unmarked, attributed to Samuel Bell's Pomona works, Newcastle-under-Lyme, c. 1724-44, 6 inches high. (Nottingham Museum, 1882-528, ex Kidd collection.)*

Colour Plate 2
Pair of flower containers *(minus perforated domed covers), rosso antico. Shape No. 199 these were referred to as 'boquet pots' in sales of 1779. No mark, c. 1779, 4¼ inches high. (Grigsby collection.)*

Colour Plate 3
Candlestick, coffee pot and cup, rosso antico. *The popularity of the red and black combination extended nearly to the end of the nineteenth century. Mark: candlestick, WEDGWOOD Z, c. 1785-1800, 5½ inches high; coffee pot, WEDGWOOD X FIY Z, February 1870, 6½ inches high; cup, WEDGWOOD (plus moustache mark), c. 1798-1805, 2 inches high. (Royal Ontario Museum, 984.18.41, 984.18.42, 995.127.34.)*

Colour Plate 4
Pyrophorous vase, rosso antico. *Mark: WEDGWOOD A, c.1805-10. (Mint Museum of Art, Delhom collection.)*

Colour Plate 5
Pot-pourri, tea cup and saucer and egg ring, *caneware with grey relief decoration. Marks: all WEDGWOOD except for egg ring which is unmarked, early 19th century. Potpourri, 3 inches high. (Pendergast collection.)*

Colour Plate 6
Pot-pourri vase and cover, *large caneware potpourri vase with pierced cover and gilt and enamel opaque Chinese flowers. A price list for cane, red and black teawares enamelled with Chinese flowers exists from the early years of the nineteenth century (p. 68). One of the most spectacular examples of this decoration on caneware is illustrated in this pot which is 12¼ inches high Mark: WEDGWOOD, c. 1807-15. (Zeitlin collection, ex Fred Tongue.)*

Colour Plate 7
Garniture of three bulbous root pots, caneware with blue enamel ground colour. These flower containers are slight variants of shapes No. 340 (centre and No.258 (flanking). Marks: WEDGWOOD (centre) and Wedgwood (right), left unmarked, c. 1786-90, 4½ inches high. (Nassau County Museum, Port Washington, New York, Buten collection of Wedgwood, 307A5250.)

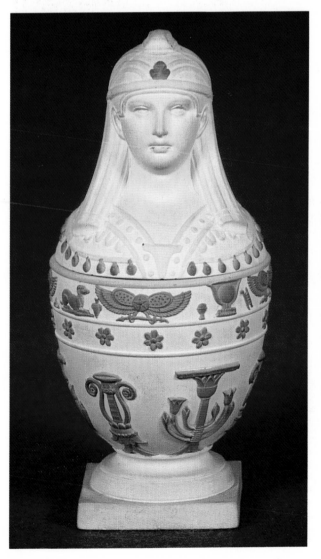

Colour Plate 9
*Portrait medallion **Benjamin Franklin** (1706-90), blue jasper with white relief of Benjamin Franklin after a terracotta by Jean Baptiste Nini dated 1777. A blue and white medallion of Franklin went for 10/6 on May 13, 1778 (Wedgwood MS 16/15220). Mark:* Wedgwood & Bentley, *c. 1778, 3½ inches high. (Manchester Museum, University of Manchester, Haworth collection.)*

(left) Colour Plate 8
Canopic inkwell, caneware with red Egyptian sprig reliefs. The source for this shape can be found in Bernard de Montfaucon's Antiquité Expliquée..., *Vol. II, Pl. 132. Mark: WEDGWOOD O, c. 1798, 5¼ inches high. (Manchester Museum, University of Manchester, Haworth collection.)*

Colour Plate 10
***Portrait medallion of* Joseph Priestley** *(1733-1804), blue jasper dip with white relief, attributed to the modeller William Hackwood. Medallions of Franklin, Priestley and Newton sold in September 1779, the three together for 21/- (Wedgwood MS 16/15292). Mark: Wedgwood & Bentley, c. 1779, 3⅜ inches high. (Manchester Museum, University of Manchester, Haworth collection.)*

Colour Plate 11
***Portrait medallion of* Viscount Admiral Keppel** *(1725-86), blue jasper dip with white relief. Medallions of Admiral Keppel sold for 7/6 and 10/6 in March and August 1779 (Wedgwood MSS 16/15268;16/15288). Mark: Wedgwood & Bentley, c. 1779, 3⅛ inches high. (Manchester Museum, University of Manchester, Haworth collection.)*

Colour Plate 12
***Medallion of* The Marriage of Cupid and Psyche**, *blue jasper dip with white reliefs. Modelled in 1774, one* Marriage of Cupid [and Psyche] *sold for 12/- on June 8, 1776 (Wedgwood MS W/M 1449). Mark:* WEDGWOOD & BENTLEY, *c. 1778-80, 11 x 16¼ inches. (Manchester Museum, University of Manchester, Haworth collection.)*

Colour Plate 13
'Bell handles' or 'Bell drops', *blue and white jasper. Left, shape No. 336 2¾ inches long; Centre, shape No. 433 2⅝ inches long; Right, shape No. 334 2⅝ inches long. All unmarked. Wedgwood c. 1777-1800. The first mention of 'bell handles' or 'bell drops' in sales records was in October 1777, (Wedgwood MS 25/18788). (Nassau County Museum, Port Washington, New York, Buten collection of Wedgwood.)*

Colour Plate 14
Plate, *solid blue jasper, press-moulded in the form of an artichoke. 5⅝ inches diameter. Mark: WEDGWOOD, c. 1786-95. (City Museum and Art Gallery, Stoke-on-Trent, 1984.)*

Colour Plate 14a
Vase with lilies, *oil on canvas by Peter Faës dated '1796', the vase is Wedgwood shape No. 40 in white bisque which sold in November 1791 for 10/-; 24½ x 18½ inches. (The Bowes Museum, Barnard Castle, Durham.)*

Colour Plate 15
Tea bowl and saucer and teapot, *white jasper with green jasper dip. The tea bowl and saucer have arabesque scroll decoration and the teapot has reliefs of* Sportive Love *and a woman kneeling next to a cinerary urn. Mark:* Wedgwood Z *(tea bowl and saucer) 2¼ inches high;* WEDGWOOD A, *c. 1786-95. (Royal Ontario Museum, teapot gift of Mrs J. H. Plummer.)*

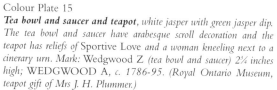

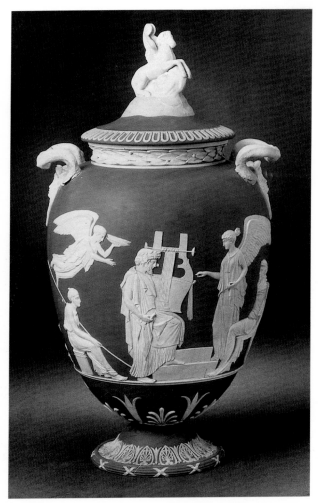

Colour Plate 16
Vase, *blue and white jasper shape. The motifs entitled* Maternal Love *and* Childhood *were designed by Emma Crewe (fl.1786-1818). The most popularly sold vase shape in the late eighteenth century, the snake-handled vase, shape No. 266, was purchased by royalty, nobility and even came to America to be sold by Philadelphia dealer John Bringhurst in 1793. Generally produced in blue and white jasper it was also made in green jasper in 1786. The vase was included as the frontispiece of the 1787 Wedgwood trade catalogue. Mark:* WEDGWOOD, *c. 1786-93, 14½ inches high. (Zeitlin collection.)*

Colour Plate 18
Pegasus vase, *blue and white jasper with white relief depicting the* Apotheosis of Homer. *A similar vase, shape No. 298, was sold to Lord Howard for the remarkable sum of £21.0.0 on 7 December 1786 (Wedgwood MS 16/15398). Mark:* WEDGWOOD, *c. 1786, 18 inches high. (Courtesy the Trustees of the Wedgwood Museum, Barlaston, Stoke-on-Trent.)*

Colour Plate 17
Bulbous root tub, *white jasper with lilac jasper dip and white reliefs of putti. No. 504 in the shape book, the large oval tub was intended to have a pierced liner. Mark:* WEDGWOOD, *4 x 10½ inches, c. 1785. (Nottingham Museum, 1892-140.)*

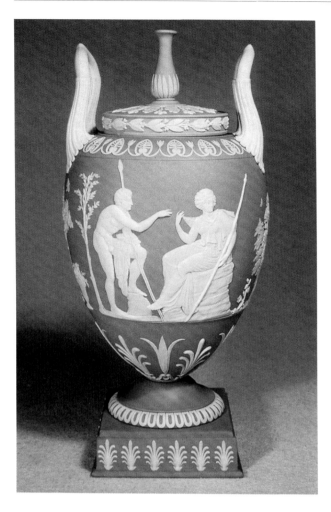

Colour Plate 19
Hercules vase, *solid pale blue jasper with white reliefs of* Hercules in the garden of the Hesperides. *Modelled by John Flaxman in 1785, this is vase shape No. 302. Mark:* WEDGWOOD, *c. 1785, 13⅛ inches high. (City Museum and Art Gallery, Stoke-on-Trent, 2060.)*

Colour Plate 20a (above right)
Tripod vase, *solid blue jasper with white jasper reliefs. This tripod, shape No. 180, is variously referred to as 'vase' and 'candelabra' in the sales records, the first recorded sale of which was to Thomas Hope Esq., sold as a pair on February 11, 1791 for £16.16.0 (Wedgwood MS 16/1529). Other sales of this auspicious vase, made also in basalt, included HRH the Duke of York on January 28, 1792, and the Archbishop of Santiago on October 29, 1792 as well as to a Mrs Billington on November 4, 1791. Mark:* WEDGWOOD, *c. 1791-92, 11⅛ inches high. (Beeson collection of Wedgwood, Birmingham Museum of Art, Alabama, 1982.190 a and b.)*

Colour Plate 20 (right)
Pair of ewers Sacred to Bacchus and Neptune, *solid blue jasper with white embellishment. Nos. 236 and 237 in the shape book, such ewers sold for £10.10.0 on 1 September 1786 (Wedgwood MS 16/15385). Mark:* WEDGWOOD K *(wine on left; water on right unmarked), 15 inches high, c. 1786. (Nottingham Museum, 1892-375 a/b.)*

Colour Plate 21a
Busts on terms, *white jasper busts on blue jasper socles mounted on blue jasper pedestals. Left to right they are tentatively identified as: young Bacchus, Venus, Jupiter and Mars. Marks on base of Jupiter and Venus: WEDGWOOD, c. 1786-93, 5¼ inches. (British Museum, Franks collection.)*

Colour Plate 21
Season candlestick *with a figure of Winter, solid blue jasper with white jasper relief. Shape No. 265, the candlestick would have been sold in sets of four each pair priced at £4.4.0 (Wedgwood MS 16/15461, March 3, 1788). Mark: WEDGWOOD, c. 1788, 10¼ inches high. (Nottingham Museum, 1892-193.)*

Colour Plate 22
Smelling bottles, *blue jasper with white reliefs in octagon and round forms. Two octagon smelling bottles were sold to Princess Elizabeth in March 1788 for £1.10.0 (Wedgwood MS 16/15461). No marks, Wedgwood, c. 1788-1800. (Nassau County Museum, Port Washington, New York, Buten collection of Wedgwood.)*

Colour Plate 23

Vase and cover, *white jasper with black dip and white reliefs. The base has black dice work with yellow stars. Shape No. 273 was popular from 1786-1792. However, this vase is a late 19th century version. Mark: WEDGWOOD, c. 1875, 8¾ inches high. (Beeson Collection of Wedgwood, Birmingham Museum of Art, Alabama, 1982–63.)*

Colour Plate 24

Jasper dice work pieces, white jasper with blue and green dip. First appearing on existing sales lists in April 1790 (Wedgwood MS 16/15473) dice work became the rage for the remainder of the decade. Marks: all WEDGWOOD, c. 1790-1800, vase (left No. 395) 5¼ inches high; custard cup (No. 333) 3½ inches high, vase (right) 5⅛ inches high. (Nottingham Museum, 1892-183, 1892-432, 1892-12T.)

Colour Plate 25

Ice pails, solid blue jasper with white jasper ornamentation. Shape No. 316, these pails sold in June 1790 for £25.4.0 for four (Wedgwood MS 16/15497). Mark: WEDGWOOD, c. 1790, 7⁷⁄₁₆ inches high. (Lady Lever Art Gallery, Museums & Galleries on Merseyside, LL1448,1449.)

Colour Plate 26

Triton candlesticks, solid blue jasper with white jasper additions. Shape No. 337, these appeared on sales lists in June 1790 in blue and white jasper for the enormous sum of £37.16.0 the pair (Wedgwood MS 16/15498). Tritons in basalt were six guineas a pair, a considerable sum for basalt. No marks, c. 1790, 11⅛ inches high. (Grigsby collection.)

Colour Plate 27

Tablet Priam begging the body of Hector from Achilles, *solid green jasper with white reliefs, described by Henry Webber in an 'Explanation of Bas Reliefs' on 12 December 1789 as 'Priam kneeling before Achilles, begging the body of his son Hector. The young man standing by Achilles is Automedontes, his Shield-bearer. The first is the car of Hector, & the second the cart with presents to Achilles' (Wedgwood MS 1526). The wax for the tablet was modelled by Pacetti from the original on the back of the sarcophagus of Alexander Severus in the Capitoline Museum, Rome. Pacetti was paid 15 zequins (£32.25) for the wax model on 10 May 1788 (Wedgwood MS 1526). The Priam tablet was among purchases made of Wedgwood wares by Thomas Hope in February 1793. Mark: WEDGWOOD, c. 1793, 6 x 15½ inches. (Walters Art Gallery, Baltimore, Maryland, 48.874. Ex Sibson collection 1877, W.D. Holt 1892, L. Huth 1895, purchased in 1911 by Henry Walters from John Harding.)*

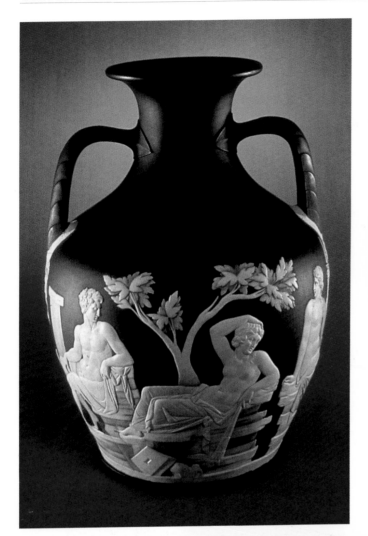

Colour Plate 29
Oval cream paterae, *in blue and white jasper with arabesque decoration. Shape No. 349, these paterae were sold with ladles for £1.5.0 each in May 1791 (Wedgwood MS 16/15543). Marks: WEDGWOOD 6, c. 1791-2, 8⅛ inches long. (Lady Lever Art Gallery, Museums & Galleries on Merseyside, LL1510, 1512.)*

Colour Plate 28 (left)
Hope Portland (Barberini) vase, *black jasper dip with white figures. Thomas Hope's copy has been in the collection of the Wedgwood Museum since 1950 when it was acquired from the collection of Eustace Calland. The vase was purchased originally by Hope for £31.10.0 on 13 June 1793, while he was still living in Amsterdam. No mark, 10 inches high. (By courtesy of the Trustees of the Wedgwood Museum, Barlaston, Stoke-on-Trent, England.)*

Colour Plate 30
Flower pots, *blue and white jasper. Left, variously described in the sales records as 'bulbous root pot', 'pedestal', 'square flower pot', shape No. 295 appeared for the first time in 1790. Right, shape No. 377 appeared first on 21 February 1792 for £1.4.0 a pair (Wedgwood MS 16/15582). Marks: left, WEDGWOOD O, c. 1790-91, right, WEDGWOOD 3, c. 1792, left 3 inches high, right, 6⅛ inches high. (Nottingham Museum, 1892-82, 1892-205.)*

Colour Plate 31
Sweetmeat basket, *oval shell-shaped with pierced trellis pattern, this dark blue jasper basket with white trim is shape No. 632. Mark: WEDGWOOD, c.1810, 7½ inches high. (Lady Lever Art Gallery, Museums & Galleries on Merseyside, LL1000.)*

Colour Plate 32
Dolphin candlesticks, *solid white jasper. No. 488 these candlesticks appear to date after 1794 as no sales are recorded in surviving records which end in 1794. Marks: both WEDGWOOD, c. 1794-1800, 8¾ inches high. (Lady Lever Art Gallery, Museums & Galleries on Merseyside, LL1365,1366.)*

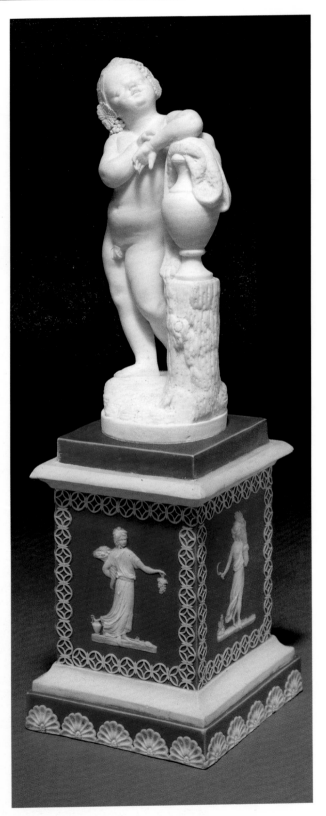

Colour Plates 33
Quiver flower pots, solid blue jasper with white relief. An unusual and not popular shape (No.507), the sole recorded sale in existing records was to the King of Naples in June 1786 for £2.2.0 (Wedgwood MS 16/15375). Other sales must have occurred because there are a few examples in museum collections. No mark, c. 1786, 6⅛ inches high. (Lady Lever Art Gallery, Museums & Galleries on Merseyside, LL1389, 1390.)

Colour Plate 34
Figure of a Young Boy, white jasper on a white jasper plinth with blue jasper dip. Mark: ADAMS, 12 inches high. (Grigsby collection.)

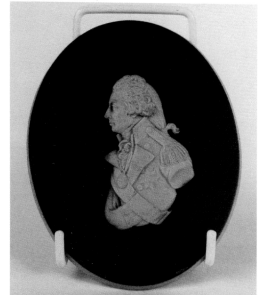

Colour Plate 35
***Portrait medallion of* Viscount Lord Nelson** *(1758-1805), white jasper with blue jasper dip. Mark: ADAMS, late 18th c., 4½ x 3½ inches. (City Museum and Art Gallery, Stoke-on-Trent, T.119.1908.)*

Colour Plate 36
***Jug**, white jasper with dark blue jasper dip and white reliefs of the Muses. Mark: ADAMS, late 18th c., 9 inches high. (City Museum and Art Gallery, Stoke-on-Trent, 2138.)*

Colour Plate 37
Teapot, dark blue jasper with white reliefs. Mark: ADAMS, late 18th c., 7¼ inches high. (City Museum and Art Gallery, Stoke-on-Trent, 250.)

Colour Plate 38
Pair of vases, dark blue jasper dip with olive green acanthus leaves in relief and olive green lily stems with white flowers. Mark: ADAMS, late 18th c., 7¼ inches high. (City Museum and Art Gallery, Stoke-on-Trent, nos. 120 and 973.)

Colour Plate 39
Vase, white jasper with blue jasper dip and white reliefs. Dimpled granular surface below central scene of Venus in her car being pulled by Dolphins.
Mark: ADAMS, late 18th c., 12¾ inches high. (Zeitlin collection, ex Fred Tongue 1969.)

Colour Plate 40
Vase, solid blue jasper with white relief of Apollo crowning Cupid. *Unmarked, probably Adams, late 18th c., 11½ inches high. (Royal Ontario Museum, gift of Mrs A.S.Bowley, the Herbert Bowley collection of Wedgwood, 920.25.50.)*

Colour Plate 41
Teapot, *white felspathic stoneware with marbling in blue, smear-glazed with a finial of* Venus and Cupid. *Unmarked, attributed to Chetham and Woolley, c. 1796-1810, 5⅛ inches high. (Collection of Olive Talbot.)*

Colour Plate 42
Candlesticks, jug, honey pot and pie dish, *caneware with enamel embellishment. Marks: all Davenport over an anchor, c. 1800-10, candlesticks 6½ inches high. (Lockett collection.)*

Colour Plate 43
Egg stand and jug, egg stand, caneware with brown enamel lines, jug, caneware with printed Egyptian decoration and enamel Greek key border. Egg stand marked: Davenport over an anchor, c. 1795-1810 6½ inches high; jug unmarked, Davenport, c. 1800-10, 5.4 inches high. (Darlington collection.)

Colour Plate 44
Part of a flower garniture, white stoneware 'D-shaped' central portion of a three part garniture with dark blue figures of bacchanalian boys and boys with goat and blue enamel painting. Mark: HACKWOOD & Co., c. 1810-20, 8 inches high. (Liverpool Museum, Museums & Galleries on Merseyside, 15.10.1909.3.)

Colour Plate 45
Sugar box and cover, fine white stoneware with moulded body and enamel painted cartouche. Mark: HERCULANEUM, c. 1805-10, 5½ inches high. (Lockett collection.)

Colour Plate 46

Jugs and tumbler and teapot, drab stoneware with silver line embellishment, sprig relief. Large jug has relief of the 'Death of General Wolfe', smaller jug has the relief of the 'Dipping of Achilles'. The larger jug and tumbler have a history of always being together. All unmarked Samuel Hollins, c. 1805, large jug 8½ inches high. (Burgin collection.)

Colour Plate 47

Teapot, blue stoneware decorated with silver overpainting. Mark:S. HOLLINS, c. 1805, 4½ inches high. (Nottingham Museum, 1882-512.)

Colour Plate 48
Teapot and sugar bowl and stand, *deep-red stoneware with metallic silver and blue decoration, both with Prince of Wales sprig reliefs. Marks: teapot, S. HOLLINS, 4¼ inches high; sugar bowl unmarked, c. 1800-05. (Darlington collection.)*

Colour Plate 49
Teapot, *fine white stoneware with blue relief. Mark: T. & J. HOLLINS, c. 1800-10, 5¼ inches high. (The Jones Museum of Glass and Ceramics, Sebago, Maine.)*

Colour Plate 50
Wine cask on wooden stand, *white stoneware with brown dip and sprig relief, bacchanalian cover. Mark:* J. LOCKETT *impressed on reverse, c. 1826-35, 13½ inches long. (Grigsby collection.)*

Colour Plate 51
Brandy barrel, *white stoneware with brown dip and sprig relief. Mark:* J. LOCKETT, *c. 1826-35, 10¼ inches high. (Blakey collection.)*

Colour Plate 52
Cup and saucer, fine white stoneware with sprig relief birds and enamel ribbon decoration. Mark: NEALE & Co., c. 1790, 2¼ inches high. (Collection of Olive Talbot, ex Godden collection.)

Colour Plate 53
Mug, white stoneware with smear glaze, turquoise enamel and gilding. The sprig relief figures are of children playing various musical instruments. Mark: NEALE & Co., c. 1790, 5⅛ inches high. (Private collection.)

Colour Plates 54 and 55
Trophy cup, *caneware with moulded body, enamel painted and gilded. The painting consists of Prince of Wales feathers with the motto* Ich Dien *and on the reverse hunting symbols and the inscription* Success to the Royal British Bowmen. *Mark:* NEALE & Co., *c. 1790, 11⅜ inches high. (Virginia Museum of Fine Arts, Richmond, Virginia, gift of David K.E. Bruce, by exchange, ex Rakow collection.)*

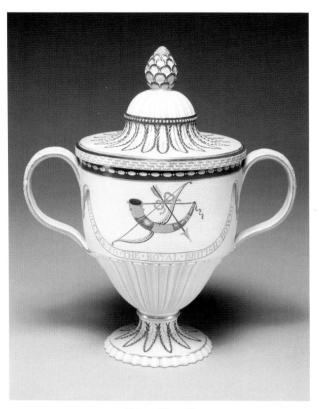

Colour Plate 55

Colour Plate 57
Jug with pewter cover, smear-glazed caneware with decoration of satyr heads between scrolling acanthus. The handle is a stylised female figure. Mark: W. RIDGWAY & SON, c. 1830-35. (City Museum and Art Gallery, Stoke-on-Trent, 38 P1977.)

Colour Plate 56
Two pot-pourri vases, grey, smear-glazed stoneware with blue sprigs and gilding (right). A similar vase (without the cover) is in the Victoria & Albert Museum (acc. #2545-1901) and another example is in the Fitzwilliam Museum (illustrated Lewis, 'Pratt Ware', page 15). Mark: left, Pratt, right unmarked, c. 1800, 5 inches and 7 inches. (Blakey collection.)

Colour Plate 58
Sugar bowl, *blue jasper dip with white relief. Mark: SPODE, c. 1805, 7¼ inches high. (City Museum and Art Gallery, Stoke-on-Trent, 2149.)*

Colour Plate 59
Teapot, *red stoneware following on Yixing prototypes, with black basalt relief and Fo lion finial. Mark: SPODE, c. 1805, 5 inches high. (Coles collection, photograph by Bill Coles.)*

Colour Plate 60
Watch holder, *deep blue jasper with white sprigged relief. Mark: STEEL BURSLEM, c. 1800-15, (Daniel Steel, Burslem), 6½ inches high. (Rakow collection.)*

Colour Plate 61
Pair of spill vases, *deep blue jasper with white neo-classical reliefs. Unmarked, attributed to Daniel Steel, Burslem, c. 1800-15, 5⅛ inches high. (City Museum and Art Gallery, Stoke-on-Trent, 2141.)*

Colour Plate 62
Spill vase, *caneware with red sprig relief. Mark: WEDGWOOD A, c. 1795-1805, 3⁵⁄₁₆ inches high;* ***Cream jug***, *caneware with moulded body and sprig relief outline painted in red enamel. Mark: SWANSEA, c. 1802-10, 4½ inches high. (Royal Ontario Museum, 920.25.45, 996.18.1.)*

Colour Plate 63
Jug, *smear-glazed caneware with blue sprig reliefs of children playing musical instruments. Mark: BRAMELD H pad mark, c. 1820-30, 8⅞ inches high. (Lockett collection.)*

Colour Plate 64
Three vases, *solid blue jasper with white reliefs on octagonal polished basalt plinths. Marks: left, TURNER 4, centre and right: TURNER 3, c. 1790-1800, centre 11½ inches high. (Nottingham Museum, 1892-310 and a.b.)*

Colour Plate 65
Flower pot, *solid jasper with white reliefs on a polished basalt plinth. Mark: TURNER 3, c. 1790-1800, 7⅛ inches high. (City Museum and Art Gallery, Stoke-on-Trent, 20P1966.)*

Colour Plate 66 (below)
Satyr mug, footed jug, cream jug and custard cup, *caneware moulded with enamel painting. Marks: satyr mug and footed jug, TURNER; cream jug, SPODE, custard cup, unmarked, attributed to Wedgwood, all c. 1790-1800, satyr mug 4½ inches high. (Burgin collection.)*

Colour Plate 67 (opposite)
Pastille burner, *caneware decorated with green, blue and red enamel painting. The burner (minus liner and cover) is supported on a tripod with eagles' heads. Mark: TURNER, 10 inches high, (City Museum and Art Gallery, Stoke-on-Trent.)*

Colour Plate 68
Pot-pourri vase and cream jug, *caneware with enamel painting. Marks: vase, TURNER, c. 1795, 6¼ inches high, ex Oster collection sold Sotheby's New York, 30 November 1971, lot 131. Cream jug, Davenport over an anchor, c. 1805, 2¹¹⁄₁₆ inches high, ex Joseph Park collection, sold Sotheby's New York, June 1980. (Zeitlin collection.)*

Colour Plate 69
Milk jug and teapot, *solid blue jasper with white reliefs. Unmarked, attributed to Turner, c. 1810, teapot 6¼ inches high. (Liverpool Museum, Museums & Galleries on Merseyside, 1167M.)*

Colour Plate 70
Double bulbous root pot, *white stoneware with rococo scroll moulded body, end of three pot garniture, sprig reliefs. Mark:* TURNER WW, *c. 1790-1800, 6½ inches high, Liverpool Museum, Museums & Galleries on Merseyside, 757M.*

Colour Plate 71
Plaque, *white jasper frame with blue dip and yellow jasper centre, with white sprig decoration of Hercules and Janus. This plaque was probably intended as a panel in an architectural site. Mark:* ENOCH WOOD *impressed in three places, c. 1789, 12 x 9 inches. (City Museum and Art Gallery, Stoke-on-Trent, 856.)*

Colour Plate 72
Figures of **Diana**,
*caneware, glazed and
unglazed. Marks:*
R.WOOD, *Ralph
Wood, c. 1783-84.
(Colonial Williamsburg
Foundation,
Williamsburg, Virginia,
1960-419, 1963-459.)*

Colour Plate 73
*Group of dry-bodied
teawares:* **Sugar bowl**,
*black basalt, 4½ inches high
(acquired in 1874);*
Teapot, *red stoneware,
4½ inches high (bequest
1931);* **Teabowl and
saucer**, *buff stoneware with
black enamel decoration,
3 inches high (bequest
1947), all Dortu & Co,
Nyon, Switzerland,
c. 1807–1813, Ariana
Museum, Geneva,
Switzerland (Photograph
by Jacques Pugin).*

CHAPTER I

Antecedents of English Dry-Bodied Stoneware

English dry-bodied stoneware developed from its predecessors in un-glazed earthenware, primarily redwares which had been made from ancient times in every culture and every society as containers for food and drink. The development of stoneware eliminated the need for harmful lead glazes to make the pottery impervious to liquids. In fact, lead glazes were almost impossible to achieve on such highly fired wares as they would melt in the kiln. When a sheen was required it was almost always accomplished by adding salt to the kiln, which in turn vitrified onto the body of the pot producing a salt-glaze. However, these wares are technically outside the area of the dry-bodied stonewares. The so-called dry bodies were just that, native or matt surfaces where a glaze was unnecessary. With the firing of pottery to temperatures of 1200 to 1300 degrees centigrade the clay partially vitrified creating a dry-body capable of safely containing liquids.

Perhaps one of the first dry-bodied stonewares, and certainly the most highly visible, was made in China in the sixteenth century in the provincial town of Yixing near Shanghai in Jiangsu province (Fig. 1, left). Little is known of the first products but the fine grained stoneware at its best imparted a slight sheen to the unglazed surface which was most admired. Some small toys and miniatures were also made in stoneware from Yixing which were coated with a bluish glaze thin enough around the edges to reveal the brown or red body underneath.[1] Thought to be the best ceramic body in which to brew a pot of tea, Yixing stoneware continued in popularity through the seventeenth and eighteenth centuries and was exported in quantity to Europe in packed crates in sago (rice) at a cost of approximately two pence per pot.[2] The arrival of eighty-two such teapots in London in 1699 is noted in the East India Company records, and in 1703 the company sold more than one thousand chocolate cups of the same ware.[3]

In Holland Yixing teapots were imported even earlier, in the 1670s. The day register of the Dutch East India Company office at Batavia has entries which read: 'From

Fig.1 **Teapot**, left, red stoneware with unglazed exterior and interior and crab-stock handles and spouts. Exterior decoration includes sprig-moulded relief of squirrels and vine leaves. Unmarked, Chinese, 18th century, large teapot 4½ inches high; right, **Punch pot,** red stoneware with crab stock handle and spout. According to David Barker, this teapot shares many motifs with the so-called Joseph Edge coffee pot in the Fitzwilliam Museum, Joseph Edge, however, was probably a workman, not a master potter. Unmarked, English, c. 1750-60, 6 inches high. (Royal Ontario Museum, 984.18.91, 984.18.93.)

Zhangzhou 7 cases of red teapots' in 1679 and '320 figured red teapots' from Macao in 1680.[4] These pots in turn spawned the Dutch and English production of the charming teawares. From about 1670 the Dutch emulated the Yixing red stoneware producing teawares often with relief decoration and foreshortened spouts. Several manufacturers, such as Ary de Milde (Fig. 2) in the late 1670s produced marked stonewares but most were left unmarked as were most of the English and German redwares.

In England the first recorded manufacturer of red stoneware was John Dwight in his London factory at Fulham. Dwight's famous patent of 1672 has long been a watershed date for the production of stoneware in general, although in the last two decades much more information has surfaced through the archaeological and documentary records to indicate that there were stoneware manufacturers in several London communities probably as early as 1620. However, these potters were making salt-glazed stonewares in the manner of the wares coming from Raeren and Frechen,[5] not the native *métier* which was later

associated with English red stoneware. Until recently Dwight was primarily known for his production of salt-glazed stonewares in both white and brown bodies; however, a few unglazed redwares have surfaced which match the salt-glazed examples attributed to Dwight which, along with the documentary record and shards recovered at the site, make it appear likely that he was among the first locally to produce these very attractive red stonewares (Fig. 3).

Certainly the Elers brothers, David and John Philip, Dutch silversmiths who came to London around 1690, were making a variety of examples which can be rather firmly attributed to one of their potworks in the late seventeenth century (Figs. 4-6). The Elers were among a considerable number of potters accused of the infringement of the Dwight's second patent of 1784. Dwight, who studied 'Civil Law and physic a little but most Chemistry',[6] used his legal background to prosecute a number of these illegal manufacturers, including the Elers. It was a partial success for Dwight who although the case against the Elers in 1793 did not go to court, was

Fig. 2 **Teapot**, *red stoneware with sprig relief. Mark: ARY DE MILDE, c. 1680-1708, 3⅜ inches high. (Private collection.)*

Fig. 3 **Partially reconstructed teapot and bowl and cover**, *red stoneware from John Dwight's factory at Fulham. Based on Yixing redware these represent the earliest examples of English teaware. A teapot 4¼ inches high; teabowl 2⅛ inches high. There is documentary evidence that John Dwight was marketing red stoneware in the 1690s. Shards c. 1675. (Photograph by courtesy of the Museum of London.)*

Fig. 4 **Teapot**, *red stoneware, slip-cast with sprig reliefs. Unmarked, probably David and John Philip Elers, Vauxhall, London, or Bradwell Wood, Staffordshire, late 17th to early 18th century, 5⅛ inches high. (Royal Ontario Museum, 984.18.88.1&2.)*

Fig. 5 **Mug**, *red stoneware, slip-cast with moulded applied reliefs and silver rim. Unmarked, attributed to David and John Philip Elers, Vauxhall, London or Bradwell Wood, Staffordshire, c. Late 17th to early 18th century, 4¼ inches high. (Weldon collection, 338.)*

Fig. 6 *Two teapots*, *left*, *red stoneware of cylindrical form, thrown and embellished with applied reliefs taken from Robert Sayer's* The Ladies Amusement *(plate 175). Unmarked, attributed to William Greatbatch of Lower Lane, Fenton, Staffordshire, c. 1765-75, 3 inches high.* **Teapot**, *right, red stoneware, slip-cast with turned horizontal ribbing and applied reliefs. Unmarked, attributed to David and John Philip Elers, Vauxhall, London, or Bradwell Wood, Staffordshire, late 17th to early 18th century. (Weldon collection, 235, 444.)*

successful in getting them to make red stoneware under licence.[7] The brothers Elers doubtless forced Dwight to make red stoneware in sufficient quantity to justify the patent which he appeared, as mentioned, from the archaeological record, to have done. His recipe books of 1689-1698 also mentioned red clay and the firing of red teapots in a muffle kiln.[8]

The wares made by the Elers are much more in evidence than those made by Dwight (Fig. 3); however, they are still scarce and highly coveted as the first well-known red stonewares produced in England. The Elers were first producing red stoneware in South London at Vauxhall. Around 1693 they moved up to North Staffordshire, to Bradwell Wood where they continued to manufacture wares indistinguishable from those made in London. All along it appears they were successful in keeping their famous slip-casting method secret, thereby stamping a secret imprimatur upon their pots for identification later by ceramic historians. In 1698 the Elers were known to have occupied Bradwell Hall [9] but by 1700 they were declared bankrupt and left Staffordshire. After that there is an hiatus in the record of red stoneware potters operating in North Staffordshire for several decades.

However, the red earthenware tradition continued, probably uninterrupted. By 1724 Samuel Bell was operating a work at the Pomona Pottery in Newcastle-under-Lyme making red earthenware (Colour Plate 1), and possibly stoneware. A patent for the manufacture of 'red

marble stoneware' was taken out by Bell on 9 May, 1729, but no actual stoneware identified with this pottery has come to light.[10] The pottery, which operated until Bell's death in 1744, was known for its lathe-turned objects, agate banding and for some slip-casting of hexagonal teapots and lids.[11]

The manufacture of red stoneware was certainly revived

Fig. 7 **Teapot**, *red stoneware with press-moulded hexagonal body, with panels of the so-called 'Indian Boy' design, serpent handle and foliate spout. Unmarked, attributed to Thomas Whieldon, Fenton Vivian, Stoke-on-Trent, c. 1755, 3¾6 inches high. (Colonial Williamsburg Foundation, 1975-45.)*

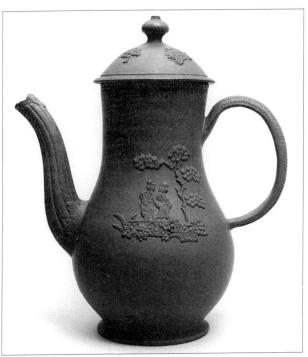

Fig. 8 **Coffee pot,** *red stoneware of baluster shape, with moulded relief decoration. Unmarked, attributed to Thomas Barker, The Foley, Fenton, Stoke-on-Trent, c. 1770, 8¾ inches high. (City Museum and Art Gallery, Stoke-on-Trent, ex Nancy Gunson collection, donated by Peter Gunson.)*

Fig. 9 **Coffee pot,** *red stoneware of baluster shape and sprigged decoration of Oriental figures and a tree. Unmarked, attributed to William Greatbatch, Lower Lane, Fenton, Stoke-on-Trent, c. 1765-70, 8⅝ inches high. (City Museum and Art Gallery, Stoke-on-Trent.)*

by the mid-eighteenth century; however, no other red stoneware was slip-cast. It was thrown on a wheel before firing and decorated with the same stamped decoration as the salt-glazed stonewares of the period or press-moulded in a style copying Chinese prototypes (Fig. 1 left). After 1760 some evidence of current ceramic fashion appeared on these humble low-market wares. Teawares with rococo decoration appeared from time to time, but the neoclassical trends which followed in all the other stonewares were not in evidence on these red stonewares, as it was later on in the century exemplified best by the dark red, drab and teal-coloured stoneware produced by Samuel Hollins (see **Samuel Hollins** Chapter VIII).

One of the first marked manufacturers of red stoneware was the elusive Joseph Edge who incised his name and the date 1760 in a red stoneware lighthouse-shaped coffee pot with rococo handle and spout and foliate rococo sprig decoration.[12] Another example, in the British Museum, appears to be from Edge's factory in a baluster shape, but very much otherwise as the signed example. A punch pot in the Royal Ontario Museum (Fig. 1 right) appears to bear some of the same motifs as the Edge coffee pots and has been suggested by David Barker to be another possible example of Joseph Edge's wares.

A group of red stonewares with pseudo-Chinese seal marks impressed in the base has long been a source of speculation among ceramic scholars. Robin Price[13] was the first one to seriously try and group these wares into categories stylistically and by seal mark. Some of these wares may have been manufactured by the Leeds Pottery, as they bear characteristics similar to Leeds creamwares. But subsequent attempts to ascribe the particular seal marks to manufacturer have proved unsuccessful.

Aside from the seal-marked red stonewares, there is another group which can be associated more closely with the Leeds Pottery, some examples are even impressed with the factory mark.

One group which Mr Price identified appears to be of Wedgwood origin. He noted that there was an integral 'W' within the seal mark which could not have been unintentional. One tea bowl and saucer in the Victoria and Albert Museum illustrated by Mr Price[14] bears this mark and is similar to a shard recovered from the Brick House, Burslem. As we shall see in the redware section of the Wedgwood chapter none of the red stonewares sold by the factory were ever marked with conventional factory marks and yet for a period of more than a decade in recorded sales redwares were sold on a regular basis.

A few redwares were manufactured by one of the Myatts. Marked with the impressed name this group will be further discussed in Chapter VIII under **Myatt** (Fig. 223).

Another manufacturer has been assigned rather tentatively to one J. Taylor on the basis that there was a Mr J. Fletcher apprenticed to Jo. Taylor among the potters at Burslem to handle and to stick legs on to the 'red porcelain'.[15] The 'Indian Boy' teawares are prominent among the red stonewares with legs and so it is possible that Taylor can be identified in that obscure way as another manufacturer. However, as we shall see the 'Indian Boy' teawares are most often associated with the Thomas

Fig. 10 **Teapots (partial reconstructions)**, *caneware with engine-turned and enamel painted decoration. Uncovered in Phase III of the Greatbatch excavations these parapet-neck teapots were glazed on the interior and are of very high quality. They were among thirteen other examples of caneware vessels found on the site. For drawings of some of the other teapots see D. Barker,* William Greatbatch a Staffordshire Potter, *fig. 45. Seal marked, c. 1780. (City Museum and Art Gallery, Stoke-on-Trent.)*

Whieldon output at Fenton Vivian (Fig. 7).

For a synopsis of the red stonewares of the various groups identified by Robin Price see the sequel to his 1957 paper, the second of which was also in the *English Ceramic Circle Transactions Vol. 5 Part 3.*[16]

In the last two decades more manufacturers of red stoneware have come to light through recent excavations, particularly in Staffordshire where the principal potters were operating. A great many potters were producing red stonewares in the middle of the eighteenth century and the problems of identification are essentially the same as for the tortoiseshell and salt-glazed stonewares, the majority of which can only be ascribed to manufacturer through the archaeological record and in many cases only tentatively. However, of those potters who have been identified as manufacturing red stoneware, it is necessary to mention them by name and illustrate the wares attributed to them.

The Foley Pottery, Fenton, Stoke-on-Trent, operated by Thomas Barker c.1765-1770s, is a site where seal-marked wares all bearing the same pseudo-Chinese seal mark were found. Several pieces (Fig. 8) excavated from the Foley pottery site can be matched with extant whole pots providing a probable attribution to the manufacturer.[17]

The early development of the pottery industry in Staffordshire is dominated by a few names. Josiah Wedgwood has been mentioned and will feature as the most prominent player in this monograph. However, other important contributors to the early development were Thomas Whieldon and William Greatbatch and both were making red stoneware.

Thomas Whieldon is associated with two pottery sites, at Fenton Vivian where he was recorded as a tenant in a newly built factory in 1747, and at Fenton Low in 1750 as the owner of the potworks which he leased out to a

number of tenants until his death in 1795.[18] David Barker concluded, however, that there was no evidence that Whieldon ever potted at the Fenton Low site. Whieldon left an account book which spans the years of 1749-62 and, of course, his partnership with Wedgwood, from 1754-59 is well-known. Archaeological finds on the Whieldon site included red stoneware (Fig. 7). The 'Indian Boy' pattern, often associated with Whieldon, was excavated at Fenton Vivian but similar shards were found in nearby sites so others were also making tewares with this distinctive design.[19]

William Greatbatch (1735-1813) has been the subject of a single monograph[20] which sets the record straight on a potter who, along with Whieldon, has been particularly subject to generalisations. Greatbatch produced both buff stoneware and red stoneware (Figs. 6, left and 9). Unfortunately, a single shard from each of two phases of the excavation of the site exists to record the buff stoneware. Of particular interest these teapot shards also used the pseudo-Chinese seal mark,[21] which insists on the addition of Greatbatch to the list of potters using such marks.

Greatbatch was also making unique canewares (Fig. 10), including oval bamboo teapots with parapet necks and enamel decoration which appear from their shape to date around 1790-1800.

In red stoneware Greatbatch offered a variety of shapes. As in most red stonewares these shapes were restricted to tea and coffee wares. Red stoneware recovered from the Greatbatch site included round globular and round barrel-shaped teapots and baluster-shaped jugs and coffee pots. Greatbatch was supplying Wedgwood with 'China' teapots and saffron pots in 1764 and 1765[22] and may have been one of his suppliers for the redware discussed in the

Fig. 11 **Coffee pot,** *red stoneware with mould-applied ornament and engine turning. Unmarked, Staffordshire, c. 1770, 6¼ inches high. (Liverpool Museum, Museums & Galleries on Merseyside, 1972-164.)*

Fig. 12 **Coffee pot,** *left, red stoneware lighthouse-shaped with sprig reliefs. Unmarked, c. 1730-50, 6⅛ inches high.* **Tea canister,** *red stoneware moulded body. Wares with similar decoration were excavated at Thomas Whieldon's site at Fenton Vivian and other Staffordshire sites. Unmarked, c. 1750-60, 4½ inches high. (Royal Ontario Museum, 984.18.1&2, 983.236.2 1 & 2.)*

Fig. 13 **Teapots**, *chocolate-brown stoneware with buff slip ground and dragon and foliate sprig relief decoration. Left, pseudo seal mark, English, probably Staffordshire, c. 1770-80, 5¼ inches high; right, unmarked, Chinese, c. 1750-70, 4 inches high. (Darlington collection.)*

Wedgwood red stoneware section. However, there is evidence that Wedgwood was 'buying in' red stonewares from Samuel Hollins and others in the late 1700s and may have even been manufacturing these wares himself so the question is moot. According to David Barker a preponderance of the Greatbatch stonewares date from 1765 to 1770,[23] more or less the height of fashion for these wares which were subsequently largely replaced by the ascendancy of creamware. Most of the Greatbatch pieces have sprig relief decoration of Chinese figures, some press-moulded in a hexagonal form, but others in addition to Greatbatch were making these wares. Serpent handles and bamboo handles also were recovered in the excavation as well as engine-turned teapots with chevron decoration which were commonly made in redware in the period. Greatbatch is also discussed in Chapter VIII in the alphabetical listing of stoneware manufacturers.

Two other potteries should be mentioned in the context of red stoneware manufacture: the Bovey Tracey potteries excavations unearthed redwares which could have been manufactured at Bovey Tracy or could have been made in Staffordshire producing no positive conclusions about source.[24] At Swinton, however, red stoneware manufacture is more conclusive. Both glazed and unglazed red stoneware in a variety of engine-turned patterns were produced.[25]

Thus red stoneware, a common denominator in the ceramic lexicon, leads us into the more dramatic dry-bodied stoneware emanating from it. In a sense the most long-lived and most popularly produced body in English ceramic history, red stoneware is the one ceramic body which transcends frontiers and tastes as a comfortable,

appealing aesthetic which can be charming left unadorned but rises to a sophistication given an Egyptian or Greek theme to embellish it. From prehistory, from the Greek and South Italians, from Samian to Elers, redware was the lingua franca of the ceramic world and yet its common elements predisposed it to exceptional fineness at times, as a body which could be slip-cast, moulded, chased and embellished to enable it to compete with its more *outré* competitors, black basalt, caneware and jasper.

Fig. 14 **Brazier,** *red stoneware with pierced decoration and on tripod grotesques, twisted rope handles. Unmarked, Yorkshire or Staffordshire, c. 1770-80, 5⅛ inches high. (Royal Ontario Museum, 983.236.15.)*

CHAPTER II

⟫—◦—⟪

The Wedgwood Contribution

The fact that Wedgwood has been written about for more than 125 years, since both Eliza Meteyard and Llewellynn Jewitt published biographies in the 1860s, is not surprising, given the many innovations he provided to the English pottery industry. That he has been made an icon in the whole scheme of English pottery production may be somewhat disproportionate to his contribution, but not by much. Such veneration has dripped from the pens of Wedgwood biographers that 'hagiography' is not too fulsome to describe the enthusiasm that his name and work inspire. In 1865 Miss Meteyard was probably the first to utilise the vast archival material, preserved by collectors of business history like Joseph Mayer of Liverpool and later Mrs William Mosley (née Mary Wedgwood),[1] who saved batches of letters and factory related material from destruction. It is, in part, because of the existence of such a wealth of material relating to the factory and to the life of Josiah Wedgwood I, augmented by the survival of much of the almost daily correspondence of Josiah Wedgwood to partner Thomas Bentley (1730-80), that we can continue to produce books with material on Wedgwood and his wares that has not previously seen the light of day.

Although Wedgwood's name is associated with the perfection or invention of any number of ceramic body types, such as Queen's ware or creamware, caneware, jasper, and basalt, in truth he was responsible for only two inventions: the jasper body and the pyrometer for measuring kiln temperature. Josiah Wedgwood himself took credit anonymously in a letter which he sent to Mr John Walter editor of *The Times* in 1788 for the invention of seven ceramic bodies.[2] The first one was Queen's ware, or creamware. It is no wonder that Wedgwood published this treatise anonymously considering that creamware was being made and dated at least as early as 1743, probably by Enoch Booth and doubtless others.[3] Six other bodies in addition to creamware were listed as inventions of Wedgwood: Terracotta, Basaltes, White Porcelain bisque, Jasper, Bamboo, or cane, and another body simply described as 'A porcelain bisque'.

It might be worthwhile to try to separate fact from fiction, in the order listed. Which, indeed, were inventions for which Josiah Wedgwood could legitimately be given credit? As described by Wedgwood in his letter to John Walter the list included the following:

Terracotta, resembling porphyry, granite, Egyptian pebble, and other beautiful stones, of the Siliceous or Crystalline order. The use of the term Terracotta is a curious one and, until recently, little understood. However,

in his own description Wedgwood elucidates it clearly enough as the body used in vases and other ornamental wares described in sales records and inventories of factory stock according to the geological prototype, such as, 'Pebble', 'Blew' (*sic*) or 'Blue necked', 'Marble' or 'Porphyry', and 'Granite'. As we shall see he even 'Jasper' in an early context to denote the surface and not the body. All of these wares were decorated in various dips or slips over a white high-fired earthenware which Wedgwood described as 'Terracotta'. This terminology presents some of the trickiest definition problems of all the Wedgwood bodies. First of all it is apparent that several bodies listed in successive catalogues are further developments of earlier ones in progress. White terracotta probably developed into 'White Porcelain bisque' that Wedgwood utilised in cameos and medallions, which in turn also laid the foundations for the basic jasper body. However, as with the 'White Porcelain bisque', which we will touch on shortly, white terracotta had its foundations ultimately in the white salt-glaze stoneware body with perhaps an extra measure of flint. Accordingly, white terracotta, with its matrix in the earlier white salt-glaze stoneware cannot be considered to be Wedgwood's specific invention.

'Basaltes' was listed as the second (or third if one includes creamware) invention of Wedgwood in the anonymous treatise sent to *The Times* in 1788. Certainly Josiah Wedgwood was the first or among the first of those manufacturers to industrialize and market basalt, but the body once again was being produced at least by 1750 by John and Thomas Wedgwood, before they built the Big House, Burslem (*c.*1750),[4] by Thomas Whieldon at Fenton Vivian in the 1750s, and undoubtedly others.

The third invention Wedgwood ascribes to himself is for White Porcelain bisque to be 'of a smooth wax-like surface, of the same properties with the preceding except that it depends upon colour'. Wedgwood's 'white porcelain bisque' is also described as a 'fine waxen biscuit' in his 1779 catalogue and, by his own definition, it was a highly vitrified or porcellaneous stoneware used principally for cameos, medallions and plaques and tablets. Certainly this was in production by 1774 as Wedgwood was sending from Etruria to the London retail rooms 'fine white heads of The Grand Duke and Duchess, Apollo, and Medusa[5] and Dr Franklin, Count Orloff, and Cleopatra'.[6] The same inventory included 'white bracelet Gems'. Although no size was given, these are probably the 2 x 1¾ inch cameos listed in the 1779 catalogue. The composition was probably similar to the antecedent of English creamware, white salt-glaze stoneware. Abroad the refined white bisque porcelain popularly produced in France in the mid-eighteenth century again argues against any specific 'invention' by Wedgwood.

Next on the list of Wedgwood inventions is Jasper. Indeed, this is the body which history has justifiably given to Wedgwood and the one with which his name is inextricably linked, his invention truly. Jasper plays a key role in any work on the dry-bodied stoneware and it will be looked into at considerable length later on in Chapter V.

Fifth was *'Bamboo'*, or cane-coloured bisque porcelain of the same nature as No. 3. Cane-coloured stoneware has been considered for some time to have been the first of the dry-bodies to have succeeded basalt and white terracotta. But, as shall be further discussed in this chapter, caneware was not produced in 1771 as has previously been suggested. Indeed the evidence makes it clear that jasper was in production much in advance of caneware. As to Wedgwood's invention of the cane body, that, again, is problematical as caneware has antecedents in both Chinese Yixing buff-coloured stoneware and in some earlier Staffordshire stoneware of the drab composition. Thus, the cane body was a refinement of earlier wares in the pottery matrix.

A porcelain bisque was the last of the inventions for which Wedgwood took credit in his 1788 article:

Remarkable for great hardness, little inferior to that of agate: this property, together with its resistance to the strongest acids and corrosives, and its impenetrability by every known liquid, adapts it for mortars, and many different kinds of chemical vessels.

In other words Wedgwood is talking about mortar and crucible ware (Fig. 222) suited for medical and scientific purposes. On this one it seems plausible to take Wedgwood's word for it. What cannot be contradicted is that Wedgwood was always experimenting with and improving bodies and glazes and looking for more scientific ways to control kiln temperatures, hence the invention of the pyrometer in 1782 for measuring such temperatures.[7]

Thus out of the seven 'inventions' for which Wedgwood gave himself credit in the 1788 anonymous letter written to the publisher of *The Times*, only jasper, and possibly mortarware, can be truly credited to his name. Jasper, along with the pyrometer, for which he was made a Fellow of the Royal Society in 1783, are the two great contributions to the ceramic world made by Josiah Wedgwood.

On the other hand there is no doubt that Wedgwood had the major hand in perfecting and, perhaps more importantly, in promoting all of the other wares from creamware to basalt. In his marketing of all these wares he was a master, ever attendant to the fickleness of an increasingly economically mobile society with an eye for the latest fashion.

Of the seven so-called 'inventions' all but creamware and terracotta fall into the arena of a work on dry-bodied stoneware. However, other works have been written about the basalt body,[8] and although basalt is a dry-bodied stoneware, because of these other books it will be eliminated from the scope of this particular work.

One particular body which is nearly anonymous, and for which Wedgwood never took credit is red stoneware which played a long and essential role and was the stock in trade of nearly all early potteries.

CHAPTER III

Wedgwood Red Stoneware and Brown Stoneware

Loo [Lady Ashburton] staying in Paris at the Hotel Westminster, rue de la Paix, agreed
to take from Hatty [Harriet Hosmer] a rosso antico pedestal with its base, amounting
to £70, hoping one day to have a handsome vase to place upon it.

Virginia Surtees – *The Ludovisi Goddess. The Life of Louisa Lady.*

Red stoneware, or redware in the vernacular, was undoubtedly a staple in the Wedgwood bread and butter trade from the outset in all the partnerships (Fig. 15). As an inexpensive, common product the forms would have been less vulnerable to the vicissitudes of fashion. That Wedgwood even produced red stoneware is not commonly known, because he rarely acknowledged its production by marking it. Nevertheless, there are the odd references to redware sales and purchases in the 1770s, which would seem to have been the end of Wedgwood's interest in this out-of-fashion teaware, and yet, as we shall see, the body hung on for more than two decades in the old shapes and continued to be revived in various other states until the middle of the nineteenth century. Charles Carroll of Carrollton, the wealthiest man in America in the period of the American Revolution, was still ordering redware in late 1771 when he ordered '6 large red stone Teapotts' as well as '2 brown stone Teapots.'[1] The description 'brown' is a problem which will continue to perplex interpretation in studying future Wedgwood sales lists. Indeed, in 1772 Wedgwood

Fig. 15 *Jug and plate*, red stoneware, jug with interior glaze. Marks: jug WEDGWOOD D, *c. 1785-1800, 3¼ inches high; plate*, WEDGWOOD T, *c. 1800-1810. (Royal Ontario Museum, 984.18.39; 984.18.40.)*

complained to Bentley that, 'Those brown T'pots had lead in their composition which material must be omitted and we must endeav'r to find out something else to make the body close.'[2] Wedgwood's description is a temptation to conclude that the so-called 'brown' wares were actually the lead-glazed red stonewares. On the subject of red teapots Wedgwood lamented to Bentley in correspondence later that year:

I do not know what we shall do with these People at the Ornamental works—we have been making a qu[ty] of common red china Teapots to sell quite cheap & now we have begun upon 70 or 80 doz. of the other sorts, after examining your stock acct. to see what you have fewest of.[3]

An examination of inventories of ornamental wares sent to Mr Bentley in London for sale on the account of Wedgwood and Bentley in 1774 yields 'Brown [bustos] of Voltaire and Montesque' @ 15/- each as well as 'Brown fox heads' or stirrup cups for 2/- each.[4] The question remains: what has happened to these so-called 'brown' wares?

By 1776 *rosso antico* (Figs. 17, 20-23; Colour Plates 2-4) was being made at Etruria and since redwares were always common denominators and not fashionable by the mid-1770s, Wedgwood accordingly lamented in a letter to Bentley: 'I am afraid we shall never be able to make *Rosso Antico* otherwise than to put you in mind of a red-Pot-Teapot.'[5]

As jasper was the current rage and since basalt continued to be exceedingly popular, Wedgwood discouraged the production of *rosso antico*, or the red and black in combination, in the form of 'subjects' saying that: 'Everybody can make that color, & composition, but nobody besides W. & B. can make Jasper.'[6] Nevertheless, 'Black & red Toylet (*sic*) Candlesticks' at 2/6 a piece were being produced in 1776 along with other forms in the so-called *rosso antico*.[7]

Brown and red bodies were made into tablets and could be as expensive to produce as jasper ones, at least in some instances, as they were being sold at the same prices as those made in jasper. The first mention of 'brown' tablets was on 26 September 1776.[8] In the same list another tablet of 'common clay; of *Bacchante & Boys* was priced at 15/-.[9] One is tempted to think that this was a redware tablet, but

Fig. 16 *Pair of vases* (with replacement covers), red stoneware with sprig relief in red stoneware. These vases are shape No. 381 in the Wedgwood shape book and are listed as being 31½ inches high. They are among vase shapes which were sold in the early 1790s and are very rare examples of a small but important group of red stonewares made by Wedgwood. Marks: both WEDGWOOD, c. 1790-95, 11¼ inches high. (Collection of the Birmingham Museum of Art, Alabama; Dwight and Lucille Beeson Wedgwood collection, 1976.228.)

in another invoice the same description is referred to as common 'white'. On 5 October 1776 the following were sent down to London for sale:

1 Brown Tablet Panther, 4 by 8½in. 1.11.6
4   do.   Boys 4¾ by 3½in. 7/6, 1.10.0
1 Red   do.   4 by 8½in. 1.11.6
4 do.   do.   4¾ by 3½in. 7/6, 1.10.0.[10]

Not surprisingly red tablets were made in the same subjects as jasper and black ones. Thus the *Dancing Hours* (15in. by 5in. £1.1.0), *Cupid & Marriage* (16in. by 8in. £1.11.0), *Boys & Goat* (oval 12in. by 8in. £1.11.6) were all subjects made in red tablets.[11] Red tablets were also made with less well-known subjects described as a *'Vase between two Sphinxes'* (8½in. by 7in.) which sold for £1.1.6.[12] A curious entry for 'Brown vases No. 142, 7½ inches' high, was listed as selling for 12/- each in the same inventory. Three large red tablets, undescribed except for size (17in. by 6in.) sold for the not inconsiderable sum of three guineas each about the same time.[13]

Wedgwood continued to denigrate the red body saying in a letter in 1777:

Red Seals wo'd be made with much greater certainty, & look very well when polished — But anybody can make Red & nobody but W & B can make Blue — & There is something in that which urges me strongly to prosecute the blue in preference to red.[14]

Yet red-and-white and brown-and-white seals were made and sold unset for 33 shillings the dozen or 2/9 each.[15]

By 1778 almost no red tablets were being sold at the Greek Street showrooms in London. There are only two sales listed for the whole year, one of which was '1 Red Bas relief Triumph of Bacchus' for the enormous sum of 63/-.[16] However, there were several sales of dual-colour bas-relief tablets, in brown and white, Nos. 22 and 23 *(Perseus and Andromeda)* which sold for 12/- and a 'Brown & White Statue framed, No. 51' *(Herculaneum dancing Nymph)* for 63/-. One 'Black & Red unframed' Class 5 No. 91 head sold for 31/6.[17]

Red teapots described as 'high' or 'upright fluted' were very inexpensive, selling for as little as 1/- each.[18] But they also constituted a small proportion of the Wedgwood and Bentley sales, and judging from the survival, were probably never marked with the Wedgwood imprimatur; indeed, they may have been 'bought in' from some other

Fig. 17 *Egg cups*, (left) blue and white jasper shape No. 324, (centre) caneware with black grape vine relief, (right) redware with black Egyptian sprig relief. Jasper egg cups are being sold in June 1786 (Wedgwood MS 16/15373) and caneware were available at least by May 1790 (16/15491) for 1/- each. Marks: all WEDGWOOD, c. 1786-1800, 2¼ inches high. (Polikoff collection.)

Fig. 18 *Oil lamp*, red stoneware with white Oriental sprig relief. Mark: WEDGWOOD, c. 1810, 1¼ inches high. (Grigsby collection, ex Byron Born collection.)

Fig. 19 **Egg cup basket with egg rings**, *red stoneware (fire damage). In spite of the poor condition, the survival of an egg basket with its four egg rings is highly unusual and worthy of illustration. Mark: WEDGWOOD 8, c. 1800, 3¼ inches high. (Royal Ontario Museum, 984.18.43.1-5.)*

manufacturer, such as Christopher and Charles Whitehead, who were selling red teawares to Wedgwood at the time.[19]

1778 was the year when *rosso antico* entered the sales records in considerable numbers. Described simply as 'Red & Black', the *rosso antico* body included such forms as bulbous root pots which sold for 5 shillings each,[20] 'Red & Black flat candlesticks' at 2/6 each,[21] and 'Red & Black low fluted Tea Potts @ 1/-' [each].[22]

In 1779 *rosso antico* continued to feature prominently. The major item of interest purveyed in redware was a tablet of the *Marriage of Cupid and Psyche* for 31/6, the standard tablet price.[23] Among the most popular items were 'Bulbous Root pots', a total of thirty-three sold in 1779, (fourteen black and red; nineteen red and black). The price varied from 2/- to 6/- per pot. Twelve red and black candlesticks were sold, two of them described as 'high' candlesticks at 15/- the pair.[24] Ten red and black teapots and seven black and red teapots were among the sales along with four red and black 'fluted' teapots and five red and black cream ewers. Teapots sold from 9d to 3/6 each. Among 'red and brown' sales were two cream ewers at 9d.,[25] priced the same as the red and black cream ewers.[26] In a single instance a red and black fluted cream 'jug' sold for 9d. in 1779.[27] As with all the rosso antico objects some were described as black and red and others as red and black. It may have been the ground colour which was described initially followed by the colour of the decoration. The survival of 'brown' wares being minimal it is fascinating to see the number of wares described as 'brown' being listed. A garniture of five 'Red and brown' bow pots, probably earthenwares, sold for a total of 10/- (5/- the central vase, 3/- the two middle vases and 2/- the smallest pair).[28]

As mentioned, the major item of interest purveyed in redware was a tablet of the *Marriage of Cupid and Psyche* for 31/6, a standard tablet subject in all bodies.[29] Simple redwares, however, were offered consistently at very low prices. Not surprisingly in 1779 teapots remained the most popular form. There were sales of 107 red teapots without further description. The most expensive red teapot sold for 2/6, the least was an order for thirty-six red teapots selling for only 9d. each.[30]

Five teapots were described as 'parapet' and sold from 2/- to 1/- each. One 'orange Red' parapet teapot went for 3/6.[31] Six red fluted teapots sold the same year ranging from 2/- to 1/- a piece and one red fluted 'upright' teapot was 1/6.[32] Four teapots simply described as red 'upright' sold for 2/- each.[33] Although by 1779 it would seem late for red sprigged wares to continue to be popular a few were still being sold. Red sprig teapots, tea and coffee cups (12 for 6d. each)[34] and chocolate inlets, as well as butter tubs linger, but not in quantity. Other forms included red foxes heads, two of which went for 2/- each.[35]

The 'brown' wares persisted and continued to be manifest themselves abundantly in inkpots, but also in inkstands which sold for 6/-,[36] as well as 'Brown Foxes head[s]' at 2/6 each.[37]

Neither the interest in, nor the variety of, red and brown stoneware increased in the early years of the 1780s. A few red parapet teapots were sold in 1780, for as little as 3/6 for one

Fig. 20 **Pastille burner**, *rosso antico with Egyptian motifs. Reilly illustrated a prototypical tripod perfume burner in ormolu probably made by Diederich Nicolaus Anderson, c. 1761. Matthew Boulton copied the design in 1771 and in 1777 when four such tripods were supplied to Earl Gower. As Reilly suggested, Wedgwood may have used Boulton or Gower examples as models. Mark: WEDGWOOD, c. 1798-1805, 15 inches high. (Courtesy the Trustees of the Wedgwood Museum, Barlaston, Stoke-on-Trent.)*

Fig. 21 **Pyrophorous vase,** *rosso antico. Pyrophorous vases, basically modern tinderboxes for lighting candles, were adapted from earlier vase forms, such as this altar flower pot which first appeared on the market as a bulbous root vase, shape No. 288, in 1788. By the early 19th century these adaptations were common. Mark: WEDGWOOD, c. 1810, 4 inches high. (Liverpool Museum, Museums & Galleries on Merseyside, Mayer collection, M3007.)*

Fig. 22 **Mark fig. 21,** *from the retailer in Cambridge, Weston Chemists.*

half dozen.[38] Brown inkpots continued to be sold in considerable numbers, along with some red and black wares but the heyday, if there ever was one, was concentrated in the late 1770s and simply lingered on into the next decade. A few brown teapots,[39] brown altar candlesticks[40] and lamps[41] showed up on lists of sales, no doubt placed there simply to confuse future ceramic historians who might be looking for such rarities to illustrate. The combination red and brown was not unknown and was made in bough pots (No. 206) selling for 3/6,[42] and in 'pipe heads', or bowls, which sold for 1/6 each.[43]

Only a few records exist for the months January to April of 1781 and none for 1782 and 1783. Oven records do exist for this period and indicate the factory was in full operation. Although the Wedgwood & Bentley sale in December, 1781, did not obviously include any red or brown wares, some ceramic bodies were undescribed. An inventory taken at Bath of the Wedgwood and Bentley stock in August, 1781 included:

14 Brown Teapots a.g. 10/6 14 do @ 14/- £1.4.6

31 Teracota (*sic*) Brown & Black & Red & Red & Wt. Teapots @ 1/6 £2.6.6

29 Do. of Different Sorts @ 2/- £2.18.0

34 Teracota (*sic*) Cain (*sic*) & Black & Red Shugar (*sic*) Dishes @1/6 £2.11.0

19 Teracota (*sic*) & Red & Black flatt (*sic*) Candlesticks @ 2/6 £2.7.6[44]

A few sales lists exist for the months of April and May in 1784 but no red or brown stonewares are listed. Sales records for 1785 do not survive and by 1786, not surprisingly, interest in and sales of red stonewares have almost been extinguished. There is a recording of '1 red China teapot stand long Square' for 2/6[45] in July of that year, but that may have been a special order, or again, something 'bought in' from another manufacturer.

No sales of redwares occur in 1787 but just when one is tempted to declare the body extinct a sale of '1 Red Teapot' at 12/- and 6 (Red) Cream Jugs at 2/- takes place in September of 1788.[46] These were ordered by Messrs C. Muller & Co. for the Continental market. After 1788 no more red or brown stonewares appear on lists of Wedgwood sales. One sale in 1791 of '18 Red & White Bisque Garden Pots' for £2.2.0[47] presents somewhat of a problem in definition, but they may have been fired at a high enough temperature to fall into the stoneware arena.

An early nineteenth century revival in *rosso antico* production yielded a great many wares (Figs. 17, 20-23; Colour Plates 2-4), both with Egyptian themes following the Napoleonic campaigns in the Nile, and in Greek revival styles, which can be confused with similar pots manufactured in the 1770s. The interest in the red and black combination continued well into the nineteenth century with sales of 'Red and Black bas-relief Grecian

Fig. 23 *Gondola escritoire*, rosso antico. *'Gondola ecritoires masque heads' were available by August 1786 for 7/- each, but these would have been basalt. Following on the revival of Egyptian themes, which had been recurrent from the Middle Ages, the last years of the eighteenth century and early years of the nineteenth produced some remarkable ceramics in the motifs spawned by Napoleon's campaign of 1798. Unmarked, early 19th c., 5 inches high. (Birmingham Museums & Art Gallery. (Tangye collection, 1885 M 2795.)*

lamps & wax' and red and black 'Egyptian' teapots in 1809.[48] The 'Red with Black Chinese ornament' in the form of 'oval creams' was ordered by merchant Mr Thomas Surr of York, around the same time.[49] The price for Black or Red & Black Incense Burners No. 493 was 15/-; No. 494, 12/6; No. 495 15/-; No. 496 10/-.[50]

The order book of Bateman, Wedgwood's traveller, included 'redware [with] black leafage flowers' and 'red with black husk' bas-relief, which were very popular in 1818 in both cane and redwares.[51]

Although no prices are given in Bateman's day book, the orders give an idea of what was being sold and often to whom. For instance, by 1818 the grape border was very frequently the subject of bas-relief decoration on both cane and on red ware; on caneware it would often be in red, but sometimes on redware the border would be grey or black. The black grape border (Fig. 17 centre) continued to appear on redware in Bateman's order book in 1837 and

1838.[52] Less descriptive was 'Redware with black ornaments' and this was produced in flower vases No. 584 'on a square pedestal, etc.' and in egg cups (Fig. 17).[53] In October, 1821 a Mr Pomfret of York was ordering redware 'Garden pots & stands [No.] 855'.[54] And in 1827 redware was still popularly produced with enamel Chinese flowers and birds, especially pheasants, as decoration.[55] Redwares with 'black rose borders' were on Bateman's order book for September, 1832. And in 1835 'club jugs' in redware with enamel Chinese decoration were also available.[56]

As a common denominator red stoneware could, when required, rise to meet the demands of almost any ethos or taste as a body which, while providing a container for the best pot of tea, could also stand alone as a vase in a garniture on a chimney piece or a tablet over a mantel. As the predecessor body to a host of more sophisticated dry bodies it was both the least pretentious and the most comfortable of all the unglazed stonewares.

CHAPTER IV

Wedgwood Caneware

Caneware was produced from local marl, the body being similar to the refined brown stoneware which was also made locally. Contrary to popular notion caneware was probably not the first dry-bodied stoneware to succeed the industrial manufacture of basalt and the white terracotta body used in the variegated vases. It did not appear on the market until late in 1776, making jasper an earlier development. Unlike basalt and jasper, caneware was a development for which Wedgwood never mustered much enthusiasm. In the past it was thought that Wedgwood's experiments in August 1771 in producing 'Fawn colour articles'[1] referred to early production of caneware. However, it becomes clear when reviewing sales in 1778 and 1779 that the description 'Fawn' is a buff-coloured, slip-decorated creamware body used primarily for garden pots. In 1778 a 'cane Tea Pott' is followed by a 'Fawn colour'd Foxes head' in a list of Wedgwood & Bentley sales giving rise to the suspicion that two distinct body or decorative techniques are being described.[2] By 1779 'Brown & Fawn fluted Garden pots' or 'Chocolate & Fawn Barrel'd [Garden pots]' make it clear that fawn and cane were not synonymous.[3] Although the records are not complete, this is further supported in the available inventories of wares sent from Etruria to the Greek Street London showrooms in 1774 and 1776. Cane teapots do not feature on lists of items sent down to London until 31 October 1776 when 'cane Teapots' (Figs. 24-26, 31, 34) 12s sold @ 2/6; 18s @ 2/- and 24s @ 1/6 appear.[4] A small number of canewares began to trickle on the market, with twelve teapots being sent down to London on 31 October 1776 and another ten on 9 November.[5] Twenty more teapots were sent to London on 23 November.[6] All these lists lacked any detail about shape or decoration. Throughout the Wedgwood listings and inventories in the 1770s details of caneware forms are sadly lacking; whereas accounts of black basalt and other tewares, such as jasper, usually include some description about shape or embellishment, such as painting or sprigging. Two more lots of nineteen and seventeen cane teapots respectively were sent down to London in December making a total sent out for sale of only seventy-eight for the year 1776.[7] No documentation exists for sales or inventories being sent to London for the year 1777; however, in 1778 there is almost a complete list of daily sales except for the month of January. Teapots were the primary form, continuing at the same price and without description, selling at about two per day throughout the year until August when cane sugar dishes at 1/- each were first mentioned.[8]

In October '2 Black & Cane Bow Potts @ 1/6 featured in sales listings,[9] and the following month 'chased' teapots were being made in both black and caneware as well as 'chased fluted Turnip'-shaped teapots.[10] A 'Fawn colour'd Foxes head' at 2/- followed an entry for a 'Cane Teapot' at 1/6 in February of 1778, further supporting the evidence that cane and fawn were two distinct bodies.

The sales listings for 1779 are complete and cane ware was produced in all the teaware shapes and in a few garden pots. Prices continued to be low and no descriptions about form or embellishment were given. Teapots predominated and the 1776 prices continued with the smallest size selling for 1/6. The range went to 2/-, 2/6 and the largest teapot selling for 3/6. A total of 227 teapots were sold in 1779. A cane 'Sugar Dish' (Fig. 27) sold for either 1/- or 1/6 and a total of fifty-one were sold in 1779. 'Sugar Basons' (sic) were distinguished from the sugar dishes, but were the same prices 1/- and 1/6. Eight of those were sold. A cane 'Ewer' sold for either 9d or 1/- with a total of twenty-five sales that year. Cream Jugs sold for 9d but only two were sold; however sixteen 'Cream Ewers' were sold, also at 9d. A few 'Milk Potts', only four, were sold at 9d. A total of thirteen garden pots were also sold and ranged in price from 2/- to 4/-.[11] Caneware continued to be less costly than basalt but descriptions for basalt and jasper, which were always considerably more expensive than either cane or redware, are much more complete so comparisons about prices between basalt and caneware or jasper and cane are not really feasible.

Although caneware had been on the market for three years, Wedgwood's indifference to the body was so complete that he did not even bother to include it in his 1779 catalogue, listing it for the first time in 1787.

Sales continue apace in caneware in 1780 with 'Cane [Bulbous] Root Pots' entering the market in February 1781.[12] Sales records end in the last week of April 1781, presumably due to arrangements for the disposition of the Wedgwood and Bentley stock consequent to Bentley's death the previous November. The sale of the stock from the Wedgwood and Bentley partnership by Christie and Ansell commenced on 3 December 1781 and continued over the next eleven days. Confirming the step-child nature of the caneware body, there were no offerings of cane in the Christie and Ansell sale, save for a few Myrtle-pans in 'Cane-leaf pattern'.[13] Whether 'cane leaf' was actually caneware is uncertain. Most of the Myrtle-pans, Bouquetiers and Pots-pourries, including those listed in the sale, were earthenware, not stoneware.

Fig. 24 *Teapot*, caneware in cane pattern. Cane teapots (undescribed) were being sold by 31 October 1776 @ 12s @ 2/6, 18s @ 2/- and 24s at 1/6 (Wedgwood MS 1449). Mark: Wedgwood & Bentley, c. 1776-80, 4 inches high. (Liverpool Museum, Museums & Galleries on Merseyside, 2912 M, ex Mayer collection.)

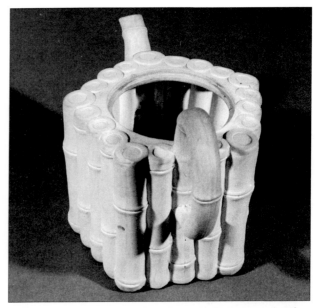

Fig. 25 *Interior of teapot* figure 24, glazed with flat strainer and uniform punch holes. Mark: Wedgwood & Bentley. (Liverpool Museum, ex Mayer collection.)

An inventory of the Wedgwood and Bentley stock taken at the Bath warehouse on 13 August 1781, presumably to settle the partnership's interests there, included the following teaware listings: '12 Cain (*sic*) Shugar (*sic*) Dishes @ 1/- for a total of 12/6 and 6 Cain (*sic*) Cream Ewers 4/6'.[14] Sales records for the years 1782-83 do not survive, but it is likely that the stock was being replaced after the 1781 liquidation. Only a few weeks of sales survive for April and May of 1784 and nothing for 1785.

Apparently, as late as 1783, cane trials were still being

Fig. 26 *Underside and mark on teapot* figure 24, three pads and upper and lower case Wedgwood & Bentley mark and Mayer collection accession number. (Liverpool Museum.)

conducted to perfect the body. In a letter to his father Josiah Wedgwood II wrote:

'Daniel sends some cane trials by a box p[er] coach & Mr Swift sends some manganese. These are the trials of the cane color.'

No. 1
3 of 84 brown   (
2 of ball clay   (Too bibulous and too pale color
                (*sic*) = red
1 of ground flint   (

No. 2
4 of 84   (
2 of ball clay   ([no comment opposite this]
1/8 of red clay

No. 3
10 dwts of No.2 & 12 qrs. of whiting

No. 4
3 of 84
1 of ball clay
1/2 of whiting[15]

By April 1784 caneware was being sold in shapes and decoration which were being described: '1 Cane Color Basrelief Jug painted Blue 14/-' (Fig. 28) 1 Oval Chased Teapot 2/6' as well as '1 [Cane Chased] patera & Ladle 2/6'. Size was also included for the first time: '1 Cane 3 pt. Basrelief Jug 14/-'.[16]

Unimportant prior to 1786, there is no doubt that by that year caneware took on a specific identity and life of its own. Records of sales for 1786 are complete from 1 May to the end of the year revealing a wide variety of new

Fig. 27 **Sugar dish** (with possibly unmatched cover), cane shape caneware. Sugar dishes were first mentioned in surviving Wedgwood sales in August 1778 and sold for 1/- or 1/6 each (Wedgwood MS 16/15233). Mark: Wedgwood & Bentley, c. 1778-80, 4⅛ inches high. (Private collection.)

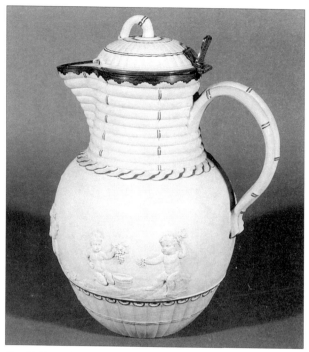

Fig. 28 **Covered jug**, caneware with blue enamel embellishment. April 1784 sales included 'Cane Color Basrelief Jug painted Blue 14/-' (Wedgwood MS 16/15367). Mark: WEDGWOOD, c. 1782-90, 10.2 inches high. (Lady Lever Art Gallery, Museums & Galleries on Merseyside, LL1100.)

articles including caneware with specific border painting such as, '1 Cane Basrelief teapot Blue Drop Border 7/6-,'[17] and for the first time 'Cane tube flower pots (Fig. 29) painted blue l.12.0.[18]

Cane tube flower pots proved to be a steady item in Wedgwood sales into the early 1790s, essentially falling out of fashion by 1792. Teapots described as 'Cane bamboo'

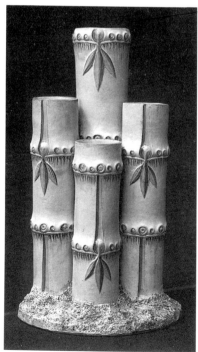

Fig. 29 **Tube for flowers**, caneware painted in green enamel. Shape No. 542, 'Cane tube flower pots painted blue' were mentioned for the first time in existing sales in June 1786 and sold for £1.12.0 (Wedgwood MS 16/15373). Mark: WEDGWOOD, c. 1786-92, 10½ inches high. (Birmingham Museums & Art Gallery, 542.)

(Fig. 31) selling at 3/6- begin to appear in July 1786,[19] leading us into questions about terminology, as 'Cane cane' teapots and 'Black cane' teapots are terms also used frequently. In November 1786, '3 Cane color bamboo pattern Teapots' sold for 4/6-, followed by 'Cane color Cane pattern [Teapots]' for 7/6-.[20] A 'Cane bamboo painted teapot & Stand' brought 10/- in August (Fig. 31).[21] To be sure no size is given but there is a distinction as Wedgwood and his staff did not use terminology loosely.

At the same time cane-coloured bas-relief oval bulbous root pots painted in green and gold and blue and red at 15/9 appear for the first time.[22] Soon thereafter 'cane [bulbous roots] blue & white [painted] for 2 [roots]' appear at 14/- (Fig. 33).[23] The adjective 'fawn' continues to be distinguished from 'cane' as a body in 1786 when 'fawn & white Mignonet pans' are offered.[24] That same year caneware was being made in the form of painted ewers and basins which sold for one guinea,[25] as well as 'déjeunes' for one with both blue painted and red Etruscan borders and the other blue with white leaves which sold for £1.11.6 each set.[26] Déjeuners (Fig. 34) were soon being decorated with a number of borders such as 'blue water Leaf' and 'blue Laurel on a red ground'.[27] The popularity of the déjeuner, or breakfast set, naturally led to the production and sale of cups and saucers independently (Fig. 32). By August, 1786, caneware chocolate cups with covers and saucers, painted blue were sold for 10/-.[28] Paint boxes in cane, burnished with gold, appear at the same time and were sold for £2.10.0 the pair.[29] Soon thereafter cane teapots with black bas-reliefs were being offered at 6/-[30] as well as 'Cane bas relief Teapot[s] painted [with] red & bl[ac]k Etruscan

Fig. 30 **Pipe tampers**, *caneware figures of a Satyr and Ariadne. These curiosities are not mentioned in existing sales, although there are a few examples of 18th century tampers in both basalt and in caneware. They are taken from the same moulds as seals with figures, the tampers having elongated stems. It has been considered that the term 'pipe head' found in sales records could indicate these objects but it is more likely that pipe heads are what we now call pipe bowls, another Wedgwood product. Unmarked, c. 1780-1800, Satyr 3⅛ inches high. (Courtesy the Trustees of the Wedgwood Museum, Barlaston, Stoke-on-Trent.)*

Honeysuckle' @ 15/- (Fig. 31).[31]

Coffee cups in caneware in 'Bamboo pattern' painted in blue appear for 2/- to 4/- each.[32] It is interesting to note that coffee cups in both basalt and cane were offered without saucers, the saucers serving alternatively either in

Fig. 31 **Teapot**, *caneware with red enamel additions. Possibly what was referred to as 'cane bamboo', teapots with this description began to appear in sales in July 1786 selling for 3/6 (Wedgwood MS 16/15373). Mark: Wedgwood 5 O and painter's mark P in red, 5 inches high. (ex Jacobs collection.)*

tea or in coffee drinking. In December 1786 several interesting items appeared in sales: a pair of square flower pots in cane painted blue and gold for £3.3.0 and one large cane flower vase painted with Etruscan borders for 15/- as well as a garniture of three 'Refraichisoir[s] [*rafraîchissoir*] painted Green cane color ware',[33] the larger selling for £1.5.0 the smaller two for £1.16.0 the pair.[34]

By 1787 an even wider variety of wares was on the market including cane garden pots at 1/-,[35] cane teaspoons also selling for 1/-, cane bread and butter plates for 1/6,[36] cane bas-relief mugs (6 for 15/-),[37] and cane bas-relief almond paste pots at 7/6 each.[38] In 1787 cane teapots were sold with stands for 8/6,[39] a garniture of three square 'Altar Flower Pot[s]' in cane colour with bas- relief paintings and two round candelabra sold for £3.13.0,[40] and a cane colour bas-relief cup painted green cost £2.2.0.[41] Bulbous root pots, by now the rage in all ceramic fabrics, were produced in blue-painted caneware (Fig. 36), selling for 15/6.[42]

By 1788 most caneware seemed to have been embellished with either painting, relief, turned, or chased decoration. Cane tube flower pots, bulbous root pots painted in green or in blue, and painted teawares are examples listed in the sales records.[43] The light cane body which was so compatible with painted decoration was indeed being thoroughly exploited. Painted teawares with 'blue Drop' borders, chased and painted green and purple or 'Cane Pattern Painted Green Laurel Border' predominate.[44]

Teapots, many of which by 1788 are offered in the latest 'oval' and 'oval fluted' shape,[45] are accompanied by sugar dishes, cream ewers and butter tubs and stands in the tea-set sales.

Fig. 32 **Teacup and saucer**, *cane bamboo with blue and white enamel decoration. Mark: Wedgwood 2 on both, c. 1786, teacup 1⅛ inches high. (Birmingham Museums & Art Gallery, 1885 M 2816-1-2.)*

By the 1780s the major theme was jasper, caneware continuing to play a minor role. Caneware, nevertheless, was elevated in status to a level never achieved in the 1770s, as highly decorative and ornamental.

By 1790 cane water ewers painted blue at 10/6,[46] as well

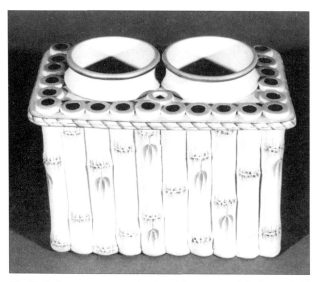

Fig. 33 **Bulbous root pot**, *cane bamboo with green enamel. In August 1786 cane bulbous roots for two roots appear in the sales lists for 14/- each (Wedgwood MS 16/15381). Mark: WEDGWOOD, c. 1786, 4½ inches high. (Lady Lever Art Gallery, Museums & Galleries on Merseyside, LL1094.)*

as chased jugs and teapots, featured in Wedgwood's sales. Other teaware forms, such as 'slop basons' were added to the usual list which included sugar dishes, cream ewers,[47] and tea canisters.[48] In general canewares were falling off in popularity with the bulk of sales in flower containers or bulbous root pots painted in blue or in green (Fig. 32). Painted cane garden pots (4/6 each)[49] occasionally feature

in sales but for the most part garden pots were earthenware, not stoneware. 'Cane tube Flower pots' or cane 'Bamboo tube,' as they were occasionally referred to, sold for 9/- for one tube.[50] Cane honeypots painted blue at 10/6 came on the market in May 1790,[51] along with caneware egg cups at 1/- each (Fig. 34; Colour Plate 5).[52] The lovely 'cane color [teapots] painted blue' sold for 12/- and to these were added 'chased Cream Boats' at 5/- the pair,[53] and cane punch pots for 12/-.[54]

By 1791 'chased' punch pots were fetching 16/-,[55] and caneware continued to be at its most desirable and attractive when painted: a 'Cane [bas-relief jug] painted Green Etruscan honeysuckle [border] & Glazed within' sold for 14/-.[56] Cane tube flower pots painted in green and blue continued in popularity and could cost as much as 16/- each,[57] the same price as a blue painted cane monteith.[58] In general, as mentioned, the tube flower pots fetched 9/-.[59] Tea cups and saucers were always unusual in the dry-bodied stoneware but '12 Cane Color Tea Cups & Saucers' sold for 18/- in July, 1791.[60]

By 1792 the shapes produced in caneware become even grander. Monteiths produced in the previous year yield to glaciers in 1792: '1 Cane color painted Red & Black Honeysuckle Glacier' sold for £1.11.6 [61] However, there are fewer caneware tewares and in general the trend seen in the previous year is emphasized in 1792 and the following two years with production, sales, or both, falling off dramatically. Towards the end of the year '2 Cane color Bas relief silver Tip't'[teapots] sold for £1.13.0 and '1 Bas relief Teapot Cane color with Green & Blue Festoons glazed within' brought a mere 6/-.[62]

Fig. 34 **Déjeuner teapot, saucer and egg ring**, *caneware with red enamel. Marks: teapot and saucer, WEDGWOOD; egg ring unmarked, c. 1785-95, saucer 4½ inches high; egg ring, 1½ inches high. (Pendergast collection.)*

Fig. 35 **Caddy spoon and cream jug,** caneware. Caddy spoons were available in jasper for 1/- each in August 1786 (Wedgwood MS 16/15380). Mark on spoon: WEDGWOOD, on jug: WEDGWOOD O, c. 1786-1810. (Pendergast collection, spoon ex Byron Born collection.)

Fig. 37 **Teapot and cover,** caneware with grey relief decoration. Mark: WEDGWOOD RK, c. 1800-10, 5¼ inches high. (Blake collection.)

Fig. 36 **Bulbous root pot,** caneware with blue enamel and gilding (shape No. 208). Mark: Wedgwood, c. 1786-92, 8⅞ inches high. (Laver collection.)

Sales records for 1793 are complete but cane colour had nearly disappeared from the lists. 'Cane color Bamboo Teapots' sold for 2/- or 2/6 on two occasions.[63] Teapots such as these and others with little embellishment continued to be sold in four sizes at 4/6, 3/6, 2/6, and 2/-; Creampots were sold for 1/6, 1/3, and 1/- each.[64] A cane teapot painted blue sold for little more at 2/6.[65]

After 1793 very few records of sales survive, and in the records for the first four months of 1794 no canewares were sold. However, there exists an undated document, which appears to be from the early years of the nineteenth century, listing wholesale and retail prices for:

Cane, Black, and Red tewares enamelled with Chinese flowers (Colour Plate 6; see Table below).

Wedgwood sales records are not the only source by which one can gauge the interest in the cane body and in other wares. Orders and invoices from both domestic merchants and those abroad, as well as from private customers, augment the information gleaned from the Wedgwood lists.

From all indications, caneware remained a saleable item well into the nineteenth century. Indeed, as late as 1836,

WHOLESALE SIZE	TEAPOTS	RETAIL	SUGARS	TEAPOT STANDS	CREAMER
9	6/-		6/-	2/-	5/6
12	5/-	7/-	5/-	1/6	4/6
18	4/-	5/-	4/-	1/3	3/6
24	3/-	4/6	3/-	1/-	2/6
30	3/-	4/-	2/6	9d.	2/6
36	2/6	3/6	1/10	9d.	2/-[66]

Table (probably early 19th century) for wholesale and retail prices for Cane, Black and Red teawares.

Fig. 38 **Vase and cover**, caneware with black and russet encaustic colours depicting an athletic trainer and a bull's head taken from d'Hancarville's Antiquities..., Vol. II (plates 38,41,71) from Sir William Hamilton's collection. The shape, No. 302, was a popular one in jasper from 1786 and enjoyed continued sales through 1793. The caneware versions are very rare indeed. Mark: WEDGWOOD A, c. 1786-95, 7⅝ inches high. (British Museum, Falcke collection, 1909.)

Fig. 39 **Teapots**, glazed caneware and unglazed drabware basket weave, both in low round form. Glazed caneware was regularly seen in the first third of the nineteenth century and was made by many other manufacturers in addition to Wedgwood. Marks: left, WEDGWOOD, right, WEDGWOOD 152 8 and 3⅛ inches high. (Royal Ontario Museum, gift of Mrs G. Edgerton Brown, 984.18.49.1 & 2.)

Fig. 40 **Hookah**, *caneware with brown relief of* Venturia *and* Volumina *entreating* Coriolanus, *taken from a wax model of 1784 by John Flaxman* (L. Miller, Proceedings of the Wedgwood Society, *No. 11, 1982, 170*). *'Hookers' or hookahs (shape No. 497) are mentioned in surviving sales in April 1790 (Wedgwood MS 16/15483). Mark:* WEDGWOOD, *c. 1790, 7½ inches high. (Birmingham Museums & Art Gallery, Tangye collection, 2814'85.)*

Fig. 42 **Covered sugar and ewer**, *sugar, white felspathic stoneware with moulded body and spaniel finial; ewer, fine white stoneware. Wedgwood felspathic stonewares are not found in abundance. Marks: both* WEDGWOOD, *c.1790-1810, 4½ inches (sugar), 8½ inches high (ewer). (Rakow collection.)*

'cane basketwork smeared' (Fig. 39) featured in such forms as honeypots, butter tubs, teapots and sugars, and 'cane-blue ornaments' were being offered in muffineers.[67]

In 1809, Wedgwood senior salesman Josiah Bateman began travelling throughout England and Scotland purveying Wedgwood wares, advising clients, and suggesting new types of merchandise to be considered in factory production. Bateman continued as the most senior

of salesmen to the factory until 1842 and the record of his orders sheds considerable light on the taste of the period. Beginning in 1809, Bateman's sales accounts include Northampton china merchants, 'Mesd'es Ann & Eliz' Horsey', who were ordering, in addition to jasper caddy spoons in various colours (Fig. 35), and red and black Egyptian tearwares and Grecian lamps (Figs. 17, 20; Colour Plate 3), '12 double egg cups' and oval teapots in

Fig. 41 **Teapot and cover**, *caneware with red stoneware relief. Mark:* WEDGWOOD *(in an arc), c. 1820. (Liverpool Museum, Museums & Galleries on Merseyside, 2913 M, Mayer collection.)*

Fig. 43 **Teapot and cover**, *fine white stoneware with blue floral sprig bands and sibyl finial. Glazed interior. Mark:* WEDGWOOD '159', *c. 1820, 5⅛ inches high. (Private collection, ex Nina Fletcher Little collection.)*

Fig. 44 **Wine cooler**, *engine-turned caneware with satyr mask handles. Mark: WEDGWOOD, c. 1800-20, 10¼ inches high. (Blake collection.)*

Fig. 45 **Pie dish**, *caneware. Mark: WEDGWOOD S, c. 1815, 7¼ inches high. (Royal Ontario Museum, 983.139.24.1&2.)*

caneware.[68] The 'low oval' form in teawares was still much in demand in all the stoneware orders. At the same time cane teapots were being described as 'embossed' in the oval form (Fig. 39).[69]

By 1818 cane colour with 'Red honeysuckle & husk bas relief' began to be seen frequently on Bateman invoices and receipts.[70] Cane flower vases No. 584 decorated with green borders and cane 'reading candlesticks' with 'green grape borders', as well as cane (jugs) with 'bas relief boys' are being sold that same year.[71]

Cane jugs with hunting subjects appear in 1821[72] Terminology begins to be a problem somewhat later when, in 1827, 'cane porcelain' enters into the descriptions of 'Pots 148' described as 'embossed with Chinese flowers' as well as others embellished with blue bands.[73] The trend continues with 'cane porcelain beehive (smeared)' describing honeypots and butter coolers and liners, ordered by Mr W. Jackson of Grafton Street, Dublin, as well as a 'cane porcelain basket weave' which included teapots and a drawing of a cheese stand for Stilton.[74] These 'cane porcelain' wares, occasionally described as 'smeared' which seems to imply the smear-glazed porcellanous body associated with feldspathic stoneware, are probably descriptive of glazed canewares in general. In the same order there was a 'cane, Chinese, embossed' group of teawares listed which implies the traditional dry-bodied stoneware. In the following two years, orders for canewares in 'arabesque' and in 'basket work' designs, described as caneware rather than cane porcelain, imply that the

original body was still in demand.[75]

Thus caneware was in Wedgwood's repertoire from 1776 to at least 1837, beginning in the 1770s as an inexpensive, nondescript teaware body which did not merit inclusion in Wedgwood's 1779 catalogue, nor descriptions of shape or embellishment in sales listings. By 1784 shapes and decoration were part of most descriptions of caneware and by 1786 much of the pale cane body was enamelled with blue or green borders. In a sense Wedgwood legitimized a body which he had previously spurned, by including it in his 1787 catalogue. In the late 1780s and early 1790s caneware was produced in a great variety of forms, from egg cups to teaspoons and almond paste pots. The last order for cane in Josiah Bateman's accounts was a 'cane porcelain beehive' [honeypot] in December 1837, probably as suggested, descriptive of glazed caneware.[76]

The body, doubtless, continued in moderate production after that, but the years from 1785 until about 1810 can be considered to be the salient ones in the production and interest in caneware. Other manufacturers produced canewares which rivalled those made by Wedgwood, some, such as Davenport (Colour Plates 42, 43; Figs. 149-155), producing wares which were so distinctive in style and decoration as to be recognized and associated with only that pottery. All the other caneware producing potteries, such as Davenport, Spode, Neale, and Ridgway, and others who may have only dabbled in its production, will be discussed individually under the various factory summaries in Chapter VIII.

CHAPTER V

Wedgwood Jasper

The King and the 2 eldest princes were in the dining-room looking at the pictures, but soon came in, and then they all went in a train thro' the great apartments to the Duchess of Portland's china closet, and with wondering and enquiring eyes admired all her magnificent curiosities.

Mrs Delany, August 1778[1]

Towards the end of 1772 the ornamental wares business of Wedgwood and Bentley was suffering one of its periodic declines. Dependent upon consumers in a fickle society, and some established competition in the form of Humphrey Palmer, as well as emerging competition by potters such as Josiah Spode and John Turner, Wedgwood sought a new product. Although the basalt and variegated wares were still admired, the partners realized that they had to anticipate, indeed, perhaps to create, the market in which they would find a voice. Jasper was that voice. And it was not *sotto voce*. It was *the* great invention. Imitated by few, but by those, such as Turner, Neale, Adams and Steel successfully; nevertheless, jasper has remained the flagship of the Wedgwood image to this day.

Jasper was conceived for ornamental wares. Unlike basalt and caneware, which adapted themselves to the manufacture of tea and coffee services, jasper was ill-suited to teaware production which tended to dilute the beauty and lower the profile of a coloured stoneware which should have exclusively remained the *ne plus ultra* of the refined ornamental market. An invention which truly can be ascribed to Josiah Wedgwood, the jasper body might be construed to have been introduced in the 1773 Wedgwood and Bentley trade catalogue when Wedgwood described the various offerings, including wares 'resembling Lapis Lazuli, Jasper ...'; however, that was not the stoneware, but another of the variegated wares decorated as natural stones.[2] Although it was doubtful if Wedgwood could actually produce all the wares he advertised in 1773, a form of the jasper body as it is now known was available in the next year. However, it remained in experimental stages for at least three years after it first appeared in August, 1774, when the two famous portrait medallions of the daughters of Lady Charlotte Finch were produced.[3]

In July, 1774, Wedgwood wrote to Bentley, 'At one time the body is white & fine as it should be ... the next we make it a cinnamon color (*sic*). One time it is melted to a Glass, another time dry as a Tob[acco] Pipe'.[4] Not withstanding the difficulties, in November, 1774, Wedgwood wrote also to Bentley that he had produced

Fig. 46 **Smelling Bottle,** *solid blue jasper with white jasper relief of Cupid Shaving his Bow. The popular Cupid theme was in full production in medallions and cameos by March 1774. 4¼ inches long. No mark, Wedgwood, c. 1788-95. (Nassau County Museum, Port Washington, New York, Buten collection of Wedgwood.)*

Fig. 47 **Pair of Pedestals,** *solid blue-grey jasper with white jasper. These pedestals appear to be the earliest surviving examples of marked Wedgwood & Bentley jasper. 3⅛ inches high Mark: Wedgwood & Bentley Etruria, c. 1780. (British Museum, Falcke collection, MLA 1909,12-1-33.)*

'seed of consequence ... of a beautiful onyx color'[5] which was to be his black jasper. By the summer of 1775 jasper production included cameos (heads) of persons of contemporary interest such as Mrs Montague and Mrs Barbault,[6] and Wedgwood was boasting that he could make 'blue grounds fine enough for *any thing or any body*'.[7]

As early as March 1774 Wedgwood was making bas–relief tablets of 'Boys' 12 inches by 8 inches representing the famous quartet: *War, Hunting, Music* and *Science*. He intended to transpose these into medallions a size larger than the popular *Cupid Shaving his Bow* (Fig. 46), proposing to make them in pairs of two each including two of *War*, about which when he wrote to Bentley he added, 'if you please to have so horrid a subject represented by innocent Babes in two more'.[8] By May of 1776 Wedgwood wrote, 'We have nine different Tablets which I hope we can make; none of them less than the Birth of Bacchus, & some of them much larger, but most of them want alterations & repairs to fit them for our blue & white Jasper'.[9] Firing and composition problems plagued the manufacture of jasper. In May and June Wedgwood complained about the firing of the body, which cracked in the process,[10] saying that jasper was certainly the most 'delicately whimsical of any substance' with which he had ever worked.[11]

There are a number of surviving documents, or partial documents, which discuss the problems with which Wedgwood was confronted when dealing with the tricky jasper composition. He finally settled on 'pool [Poole, Dorset] clay',[12] purchased from a Mr Hyde, which produced the whitest body. If the clay was not cleared of sand it would fire with yellow specks. This was also true of Devon ball clay which had to be thoroughly inspected for impurities and the clay houses kept very clean.[13] Grinding was a key, the more finely ground the more vitreous the

Fig. 48 **Medallion Sacrifice to Hymen,** *white jasper with blue jasper wash. In March 1778 an imperfect medallion sold for 10/6 (Wedgwood MS 16/15214). 2¹¹/₁₆ x 3¼ inches. Mark: Wedgwood & Bentley, c. 1777. (Nassau County Museum, Port Washington, New York, Buten collection of Wedgwood, 284 'B' 5150.)*

body. If the body was coarse it was more likely to warp or bend in the firing and the surface would likewise be coarse.[14] If he ground the clay more finely the jasper fired to a sheen which made the surface appear almost to have been glazed.[15] By late 1777 Wedgwood was able to produce jasper dip or surface jasper wares using some of the jasper composition (composed of 10% flint, 59% barium sulphate, 2% barium carbonate, and 29% clay) ground smoothly and made into a slip, in which the pieces were dipped, and when dried, polished. The slip could be very thin, so thin, according to Wedgwood, as 'not to injure a figure'.[16]

Three slips were necessary to make one tea cup, for

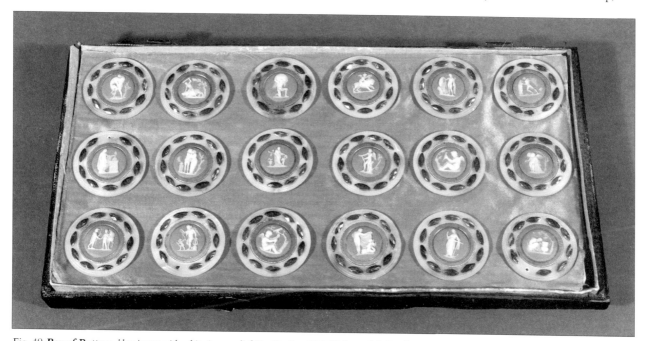

Fig. 49 **Box of Buttons,** *blue jasper with white jasper relief. By October 1777 Wedgwood & Bentley were manufacturing buttons as well as a variety of other jewellery. No visible marks. Probably late 18th century. (Grigsby collection.)*

Fig. 50 *Box of medallions and cameos*, jasper. Presented to Joseph Clarke of Saffron Walden by Joseph Mayer of Liverpool, September 27, 1854. Box 10 x 12 inches. (Zeitlin collection, Christie's, 30 November 1964, lot 50.)

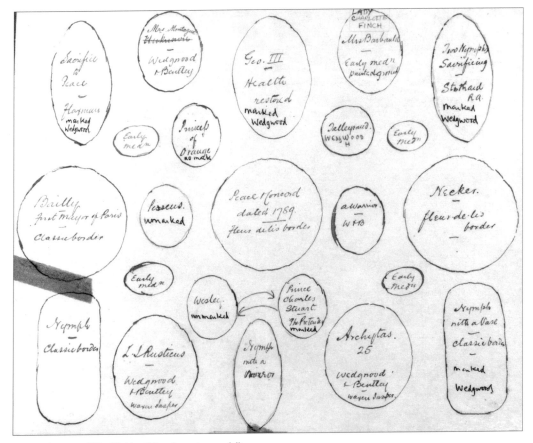

Fig. 51 *Reverse* of Fig. 50, identifying the various medallions.

Fig. 52 *Paint box, palette, paint pots,* solid blue jasper with white jasper relief decoration of Bringing Home the Game. *In May 1778 '1 Ecritoire jasper with painting cups was sold [for] 21/-' in June 1778 (Wedgwood MS 16/15226). Mark:WEDGWOOD A, c. 1786-95. (Nassau County Museum, Port Washington, New York, Buten collection of Wedgwood, 32.70.)*

example: blue, fine enough to take a semi-polish in firing, white of the same quality and a coarser white. First the mould was filled with the blue slip, and emptied again very quickly. When it was slightly dried it was filled with a coarse white and let to stand until the cup was of 'sufficient thickness'.[17] It was again emptied and let to dry and then filled briefly with the fine white slip which would be the interior finish. After leaving the mould the cup was polished on a lathe and had a foot put on, 'as it could not have one in the mould without leaving a mark on the inside'.[18] Wedgwood instructed that if throwing were preferred to casting, the vessel must be thrown in the coarse body, slipped within with the fine white before it is turned, and dipped in the fine blue after turning. The principal danger, Wedgwood advised, was in the dissimilarity of the coarse and fine bodies as they would not diminish alike in the kiln and may 'tear one another to pieces in the first cooling, or in heating & cooling afterwards'.[19] He went on to suggest that if the middle part were thick and the fine washes as thin as could be, the middle part may be too strong to be broken by the others.[20] In the early years Wedgwood was not able to develop a deep blue for his jasper, so the early pieces were often of a grey-blue hue (Fig. 47). The cost of cobalt at 36 shillings a pound was too expensive for producing wares for ordinary markets and consequently Wedgwood introduced the aforementioned dipping process to produce a visible likeness at a lower cost.

About the same time, at the end of 1777, Wedgwood felt that he had mastered the composition saying that he was now 'ABSOLUTE in this precious article & can make it with as much facility, & certainty as black ware.- We have only now to push it forward into the World - keep our secret &c-&c-&c'.[21] The secret included a portion of Cherokee clay which Wedgwood considered might be worth making known to the world at large, as it would

impress the public which wants only '*age & scarcity* to make them [jasper tablets] worth any price ...'[22]

In examining weekly inventories[23] of wares sent from the factory at Etruria to the Wedgwood and Bentley showroom in Greek Street, Soho, it is possible to see the emergence of the product which was to become the imprimatur of the Wedgwood name from the mid-1770s to the present day. The precursor body was the 'fine white' which was made into heads (cameos and intaglios), and was being produced in November 1774. Heads of Count Orloff, Dr Franklin and Cleopatra sold for 3/- each.[24] In the spring of the following year the factory was producing fine white tablets with bas-reliefs 9 inches by 4½ inches which were sold at £1.16.0 the pair.[25] But problems in both the composition and firing of the white clay persisted into the summer of 1775 when Wedgwood was still experimenting with sources of supply locally and from Bruges in Flanders.[26] In the autumn Wedgwood seemed relieved to hear from Bentley that the jasper proved to be a successful ground for enamelling, which he also conceived would make suitable gems for bracelets and rings [27]

In January of 1776 heads were being made with blue grounds of all the Kings and Queens, and a number of modern luminaries such as Solander, Linneaus, Newton and Hamilton, all of which sold for 7/6 each. Antique subjects including Socrates and mythological subjects such as Medusa were among the first of their kind produced by the factory.[28] Bas-reliefs with blue ground of an undisclosed subject, 7½ inches, were being sold for 21/- each around the same time, as were 3½ inch medallions of 'Fawn faces' for 5/-.[29] Plain white Medusas 5 inches in diameter were more than twice as expensive at 10/6 as the blue ground 3½ inch ones which sold for only 5/-.

By 1776 jasper was a formidable market item even as it was being perfected, which, according to Wedgwood was

Fig. 53 **Déjeuner** *set for one, white jasper with lilac jasper dip. In May 1786 a lilac and white déjeuner set for two sold for £3.13.6 (Wedgwood MS 16/15368); a déjeuner for one was £2.12.6 (16/15374). Teapot 3¾ inches; cream jug 3⅞ inches high; covered sugar 3¾ inches high; teabowl 2 inches high. Marks: all WEDGWOOD except teabowl which is Wedgwood, c. 1786-95. (Nottingham Museum, 1892-182 1-4.)*

not until the summer of 1777. Modeller William Hackwood had nearly finished the two famous tablets relating the *Birth of Bacchus* and the *Triumph of Bacchus*, the latter of which was fired on 21 February 1776.[30] An oval tablet of the *Birth of Bacchus* was sent up to London on 17 February 1776 priced at £1.16.0.[31] The firing of tablets continued to plague Wedgwood for several years. In the same inventory a note was appended [to Bentley ?]:

Tablet for Mr Weddal. Another was drawn out of the Bisket oven today - cracked & broke in several places, though it has been several months made and drying. Another will go in tomorrow, & if that does not succeed, we will either give it up, or try again as Mr Bentley shall direct.[32]

At the end of February Wedgwood talked of sweeping the cabinets of all the black seals and producing only white, blue and white and other coloured seals, a threat which never actually materialised.[33]

There is a suggestion, indeed, around the same time, that had Wedgwood not been so concerned with the perfection of his jasper and 'onyx', or black jasper, he might have spent more time experimenting with porcelain production.[34]

By February of 1776 the range of blue and white jasper was considerably expanded with offerings of statues (unspecified subjects) at 9/-, and a wide variety of medallions including *Cupid & Psyche* and *Cupid Shaving his Bow* (Fig. 46) also for 9/-.[35] Statues, described as 'fine' and 'very fine', but otherwise undescribed, appeared in March and April for 9/-, one identified as *Minerva*, and another as *Aspasia*, in blue and white sold for 10/6.[36] A note from William Cox to Thomas Bentley, appended to the inventory list, reads that 'if Mr Bentley perceives any faults in these [goods sent to London] or any other of the heads cast ... Mr Hackwood will endeavour to Refire it & D. Greatbatch hath at last tried a lamp or two from the pattern Mr Bentley sent'.[37]

In May 1776 tablets of *Cassandra, Night & Day, Bacchus & Panther* were sent up to London priced at £1.1.0 each.[38] A smaller *Cupid on a Lion* 4¾ inches was 10/6.[39] Bas-reliefs of *Vestal & Aspasia* in fine blue and white went for 12/-.[40] By 1776, cameos with blue grounds of the Roman Emperors and Empresses were regularly made, priced at 5/- each, and in white of the Kings of France, sixty- three of which were £1.11.6.[41] Medallions in blue and white of *Cupid, Lyon (sic)*

Fig. 54 *Custard cup and cover, drab green jasper, 'artichoke' shape custard cup[s] appeared on sales records in May 1786 (Wedgwood MS 16/15368). Cup 2¼ inches high; stand 4½ inches diameter. Mark on cup: Wedgwood; on stand: WEDGWOOD, c.1786-95. (Lady Lever Art Gallery, National Museums & Galleries on Merseyside, LL1355, 1356.)*

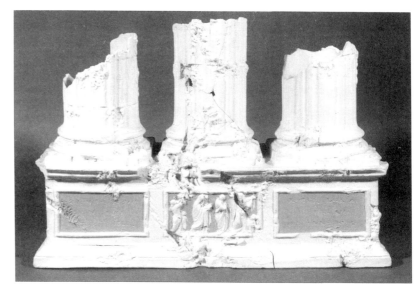

Fig. 55 **Ruined flower column**, *caneware. Ruined flower vases appeared for the first time in Wedgwood sales records in June 1786 where a pair of blue and white columns sold for £3.3.0 (Wedgwood MS 16/15372). 7⅛ inches high. Mark: WEDGWOOD. (Liverpool Museum, National Museums & Galleries on Merseyside, 2914M, ex Mayer collection.)*

Fig. 56 **Vase of three ruined columns**, *white stoneware with blue ground. Vases of one and two ruined columns were first mentioned in sales records in June 1786. 8⅜ x 12½ inches. Mark: WEDGWOOD. (Liverpool Museum, National Museums & Galleries on Merseyside, ex Mayer collection.)*

& *Boys* for 15/-, a head of *Christ* at 10/6, and of the *Marriage of Cupid* [and Psyche] (Colour Plate 12) at 12/-, and *Perseus & Andromeda* for £1.11.6 were sent up to Greek Street in June.[42] In July a pair of bas-reliefs depicting *Cupid Burning a Moth* was listed for 15/- each, as were four others representing *Cupid & Hymen*.[43] In September a blue ground *Panther & Boys* 10 inches was priced at £5.5.0.[44] Lord Warwick ordered a blue and white *Medusa* for 15/- to be sent to Warwick Castle in September.[45]

At this point one begins to see listings for these grander tablets. In October one blue and white tablet of the *'Tryumph* (sic) *of Bacchus'* (no size indicated) was also five guineas, listed along with another, probably smaller, *Birth of Bacchus* for two guineas.[46] Black ground bas-reliefs (subject not described) at 9/- each began to appear in the lists in October, 1776. Black ground cameos of *George and Charlotte* were among the first examples, four priced at a total of £1.1.0.[47] These would doubtless be what are now referred to as black jasper.

Chimney pieces were by now in production, one early set included a central panel of *Pan and Young Fauns* (£1.1.0) flanked by two bacchanalian figures of *Thalia and a Piping Faun* (15/-).[48]

'Green jasper' was being sent up to the London showrooms at the end of June, 1776, when 'Green Jasper Vases No. 57' at 13/6 and 9/- respectively and No. 25 at 9/- each appeared in the inventories.[49] This 'green jasper' is another one of the variegated coloured glazes used on the terracotta body and not to be confused with the sea-green stoneware produced later on in the decade. Solid fine white continued to be marketed in cameos, and small bas-reliefs, as well as a few busts, such as a pair of 'white Busts 'Anty [Anthony] & *Cleopatra*' for 21/-each.[50]

Faulty blue and white jasper statues, and 'Heads' (cameos) were sent up to London to be sold as imperfect, a practice

which had occurred in basalt since 1769.[51] A wide range of subjects was to be seen in cameos, cameo-medallions, and medallions themselves, from the earliest entries of blue and white jasper. Bas-relief portraits in a typical week in August 1776 included: '1 Blue & White Vitellius for Mr Constable' as well as 12 small portraits of Mr Constable', *Madam Diede, Geo(rge)*, *Cassandra & Ariadne, Jesus, Hercules, Homer, Sappho* and *Socrates*, a combination of tastes indeed.[52] The public preferred a 'full-color'd' example over a 'pale blue' if given

Fig. 57 **Pair of fluted columns**, *white jasper columns with blue dip and solid jasper bases. Number 287 in the Wedgwood shape book, the first mention of these columns by number in sales records was 29 June 1786 when the Rt. Hon. Mr Eden purchased a pair of 'columns fluted' for £2.12.6 (Wedgwood MS 16/15375). The terminology for these objects varied from 'columns' to 'pillars' leaving the function undisclosed until 1790 when they began to be described as 'candlesticks' (Wedgwood MS 16/15497). 6¼ inches high Mark: WEDGWOOD, c. 1786-95. (Lady Lever Art Gallery, National Museums & Galleries on Merseyside, LL 1549.)*

Fig. 58 *Gondola escritoire, solid medium-blue jasper with white relief decoration. Number 328 in the shape book, these inkwells are mentioned in May 1786 as 'Gondola ecritoires with masque heads' for £1.11.6 (Wedgwood MS 16/15370). Mark: WEDGWOOD, c. 1786-1800. (Nassau County Museum, Port Washington, New York, Buten collection of Wedgwood, 6955150.)*

a choice[53] and in late 1776 indications of variations in ground colour began to be seen in the descriptions. Thus 'dark ground bas-reliefs of *Cupid & Psyche, Cupid & Swan,* and a *Sacrifice'* are singled out.[54] And word began to filter in from the various Wedgwood warehouses about the local

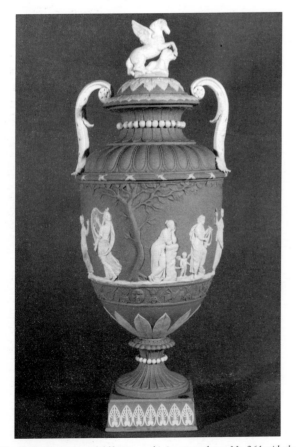

Fig. 59 *Pegasus vase, solid blue jasper, this 'ornamental vase No. 261 with the Muses in blue jasper with white reliefs' sold for five guineas to the King of Naples in June, 1786 (Wedgwood MS 16/15372). In March 1791 a larger version sold for eight guineas. Mark: WEDGWOOD, c. 1786-91, 16 inches high. (Lady Lever Art Gallery, National Museums & Galleries on Merseyside, LL1013.)*

preferences. In Dublin, Wedgwood agent Mr Brock acknowledged that jasper was very much admired and that he had sold all except for a 'few Banks [Sir Joseph Banks], and modern heads which they do not admire'.[55] In October, 1776, a note appended to the lists of wares sent up to London said: 'Sundry blue & white Bas reliefs & new vases by Mr Wedgwood',[56] probably indicating that he had designed them, as it is unlikely that Wedgwood was actually making vases himself. A potter who concerned himself with all aspects of the business, Wedgwood acknowledged in 1777 that he was busy 'mixing near two tons of Jasper which takes all the material I have'.[57] Jasper found an early market abroad. In September, 1776, fine white heads of Anthony and Cleopatra, a gilt framed head of Voltaire, bas-reliefs of Perseus and Andromeda and '5 Blue ground Cupid with Bow' went off to Mr Baumgartner, Wedgwood's Frankfurt agent.[58] Thus foreign monarchs became popular subjects of bas-reliefs. In a note of 8 November 1776 to William Cox, the Greek Street showroom manager, Wedgwood wrote: 'Fine white heads with blue ground of the King and Queen of France are now in the Fire'.[59]

By 1777 Wedgwood had begun making door knobs, buttons (Fig. 49) and jewellery inset with cameos and intaglios.[60] He declared that they now had four new subjects of a proper size for bracelets and other jewellery: *Scevola, Curtius, A Sacrifice with Esculapius, Hygeia and other figures,* and another companion sacrifice.[61] Jewellery inset with jasper and basalt was to feature prominently in Wedgwood's sales over the next two decades. In the same letter, but on another subject, Wedgwood suggested that Flaxman go ahead with the 'Muses of the size he had begun'.[62] Flaxman had completed half of the twelve muses leaving six to be finished. Concurrently another modeller, William Hackwood, was occupied repairing and making good damaged or imperfect bas-reliefs which were languishing in storage.[63]

From 1778 until 1794 there are intermittent listings of day-by-day sales from the Wedgwood and Bentley showroom in Greek Street, Soho. For the year 1778 only the month of January is missing. In February blue and white relief listings include *Ganemeade* (*sic*) and the Eagle which sold for 21/- as well as four statues of *Hope, Ganemeade* (*sic*), *Juno* and *Sophonista*.[64] Blue and white statues of *Apollo* and *Bacchus* were also sold for 12/- the pair.[65] The most extraordinary listing was for '1 Green Venus of John of Bologna & Black Pedistal (*sic*)'.[66]

The green *Venus* was doubtless another of the variegated glazed wares and probably inspired by the so-called 'Crouching Venus', or one of the imitations dating from the time of Giambologna, now in the Ufizzi Museum in Florence.[67] It was only mentioned once in the sales over many years and the purchaser is unknown.

Five blue and white 'heads' of *Mendelssohn* were listed in March 1778 along with two blue and white pedestals with the *Seasons* @ 21/-.[68] These are the first listing for a jasper hollow ware and may be like the pair in the British Museum (Fig. 47). An imperfect blue and white *Sacrifice to Hymen* (Fig. 48) sold for 10/6 at the same time. The most interesting item listed in March was definitely '1 *Venus Rising Out of the Sea*' for 21/-.[69] Later that year a blue and white '*Venus* on a Pedestal' sold for 31/6.[70] A blue and

white '*Venus* on a Pedestal' for the same price sold in October of 1778 accompanied by a 'Bell Glass' for an additional 6/-.[71]

In April 1778 three blue and white tablets of the *Marriage of Cupid & Psyche* sold successively for £7.17.6, £10.10.0 and £5.5.0.[72] 'Statues' (medallions) in blue and white of *Bacchus* and *Summer* (?) were 12/-, *Cupids* 7/6 and one of a *Horse* 12/-.[73] In the 1770s it was not common to have the name of the buyer written into the margin as it was in the succeeding decades when, it appears, the buyer was buying on credit. However, on 16 April, 1778, Sir Roger Newdigate is acknowledged as purchasing a number of blue and white medallions: *Silenus* 21/-, *Venus Belsesses* 15/-, *Ganemeade* (*sic*) 15/- and *Ganemeade & Eagle* 21/-. He also purchased one black '*Venus Rising out of the Sea*' for 21/-.[74]

Sales of heads of statesmen in blue and white, including the *Emperor of Germany* and surprisingly, considering the period, *George Washington*, sold for 10/6 each in the spring of 1778.[75] The other American statesman who featured in sales in that period was *Benjamin Franklin*, of whom a cameo in white went for as little as 5/-.[76] A blue and white head of *Franklin* (Colour Plate 9) went for 10/6 with an additional 4/6 if framed.[77] By August 1778 a blue and

Fig. 60 ***Ewer and vases***, *black jasper dip with white reliefs. Ewer no. 262 sold for £3.3.0 beginning of June 1786; vase (centre) no. 279 sold for £2.2.0 and vase no. 275 (right) for £6.6.0 the pair at the same time (Wedgwood MS 16/15374). A pair of ewers no. 262 was purchased by the King of Naples on 13 June 1786 for six guineas and both vases no. 275 and 279 were among the most popularly purchased shapes from 1786 to 1792. Ewer 9¼ inches high. Marks: all WEDGWOOD, c. 1786-92. (Nottingham Museum, Felix Joseph collection.)*

Fig. 61 *Vase and cover*, solid blue jasper with white relief of a sacrifice. Shape No. 273, the vase was popularly sold from June of 1786 through 1793 to various dignitaries including the King of Naples (14 June 1786), John Wilkes, Esq. (11 Sept. 1788), the Archbishop of Santiago (27 October 1792) and Philadelphia dealer John Bringhurst (7 January 1793). Produced in both green and blue jasper, the relief scenes were often of the Marriage of Cupid and Psyche *from the Marlboro gem and its companion* Sacrifice to Hymen *and the vase generally sold for two guineas, but prices varied according to size. Mark: WEDGWOOD, 7½ inches high. (Lady Lever Art Gallery, Museums & Galleries on Merseyside.)*

Fig. 62 *Teapot*, solid medium blue jasper with Lady Templetown figures in white relief and a seated boy finial. The ground is stippled. Shape No. 303 may have entered the sales records in 1787 but it was not mentioned by shape number. Few seem to have been specified by number but the shape was still being sold in 1790. Mark: WEDGWOOD, c. 1787-90, 6 inches high. (Nottingham Museum, 1892-412.)

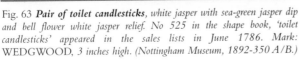

Fig. 63 *Pair of toilet candlesticks*, white jasper with sea-green jasper dip and bell flower white jasper relief. No 525 in the shape book, 'toilet candlesticks' appeared in the sales lists in June 1786. Mark: WEDGWOOD, 3 inches high. (Nottingham Museum, 1892-350 A/B.)

Fig. 64 *Reading candlestick*, solid medium blue jasper with white relief. In January 1791 a 'Blue and white reading candlestick No. 309' sold for £1.11.6 (Wedgwood MS 16/1557). Mark: WEDGWOOD Z, c. 1791, 5¼ inches high. (Nottingham Museum, 1892-364/364A.)

white 'new head Dr Franklin' (Colour Plate 9) was being offered at 10/6.[78] Blue and white bas-reliefs of *Night* and *Day* sold for 21/- each in May of 1778.[79] Fine white 'Statues' (medallions) *Night* and *Day* sold for 15/- each.[80]

An unusual entry for '1 Ecritoire (*sic*) Jasper with painting cups' (Fig. 52) for 21/- featured in June.[81] As mentioned the term 'jasper' was not used at this early date to denote the body with which we now associate it and thus this was probably a terracotta body with a variegated glaze. Whether this was a painting box or a writing box with paint cups as it suggests is not certain. Likewise five 'Jasper Gilt' vases were among sales in July 1778. Clearly intended as a garniture, the largest vase, shape No. 40, was 31/6, of the two smaller pairs, No. 221 were 7/6 each and No. 124, 10/6 each.[82] In a listing with other vases described as 'porphyry' these 'jasper' vases were also probably of the variegated variety.

Tablets in blue and white continued as a rare occurrence. One of *Homer & Orpheus* sold for £10.10.0 along with two of *Apollo & the Nine Muses* for £8.8.0 each late in the year.[83] The following week blue and white tablets of the *Birth of Bacchus* and *Triumph of Bacchus*, sold for £7.17.6 each.[84] One *Sacrifice to Bacchus* in blue and white went for £15.5.0. Blue and white medallions of *Medusa* continued to be popular, selling for 15/-.[85]

Basalt and jasper were popularly inset into jewellery, often in gold. Blue and white jasper rings in unspecified settings sold for 28/-, 24/- and 21/- respectively in December 1778.[86]

For the year 1779 there are full records of sales from Greek Street and therefore data in this last full year of the Wedgwood and Bentley partnership is complete. Cameos, medallions and tablets continued to comprise the only blue and white forms produced by the partnership. The most expensive tablet was one tablet of the *Muses* for £18.18.0.[87] A tablet of *Homer & Orpheus* sold on 1 March for 12 guineas,[88] and the first *Apotheosis of Homer* tablet seems to have been sold on 3 September 1779 for £10.10.0.[89] Another *Sacrifice to Flora* in a gilt frame sold for £6.6.0.[90] One *Birth of Bacchus* and a *Bacchus & Panther* (7½ inches) sold for 42/- each,[91] and one round 10 inch *Sacrifice* and another *Triumph of Bacchus* for 105/- respectively.[92] Tablets of the *Marriage of Cupid & Psyche* sold for a variety of prices depending on the size. Five were sold in 1779: one for £10.10.0, another for £7.17.6 and three for 63/-.[93] A *Judgment of Hercules* tablet also sold for 63/-.[94] Two tablets of *Dancing Boys* went for 94/6,[95] two *Boys at Play* were 63/- each and four *Herculaneum Nymphs* sold for 42/- a piece.[96] The final tablet subjects completing the group of sales for 1779 were: one tablet of *Apollo & the two Muses* and two *Dancing Nymphs* in burnished gold frames sold for 63/-.[97] At the same time a tablet of *Ganymede & the Eagle* sold for 42/-. By and large medallions seemed to sell for 21/-, 18/- and 15/-, probably depending on size and subject. Cameos ranged in price from 10/6 to as little as 4/- or 5/-.

The 1779 catalogue listed subjects but not prices. Blue and white jasper prices were four or five and up to ten times as expensive as their basalt counterparts, basalt cameos generally selling for one shilling. The subjects were generally mythological or hybrid mythological such as *Cupid & Lyon* (*sic*), but included among the offerings in 1779 modern subjects such as *Isaac Newton, Benjamin Franklin* (Colour Plate 9) and *Joseph Priestley* (Colour Plate 10). Specific subjects of interest sold in the year included, in addition to *Newton, Franklin* and *Priestley* (3 @ 21/-),[98] *Admiral Keppel* (Colour Plate 11), 2 @ 15/- and 1 @ 10/6,[99] the *King and Queen* (17 from 15/- to 5/-),[100] *Shakespeare* was often paired with *Garrick* (19 from 15/- to

Fig. 65 **Plate** *showing shape No. 266 in the 1787 Wedgwood trade catalogue. Vase shape No. 266 illustrated in the catalogue proved to be the most popularly sold jasper shape of the Wedgwood factory offerings. The stipple engraving (8¼ by 5⅛ inches) depicts what the catalogue describes as 'Venus in her car being drawn by swans with attending Cupids &c,' after a design by Charles Le Brun (1619-90). (Private collection.)*

Fig. 66 **Egg cups,** *white jasper with dark blue jasper dip, left engine-turned vertical fluting with yellow ground band at neck; right arabesque band at neck. Egg cups in jasper appear in sales records for the first time on 3 August 1786 for 4/6 (Wedgwood MS 16/15380). Marks: both WEDGWOOD, 2 inches high, c. 1785-95. (Liverpool Museum, Museums & Galleries on Merseyside, 2757M, 2756M.)*

Fig. 67 **Two medallions,** *blue jasper with white reliefs of a woman kneeling at a cinerary urn (left) and a medallion commonly known as 'Sportive Love'. This may be the medallion described in the Wedgwood sales as 'Lady Templetown's Children toe Charlotte' on 22 July 1786 (Wedgwood MS 16/15378). Unmarked, Wedgwood, c. 1786, 3⅛ inches high (including frame). (Grigsby collection.)*

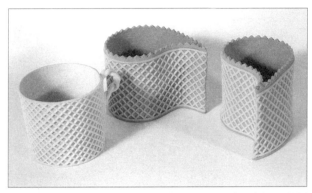

Fig. 68 *Custard cups*, two blue and white jasper tear-shaped (Nos. 460/ 461) and one jasper dip yellow ground cup, all with white lattice. Custard cups in these shapes first appeared in existing sales records in the autumn of 1786. Marks: all WEDGWOOD, c. 1786, tear-shaped cups 1¼ inches high, handled cup 1¹¹⁄₁₆ inches high. (Polikoff collection, ex Byron Born.)

Fig. 69 *Vase,* light blue jasper with white reliefs of boys playing blindman's-buff and other games. Vase shape No. 302. A pair of these vases sold for four guineas in the autumn of 1786 (Wedgwood MS 16/15390). Mark: WEDGWOOD V, c. 1785-1793, 10½ inches high. (Nottingham Museum, 1892-177.)

5/-),[101] *Hercules* (1 at 21/-),[102] and *Medusa* (9 ranging from medallions at 15/- to cameos at 10/-, 9/- and 6/-).[103] Although it is impossible to determine from the price exactly what the object was, certain subjects such as *Erato*[104] and *Night and Day* at 21/-[105] and *Lyon* (sic) *and Cupid* at 15/- and *Lyon and Two Cupids* at 21/-,[106] were probably medallions. All these were single sales as were *Lyon* (sic) *and Boys*[107] and *Venus, Ganymede*[108] and *Venus Belsesses* at 21/-.[109] Other subjects which were single sales included *Jupiter, Juno,*[110] and *Hercules,*[111] and *Newton, Franklin* and *Priestley* (Colour Plates 9 and 10) all at 21/-.[112] Multiple sales of medallions included *Apollo and the Nine Muses* (10 at 21/-)[113] as well as five unspecified 'heads' at the same price.[114]

At 18/- the only sales during the year were four medallions of *Anthony and Cleopatra* and one single of *Cleopatra.*[115] At 15/- medallions were sold of themes ranging from *Medusa,*[116] and *Cupid Burning a Butterfly,*[117] to *Keppel* (Colour Plate 11),[118] *Bacchanalian Boys,*[119] and *Venus Belsesses* and *Ganymede.*[120]

Framed medallions and cameos added to the basic price. Thus a blue and white framed head of *Edwards* was sold for 14/6[121] and another framed *Pythagoras* was 13/6.[122] It appears that small medallions (4½ inches and 5 inches) were still sold for as low as 12/- while cameos ranged from 10/6 to 2/6, and intaglios from 5/- to 1/6. The greatest number of cameos were sold at 10/6.

Small medallions selling for 12/- in 1779 included the following subjects: *Ganymede and Eagle,*[123] *Sacrifice to Hymen* (Fig. 48),[124] *Marriage of Cupid and* [125] *Psyche* (Colour Plate 12), *Apollo,*[126] *Bacchanals* (5 inches),[127] and *Bacchanalian Boys* (4½ inches).[128] Companion pieces sold individually at 12/- included pairs of *Marriage of Cupid and Psyche and Companion,*[129] *Cupid and Psyche* and *Sacrifice,*[130] and *Philip and Alexander.*[131]

In 1779 the following quantities of cameos were sold: 161 @ 10/6, 2 @ 10/-, 23 @ 9/-, 2 @ 8/-, 88 @ 7/6, 12 @ 6/-, 3 @ 5/6, 94 @ 5/-, 2 @ 4/-, 3 @ 3/6, and 3 @ 2/6. Intaglios sold in the following numbers and prices: 7 @ 5/-, 19 @ 3/6, 28 @ 2/6 and 5 @ 1/6. Twenty cyphers were sold at 3/6. Arms were offered and sold at 3/- (2), and 1/6 (1) and seals 2/6 (2) and 1/6 (1).

Popular contemporary figures continued to sell in cameos. Sixteen cameos of *Frederick, King of Prussia* and his son *Prince Henry* sold at 5/-[132] and eighteen of the *King of Denmark.*[133] The *King and Queen,* fifteen sold in 1779,[134] continued to be outsold by the *Kings of Prussia and Denmark* as well as by *Shakespeare* and *Garrick* (27),[135] *William Penn* (2),[136] *George Washington* (1) [137] and *Benjamin Franklin* (2 at 10/6, 1 at 5/-; Colour Plate 9)[138] trickled along in sales, the latter often paired with *Lord Chatham* or with *Cook. Chatham* was more frequently sold in tandem with *Camden,* and *Washington* with *Cook.* Other figures of contemporary interest included: *Linneaus* (2) and *Banks* (1),[139] *Locke* and *Newton,*[140] *Dr Solander,*[141] *Voltaire* and *Rousseau.*[142] Of the specified subjects, and indeed many were not described, cameos of *Apollo and the Nine Muses* continued to be among the most popular with twenty sold at 10/6.[143] Classical figures such as *Terrence* and *Seneca* (2 at

Fig. 70 *Vase*, light blue jasper with white reliefs. Shape No. 271 was sold to Lady Kivers for £3.3.0 in August 1786 (Wedgwood MS 16/15380). The shape remained popular until 1791. Mark: WEDGWOOD, c. 1786-90, 9⅝ inches high. (Lady Lever Art Gallery, Museums & Galleries on Merseyside, LL1458.)

Fig. 71 *Vase*, blue jasper with white jasper depicting Leda and the Swan. Vase shape No. 274 first appeared in surviving Wedgwood sales in August 1786 (Wedgwood MS 16/15380). Sold for £6.6.0 the pair, such vases were purchased by Henry Hope, Esq., the Amsterdam entrepreneur, in May, 1787 (Wedgwood MS 16/15422). Mark: WEDGWOOD. c. 1786-7, 11 inches high. (Lady Lever Art Gallery, Museums & Galleries on Merseyside, LL1468.)

5/-), *Horace & Ovid* (2 at 7/6), *Cicero* (1 at 10/6),[144] and *Esculapius* (2 square at 9/-, 3 oval at 9/- and 4 at 7/6-)[145] and *Esculapius & Hygia* (2 at 5/-).[146]

As we have seen in 1779, with only one exception, the only blue and white jasper wares were tablets, medallions, cameos and intaglios. The one exception was sales of three blue and white entries described as *Venus Rising from ye Sea*[147] for 31/6 each. These were probably mounted on pedestals such as the blue and white jasper Wedgwood & Bentley examples in the British Museum (Fig. 47). Thus these pedestals were probably the first or among the first hollow wares produced by the factory.

Sales records for 1780 survive from 1 May to 27 June and from 27 July to 11 August and from 21 August to the end of the year. On 26 November 1780 Thomas Bentley died. The Greek Street emporium was open from 28-30th November but closed until the 11 December.[148] Bentley's death brought to an end the famous partnership which was, by then, recognized throughout the Western hemisphere.

Surprisingly little jasper continued to be sold in 1780. Most of the bas-reliefs were cameos and small medallions, often with unspecified subjects. No major tablets and no

obvious hollow wares were sold during the year in the surviving sales records. What does appear are a few sales of black and white in both pearlware and in jasper. For instance, a listing for a black and white Medusa at 15/-[149] would probably be a jasper medallion whereas a black and white 'bough' at 4/-[150] would undoubtedly be pearlware. A perhaps larger blue and white framed *Medusa* sold for 31/6 on 3 May 1780.[151] One unusual entry was a 'bisque statue' of *Rousseau* for 21/- sold 12 June, 1780.[152] The following day a cameo of the *Vestal* was sold for 10/6.[153] Another first mention of the *Indian Bacchus* figure appears in a sale of 2 October[154] for 10/6 although it was undoubtedly in production prior to that in basalt as it is listed as No. 146 in the Class II bas-relief section of the 1779 trade catalogue. One final entry of note was '2 White figure Candlesticks with Blue Nossells (sic) 21/-' sold 10 November 1780.[155] These would rank among the earliest free-standing ornamental jaspers, along with a blue and white *Venus* for 31/6 sold on 30 October.[156]

Between the end of 1780 and April of 1784 no sales records survive. However, oven records survive and indicate that Wedgwood was embarking on the production of jasper in large and showy ornamental wares. The jasper in the

Fig. 72 *Lamp case, white jasper with blue jasper dip. Lamp case No. 306 was intended for one of the several patent lamps available in the late 18th century. The base on these cases is cut out in various shapes to accommodate the oil fuelled apparatus. Lamp cases are mentioned in Wedgwood sales records in the autumn of 1786 (Wedgwood MS 16/15387). Mark:* WEDGWOOD, *7⅛ inches high, c. 1786. (Nassau County Museum, Port Washington, New York, Buten collection of Wedgwood, 1636B.)*

Christie and Ansell sale of the Wedgwood and Bentley stock in December 1781 generally reflected merchandise which had been sold in the previous years, that is, tablets for chimney pieces, medallions, cameo-medallions and cameos for cabinets and for jewellery. The only difference was a current reference to 'jasper' in place of the 'blue and white' used to describe it previously. In addition there were bas-reliefs offered in terracotta and in 'fine white bisques, Porcelain'. In the main the offerings continued to be of basalt and all teawares were in basalt.

Bas-reliefs for chimney pieces were sold in suites of five to seven pieces: one tablet, two to four flanking friezes and two blocks for vertical chimney surrounds. The 1781 sales include thirty-two suites for chimney pieces in jasper, nine in terracotta and one set in 'white Porcelain bisque'. Some friezes and blocks were sold individually, but the vast majority were offered in suites. Other groups were sold of two or three pieces listed as 'Suites of three for Pictures'. A vast quantity of cameos, either set or to be set in jewellery, were offered as well as boxed sets of cameos in jasper. For the most part the colour of the jasper was not indicated. However, one unusual entry for 'A Suite of three Cameo-Medallions, with red Grounds, in black frames; Death of *Julius Caesar, Apollo, Three Graces,*' was listed as lot 247 to be sold on the third day, 5 December, 1781.

Only a week of sales records exist for 1784, but they indicate vast changes in the forms available in jasper. By now teawares were in the shop as well as *'déjeune'* sets which sold from £2.4.0[157] to £3.0.0 per set.[158] 'Bell handles', or bell pulls (Colour Plate 13), first appear in the inventory sales for the price of 3/–,[159] the same price as for jasper 'bell handles or bell drops' in 1786.[160] Jasper blue and white teapots could be expensive at the outset, priced at the same level as a jasper butter tub and stand at £1.1.0.[161] Other teapots were somewhat less expensive, six for £4.1.0,[162] but still very much dearer than basalt ones which sold for as low as 3/– including a stand.[163]

Cane teapots were also a fraction of the jasper versions at 3/6.[164]

Other hollow wares included 'Blue Jasper Altar Flower Pot[s]' at £3.3.0 each.[165] Jasper canisters were five for £2.5.0, sugar dishes, five for £2.4.0 and cream ewers five at £2.4.0.[166] Tablets and medallions continued to appear but sizes were not given so it is difficult to determine if they had dropped in price since 1780 when they last appeared in sales accounts.

Sales records do not survive for 1785 nor the early months of 1786. However, from 1 May 1786 to the end of the year the records are complete and the augmentation of the jasper inventory is, by this time, staggering in its breadth. In pursuing the first week of May 1786 one finds a myriad of items not previously listed: lilac and white *'déjeune'* sets for two at £3.13.6 (Fig. 53), a white jasper artichoke shape custard cup for 3/– (Colour Plate 14; Fig. 54), muffin plates at 15/–, one 'Blue & White Jasper Saucer ornamented with figures & other decorations £1.1.0,' as well as jasper teawares more competitively priced than

Fig. 73 *Ice Pail for glass cooling, solid blue jasper with white jasper and icicle border around base. In 1790 shape No. 348 was described as a 'Glass pail' and they sold for 21/– each, at other times they were referred to as 'ice pails' and sold for £3.3.0 a pair (Wedgwood MS 16/15398). The latter were presumably a larger size. Mark:* WEDGWOOD, *c. 1786-90, 4 x 7¼ inches. (Lady Lever Art Gallery, Museums & Galleries on Merseyside, LL1515.)*

Fig. 74 *Dolphin lamp*, solid blue jasper with white embellishment. These oil lamps varied greatly in size, one large lamp selling for £21.0.0 to Sir John Webb on 7 December 1786 (Wedgwood MS 16/15398). Other smaller versions, of which this is one, sold for a mere two guineas. Mark: WEDGWOOD, c. 1786-92, 4⅛ inches high. (Lady Lever Art Gallery, Museums & Galleries on Merseyside, LL1467.)

Fig. 75 *Flower pot*, solid jasper with white reliefs of Apollo and the Nine Muses. Shape No. 369, these flower pots were made in 7, 9, 10 and 11 inch sizes. HRH the Duke of York purchased one green and white jasper vase shape No. 369 for two guineas on 11 February 1792 (Wedgwood MS 16/15580). Mark: WEDGWOOD V, c. 1791-92, 8¼ inches high. (Birmingham Museum of Art, Alabama, Beeson collection of Wedgwood, 1982.232 a & b.)

initially: a teapot for 17/-, sugar dish at 12/-, tea canister at 9/- and cream ewers at 6/- and 8/-. Black and white jasper cameos are listed as selling at £1.2.6 for a set of three. On 5 May 1786 the first listing for a jasper vase is described in surviving records as, '1 Vase blue jasper with Lady T's friendship Consold (sic) by love £2.2.0'. A note in the margin indicated the vase was purchased by a Mrs Rouse as a gift to Lady Templetown.[167] Two blue jasper 'Bell Drops' (Colour Plate 13) were 5/- and one white jasper bell drop 2/6. Imperfect tablets were so described and priced accordingly, one described as '1 imperfect Freze (sic) D. Hours £2.2.0' which was destined for a 'Builder at Bath' who had before selected imperfect tablets.[168]

Flower pots were to become the rage in blue and white jasper as well as in other coloured jasper bodies. On 8 May 1786, a blue and white jasper 'term flower pot' was sold to the Hon. Mr Wyndham for £3.3.0.[169] Two blue and white 'ruin flower pot vases' (Figs. 55, 56) for three guineas sold on 8 June 1786 along with several other flower containers: '1 Term flower pot on Lion's paws' for one guinea and '2 pillar flower pots' (Fig. 57) for one guinea.[170]

Writing accoutrements had always been a popular item in the Wedgwood inventories. By 1786 that included 'Gondola Ecritoires' with masque heads in lilac with white bas-reliefs which sold for £1.11.6. (Fig. 58)[171] During the 1770s the Wedgwood jasper reputation rested principally on the great tablets and medallions which the factory produced. In the next decade it was vases.[172] Vases were the most fascinating aspect of the Wedgwood jasper

production. The early to mid-1780s was the beginning of the great jasper vase-making tradition which was the diadem on which the Wedgwood reputation was secured. Vases with the *Muses* in jasper seems to have been popular from the beginning. These sold for £5.5.0.[173] The first entries do not specify the shape number but in the entry on 14 June 1786 the shape is listed as No. 261 (Fig. 59) in an order of ornamental jasper sent to the King of Naples, Ferdinand IV,[174] (see Wedgwood Sales Abroad, Chapter VII).

The first set of chessmen in jasper appeared in surviving sales records in June, 1786, selling for £5.5.0.[175] A 'déjeune

Fig. 76 *Escritoire and stand*, solid jasper with white reliefs. Jasper inkstands in shape No. 311 first appear in the surviving records of sales in August 1786 and sold for two guineas. Mark on inkwell: WEDGWOOD; on stand: WEDGWOOD V, c. 1786-88, 3⅝ inches high. (Birmingham Museums & Art Gallery, 1885 M2680.)

Fig. 77 **Escritoire and stand**, solid blue jasper. Shape No. 310 was not mentioned frequently by number in Wedgwood sales, in fact only one entry exists for a sale in August 1786 to Wedgwood agent Le Coq in Paris for £1.5.0 (Wedgwood MS 16/15385). Marks: WEDGWOOD, c. 1786, 4⅕ inches high. (Lady Lever Art Gallery, Museums & Galleries on Merseyside, LL1478.)

for one' in jasper was £2.12.6 (with a teaspoon add 1/-) and a *déjeuner* for two (with only one cup and saucer) was £3.4.6.[176] A *déjeuner* for two in basalt painted with a Greek border was much less expensive at £1.16.0.[177]

Initially the mania for vases began with the reproduction in jasper of shapes which had previously been made in basalt and in imitation of crystalline stones such as porphyry, pebble and marble. On 24 June 1786 a Mr Forster purchased a number of vases in blue and white jasper: 2 No. 275 at £6.6.0 (Fig. 60, right), a pair smaller No. 276 for £4.4.0, 2 smaller No. 273 (Colour Plate 23; Fig. 61) with the *Marriage of Cupid & Psyche* and *A Sacrifice to Hymen* for £3.3.0, a pair smaller No. 289 for £2.2.0, a ewer No. 262 (Fig. 60, left) for £3.3.0, and another single vase No. 279 (Fig. 60, centre) for £2.2.0. At the same time he purchased a *déjeuner* for one with a teaspoon for £2.13.6, an escritoire in lilac jasper with white reliefs for £1.1.6, a green jasper teapot with white bas-reliefs for £1.2.0 (Colour Plate 15) and a pair of toilet candlesticks in blue and white jasper for £1.11.6 (Fig. 63).[178]

Another large purchase of vases by the Rt. Hon. Mr Eden included the first mention of an ornamental vase with a green ground and white bas-reliefs of 'Lady T's No. 266 2nd size' for £4.4.0 (Colour Plate 16). A pair of 'Temples of Flora' with bas-reliefs (No. 260) were the same price, a set of flower pots in blue jasper No. 269 was 10/6, a pair of fluted columns No. 287 (Fig. 57) £2.12.6 and a smaller pair No. 252 were £1.1.0. He also bought a pair of square altar flower pots with the Seasons in relief No. 293 for six guineas; a pair of bulbous root pots for growing 'flowers, Corals & Sea Weeds' for two guineas and a pair of tripod dolphin lamps for four guineas.[179] Other ornamental wares appearing around this time were the 'Ceres and Cybele' candlesticks (No. 272) which sold for £6.6.0 a pair.[180]

Teaspoons were made in jasper and sold for 1/- each in 1786. A blue and white cup and saucer was 9/- and egg cups (Fig. 66) 3 for 4/6.[181] Caddy spoons (Fig. 35) were also produced in blue jasper selling for 1/-.[182] A large jasper teapot was £1.11.6 and a pair of bulbous root tubs in lilac ground with white reliefs (Colour Plate 17) went for three guineas. A jasper muffin plate and cover was 15/-.[183]

Recent additions to the inventory were often so-described. Thus 'a pair of New Reading Candlesticks' in jasper sold on 28 June, 1786 for £1.11.6.[184]

In July 1786 the Duchess of Devonshire purchased some jasper including a *déjeuner* set for one with the cups 'polished within' for £3.13.6 along with four jasper medallions for £1.10.0.[185]

Chocolate cups in jasper with bas-relief decoration were sold individually or in pairs for 15/- each. In late July 1786 a 'New blue jasper' was being sold in chocolate cups,[186] and a little later there was a description of a 'pale blue Jasper teapot old [?] bas reliefs' for 16/-, suggesting that the bas-reliefs, not the colour, were old.[187]

Boat-shaped jasper escritoires with masque heads were sold at the same time for two guineas. Medallions of Lady Templetown's 'Children toe Charlotte' (Fig. 67) were 15/- each and two of 'Maria & figure reading' were £1.4.0. Two

Fig. 78 **Season candlestick** with a figure of summer ?, solid blue jasper with white jasper relief. Shape No. 265. Mark: WEDGWOOD, c. 1788, 9¼ inches high. (Grigsby collection.)

Fig. 79 *Altar flower pot*, shape No. 288 in solid blue jasper with white relief. These flower containers, also made in green jasper, were popular sellers between May 1788 and 1792, a pair going for as little as £1.11.6 (Wedgwood MS 16/15464). Sales records listed them under various names, including 'bulbous root pots' and 'Altars' and they were frequently sent to France to agents Sykes and Le Coq who apparently found a ready market for them. Mark: WEDGWOOD, c. 1788-92, 5 inches high. (Grigsby collection.)

Fig. 80 *Glacier*, solid blue jasper with white relief decoration including icicle sprigged border on cover and shivering boy finial. Shape No. 338 has ear-shaped grotesque mask handles. The shape is first mentioned in Wedgwood sales lists in April 1789 when six glaciers No. 338 were sold for 83/- each (Wedgwood MS 16/15715). Other sales of the glaciers occurred in 1790 and 1791. Mark: WEDGWOOD (on base of foot only), c. 1789-91, 10½ inches high. (Nottingham Museum, 1892-83 a/b.)

six inches high by four and a quarter inches wide of a 'Girl reading Tripod Lamp &c its pendent (sic)'[188] were £1.16.0. An unusual entry in the sales records for July included '5 white fluted Jasper Egg Cups' for 7/6 and a more common entry for three jasper custard cups (Fig. 68).[189] By the autumn of 1786 blue and white jasper egg cups were being sold for 2/6 each.[190] At the same time a Mr Wilson of Gower Street purchased a pair of blue and white jasper vases No. 302 (Fig. 69) for four guineas and an altar flower pot for three guineas.

On 31 July, 1786 'Alexandra Allerdyce Esqss.' recently married daughter Alexandra Barter purchased twelve teacups and saucers and coffee cups, one slop basin, a bread and butter plate, a cream ewer and three butter prints in blue and white jasper for a total of £11.19.6.[191]

Individual purchasers of jasper continue to be acknowledged when the buyer was probably purchasing on account and the lists are vastly enhanced by naming the buyer. Lady Kivers 'for a new house at Nice' selected a tablet of *Boys & Goat* in blue and white jasper measuring 9⅜ by 6⅛ inches for four guineas, accompanied by two upright blockings of *Boy & Horn* for £1.4.0. At the same time she bought one vase No. 271 (Fig. 70) for three guineas, two figures of *Cupid & Hebe* on blue pedestals for £2.14.0 as well as a 'Grecian Figures candelabra No. 25' for £2.12.6 and a black tripod (candelabra) for £2.10.0.[192]

Earl Cowper purchased a number of blue and white medallions: *Sir William Hamilton, Mr Pitt, Lord Camelford* for 10/6 each and some vases in jasper, all of which were the most popular ones of the day: 1 each No. 302 (Fig. 69), No.

Fig. 81 *Vase,* white jasper with green jasper dip and relief decoration of The Three Graces in a central medallion and a zodiac border at the neck. The signs of the zodiac began to be seen as decoration on jasper in 1789 and continued in popularity for the following few years of the next decade. Mark: WEDGWOOD UMX, this example 1869, 8¼ inches high. (Liverpool Museum, Museums & Galleries on Merseyside, 1971-133-6.)

Fig. 82 *Garden pot with figures*, medium blue jasper with solid white figure of Cupid. A pair of 'garden pots with figures' (for a plateau; shape No. 259) appeared for the first time in sales records of 8 January 1790 purchased by Lord Auckland for £6.6.0 (Wedgwood MS 16/15467). Mark: WEDGWOOD, c. 1790, 8½ inches high. (Nassau County Museum, Port Washington, New York, Buten collection of Wedgwood, 3555.)

275 (Fig. 60, right), and No. 266 with snake handles Fig. 65); and a pair of altar flower pots with relief decoration of the Seasons.[193]

Certainly the most outstanding purchase at this time was by Lord Howard of a vase described as: '1 large Ornamental Vase bas relief Apotheosis of Homer No. 298' (Colour Plate 18) for the remarkable sum of £21.0.0. At the same time Lord Howard bought one altar flower pot with decoration of the 'Seasons' in blue and white jasper for £2.12.6 and two Grecian figure candelabra for the same price, as well as a pair of ewers *Sacred to Bacchus and Neptune* for £10.10.0 (Colour Plate 20).[194]

A great deal of jasper was going abroad at this particular time and that is covered in the section under **Wedgwood Sales Abroad' – Chapter VII.** Also detail regarding the retail trade in England is listed in a separate section entitled **'Wedgwood Retailers at Home' – Chapter VI.**

On 22 August 1786 an entry for '2 blue jasper Garden pots basket work & white wrought border' for two guineas has a margin entry which reads: 'extremely admired' beside it.

Patent lamps were becoming an important part of interior decoration, providing a more reliable source of lighting than the candle. Wedgwood offered lamp cases in jasper (Fig. 72) and patent lamps in blue and white jasper for £2.15.0.[195] Another 'Jasper lamp complete' sold for £2.12.6.[196] Exactly what these lamps were is not known but they began to make frequent appearance in sales lists from late 1786 in listings such as: '4 cases for the Patent Lamps or for Girandoles' £8.8.0.[197]

Colours such as pale blue and olive green began to be specified in the sales records. Medallions in 'olive green

ground from a design of Lady Diana Beauclerk' were so-detailed. That particular one sold for 18/-.[198] Every conceivable form found its way into the jasper repertoire, including bird fountains in green and white jasper for 5/3.[199]

Groups of jasper vases were complementary and thus frequently sold together. No. 271 (Fig. 70) as the central vase was often set off with two flanking smaller No. 264 vases.[200] No. 271 was made in at least two colours of blue and white jasper. The usual colour was not specified any further than 'blue and white' and it was either two or three guineas depending, one assumes on size. Another No. 271 blue and white was further described as 'dark color' (*sic*) and sold for two guineas.[201] At the same time a green and white tripod candelabra pair sold for four guineas. Tripods were frequently made in blue but were uncommon in green.

The first description of 'drab color (*sic*) Jasper' occurs in the form of two bell drops sold in October, 1786 for 5/-.[202] Bells drops with 'words up & down in relief' were sold for 8/- a few days later.[203] From 1786 well into the next decade snake-handled jasper vases, usually in blue and

Fig. 83 *Portland vase*, black jasper with white jasper reliefs. One of the first fourteen copies of the so-called Barberini vase, this copy was originally purchased by glass dealer and collector Apsley Pellatt from the Wedgwood York Street showrooms in 1829. Mark: pencil mark of numeral 1 on base, c. 1790s, 9¾ inches high. (Colonial Williamsburg Foundation, 1991-160, ex Pellatt, to Holt, to Alfred Spero, to Duff-Dunbar, to Mellanay Delhom, to the Drs Brown, to Lindsay Grigsby.)

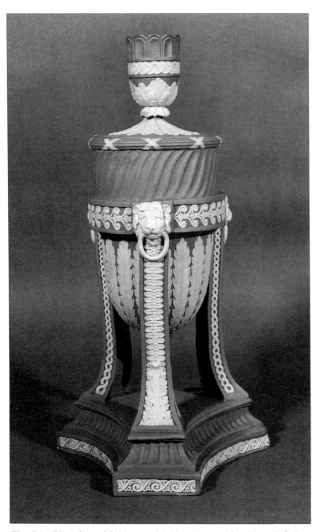

Fig. 84 *Tripod candelabrum*, solid blue jasper with white relief, these candelabra, No. 255, appeared for the first time in sales in February 1790 and sold for four guineas a pair (Wedgwood MS 16/15473). Mark: WEDGWOOD M, c.1790-93, 11 inches high. (Nottingham Museum, 1892-94.)

Fig. 85 *Tripod candelabrum*, white jasper with blue jasper dip and dice work. Shape No. 255 was a popular item in the early years of the 1790s. Produced in basalt, jasper and in the latest of fashions, dice work which appeared for the first time in 1790 (Wedgwood MS 16/15473). Mark: WEDGWOOD, c. 1790-93, 11 inches high. (Royal Ontario Museum, 925.13.68 A-B.)

white, but occasionally in green,[204] were popular. The most desirable shape was No. 266 (Colour Plate 16; Fig. 65) and generally sold for six guineas. A pair were sold October, 1786 for £12.12.0.[205] Henry Hope, Esq.(1735-1811), the manager of the Hope & Co. bank in Amsterdam and second cousin of Thomas Hope (1769-1831), purchased among other jasper wares, a snake-handled No. 266 blue and white jasper vase in 1787 for six guineas.[206] Philadelphia dealer John Bringhurst purchased the same shaped vase in 1793 for slightly less, five guineas.[207] The snake-handled vases often had relief decoration of *Chariot of Venus* or *The Muses*. Another purchase by Henry Hope, Esq. was vase shape No. 274 (Fig. 71) in blue jasper with swan handles for six guineas a pair.[208] The vase depicts *The Story of Leda* and the first appearance of the shape in surviving sales lists was from 6 December 1786.[209]

Continuing on with the same sales of 6 December 'A pair of *Sceaux* for Bottles very richly furnished not quite

round at top' sold for £10.10.0 along with twelve small flower vases on pedestals for a dessert plateau for £6.6.0 and a dozen chocolate cups with inlet saucers for £6.6.0. On the same day a pair of octagon frames richly gilt and set with Antique gems were sold for £7.7.0. It is difficult to imagine from the description what the nature of the fabric was in the frames. A number of medallions were sold that day but the last entry of interest was a pair of jasper blue and white tub-shaped ice pails for £3.3.0 (Fig. 73).[210]

The following day several other grand scale jaspers were sold including the first recorded entry for a large blue and white jasper vase No. 290 (Fig. 74) for £21.0.0. The shape book shows a round covered vessel supported on three dolphin tails. At the same time a pair of jasper *Sacred to Bacchus and Neptune* (Colour Plate 20) wine and water ewers sold for £21.0.0 and a pair of *Ceres and Cybele* candlesticks for ten guineas, a pair of bulbous root baskets 'with rich foliage' were £3.3.0 along with a single with a

Fig. 86 *Pair of flower containers* No. 256, *solid blue jasper with white figures. Described as 'rococo flower containers with cupids' in 1790 these pots sold for 42/- each Marks: WEDGWOOD, c.1790, 8¾ inches high. (Lady Lever Art Gallery, Museums & Galleries on Merseyside, 1474, 1473.)*

Fig. 88 *Tablet* Apotheosis of Virgil, *blue and white jasper. Designed by John Flaxman this was the companion tablet to the* Apotheosis of Homer, *which sold for £10.10.0 each. A pair of these was sold on 17 April 1790 (Wedgwood MS 16/15484). Mark not visible as the tablet is inset in a carrara marble fireplace surround which measures 63½ x 81¼ inches. (Lady Lever Art Gallery, Museums & Galleries on Merseyside.)*

Fig. 87 *Flower container, white jasper with blue and green jasper dip. Shape 394 exhibits an undulating vertical pattern combined with horizontal dice work which culminates in a particularly attractive vase. Produced in 8, 7, and 6 inch sizes this vase must have been popular although it was not referred to by shape number in Wedgwood sales prior to 1794. Mark: WEDGWOOD, c. 1795, 7⁵⁄₁₆ inches high. (Zeitlin collection.)*

lilac ground for £1.11.6. A pair of lilac vases with no further description were £3.3.0. Two altar flower pots (Fig. 79) were five guineas and the next entry listed the same 'richly gilt' at the same price. The last two jasper entries of interest are: a set of six basons *(sic)* with stands for bouillon at £6.6.0 and a pair of white figures of *Jupiter* and *Mercury* with blue and white pedestals for £4.4.0.[211]

A number of tablets were sold during the week of 14 December 1786, among them an *Apotheosis Of Homer* in a gilt frame for twelve guineas.[212]

A grand vase No. 261, (Fig. 59) which the shape book illustrates as having a *Pegasus* on the cover and *The Muses* in relief, was sold in February 1787 for £5.5.0 along with a pair of shape No. 271 (Fig. 70), also with *Muses* in relief, for £6.6.0. Another pair of vases No. 276 was £4.4.0 and a third pair No. 279 (Fig. 60, centre) went for £3.3.0.[213]

Coventry Bulkeley, Esq. bought a *déjeuner* for two in blue and white jasper on 17 May 1787,[214] and Sir Richard Hoare, Bart. purchased one jasper escritoire for £1.11.6 shortly thereafter.[215] At the same time Henry Fawkener, Esq. bought five 'Portraits' (cameos) for £2.2.0 and one oblong tablet 'Lady T's' for £1.5.0.

An unusual entry for 25 May 1787 was a brown and

white jasper *déjeuner* for one for £3.3.0.[216] In June, Lady De Verey purchased a jasper inkstand for £1.1.0,[217] and Lady Leitrim bought a jasper chocolate cup for one guinea, two escritoires and stands in jasper for three guineas (Figs. 76 and 77) as well as two reading candlesticks (body unspecified) for £1.11.6.[218] A Mr Bury, Esq. purchased a green and white jasper snake-handled vase (probably No. 266, Colour Plate 16) for £6.6.0.[219]

The Hon. Warren Hastings, Esq. bought a pair of jasper bulbous root baskets for two guineas in July 1787.[220] In the same week a lilac jasper teapot was sold for £1.0.0 as well as two blue and white jasper ice pails for £6.6.0[221] but they must have been cash purchases because the buyer was not annotated in the margin.

A Mr Robinson, Esq. of Charterhouse Square made a large purchase of jasper including a pair of wine and water ewers *Sacred to Bacchus &c* (Colour Plate 20) for the usual price of ten guineas along with a pair of vases No. 266 for twelve guineas which was also the usual charge of these, two altar flower pots for six guineas, a pair of *Ceres and Cybele* candlesticks for five guineas and teaware in jasper and in black and in cane.[222]

Lord Dalrymple bought five jasper portraits in frames in

August 1787 for £3.5.0.[223] Dr Priestley purchased a number of scientific dry-bodies such as retorts, mortars and pestles and bended tubes in October 1787.[224] Lady Templetown purchased a tablet of an unidentified subject for eight guineas in early 1788[225] and Sir Joseph Andrews bought a ewer and basin in blue and white jasper for £5.5.0.[226] The Countess of Stamford was also on the list of those buying jasper with the purchase of a blue and white escritoire and stand for £1.1.0.[227] Lady Gallway bought a pair of candelabra of *The Seasons* for £4.4.0 (Colour Plate 21; Fig. 78) and a green jasper vase for £3.3.0 in March of 1788. At the same time Princess Elizabeth purchased, among other Wedgwood wares, two octagon smelling bottles (Colour Plate 22) for £1.10.0 along with a jasper tea tray for one guinea.[228]

A Miss Conyers purchased one blue and white jasper vase for £2.2.0 and one jasper egg cup for 2/6.[229] Lady Honeywood purchased a garniture of three blue and white jasper vases for a total of £9.9.0 and a pair of 'Season Candlesticks' for four guineas (Colour Plate 21; Fig. 78).[230] An extraordinary entry for 1788 was a purchase by a Mr Locke of '1 camel Shape Teapot Silver Spout & chain' for 12/6.[231] Surely this is salt-glazed stoneware and a very late example of that shape and body, but may have been residue of very old stock.

The Duke of Argyll purchased a jasper vase No. 271 (Fig. 70) for three guineas along with two smaller ones with which No. 271 is often paired, No. 279 (Fig. 60, centre), for two guineas as well as another pair of flower pots No. 227 for one guinea.[232] At the same time the Countess of Uxbridge bought two flower pots, stands and linings in blue jasper for £2.12.0.

Sir Roger Newdigate bought one of Lady Templetown's oblong tablets for six guineas and four oval medallions for £3.0.0 in April 1788.[233] A Mr Gray, possibly a retailer, purchased 12 smelling bottles with the *Prince of Wales* in relief for six guineas and two jasper flower pots No. 288 for £1.11.6 (Fig. 79).[234] This is the first mention of this shape in any of the sales records. Smelling bottles with the *Prince of Wales* and *Duke of York* were popularly seen in the lists of sales from this time, as were portrait medallions of the *Rt.Honourable William Pitt* and *Benjamin Franklin* (Colour Plate 9), mostly sold at 10/6.[235]

It was in 1788 that Josiah Wedgwood II wrote from Etruria to his father on holiday at Blackpool that 'The beads will come out tomorrow' and 'will send you also the cameos for the sword hilt & a narrow cameo with the scroll'.[236] From this time jasper beads appeared with frequency in the sales lists.

John Wilkes, Esq. selected a pair of blue and white jasper vases No. 273 (Colour Plate 23; Fig. 61) for two guineas as well as other items in basalt and in ornamental earthenware in

Fig. 89 **Tripod vase,** *solid blue jasper with white embellishment. This vase in bisque, shape No. 281, appears in sales records for the first time on 24 April 1790 and sold for a mere £1.10.0 (Wedgwood MS 16/15485). One in blue and white jasper went for £2.2.0 in the next month. (16/15488). Mark: WEDGWOOD, c. 1790-91, 8¼ inches high. (Lady Lever Art Gallery, Museums & Galleries on Merseyside, LL1466.)*

Fig. 90 **Flower pot,** *white jasper with black jasper dip and white relief decoration. Shape No. 382 entered the sales lists in May 1790 and an imperfect example sold for 83/- (Wedgwood MS 16/15491). Mark: WEDGWOOD, c. 1790-93, 7¼ inches high. (Nassau County Museum, Port Washington, New York, Buten collection of Wedgwood.)*

Fig. 91 **Opera tube** in blue and white jasper, mounted in steel for a monocular. Tubes for opera glasses were popular after 1790, particularly with European dealers. Sold mounted and unmounted '6 deep blue Tubes for Opera Glasses' sold for £4.10.0 in September 1790 (Wedgwood MS 16/15510). No visible mark, 2½ inches high. (Nottingham Museum, 1892-173.)

Fig. 92 **Medallion** with zodiac border, lilac, green and white jasper with lapidary polished edge set in gilt metal frame. The central scene is a sacrifice. Mark: WEDGWOOD, c. 1790-95, 2⅜ inches diameter. (Zeitlin collection, ex Pereira collection.)

September 1788.[237] The Duke of Devonshire and Lord Viscount Duncannon both made purchases of blue and white jasper inkwells in shape No. 311 (Fig. 76), the Duke buying six and Lord Duncannon three at two guineas a piece.[238]

The first combination of green and lilac jasper was listed in surviving sales records for 28 December 1788 when '1 Green & lilac Jasper cream Ewer' for 7/6 was recorded.[239] The year 1788 drew to a close with a single sale of '6 oval [cameos] *Aurora*' for £1.16.0.[240]

Very few records survive for sales in 1789. In February there were invoices of wares sent to Mr Thomas Byerley in London which included lilac and white bezel polished oval medallions as well as cameos and beads.[241] Five jasper vases No. 266 (Colour Plate 16; Fig. 65), 14 inches high were sent for 105/- each. The famous snake-handled vase continued in popularity. As did the No. 275 vase (Fig. 60, right), six of which Wedgwood also sent up to London for a total of £18.18.0.[242] There exists another long inventory[243] of wares, sent up to London in April, which itemizes cameos, medallions and beads, as well as other jaspers such as green and white salvers 8½ inches (9/- each), custard cups and saucers (4/6), lemonade cups (3/6), and bouillon cups with handles and stands (31/6). In blue jasper with white 'leafage' there were also round salvers at 9/-, egg cups at 2/6 and butter tubs and stands for 23/- each. In blue jasper with white bas-reliefs, the factory sent up six glaciers No. 338 (Fig. 80) at 83/- each, round and

flat smelling bottles with festoons and laurel borders and a quantity of those with Prince of Wales effigies and feathers and somewhat fewer of those depicting both the Prince of Wales and the Duke of York, all at 17/8 each. Vases in shapes No. 262 (Fig. 60 left), 12 inches 63/-, No. 302 (Fig. 69), 11 inches 63/-, No. 282, 8 inches 21/-, and No. 277, 12 inches, all at 63/- each were included. At the end of the list was a pair of semi-circular bulbous root pots finely enriched with Etruscan figures and borders. Appended to the inventory was a note: 'The Price of these Bulbous root pots Mr Wedgwood thinks will be about 4½ G's [guineas] or 5 G's the Pair but Mr Byerley will sample them to the Etruscan Vase & fix the price'.[244]

Somewhat earlier in the year Josiah Wedgwood had devised a mould for one-piece earrings, instead of the three-piece ones which had been made previously. Josiah Wedgwood II wrote accordingly to his father:

On Monday we put into the oven about 6 doz. pair of ear drops made in the way you settled before you left. It answers extremely well & Nixon can turn about 3 or 4 times as many as he could of those made in three parts.[245]

Sales records for 1790 are complete, beginning with Friday, 1 January when a 'new Vase with Zodiac' (Fig. 81) was listed in jasper for four guineas, along with a fluted teapot with a lilac spout for 13/-.[246] On the following Monday, 4 January 1790, several sales for 'lavender bottles' in oval and

Fig. 94 *Flower pots* (minus pierced tins), white jasper with lilac and green jasper dip dice work. These match descriptions of vases purchased by Thomas Hope, although one cannot be certain as no shape number was mentioned. Similar to shape No. 270 which are referred to as 'Temples of Flora,' the flower containers are pictured in the shape book with domed tops and were sold in double pairs for ten guineas in 1791. Marks: WEDGWOOD 3, c. 1790-95, 6½ inches high. (Lady Lever Art Gallery, Museums & Galleries on Merseyside, LL1175, 1176.)

Fig. 93 *Pedestal*, solid blue jasper with white reliefs. One of the purchases of Wedgwood jasper made by Thomas Hope in 1793 was a pair of pedestals (No. 506) with 'rams heads at top & Sphinxes at bottom' for £10.10.0 (Wedgwood MS 16/15627). Mark: WEDGWOOD, c. 1793, 8¼ inches high. (Nottingham Museum, 1892-78.)

Fig. 95 *Teapot*, solid blue jasper with white arabesque relief decoration. In March 1791 a group of teapots with arabesque decoration was sent back to the factory because they leaked at the spout (Wedgwood MS 16/ 15537). Mark: WEDGWOOD, c. 1790, 3⅜ inches high. (Liverpool Museum, Museums & Galleries on Merseyside, 2704M, Mayer collection.)

octagon shapes were listed. This is the first use of the term 'lavender bottle'. The next entries are for 'Smelling Bottles' so the terms are not synonymous.[247] Flower pots No. 327 appear in the existing records for the first time in early 1790. These are small urns on top of a round pedestal.[248]

A Mr Flower, perhaps a retailer, bought a number of jasper wares including a garniture of five vases with zodiac borders, the larger was £4.4.0, the smaller ones, shape No. 275 (Fig. 60 right), were £3.3.0, another smaller pair yet, £2.2.0. He also purchased several *déjeuner* sets, in two instances substituting a coffee pot for the teapot which added an extra 2/- on to the basic price of three guineas.[249]

His Excellency Lord Auckland purchased ornaments for a 'Plateau' including one large vase No. 266 (Colour Plate 16) for £7.17.6, two smaller ones No. 275 (Fig. 60 right) for £6.6.0, two small flower pots and pedestals for £1.18.0, four bisque figures with round pedestals for £5.8.0, and a pair of garden pots with figures No. 259 (Fig. 82) for £6.6.0.[250] One can visualise the elegant display on Lord Auckland's table with this combination of vases, flower containers and figures.

Bell drops continued to be sold nearly every day in a variety of combinations including Etruscan painted, and green and white fluted.[251] Another vase, shape No. 27, appeared for the first time on surviving lists in January 1790.[252]

By early 1790 cameos were being specifically identified as 'pale blue'.[253] There were other blue colours, those referred to by Wedgwood as 'Birmingham blue' and 'London blue', the Birmingham blue, naturally, being the less expensive.[254]

Studs sold by the dozen began appearing at this time in the Wedgwood sales at 4/3 per dozen. By the autumn of 1790 Josiah Wedgwood, writing from Etruria to his son in Frankfurt who was parading the Wedgwood copy of the Portland Vase (Fig. 83) around the Continent securing orders, complained of the dwindling cameo sales:

We are now at a dead lift [?] for orders in the cameo & bas relief line, having scarcely orders for one days work, except 15 gro[ss] of studs largest size from Burley, which are cheifly (*sic*) for Clays slate buttons.[255]

Fig. 96 *Flower pot*, solid blue jasper with white jasper decoration of the Muses. Shape No. 369 entered the sales lists by number for the first time in April 1791 when a pair of vases sold for £2.10.0 (no size given; Wedgwood MS 16/15541). The shape book indicates the vase was available in four sizes: 11, 10, 9, and 7 inches. It was a popular item and many were sold in the years 1791 and 1792. Mark: WEDGWOOD V, c. 1791-95, ? inches high. (Birmingham Museum of Art, Alabama, Beeson collection of Wedgwood.)

The first mention of candlestick No. 263 occurred in surviving records in February 1790. This is the candlestick which resembles a seated Britannia holding a foliate term with another foliage candle holder emanating from her helmet.

In February 1790 tripod candelabra No. 255 (Fig. 84) appeared. This was a sophisticated item which was to feature in successive purchases by Thomas Hope and others in the next few years. No buyer was listed in the entry and the pair was only £4.4.0.[256]

Temples of Flora No. 260 had been purchased since 1786, often by the nobility such as the King of Naples.[257]

They were not wildly popular with only a few sales during the last four years and they varied in price, probably due to size, from £2.14.0 a pair to £5.5.0. Another small pair sold in February, 1790 for £2.14.0.[258]

Garden pots and stands were produced in a variety of forms in jasper with varied decoration within the same form. For example, No. 332 came in five sizes from 9 inches down to 4 inches ranging in price from 21/- to 9/- each in foliage relief or foliage and strap work relief. Another flower pot, No. 358, was offered with festoon relief in 8½, 6, 5¼, or 4 inch sizes at 12/- to 6/-. Rectangular garden pots with *Zephyrs* No. 259 (Fig. 82)

Fig. 97 **Temple of Flora**, *white jasper with lilac jasper dip. Shape No. 270 has a domed cover with a figure of Diana on the top. These were apparently used for table decoration as four were sold in the autumn of 1791 for £10.10.0 (Wedgwood MS 16/1559). The Temple of Flora had been in the inventory since 1786 and had enjoyed steady sales. Mark: WEDGWOOD, c. 1786-95, 8¼ inches high. (Lady Lever Art Gallery, Museums & Galleries on Merseyside, LL1308.)*

Fig. 98 **Temple of Flora**, *solid light blue jasper with white relief decoration, shape No. 270 without the domed cover and the liner. Mark: WEDGWOOD, c. 1786-95, 5½ inches high. (Colonial Williamsburg Foundation, ex Brown collection, G1985-72.)*

were 63/- each, a rococo flower container with cupids No. 256 was 42/- (Fig. 86) and a pair of Grecian figure candlesticks No. 25 were 26/3.[259]

About this time 'meltor/melton[?]'-shaped teapots entered the inventories as terminology for a shape which was hitherto unheard of, the configuration of which cannot be determined at this time.

In 1790 jasper painted boxes sold for £1.5.0[260] and 'hookers [hookahs]' (Fig. 40) appeared for the first time as well. These were basalt with silver borders but other coloured bodies were to follow shortly. Dice work pattern appeared for the first time in sales in April, 1790 (Colour Plates 23 and 24; Figs. 85, 87 and 94).[261]

A most unusual set of four 'Vases Blue & White Jasper' No. 476 in the form of follies sold for the first time in surviving records in April 1790 for £4.4.0.[262] Another first appearance was a 'foliage pot pourrie 292' for £2.12.6.[263]

More tablets appeared that week: an *Apotheosis of Homer* and its companion *Apotheosis of Virgil* (Fig. 88) for ten guineas each, a *Hercules in the Garden of the Hesperides*, also for ten guineas, and a *Judgment of Hercules* for six guineas.[264]

'Dark blue and white jasper' teawares were mentioned specifically for the first time in April, 1790.[265] Other 'bisque' ornamental vases were sold at the same time, a newly mentioned shape, No. 281 (Fig. 89), a grand tripod vase in bisque with ram's heads and hooves sold for only £1.10.0.[266]

The same vase sold later on in the spring in blue and white jasper for relatively little but almost twice as much as the bisque one, for two guineas.[267] Another introduction was shape 283, a blue and white jasper bulbous root pot with, in this instance, 'a flat wire cover' for £2.2.0.[268]

The so-called 'tube flower pots' simulating bamboo shoots were popular in caneware (Fig. 29), painted blue or green but were rarely produced in blue and white jasper. However, five of these were listed in May 1790 selling for £3.8.0. At the same time a blue and white jasper plateau complete with egg cups sold for £1.10.0. The following day a syllabub cup 'blue within' went for five guineas.[269]

On 6 May, 1790 there was an interesting purchase of six *déjeuner* sets in light blue jasper and white reliefs and borders consisting of one teapot, one canister, a cream ewer and sugar dish, two teacups and one *déjeuner* board in an octagon case covered with black leather and lined with green cloth for £6.5.6 each or a total of £37.13.0. Another six sets, each containing the same items without white relief and only white borders, sold for £5.0.0 each plus two other variations of sets of four with one also in a leather case. In addition, two jasper gondola escritoires sold for six guineas.[270] Unfortunately, no buyer was annotated in the margin of the listing.

A first listing for shape No. 382 in a flower container (Fig. 90) appeared in late May 1790 and was sold for 63/-

and noted as being imperfect.[271] This flower pot initially appeared in blue and white jasper but was also produced in black jasper. An entry for blue and white jasper salts was on the list for £1.4.0 the pair around the same time. Two white jasper figures at £1.16.0 also seem a rarity, but there is no further description about the subject or buyer.[272]

Vases such as No. 266 with snake handles (Colour Plate 16), No. 275 (Fig. 60, right) and 279 (Fig. 60, centre) remained the most popularly selected from 1786 and continued so through 1790.

Another pair of wine and water ewers, No. 236 (Colour Plate 20) sold in June 1790 for £10.10.0.[273] An interesting contrast in price is illustrated by the sale the same year of a pair of basalt wine and water ewers for £6.6.0.[274]

'Lamp vase', or 'lamp case' No. 305 (similar to Fig. 72) as it was sometimes referred to, is a mystery. The base is cut out in a way to accommodate one of the many patent lamps on the market at the time, but the type of a lamp which went into the case is unknown. The first mention of this form was in June 1790 and a pair sold for four guineas.[275]

The end of June 1790 found a number of newly described shapes appearing in the lists of sales from Greek Street. Ice pails in blue and white jasper No. 316 (Colour Plate 25) four for £25.4.0; another form of ice pail was less expensive, No. 357, 12 of which sold for £15.4.0; monteiths No. 355 sold for 63/- and glaciers No. 338 (Fig. 80) which were sent up to London from the Etruria factory in 1789 were sold for £8.8.0 a pair. 'Foliage flower pots' No. 345 appeared also for the first time selling for one guinea each and a pair of 'oval Zephyr' flower pots No. 259 (Fig. 82) were £6.6.0. The latter were not totally new, having been sold earlier on in 1790. A large sale of 'Glass pails' No. 348 (Fig. 73) for 20/- each was included in the

list. A group of new bulbous root pots No. 297 was listed at £3.3.0 for a pair, and No. 340 at £2.2.0 a pair.[276]

At this time 'Cabinet Cups', covers and stands became popular and Wedgwood offered three shapes, No. 384 for £1.7.0, and Nos. 385 and 386 each for £1.6.0. The first mention of No. 384 (Fig. 106) occurred on 1 July, 1790.[277]

Newly listed vase No. 372 was made in seven sizes from 14 inches to 4¾ inches. Although it does not list the size, one vase, probably a rather large one, sold for four guineas in July 1790. At the same time cameos commemorating the 'Bastille' were sold for 15/- each.[278] In August an 'Antique Ewer' No. 319 and 'Bason' (sic) No. 321 sold for five guineas, another first mention.

In September another pair of white figures of Cupid and Hebe on pedestals were sold for £4.4.0. and a Mr Davis bought '6 Deep Blue Tubes for Opera Glasses' (Fig. 91) for £4.10.0.[279] Mr Davis bought twelve more opera glasses in December 1790.[280]

Vases with the Zodiac continued in popularity with shapes No. 275 (Fig. 60, right) and No. 294 decorated with the signs.[281] Vase No. 273 (Colour Plate 23; Fig. 61), one of the most popular forms, was made in green jasper and decorated with festoons and signs of the zodiac as well.[282] In late 1790 a number of sales of jasper medallions of Lord and Lady Auckland occurred, 12 for six guineas in the initial sale.[283]

Miss Crewe, probably the same one who was the designer for Wedgwood, purchased two round medallions (4⅝ inches) described as having a green ground with a black cameo in the middle and a white arabesque border for two guineas, as well as five other oval cameos and one oblong octagon, the remainder of the cameos being undescribed.[284]

Fig. 99 *Smelling bottles,* left, *blue and white jasper with a portrait of George III, 2¾ inches diameter, centre, blue and white jasper, 2⅛ inches high, right, blue and white jasper, shape No. 199, 3¼ inches high. Oval smelling bottles in 'tri'-colour jasper appeared in sales records for the first time in late December 1791 (Wedgwood MS 16/15573). No marks, c. 1788-1800. (Grigsby collection.)*

Fig. 100 **Chocolate cup, cover, and stand,** *solid medium blue jasper with white jasper. Shape No. 329 had probably been in existence for some years but was not mentioned by shape number until February 1792 when it sold for £2.4.0 for two (Wedgwood MS 16/15582). Marks: cup, Wedgwood 5; saucer, WEDGWOOD, 5 inches high. (Nottingham Museum 1892-180.)*

Fig. 101 **Hanging lamp,** *white jasper with lilac and green jasper dip. Shape No. 531, this oil lamp seems to be the only surviving example, which was never sold by number in existing records. One 'hanging lamp' was mentioned selling for three guineas in 1792 but that would seem to be too small a cost for such an item. It seems possible that this lamp was made after surviving sales records have ended, that is after 1794. No mark, c. 1795-1800, 7½ inches high. (Lady Lever Art Gallery, Museums & Galleries on Merseyside.)*

Early in 1791 another oblong tablet of *Hercules in the Garden of the Hesperides* (14 by 5½ inches) sold for six guineas along with two of Lady Templetown's *Boys* (5¾ by 4¼ inches) for £2.6.0.[285]

In February 1791 Thomas Hope, Esq., made the first of five surviving records of purchases from Wedgwood. Although Hope was only twenty-one or twenty-two at the time, and still resident with his family in Amsterdam, he was to move to London in 1795, fleeing the invasion of Napoleon's armies. In London he became a major figure about town in circles of art, taste and fashion. The first group of Wedgwood purchases made by Hope consisted of a pair of jasper vases of No. 275 (Fig. 60, right) decorated with the *Muses* which sold for £6.6.0. Hope selected a group of jasper teawares with arabesque relief decoration as well as a pair of jasper tripod candelabra No. 180 (Colour Plate 20a) for which he paid £16.16.0. A pair of lamp cases No. 305 (Fig. 72) was included in the initial group of Wedgwood purchases by Hope as well as two blue and white jasper tripod candelabra No. 255 (Figs. 84 and 85) for £4.4.0. He purchased a second pair of candelabra in the same shape in basalt the same day for £2.10.0.[286] In March 1791 Hope made a major purchase of five tablets, an oblong tablet (15⅛ by 6⅛ inches) of *Priam Begging the body of Hector* (Colour Plate 27) and two round and two lozenge-shaped, probably for a chimney piece, for a grand total of £18.18.0 for the five.[287] In February 1793 Hope bought several other tablets, the most important of which were the *Apotheosis of Homer* and the *Apotheosis of Virgil*

(Fig. 88) each of which cost £10.10.0. Other tablet purchases included four medallions of an *Offering to Flora* as well as eleven medallions of a *Sacrifice to Bacchus*. He also bought a tri-colour jasper medallion with a zodiac border (Fig. 92) for 9/-. In the same order Hope selected '2 Square pedestals rams heads at top & Sphinxes at bottom' (Fig. 93) for £10.10.0 the pair and a pair of lilac and white jasper garden pots with green stars complete with stands and tins and wires inside were purchased by Hope for four guineas (Fig. 94).[288]

On 13 June, 1793 Hope took delivery of one of the first successful copies of the Barberini vase (or Portland vase as it is frequently called). The vase (Colour Plate 28) sold for the enormous sum of £31.10.0 plus £2.10.0 for the case. The delivery of this famous vessel was probably much anticipated by Hope who first learned about it while Josiah Wedgwood II was touring abroad with the first good copy of the vase in the summer of 1790. Wedgwood showed it to Lord Auckland in the Hague who in turn gave him a letter of introduction to Hope.[289] Hope's copy of the Barberini vase is now in the Wedgwood Museum, Barlaston. What became of Hope's other Wedgwood purchases is not known.

In March 1791 a group of sixty-eight jasper teapots with either arabesque or foliage decoration (Fig. 95) was sent back to the factory because they leaked at the spout.[290] At this period the factory was manufacturing large quantities of basalt painted in blue and silvered, or in other combinations of colours, so the lists are replete with sales

variegated decoration, sold in white bisque (Colour Plate 14a) for a mere 10/- in late 1791, the same price as the pebble ones in 1779.[294] Oval cream paterae in blue and white arabesque jasper (Colour Plate 29) with handles and ladles sold for £1.5.0 each in 1791.[295] The same day thirty-three dozen cameos with lilac, blue and green borders were sent to the Birmingham warehouse along with six dozen grooved beads.

In June there was an unusual entry for two garden pots 'VELVRETT GROTTO' for 12/-. The following day a white jasper figure of *Cupid* on a pedestal sold for £2.2.0.[296] Another interesting entry was a portrait of the Marquis of Rockingham in a black frame for 13/-, perhaps not jasper but basalt.[297]

In September 1791 another Temple of Flora was introduced into the inventory of sales, No. 270 (Fig. 97), four of which sold for ten guineas. The No. 260 Temple of Flora had been in the inventory since 1786 and had enjoyed steady, but not spectacular sales. At the same time griffin candelabra went for six guineas a pair along with glaciers and monteiths, both of which had appeared in previous sales.[298]

In September a W.J. Derby, Esq. purchased five tablets in pale blue jasper, one oblong for fifteen guineas and four oval for nine guineas. Unfortunately the subjects were not divulged.[299]

Fig. 102 *Vase, blue jasper dip decorated with white jasper arabesques. Shape No. 443 this vase, often referred to as a candlestick vase is pictured in the shape book with a figure for a finial on the reverse of the candlestick. Mark:* WEDGWOOD H, *c. 1790-1800, 8⅞ inches high. (Nottingham Museum, 1892-109.)*

Fig. 103 *Viola da Gamba vase, white jasper with blue jasper dip and white embellishment. Shape No. 492. Mark:* WEDGWOOD, *c. 1801, 6⅞ inches high. (Courtesy of the Trustees of the Wedgwood Museum, Barlaston, Stoke-on-Trent.)*

of these items which, although interesting, are not germane to this work. Other large basalt ornamental wares seemed to be experiencing a revival as was Etruscan painted basalt, both of which were reflected in sales.

In April 1791 flower pot No. 369 (Fig. 96) entered the sales lists, a pair (no size given) selling for £2.10.0. These were made in four sizes 11, 10, 9, and 7 inch heights.[291] Another pair, obviously larger, was sold for £4.4.0 a few days later.[292]

There are occasional sales of white 'bisque' ornamental vases which are invariably much less expensive than their jasper counterparts. For example, a pair of white bisque ewers No. 262 (Fig. 60, left) was sold in 1791 for £1.4.0. Only days later the jasper version sold for £6.6.0 a pair.[293] Vase No. 40, a well-known shape in basalt and in pebble

Fig. 104 **Pot-pourri vase**, solid blue jasper with white reliefs and a central cartouche of the Marriage of Cupid and Psyche. Shape No. 501, this seems to have been a product of the post 1794 era as no sales are mentioned of this piece in surviving records. Mark: WEDGWOOD, c. 1794-1800, 6¼ inches high. (Nassau County Museum, Port Washington, New York, Buten collection of Wedgwood, OG774.)

Fig. 105 **Bonnet/Dome**, solid blue jasper with wafer decoration and white jasper embellishment. The dome was No. 520 in the shape book but regrettably no sales of this piece occurred before 1794 so the function of this curious object with its slats open to the air remains a curiosity. No mark. c. 1795-1800, 5⅞ inches high. (Lady Lever Art Gallery, Museums & Galleries on Merseyside, LL1503.)

Eye cups in green, probably jasper, appear for the first time in September 1791 for 1/6 a pair.[300] Other small objects include blue jasper caddy spoons which sold for 6d each[301] and '2 New oval Smelling Bottles Lilac & Green' for £1.1.0 (Fig. 99).[302]

Later that year a Mrs Billington bought the very sophisticated tripod flower pot No. 180 (Colour Plate 20a) sometimes known as the 'Michelangelo' vase.[303] There is a copy at Saltram in basalt and another in the Wedgwood Museum. One of the few jasper examples is in the Birmingham Museum in America. The first appearance of this vase in the records is the sale to Thomas Hope in February 1791.

In 1792 H.R.H. the Duke of York purchased four ice pails with 'Stars' for £12.12.0, and four smaller ones for £8.8.0. This is the first mention of the star decoration often associated with dice work on ornamental wares. He also bought one 'flower pot' No. 180 (Colour Plate 20a), the same 'Michelangelo' vase purchased by Mrs Billington late in the previous year for £8.8.0 and two of the new flower pots No. 369 (Fig. 96) for £6.6.0.[304] In February the Duke bought several green and white jasper vases in forms previously popular in blue and white jasper, one, No. 266, with snake handles (Colour Plate 16; Fig. 65) for five guineas, two No. 275 for six guineas, two No. 279 for four guineas and two No. 273 (Colour Plate 23; Fig. 61) for two guineas, clearly intending these to form a garniture of seven.[305] Sales begin to reflect green and white jasper as clearly ascendant in popularity. Variegated wares continued to appeal after two decades of production and vase No. 266 sold in marble and gold at the same time for £2.12.6[306] The Duke of York continued to purchase green and white

jasper the following week with ten more vases, most of which were first appearances in green and white jasper: one foliage vase No. 294, two ditto No. 277, two flower pots No. 377 (Colour Plate 30, right) for £1.4.0 were a first in this shape, and a pair of tripods No. 255 (Figs. 84 and 85).[307]

The same day another sale of one round cameo *Virgo* 'and fixing it in a Tooth pick case' cost the buyer 4/6.[308] Two newly mentioned shapes appeared on 11 February, 1792 which probably had been in the inventory for some time but had not previously been listed by number in the sales: chocolate cups and saucers No. 329 (Fig. 100), a pair of which sold for £2.4.0; and broth basins and covers, No. 331 for £3.0.0 a pair.

In July 1792 the first mention of '1 Hanging Lamp' appeared for £3.3.0. The only example of a hanging lamp known is the one in the Lady Lever Art Gallery (Fig. 101) which seems to be a unique survivor but would also seem to have been much more expensive than three guineas. At the same time a portrait of Mr Dundas was sold for 10/6.[309] Soon thereafter portraits of Sir Joshua Reynolds and Jonas Hanaway were sold in black frames for £1.8.0 a pair.[310]

Probably the first copy of the Portland Vase (Colour Plate 28; Fig. 83) was sold in August, 1792, the buyer being unknown and a cash purchaser.[311] Certainly many other copies were sold privately, or given by Josiah Wedgwood to his friends and benefactors. A great deal of this is laid out in Aileen Dawson's book, with Ann Eatwell's contributions, *Masterpieces of Wedgwood in the British Museum* (1984, revised 1995). According to the Wedgwood oven books six copies came off the line in 1792.[312]

1792 may have also been the beginning of the rage for

Fig. 106 *Flower container, white jasper with lilac and green jasper. A variant of shape No. 384 this vase was made in 9⅜, 8, 6, and 5 inch sizes and it was sold on April 10, 1794 in white jasper with green stars for £2.10.0 a pair (Wedgwood MS 17/15678). Mark: WEDGWOOD, c. 1794-1800, 5 inches high. (Newark Museum.)*

tri-colour dice work. Certainly it began to feature most prominently in the sales that year, particularly with lilac and green dice work in *déjeuner* sets which sold for three guineas, or a little more if the sets were for two persons.[313] The year continued the trend set by late 1791 with a preponderance of green and white jasper vases, even the odd lilac and white vase, a combination which had hitherto been seen only in teawares, bell drops and other smalls. Special orders for grand vases could be paired with covers from other vases if desired. For example, a new vase shape offered in jasper, No. 26, was decorated with the *Muses* and paired with the cover from Vase No. 372. This 16 inch pair of vases went for ten guineas.[314] In another case the base of a four part flower pot (Fig. 107) was sold separately for 31/6 to be used as a pedestal for Vases No. 266 (Colour Plate 16; Fig. 65) and No. 289.[315]

Viscount Lowerscourt bought several pieces of pale blue and white jasper, including a vase No. 294 (15 inches) and two smaller with zodiac borders and figures of the *Muses* and Lady 'T's' *Friendship Consoling Affliction* No. 266 (Colour Plate 16; Fig. 65) – 14½ inches high – for £10.10.0, and a pedestal No. 295 (Colour Plate 30, left) as well as two tube flower pots for £1.10.0.[316]

At the same time Lady A. Waley bought one vase No. 302 (Fig. 69) – 11 inches high – with the *Muses* for three guineas, and a pair of tripod candelabra No. 255 (Figs. 84 and 85) for four guineas.[317]

The Countess of Leitrim, probably resident in Ireland,

bought a lilac and green dice work part tea and coffee set in October 1792.[318] Thomas Ivory, Esq. bought a large blue and white jasper vase, unfortunately of unspecified shape, for £15.5.0 and an accompanying pedestal for an additional five guineas in November 1792.[319]

The year 1793 began with Henry Howard, Esq.'s purchase of nine medallions, mostly classical subjects except for one of *Montesquieu* and *Dr Franklin* (Colour Plate 9).[320] Mr Webber, perhaps the artist John Webber RA (1750-93), made a purchase of the largest version of the snake-handled vase and two griffin candlesticks, both in basalt for £6.6.0 the three in March 1793.[321] Jasper 'fionningo [fiammingo]' boys are recorded specifically as such at this time for 15/- for two.[322] These famous boys had been commonly made in basalt for two decades and it is not surprising that some were turned out in jasper. Sybil lamps are mentioned for the first time as such but were probably in basalt and sold for a mere two guineas a pair.[323] Egg cups in jasper with star patterns are being sold by this time costing a little over 2/- each.[324]

By 1793 many shapes of flower pots were produced in the current rage, lilac and green jasper and blue jasper was even embellished with painted decoration from time to time. It could not have been a successful combination because few examples were listed and few survive. One blue and white ink with Etruscan painting on the top sold for 15/- in April 1793.[325] Around the same time one Doctor Smith was buying flower pots Nos. 358, 378 and 382 (Fig. 90) in lilac and green jasper. Sir James Sidney (?) Lang, Bart. bought green and white jasper vases No. 279

Fig. 107 *Pedestal for a four tier tulip vase, solid blue jasper with white jasper relief. Shape 291 was a vase which sold to the King of Naples in 1786 for £7.17.6 (Wedgwood MS 16/15375 June 14, 1786). The pedestal or base was also sold separately for 31/6 and used as a pedestal for snake-handled vase No. 266 (Wedgwood MS 16/15611). Mark: WEDGWOOD, 5½ inches high. (Lady Lever Art Gallery, Museums & Galleries on Merseyside, LL1440.)*

Fig. 108 **Bulbous root pot**, *white jasper with green jasper dip and relief figures of the Muses. One of the purchases made by the King of Naples in 1786, shape 296 was popular from 1786 to 1792 and sold for £3.3.0 a pair. Mark: WEDGWOOD, c. 1786-92, 5½ inches high. (Nassau County Museum, Port Washington, New York, Buten collection of Wedgwood.)*

and four Temples of Flora in green and white at a mere 10/6 each and James Strachan, Esq. was purchasing more conventional blue and white jasper vases Nos. 275 and 279 (Fig. 60, right and centre), while the Countess of Westmoreland bought two white bisque tripods No. 281 (Fig. 89) for only £1.10.0.[326] At precisely the same time 'Bisque porcelain' began to be seen in the recorded sales.[327] No descriptions or shape numbers are given for the bisque porcelains, simply dimensions.

By mid–May 1793 silver and green dice work combinations appear in flower pots No. 380, the first mention of this shape both by number and this decoration. At the same time the decoration appears in 'bellhandles'.[328] In June the first suggestion of 'artichoke' jasper in a cream ewer occurs.[329] An example in the Lady Lever Art Gallery of an artichoke pot, cover and stand is a rare example of this colour in jasper (Fig. 54). Later on in the month '2 Grey & White Fluted Columns' were listed selling for £1.1.0. The 'fluted columns' previously so-described were shape No. 287 (Fig. 57) and this is the first mention of these being made in grey and white.[330]

A Mr Byerley, probably Wedgwood's nephew and partner but possibly the London journalist of the same name, was also making some purchases from the company. In July 1793 he bought four flower pots in lilac and green dice work with stars No. 382 (Fig. 90) for two guineas the four.[331]

Portraits of American political figures were sold regularly throughout the American Revolution and afterwards, *Benjamin Franklin* (Colour Plate 9) being a steady seller and *Washington* less so but not infrequently mentioned; however, it is assumed that these were basalt cameos and medallions. The first mention of a blue and white jasper portrait of *Washington* in existing sales lists was on 19 July

1793.[332]

Likewise a blue and white jasper seal mounted in gold of *Homer* was sold a few days earlier.[333] An oval medallion of *Inigo Jones* in blue and white jasper went for 10/6 in September.[334]

Late in 1793 blue jasper 'hand Candelabras mounted with brass nossles *(sic)*, Extinguishers & Steel Snuffers' were listed at 15/- each.[335]

Regrettably sales records do not survive after April 1794. However, early in that year girandoles in blue and white jasper and ormolu appear at £8.8.0 a pair.[336] William Adams was also producing jasper girandoles (Fig. 119) in competition with the Wedgwood ones. Jasper was utilised in many other ways in combination with other metals, as we have seen in opera glasses, and in knife handles.[337] Vases were being mounted by Pinton (?) & Co., who ordered four vases of deep blue and white jasper with yellow bands for mounting in January 1794.[338]

In February, a 'Yates Esq.', possibly the potter, purchased three flower pots in shape No. 388, a new form, in deep blue and white jasper with green stars, one pair for £1.10.0 and another single for one guinea.[339] At the same time a Mrs Wollaston was buying vases and flower pots in lilac and white fluted with green stars, green stars on all combinations of colours being the current height of fashion.[340] In April, flower pots No. 384, a shape which had

Fig. 109 **Bulbous root pot**, *solid blue jasper with white relief decoration. Shape No. 268 was sold abroad in 1788 to Wedgwood agents Sykes in Paris and Veldhuysen in Amsterdam for 18/- each. Mark: WEDGWOOD, c. 1788, 6¼ inches high. (Lady Lever Art Gallery, Museums & Galleries on Merseyside, LL1527.)*

Fig. 110 *Canopic vase, white jasper with green jasper dip and Egyptian and zodiac emblems. Shape No. 148. Mark: WEDGWOOD W/W, 19th c., 9¼ inches high. (Liverpool Museum, Museums & Galleries on Merseyside, 1981-382, a,b.)*

first appeared on sales lists in 1790, were sold in blue and white jasper with the green star combination for £2.10.0 a pair (Fig. 106).[341]

In April 1794 a Miss Berry, probably Mary or her sister Agnes, Horace Walpole's protégés, purchased a blue and white jasper smelling bottle with a gold cap and a red case for £1.14.0.[342] Mary Berry was also a friend of Thomas Hope and from about 1795 until Hope married Louisa Beresford in 1806, Mary hoped to form a more permanent relationship with the famous collector.[343]

Sir Gilbert Heathcote was among the last purchasers of blue and white jasper before the records cease. He bought two flower pots No. 345 with foliage relief decoration for £1.16.0.[344]

In January 1795 the balance of the London stock account set down at retail prices was £431.0.0. The balance at Etruria was £7,667.0.0.[345] 1795 was the year of the death of Josiah Wedgwood I, perhaps, in a sense, the end of the eighteenth century Wedgwood production in its own way.

It is impossible to determine exactly when other manufacturers began making jasper. Most certainly in the late 1770s James Neale and John Turner were also producing the desirable blue stonewares and in the 1780s William Adams was manufacturing jasper both at Burslem and at Tunstall. By the end of the century a number of other manufacturers were moving into the market established by Wedgwood, including Enoch Wood who was making both solid jasper and jasper dip, Ralph Wedgwood at Burslem and perhaps at Ferrybridge, and Spode, who was manufacturing blue jasper and tri-colour wares. On the Continent Sèvres produced some very fine jasper in limited quantities (Fig. 356), but jasper was not emulated abroad to the extent which basalt was, nor were the other English-style dry-bodies.

CHAPTER VI

Wedgwood Retailers at Home

Messrs Webb & Riggs, Merchants & Hardwaremen, located at 34 Cheapside,[1] were purchasing jasper teawares from Wedgwood in August 1786 in both blue and white and green and white as well as escritoires in blue jasper, No. 311, (Fig. 76) for £2.2.0, egg cups and vases, No. 276 one for 2 guineas and No. 279 (Fig. 60, centre) two for three guineas.[2]

These appear to be retail prices as it is not easy to tell what wholesale price, if any, existed on Wedgwood wares. In the case of vase No. 276 another sold retail on 24 June, 1786 for four guineas[3] but there were several sizes and when no size is given the price becomes immaterial. Likewise, with vase No. 279, one single sold on the same day for two guineas and the pair for Webb & Riggs sold in August were only three guineas but size is the unknown factor in both instances. It is likely that wholesale discounts existed but records are unclear on the percentage. Webb & Riggs appear to be concentrating their purchases on jasper with another group of ornamental wares later in the month: vase No. 271 (Fig. 70) for £2.2.0, two smaller No. 264 at £3.3.0, a pair of flower pots with dice work for £2.2.0, a pair of toilet candlesticks £1.11.6, a pair of reading candlesticks £1.1.0, a pair of figure candelabra £2.12.6, and one escritoire £1.5.0.[4] In September Webb & Riggs purchased six cane coloured teapots with black bas-reliefs for £1.16.0 and six half-pint blue jasper mugs with white reliefs for £3.3.0.[5] In 1788 the firm was purchasing cameos and twenty-four heads of the King of Poland.[6]

Messrs Miller and York were buying cameos in a variety of shapes, oblong, octagon and double in October, 1787.[7]

Messrs Trout & Bourgeois, operating from 26 Love Lane in Eastcheap in 1780,[8] and located in 1790 in the Minories, 32 George Street,[9] bought a number of jasper teawares in the autumn of 1788.[10]

In 1788, a Mr Bramley was buying similar objects in enough quantity to suggest that he was in a retail business of some sort. In March he bought a total of 288 cameos totalling £18.6.0.[11] He made other purchases later in March of dry-bodied stoneware[12] and in May of green and white jasper teapots and canewares.[13]

Messrs Whitbread and Messrs Willerton and Green, Jewellers & Toymen, 21 New Bond Street,[14] were making small purchases of jasper in March of 1788.[15] In 1790 Messrs Richards & Marinden, merchants operating from Cannon Street, Birmingham,[16] were purchasing quantities of basalt cameos and some small white jasper busts of *Pindar* and *Aristophanes* as well as a white figure of *Venus Rising* from *Venus Rising from the Sea* on a blue pedestal (Fig. 47),

probably similar to the ones in the British Museum from the last years of the Wedgwood & Bentley partnership.

Messrs Green & Reynolds purchased two *déjeuner* sets in April 1791, one for two with coffee pots and coffee cans in green jasper with white interiors for £5.2.0 and another in blue jasper with white reliefs and white within for £3.13.6.[17]

Messrs Stratton Gibson & Schonberg, described as Russian Merchants, Leadenhall Street,[18] London purchased a pair of vases in blue and white jasper No. 294 for six guineas, a pair, No. 292 for five guineas and one coffee pot No. 303 for £1.0.0 in May 1791.[19] This is the first mention by number of this coffee pot in the sales records; however, coffee pots were often substituted for teapots in *déjeuner* sets and this may have been one of those forms which had been in the inventory for some time but not mentioned by shape number.

J.C. Pinder & Co. were purchasing some blue and white jasper vases in 1791, three popular forms, No. 302 (Colour Plate 19) and two No. 273 (Colour Plate 23; Fig. 61) as well as some other non jasper items.[20] Messrs A. Williamson bought three jasper vases of an unspecified shape for six guineas and many tablets: two oval tablets of *Love Consoling Affliction* for four guineas; one imperfect of the same subject for £1.5.0; two oval of *Juno and Companion* for £1.16.0; two horizontal of the same subject for £1.10.0; two oval of *Flora* for one guinea and two round of Lady T's *Charlotte* for £1.16.0.[21]

William and George Russell Esqs. & Co., merchants at Paradise Street, Birmingham,[22] purchased a group of 'brown inks' and eight flower pots in jasper in 1792 including two pairs which appear in the list of sales for the first time, No. 376 at £1.0.0 and No. 388 at £1.4.0.[23]

A substantial group of tablets were returned to the factory in May 1792 without any explanation by an R. Brown & Co. The tablets included a *Muses with festoons* for three guineas and a number of smaller ones for around a guinea each totalling £11.12.6.[24]

Richard Hurtman Esq. & Co. may have been a Continental company, but it is difficult to tell from a name alone and there is rarely a location given in the marginal notations of buyers. The purchases by Hurtman were for expensive vases and pedestals including '1 Vase No. 294 with bas-reliefs copied from the Borghese Vase 19 inches high' for £15.15.0 and a round pedestal 'life of Achilles' (10¼ inches) for £5.5.0, and a new listing for two 'pot pourries with festoons & Medallions' (13½ inches high) No. 383 for £10.10.0. Notations beside the shape book drawing do not include anything higher than a 12 inch vase in this shape. These were apparently intended to be displayed on pedestals as two single pedestals No. 295 (Colour Plate 30) were the next entry followed by vase No. 266 (Colour Plate 16; Fig. 65), 18 inches high with bas-reliefs depicting the *Birth of Bacchus* for £10.10.0. Although this was the most popular jasper vase shape produced since 1786, even one produced occasionally in variegated porphyry or marble and gold surfaces, this is the largest and most costly version to date, the usual charge being five or six guineas per vase. This version was intended to be displayed on a round pedestal 10¼ inches high illustrating the *Life of Achilles* which cost £5.5.0. The last pair of vases and pedestals was No. 161, another new form in jasper, 16½ inches high with *Muses* for £10.10.0 and another pair of pedestals No. 295 for an additional £3.3.0.[25]

Pinton & Co., another unrecorded retailer, made a first purchase in surviving records of twenty-seven round blue and white jasper bases totalling £18.7.6 in June 1793.[26] A second purchase of twenty-three bases for £12.1.6 was made in September of the same year.[27]

Messrs Davies were purchasing cameos in deep blue and white jasper for inclusion in 'almanack (*sic*) bases', ten of these were £3.9.0.[28]

Concerns similar to those expressed in the next chapter regarding trade abroad apply to information gleaned from the Wedgwood sales records on the domestic retail trade. Nevertheless, the skeletal information annotated in the sales margins, combined with the information about purchase of objects, is a step in augmenting the very limited understanding of the ornamental ceramic trade in the late eighteenth century.

CHAPTER VII

Wedgwood Sales Abroad: Patrons And Connoisseurs

'Apparently when he wasn't collecting women he was collecting china!'

Edith Wharton, *Age of Innocence.*

Jasper was immediately popular abroad. In Frankfurt Baumgartner & Co. had been the major retailers purveying Wedgwood's useful and ornamental wares since 1769, but there were others of importance in the general vicinity such as C.C.H. Rost in Leipzig who sold to Prince Friedrich Franz von Anhalt-Dessau. An Anglophile who had travelled to Italy on the Grand Tour, Anhalt-Dessau was influenced by Sir William Hamilton and even designed one of his follies at Schloss Wörlitz after the *naiskos*, or horse guard house, depicted on one of Hamilton's Apulian vases.[1] The Prince had a long relationship with Wedgwood wares, having first visited London in the mid-1760s. In 1769 he visited the Wedgwood and Bentley showrooms, probably making purchases at the time. The first mention of correspondence between the Prince and Thomas Bentley was in November 1772 when Wedgwood wrote, 'I congratulate you upon your good letter from the Prince Anhalt Dessau. He seems to be a thorough good man & very sensible of the politeness of your letter to him.'[2] There were probably earlier communications and purchases. But certainly from 1774 onwards there are orders for basalt.[3] Receipts for purchases of '2 Red and Black fluted Bowpots' for 12/- exist from July 1775 and a larger order was placed in August of the same year with a total purchase of £8.2.6.[4] These, of course, were not jasper. But in 1772 one surviving letter, written in French, indicated that the Prince wished to purchase, '*J. ferai choixe de quelque garniture de Vases ...*'[5] Again these would be basalt, not jasper. In November 1779 Anhalt-Dessau placed a long order, also in French, for garden pots, vases, and escritoires directly from the 1779 catalogue.[6] Around the same time C.C.H. Rost also placed a sizeable order from the catalogue for cameos, intaglios, medallions, busts, lamps and flower containers as well as bas-reliefs in 'fine Jasper'.[7] Soon Rost placed another order for large figures of *Bacchus* (17 inches), *Fawn* (10¾ inches), *Apollo* (17 inches), *Venus Medicis* (10½ inches), and *Venus Rising from the Sea* (8½ inches) as well as two pairs of sitting 'Sphinxes to hold candles'.[8] All but the *Venus Rising from the Sea* were doubtless basalt at that date. Rost ordered more busts in basalt in 1780[9] and the next surviving orders are in 1785 when Rost ordered *Ceres and Cybele* candelabra, and '*un beau vase avec les Muses et le Pegase mais le prix de 5 guinéas est trop cher*'. Rost suggested that if

there was a less grand model to send it to him. He also ordered in a mixture of French and English, teawares in basalt, flower pots, ink pots, eye cups and bell drops in lilac, blue and grey. Tablets were ordered of '*Les Muses No. 204, et les heures Dansantes No. 205, Mariage de Cupid No. 30, Sacrifice a l'amour No. 208, grandes Vasesells Sacré a Bacchus, une autre Muses et Pegase*', &c.[10]

In 1787 Rost ordered another *Ceres and Cybele* candelabra, as well as triton candlesticks and a '*pot à fleurs en colonne ruiné*'.[11]

Rost frequently placed orders through Paris agent M. Le Coq and on 2 October, 1787 he received a bill for £56.9.6 from le Coq for his Wedgwood purchases.[12] Further purchases were made through M. Le Coq in 1788 and at one point Rost acknowledged a bill totalling £115.10.1 from him.[13] On several occasions Rost begged Le Coq to send the latest example of a vase or candelabra in the best pattern '*mais pas trop grands et pas trop cher*'.[14] Obviously he had a market but not one which would pay exorbitantly.

The 1788 order sent from Rost to le Coq included: *déjeuner* sets in basalt painted blue and white and others in lilac jasper, as well as basalt vases painted in blue and white,[15] perhaps the blue and white was a Continental preference as it does not often appear on sales of basalt within England at the time and never before 1788. February 1789 had Rost ordering more blue jasper *déjeuner* sets, 'pot pourris pots *pas trop grands*', garnitures of jasper vases, teawares, medallions and tablets.[16] Later the same year he ordered, along with basalt ornamental wares, blue jasper bulbous root pots, altar flower pots (Fig. 79), '1 pair little flower pots *en coloumne*' (Fig. 57), and caneware root pots and *déjeuner* sets with Etruscan painted borders.[17] In August 1790 Mr Rost placed a large order which included a number of garden pots in earthenware, some basalt busts, inkstands and '2 Bas relief in fine Jasper *Herculaneum Nymphs* (10 inches) £4.4.0, and 1 *Birth of Bacchus* (7½ by 5½ inches) £2.2.0 as well as a number of other tablets and fourteen heads in gilt frames and a set of heads or cameos of Roman Emperors'.[18] The body not being designated suggests that most of these were basalt bodies, not jasper. In November 1790 Rost wrote to Le Coq, who, along with M. Daguerre and M. Sykes, was acting as Wedgwood's Paris agent requesting information, among other things, about '*le prix de votre Vase Portland*' (Colour Plate 28; Fig. 83).[19]

An undated document indicated that of the German princes buying 'on account' from Wedgwood the largest sum was owed by Frederick Augustus Elector of Saxony, for a bill totalling £78.4.6, followed by Prince Anhalt Dessau with £39.5.6 and then by Prince Anhalt Zerbst with £32.1.0.[20]

In 1786 Ferdinand IV of Naples made a substantial purchase of ornamental jaspers. The Neapolitan king may have been inspired by Sir William Hamilton to seek out Wedgwood wares. It is certain that in the previous decade Hamilton's sister Lady Cathcart and her husband acted almost as agents for Wedgwood and Bentley in promoting their wares with Catherine the Great who received gifts from Wedgwood in order to encourage her patronage and ensure the custom of the Russian nobility. Wedgwood's initial success with the court ensured Russian patronage for many years. In 1786 an order for ornament wares amounting to £147 was sent to St. Petersburg, with £44.5.0 allotted to jasper vases.[21]

Although there is no actual proof, Sir William Hamilton may have been acting in a similar capacity with the Neapolitan king. A list of the pieces ordered by Ferdinand IV on 14 June, 1786, is worthy of publication in its entirety:

Ornamental Vase with the Muses & ec No. 266 (£) 5.5.0 (Colour Plate 16; Fig. 65)
a pyramidal flower pot in four parts 291 7.17.6 (Fig. 107)
a pair of pro(illegible) [Ewers] No. 262 6.6.0 (Fig. 60, left)
a pair of Chased Tripod Candelabra 4.4.0
a pair of Boquetiers antient Altar form 293 6.6.0
A pair of Vases with a bas-relief on each marriage of Cupid & Psyche from the Marlbro (*sic*) Gem & its companion sacrifice to Hymen 273, 2.2.0, (Colour Plate 23; Fig. 61)
a pair of Quiver flower pots 2.2.0 (Colour Plate 33)
a pair of round Temples of Flora No. 260 4.4.0
a pair of Bulbous Root pots No. 296 3.3.0 (Fig. 108)
a pair of ruinated Columns with inscriptions
3 Columns   (no price) (Fig. 56)
a pair do. 2 Columns (Liverpool) (no price)
1 figure white Jasper on blue pedestal Venus 2.2.0
2 do. Cupid & Hebe   2.14.0
1 do. Jupiter   1.7.0
2 do. Venus & Marin   3.3.0
4 White figures on blue pedestals   2.14.0
6 White busts on blue terms   1.1.0
3 pairs of sleeping boys from Fiamingo   1.1.0

All but the last entry were probably jasper bodies. Although Hamilton told Wedgwood it was an order for jasper, the price of the 'sleeping boys' suggests they were probably basalt. Occasionally the 'boys' were produced in jasper. Later on that month there was a sale of '1 Fiamingo white boy' for 10/6.[22]

Frankfurt dealer Baumgartner purchased a number of jasper tea wares in July 1786, including eleven blue jasper teapots, seven tea canisters, four milk pots, and two tea cups and saucers as well as a considerable number of items in black basalt.[23] In August Baumgartner made a small purchase of eight octagonal cameos for bracelets for £3.3.0 and two cameos for girdles for 18/- as well as four black ground cameos (probably jasper) for £1.10.0.[24] Prince Charles of Mecklenburg purchased thirty-one cameos in blue jasper with specific named subjects and four of the Roman emperors, as well as eight medallions in 'basalt', some wine labels and a retort in August 1786.[25]

Purchases by a Mr Nuelle for an unnamed Dutch Countess included a pair of small ornamental vases in green jasper with white reliefs of the *Marriage of Cupid & Psyche* and *Sacrifice to Hymen* for £2.2.0, and a cream ewer in jasper for 9/-.[26]

In Paris, Messrs Le Coq were providing for more than just the German princes, such as Anhalt-Dessau. Le Coq were buying the latest jasper productions for the French and other Continental markets, including *Ceres and Cybele* candlesticks for £5.5.0, chased tripod candelabra for £4.4.0, and sophisticated antique tripod lamps in basalt for £1.1.0 each. Listed were '2 *paires Paniers pour les Ognions* in jasper blue & wt. with Arabesque ornaments' for £6.6.0, and among other wares a pair of bulbous root pots for two roots in blue jasper with rich foliage burnished in gold for £3.3.0 as well as a pair of triton candelabra in blue and white jasper for £4.4.0. Two escritoires in jasper, Nos. 308 and 310 (Fig. 77) were purchased for £1.5.0 each, with a third No. 312 for £2.2.0. An entry for fluted flower cups, No. 304, at £1.11.6 for two and a pair of ruinated columns with inscriptions for £2.2.0 and another for pillar candlesticks for £2.12.6 completed the interesting jasper purchases by Le Coq on that day.[27]

Mr Baumgartner, purchasing for 'Grandry of Paris', bought a number of green ground cameos including the *Marriage of Cupid & Psyche* and the *Education of Bacchus,* and *Mutius Scavola* for 10/6 each, a pair of *Offering to Victory* and *Juno* for 10/- and a large oval cameo of *Neptune* for 9/-. He also made purchases of some blue ground cameos of *Conquering Hero and Priestess*.[28]

Herebigius (?) and Hawkesford, Russian Wedgwood agents in St Petersburg,[29] made a large purchase of ornamental wares on 1 September 1786. Among the jaspers were two pairs each of square altar flower pots in blue jasper and in green jasper with bas-reliefs of the 'Seasons' for £5.5.0 each pair. Another pair of chased tripod candelabra were £8.8.0 and four more altar flower pots in blue and white jasper were twelve guineas. One vase, No. 277, was three guineas, and four ink stands, No. 308, were four guineas, along with a quantity of ornamental cane ware and basalt.[30]

The Archduke of Austria was another customer who purchased '8 white Jasper Busts on Terms' for £5.8.0.[31] These were probably like the ones which are in the Franks collection in the British Museum (Colour Plate 21a), which sold to John Bringhurst of Philadelphia in 1793 for the same price.[32] In September 1786 a great deal of jasper, particularly teawares and *déjeuner* sets, was going to 'Bataglia'. A specific buyer, Herend Bataglia, purchased a pair of figures of *Cupid* and *Hebe* on blue and white pedestals for £2.14.0.[33] These may also have well been two of the same figures as those the Archduke purchased as the subjects are the same as two in the Franks collection.

In 1786 a Mr Marsh in Lisbon was purchasing some small quantities of Wedgwood including a blue and white jasper slop bason (sic) for £1.1.0.[34]

Messrs H. Sykes, another of Wedgwood's Paris agents, purchased '12 Jasper Seals' for £3.3.0 in May 1787.[35] In June there were two more purchases[36] including a large group of earthenware garden pots, basalt vases and busts, and Etruscan vases as well as jasper teawares and two dozen jasper egg cups priced at £3.3.0.[37] In the week of 16 July 1787 both Messrs Sykes and Baumgartner made large purchases of jasper, cane and black from Wedgwood. M. Sykes' purchases included '2 Antique Boat Shape candelabra 2 lights' £2.2.0.[38] Another Paris agent M. Daguerre placed an order the following week for a variety of the latest dry-bodied Wedgwood wares.[39] Throughout the autumn of 1787 Messrs Sykes and Daguerre and Baumgartner all continued to buy from Wedgwood.

European nobility were drawn to the Wedgwood name. His Excellency Prince Prozonnico ordered cameos, jasper altar flower pots and other useful and ornamental wares in basalt in May, 1787.[40] Her Royal Highness Princess Lubermacka purchased tablets in green jasper and blue and white jasper lamps, a total of four for £10.6.0 and green jasper teawares.[41] She made another purchase of an 'oval' tablet in jasper for ten guineas shortly thereafter.[42] 'Le Conte François D'Esterhazy' bought a number of jasper tablets and jasper and caneware teawares in June of 1787.[43] In February 1788 the Duke of Württemburg bought cameos, smelling bottles and jasper tea and chocolate wares.[44] Smelling bottles appeared for the first time in existing sales records at the end of 1787.[45]

In January 1788 Messrs Daguerre bought a tablet of the *Apotheosis of Homer* for ten guineas and a set of chessmen for five guineas, along with smelling bottles.[46] In September the firm purchased four oblong octagon medallions 'upright single figures 6⅛ x 4⅛' for £6.6.0.[47] Sykes continued to purchase, buying eleven oblong smelling bottles and eleven square ones for 15/- each in March of 1788, along with six jasper triton candlesticks for £15.15.0 (Colour Plate 26).[48] In April M. Sykes bought a smelling bottle depicting *Henry IV and Sully* for 13/6 and '2 bent oval cameos' for 9/- each, several unidentified jasper vases as well as a No. 266 vase with snake handles (Colour Plate 16) for five guineas.[49] M. J. Le Coq, Esq. bought a lilac *déjeuner* for £3.13.6 as well as a group of medallions in March of 1788.[50] Le Coq purchased a number of jasper wares in September including *déjeuner* sets in both blue and white and in lilac and white, jasper vases Nos. 275 and 279, (Fig. 60, right and centre) both popular forms of the time and a pair of basket work jasper garden pots.[51] Le Coq continued to purchase in 1790, *déjeuner* sets in jasper with arabesque reliefs which were very popular at the time, jasper bell drops in green and white, and beads.[52] In March John Le Coq bought a punch bowl, stand and cover in blue and white jasper for £5.14.0, a jasper lamp for £3.3.0, twelve ice cream cups and covers in jasper for £2.14.0, two plateaux for the ice cream cups at 18/- and bouillon cups

and covers and vases No. 302 (Fig. 69) and No. 273 (Colour Plate 23; Fig. 61). The last items were a pair of ice pails No. 351 for six guineas and a jug, No. 356, for 15/-, the first mention of these two items in surviving records.[53] M. Sykes made a large purchase of jasper, basalt, caneware and ornamental earthenware items in May 1788, including jasper bulbous root pots No. 288 (Fig. 79) for £1.11.6 the pair and No. 268 (Fig. 109) for 18/-, both of which were recently released in the sales lists. Sykes also bought four blue and white jasper coffee cups for £1.10.0 as well as medallions of *Pitt* and *Franklin* for 10/6 each.[54]

Messrs Brunt & Hook were buying cameos and employing them in unusual ways. For example, in September 1788 they purchased '1 doz[en] round [cameo/medallions] with the middle cut out Signs of the Zodiac (for Eye Glasses)' £7.4.0. At the same time they purchased four dozen 'Shield [cameos] bent with festoons, patera & shell' for £7.4.0, and two 'dozen square double [cameos] with holes through and [a] hole in the middle with husks' for £4.16.0.[55] These cameos with holes must have been for sewing onto clothing, perhaps a Continental fashion. In another order Brunt & Hook bought more cameos, twelve octagon shaped with Zodiac signs for £1.10.0, and four dozen lozenge-shaped for £9.12.0.[56]

In this last order there were quantities of caneware with painted borders.

Messrs L. V. Veldhuysen & Son, Wedgwood's Dutch agents after Du Burk, purchased a quantity of jasper in blue and white about the same time: two vase ewers *Neptune & Bacchus* No. 236 (Colour Plate 20) for £10.10.0, a No. 266 snake-handled vase (Colour Plate 16; Fig. 65) for £5.5.0, one vase with swans, No. 294, for £3.3.0, oval bulbous root pots, No. 296, (Fig. 108) for £3.3.0 a pair, and a pair of caudle cups, stands and covers, No. 285, for £2.14.0. This is the first appearance of caudle cups in the existing sales records. They also bought ink stands, No. 308, for one guinea each and a lilac *déjeuner* set for £3.13.6 and some Etruscan painted vases in basalt and other blackwares.[57]

In January 1790 Messrs Daniel Baudisson from Berlin purchased over two hundred cameos including the newly popular, open-centre, zodiac cameos for eye glasses. In addition they bought ten tablets including two of 'Lady T's [Templetown]' and two of 'Lady D's [Diana Beauclerk]', as well as a number of jasper beads which were being sold in quantity at the time.[58]

Messrs Boule Bremer & Co. were another of the continental purveyors of Wedgwood jaspers. In March 1790 they purchased salvers and custard cups, garden pots and stands, and flower pots, No. 288 (Fig. 79), as well as medallions of the *King, Mr. Pitt, Mr. Hastings* and the *Emperor of Russia*.[59]

Another probable French retailer, Madame La Vueve Wendel, made a large purchase of hundreds of cameos including coats of arms; open-centre zodiac medallions, bent, 'scroll & heads border cameos for rings'; lilac and blue, lilac, and green pyramid seals, ear drops, studs and beads and many more. She also ordered two 'new' oval lavender bottles for 18/- each.[60] She made another, somewhat smaller, purchase of similar items later in the same week.[61]

Messrs Dacogne Fils Delonnie & Co. were also buying hundreds of cameos, beads, bell (drops), ear drops and studs at the same time.[62]

Messrs B. Schilling purchased a number of the new jasper ornamental forms which appeared for the first time in June 1790 as well as some shapes which had been in the inventory since 1786. Of those wares which had been in the inventory they bought four 'Season' candlesticks No. 265 (Colour Plate 21; Fig. 78) for £8.8.0, four 'Grecian' figure candlesticks No. 257 for £5.5.0, four *Ceres & Cybele* (candlesticks) No. 272 for £10.10.0, and two 'Temples of Flora' for £3.3.0. The first appearance of triton candlesticks (Colour Plate 26) in the sales was listed in this order, in June 1790, and the twelve were sold for a total of £37.16.0.[63]

Messrs Van Alppen & Co. in Frankfurt bought punch bowls, with and without covers, broth basins and stands, chocolate cups and covers and '4 Cabinet Cups, Covers and Stands No. 285' for £5.8.0.[64]

The latter had previously been sold in 1788 to Messrs Veldhuysen, described as 'caudle cups'.[65] In addition Van Alppen's bought another pair of 'Cabinet Cups, Cover & Stands' No. 286 for £3.3.0, the first listing for this shape as well as for the six 'Pillar' candlesticks No. 307 which were sold for £9.9.0.[66]

H.R.H. the Duchess of Brunswick purchased blue and white jasper vases No. 266 (Colour Plate 16; Fig. 65) and No. 289 with two pedestals No. 295 (Colour Plate 30, left) for £13.13.0 along with other flower pots including four No. 364 for £3.12.0, another shape which had previously not been mentioned in sales. She also bought a complete tea and coffee service for twelve in September 1790. At the same time the Prince of Brunswick bought vase No. 302 (Colour Plate 19) and a pair of No. 279 (Fig. 60, centre).[67]

In 1790 tubes for opera glasses (Fig. 91) were made in dark blue jasper and began to appear frequently on sales lists. In December H. Sykes, Esq. purchased eighteen tubes in blue and white jasper for £13.10.0.[68]

In France forty dozen cameos went to Messrs Daguerre, and the same amount to Henry Sykes, Esq. and to Messrs Ellis & Co. in May 1791, each transaction amounting to £95.14.0.[69] Daguerre purchased eight more sets of cameos with signs of the zodiac (Fig. 92) in late 1791 for £24.0.0.[70] Sykes' only other purchase that year was a small one in December.[71] Tablets and vases were also going to France through another source, M. LeFevre. In July 1791 he purchased twenty-four tablets and some vases in jasper. Among the tablets were three round 8½ inch *Marriage of Cupid & Psyche* for nine guineas and three boat-shaped of the same subject for £3.15.0. In the vases, Nos. 279 (Fig. 60, centre), 276, 264 and 294 were among the purchases.[72] Another French client, a M. Laurent, bought several of the most popular vases including Nos. 266 (Colour Plate 16; Fig. 65), 279 (Fig. 60, centre), 372, 276 and 275 (Fig. 60, right); as well as a pair of *Ceres & Cybele* candlesticks for five guineas.[73] In August 1791 Messrs John Le Coq & Son

were adding to their stock in Paris with highly ornamental vases such as tripod No. 281 (Fig. 89), vase candelabra No. 278, Temples of Flora No. 260 and bulbous root pots Nos. 288 (Fig. 79) and 295 as well as salvers and egg cups (Fig. 66) in jasper.[74]

An order, perhaps from a retail customer, for several ornamental jaspers and other earthenware garden pots was sent to a Mr James Hawksley of Paris in late 1791.[75]

In Poland, Messrs Splitgorba & Co.(?) bought a number of medallions of various Polish families as well as some of the King of Poland.[76]

Dutch agents Messrs L.V. Veldhuysen & Sons continued to make purchases. In 1792 forty-two medallions were sold to them at a cost of £48.15.0.[77]

One of the largest purchases and one of the most unusual in composition was made in 1792 by Messrs Michailo Iwanow (Ivanov) Samoyloff in St Petersburg of a composite set of patterns of jasper, cane, and basalt in duplicate, the total order amounting to £919.12.8.[78]

Messrs Vining made a large purchase of jasper destined for America consisting mainly of flower pots in blue and white: bulbous root pots No. 295 (Colour Plate 30, left) and No. 288 (Fig. 79) as well as flower pots Nos. 358, 376 and 377 (Colour Plate 30, right), the latter two having been introduced in the last few months. In vases Messrs Vining bought Nos. 279 (Fig. 60, centre), 273 (Colour Plate 23; Fig. 61), 365 (a new form which came in three sizes 8, 7 and 6 inch), 276, 280, 367 (another new form which was made in 6½ and 5¾ inch heights) and 294, and ewers No. 262 (Fig. 60, left). In green and white jasper Vining bought vase No. 279 (Fig. 60, centre), No. 273 (Colour Plate 23; Fig. 61), and flower pots No. 358, all popular shapes in blue and white jasper.[79]

M. Le Coq was availing himself of the current rage for green and white jasper by purchasing bulbous root pots No. 288 (Fig. 79) and dice work flower pots and tri-colour jasper among other items in a large order executed in August 1792. At the same time he bought a lilac and white vase No. 275 (Fig. 60, right) and Vases No. 372 with zodiac borders.[80]

Le 'Comt d' Andlow' made some small purchases of two escritoires in jasper for three guineas, an *ecuelle*, cover and stand for £1.10.0 (perhaps basalt) and one coffee can in lilac and green dice work for 6/- in October 1792.[81]

One of the largest orders for ornamental jasper in deep blue and white was placed by the Archbishop of 'St Yago [Santiago]' for a total of fifty-five pieces costing £166.0.0.[82] Heading the list was a vase and pedestal for £31.10.0 which was the price for the Barberini vase. No other vase in the Wedgwood stock cost more than twenty-one pounds prior to the sale of the Barberini so it is likely that this was indeed the Bishop's purchase. He also bought four copies of the most popular single vase, No. 266 (Colour Plate 16; Fig. 65), for five guineas plus a pedestal for another 31/6 or £13.13.0 each pair. He bought four vases No. 277 for £10.10.0 and many pairs or quartets of the most fashionable flower pots (Nos. 358, 376, 345).[83]

In 1793 Messrs Guitton & Brothers purchased four oval

5 inch tablets (unspecified subjects) in 'light color' (sic) for 18/- each and twenty-five oval and round 'dark' tablets.[84]

Records of sales of Wedgwood ornamental wares in America are scarce. Aside from the odd purchase made by Mr Vining, the only other documentation listed in the existing Wedgwood sales for a dealer specifically residing in America is for John Bringhurst of Philadelphia. John Bringhurst (1764-1800) was a fancy goods merchant, located on South Third Street, Philadelphia. In early 1793 Bringhurst placed two orders for Wedgwood ornamental and useful wares, all dry-bodies.[85] A total purchase of £177.4.8 reflected these two orders. Another eight were placed with Wedgwood totalling £285.6.2 but, regrettably, specific details of those do not survive.[86] In Bringhurst's order of 7 January 1793 we see the sophisticated market which Philadelphia provided to the entrepreneur of ornamental ceramics. Bringhurst's order included approximately twenty-five cameos and medallions including mythical subjects such as *Diana* and *Hercules* as well as contemporary figures such as *David Garrick*. Four tablets 5½ by 12 inches of *Hunting, Bringing Home the Game, Music and the Arts* were among those listed in the first order. He ordered six smelling bottles (Colour Plate 22), three with gold tops and three with silver, and a lilac and green 'déjeuner' set as well as bell drops (Colour Plate 13) in blue, black, green and lilac jasper. Among the vases ordered was the famous No. 266 with snake handles (Colour Plate 16; Fig. 65) for five guineas as well as Nos. 279 (Fig. 60, centre) and flower pot No. 382 (Fig. 90). Four small busts on terms (Colour Plate 21a) for 13/6 each were among the most interesting purchases made in 1793. These had been listed occasionally in sales since 1786, more often in pairs than in quartet and sometimes as many as eight.[87]

Back in Paris, Messrs Le Coq & Son were continuing to stock the most fashionable merchandise in the Wedgwood inventory including lilac and green vases No. 272 which were £8.8.0 a pair and others in the same colour combination, and Nos. 289 and 277 for three guineas the

pair each shape. They also bought a blue and white jasper arabesque lamp for three guineas and another deep blue and white jasper vase, No. 276, for two guineas.[88] Le Coq bought a 'Temple flower pot' in jasper blue and white dice work for £3.3.0 and a smaller one in green and white for £1.12.0 as well as other objects in March 1793.[89]

About the same time a Mr John Valentine living in Madrid bought a pair of jasper vases, No. 302 (Colour Plate 19) for £6.6.0 and other vases Nos. 279 (Fig. 60, centre) and 275 (Fig. 60, right) as well as lilac and green root pots and *déjeuner* sets.[90]

Back in France a new retailer appears, Doute & Co. (?), who bought a group of tri-colour cameos very specifically described. For example, entries run 'Lilac Ground blue frame & white Etruscan border 1 oval cameo 305 15/6'; 'Green Ground blue frame & white honeysuckle border 1 oval cameo 307 D B I 12/6' and 'Black Ground, green Maroon & white flower border 1 long octagon 325 K A C 9/6'.[91]

The records of sales, regrettably, ceased after April 1794. However, one of the last sales recorded was a purchase by M. Le Coq for thirty-two opera tubes of blue and white jasper with bas-reliefs and coloured borders for £10.2.0. He also purchased a 'déjeuner' set of deep blue and white with 'cameo jasper'.[92]

The glimpses obtained from the Wedgwood sales to the Continent give us a small indication of who was buying and what was being purveyed in the way of Wedgwood ornamental and tea and coffee wares in the last quarter of the eighteenth century. The researcher, always frustrated by lack of information in records which were not being provided for posterity but being made merely as a sales list, would like to know more, specifically about the location of retailers and the existence of private buyers. Nevertheless, what one does garner from these sales is an indication of a brisk trade in the most fashionable ornamental dry-bodies available, in particular, the jaspers, undeniably the flagship of the Wedgwood reputation.

CHAPTER VIII

Contemporary Manufacturers

ADAMS:
William Adams (and Son), 1779–1805;
Benjamin Adams, 1805–21; Tunstall, Staffordshire;
William Adams & Co., c.1781–c.1788,
Burslem, Staffordshire.

Members of the Adams family had potworks in Tunstall, Burslem and Cobridge at the end of the eighteenth century.[1] This note is limited to the Adams family's pottery businesses at Burslem between c.1781 and c.1788; and at Tunstall between 1779 and 1821, where they are said to have made stoneware and jasper at the Greengates factory.

William Adams of Tunstall was born in 1746, son of Edward and Martha Adams of Bagnall.[2] He was apprenticed to John Brindley, a Burslem potter, and married Mary Cole on 12 September 1771.[3]

Documents appear to confirm that William Adams of Tunstall occupied the Hill House Works at Burslem between 1781 and 1788, to be succeeded in 1788 by Ralph Wedgwood, the works later rebuilt by the Riley brothers.[4] Their building still stands in 1997 as Wades' Royal Victoria Works, Westport Road, Burslem.

William Adams of Tunstall (1746–1805) and William Adams of Cobridge (1748–1831) were both master potters in the late eighteenth century. It is necessary to distinguish between them, and show which one was potting in Burslem in the 1780s.

Josiah Wedgwood wrote in November 1769 that he had notice from his landlord William Adams to leave the Brickhouse Works the next year, as Adams was married and would come to them himself.[5] This was William Adams of Cobridge, who married Mary Bourne 30 April 1769 and received the Brickhouse Works as part of his marriage settlement.[6] Wedgwood did not leave the Brickhouse Works until 1772, and Adams could have spent very little time there, as he leased out the works again in 1774.[7]

William Adams of Cobridge's stepfather was John Hales of Cobridge (1736–1791), potter.[8] Directories of 1781 and 1784[9] list 'Hales and Adams, Cobridge'; and it seems probable that Hales and Adams of Cobridge was William Adams of Cobridge and his step-father John Hales. Hales died in 1791 and the 1796 Directory[10] duly listed 'Adams, William', alone at Cobridge.

The same 1781 and 1784 Directories also list 'Adams, William & Co., Burslem', and the evidence suggests that this was William Adams of Tunstall, with an unknown partner. There are accounts in the Wedgwood papers for tableware supplied by Wm. Adams & Co., Burslem in 1783 and 1787;[11] and in July 1788, Josiah and Thomas Wedgwood were charged for the carriage of four crates from W. Adams, Tunstall and three crates from the same person in Burslem.[12] There is thus evidence of William Adams and Co. in Burslem from 1781 to 1787, and William Adams alone in 1788, but not in a specific factory.

Fig. 111 **Jug**, *fine white stoneware, smear-glazed with brown neck and upper handle and silver lid. The body has sprig relief decoration of Bacchanalian boys. Mark: ADAMS, c.1800, 3⅝ inches high. (Private collection.)*

Fig. 112 **Cameo**, *white jasper with blue jasper dip and relief of a warrior with a spear and shield. Mark: ADAMS & Co, c. 1780s, 1⅝ inches high. (Rakow collection.)*

Fig. 113 **Medallion,** *dark blue jasper and white reliefs of* Venus, Cupid and Aesculapius. *Mark:* ADAMS, *late 18th c., 4⅛ inches diameter (without frame). (Fisk collection.)*

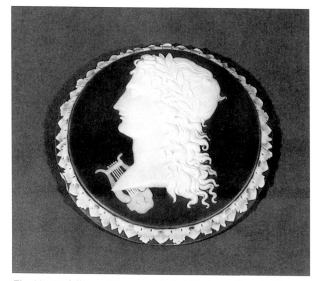

Fig. 114 **Medallion,** *white jasper with dark blue jasper dip and white relief of* Apollo. *Incised mark: "Dip No T.12 Body No 92 I", possibly Adams trial piece, late 18th century, 4¼ inches high. (Grigsby collection.)*

Fig. 115 **Oil lamp,** *white jasper with dark blue jasper dip. Figures of* Flora *and signs of the Zodiac are in white relief. Mark:* ADAMS, *c. 1790- 95, 1⅞ inches high. (Fisk collection.)*

In 1802, Wedgwood's partner, Thomas Byerley was contemplating leasing out the Hill House Works, Burslem, to John Heath. Byerley wrote from Etruria to Josiah Wedgwood II that he had got Mr Adams of Tunstall to look over the Hill House Works *which Adams had formerly rented,* and he said it was worth £120 a year.[13] Here is a clear statement that William Adams of Tunstall had rented the Hill House Works in Burslem at some time before 1802, but not when. To establish that, it is necessary to rehearse the history of the Hill House Works, so far as it can be discovered.

The Hill House Works had been owned by John Taylor.[14] Josiah Wedgwood I's future partner, 'Useful' Thomas Wedgwood, married John Taylor's daughter in 1765.[15] Twenty-three years later, in 1788, 'Useful' Thomas proposed to leave his partnership with Josiah Wedgwood and set up in business at his father-in-law's Hill House Works,[16] but died in October of that year.[17] Instead, his eldest son, Ralph Wedgwood, took over the Hill House Works,[18] and operated it with diminishing success until he

was bankrupt in 1797.[19] The next evidence of the ownership of the Hill House Works is in 1797 and 1798, when Ralph Wedgwood was bankrupt, and the works was offered for sale: 'Valuable Freehold Premises late belonging to Ralph Wedgwood'.[20]

The Etruria Wedgwoods must have bought the Hill House Works in 1798 or soon after, in order for Thomas Byerley to be negotiating the lease of it in 1802. The lease was available because Ralph Wood III died in 1801,[21] and his utensils etc., at his manufactory, The Hill, were to be auctioned in November 1802.[22] Ralph Wood III must have succeeded Ralph Wedgwood in the Hill House Works. The next tenant was John Heath, who was insolvent in 1810.[23] Josiah Wedgwood II was still the owner of the Hill House Works in 1811, when it was sold to John and Richard Riley.[24]

It has been shown that William Adams & Co. were in Burslem between 1781 and 1788 and that William Adams had once occupied the Hill House Works. As the works was occupied by Ralph Wedgwood from 1788 to 1797/98, and then by Ralph Wood III until 1801, William Adams of Tunstall must have rented the Hill House Works before 1788.

William Adams leased a potworks at Tunstall in 1779, later called Greengates.[25] He bought the property in parts from 1784 to 1794,[26] and operated the Greengates potworks from 1779 until his death on 6 January 1805.[27]

William Adams of Tunstall insured his house and contents, potworks and contents, stables, granary and four cottages on 9 July 1789.[28] In 1799, William Adams was a founding partner in the Hendra Company, formed to obtain china clay from Cornwall. His one-eighth share was surrendered in 1807, after his death.[29]

The 1802 map (see Appendix 1) shows only one works in Tunstall (No. 11) as occupied by William Adams,[30] on the south of the road leading from Tunstall to Chell. William

Fig. 116 **Teapot, jug and sugar bowl**, *teapot and sugar solid blue jasper, jug blue jasper dip, all with white reliefs. Marks: Teapot unmarked, att. to Adams, jug and sugar marked ADAMS, all late 18th c., jug 7 inches high. (City Museum, Stoke-on-Trent, 38P1933; 3902;2138.)*

Fig. 117 **Jug**, *solid blue jasper with white reliefs. Unmarked, attributed to Adams, late 18th c., 5½ inches high. (Lady Lever Art Gallery, Museums & Galleries on Merseyside, LL1624, ex Flaxman collection via Tangye.)*

Fig. 118 **Vase**, *white jasper with blue jasper dip and white reliefs. Mark: ADAMS, late 18th c., 13 inches high. (Blake collection.)*

Adams's eldest son, William Adams (born 1777),[31] died unmarried on 10 May 1805, only four months after his father.[32] His mother died five months later.[33] The only surviving son, Benjamin Adams (born 1787)[34] was then aged eighteen. It is assumed that Benjamin Adams had the help of competent managers to run the Greengates works until he was twenty-one, in 1809, although, confusingly, a directory of 1809–11 gives the occupant then as 'Adams J. (*sic*) china & earthenware manufacturer, Tunstall'.[35]

Benjamin Adams continued in business until 1821, but appears to have been insolvent in 1819. In October 1819 his creditors were offered a first dividend of 3s.4d. in the pound,[36] followed by 10s. in the pound on debts under £100 in January 1820,[37] both on application to J. H. Clive, himself a neighbouring master potter at Newfield works.

Benjamin Adams's house, potworks and twelve acres of land were offered to be let or sold in August 1821.[38] His utensils etc., including common and engine lathes, figure and other ornamental moulds, engraved and plain copper plates and under-glaze colours were offered by auction in December 1821,[39] as he was 'declining business'. Two months later, Benjamin Adams's furniture etc. was offered by auction as he was 'going to reside in another part of the kingdom'.[40]

John Meir, a Tunstall potter, bought the works in 1822.[41] Benjamin Adams died in 1828 and was buried at Sandbach, Cheshire, his wife's home.[42] The Adams family again acquired the Greengates Works in 1896.[43]

William Adams also occupied the Newfield Works, Tunstall after 1802 and until his death in 1805. This works (No. 10 on the 1802 map, Appendix 1, Caleb Cole and Co.)[44] and Newfield mansion were offered to be let in June 1802 by Admiral Smith Child, then occupied by Caleb Cole.[45]

Fig. 119 *Candelabrum*, *gilded bronze and glass on blue and white jasper base. Mark: ADAMS, late 18th c., 29 inches high. (The Chrysler Museum, Norfolk, Virginia, gift of Walter P. Chrysler, Jr., 71.1298A.)*

Fig. 120 *Vase, solid medium blue jasper with white jasper swags and a pendant medallion of Apollo. Mark: ADAMS, late 18th c., 11 inches high. (Nottingham Museum, 1892-320.)*

Fig. 121 *Crocus pot (three or four tiers), solid blue jasper with white reliefs this portion of a four-tiered bulb pot is similar to shape No. 291 in the Wedgwood shape book, a shape purchased by a number of royal patrons of Wedgwood from 1786 to 1792. No mark, probably Adams, c. 1790, 13¼ inches high (this portion). (Nottingham Museum, 1892-313.)*

Cole's earthenware utensils, including common and engine lathes, copper plates and black clay were for auction at the end of October 1802,[46] presumably prior to vacating the works at Martinmas, 11 November. Caleb Cole was the brother of William Adams's wife, Mary. Soon after William Adams's death in January 1805, the Newfield potworks (stated to be lately occupied by William Adams deceased and making eighty crates a week) and house were offered to be let by Admiral Smith Child.[47]

Adams-marked wares exist in considerable numbers in both white stoneware and in jasper, but only very rarely in caneware. Hunt jugs and mugs are the most common forms produced in white stoneware, often fitted with silver rims or lids (Figs. 123–125); but there are also wine coolers illustrated in the William Turner book on the Adams family of potters. In jugs the pouring spout is often rounded as if pulled in *ADAMS* marked white pieces and not the so-called sparrow-beak spout common to other factories. The sprig relief on the white stoneware pieces is often very high. However, the spout on the jasper wares is almost never rounded as it is on the white stoneware examples.

In jasper the shapes are far more interesting, including ornamental vases (Colour Plates 38, 39; Figs. 118, 120, 122), and teawares, as well as cameos and medallions (Colour Plate 35; Figs.112–114). Unusual forms include oil

Fig. 122 **Tripod vase** (with possible cover replacement), white jasper with black jasper dip, this tripod is similar to shape No. 281 (illustrating another cover) in the Wedgwood shape book popularly purchased in the early 1790s. No Mark, probably Adams, c. 1790-95, 9 inches high. (Nottingham Museum, 1892-331.)

County Durham, nearly identical to those made by Wedgwood. However, in jasper the shapes and applied reliefs were not usually recapitulated Wedgwood ones, but often distinctive. Indeed, the bases of both jasper vases and basalt ones, which are exceedingly rare in Adams manufacture, frequently have a characteristic white stylized relief palmette running around the outside. However, there are at least two vases (Colour Plate 40; Fig. 122), both unmarked so not definitely Adams, which are nearly direct copies of shapes from the Wedgwood shape book. If not Adams some other manufacturer capable of equal calibre vase production was using the shapes book to make high-quality Wedgwood copies.

The range of jasper colours runs the gamut from light to dark blue with hues which are specific to Adams and, again, not Wedgwood colours. Adams also produced jasper in black jasper dip, some of which is marked, and others which are not (Fig. 122). The tripod vase in the Nottingham Museum, tentatively attributed to Adams, has some characteristic decoration seen in other Adams-marked wares. Other tripod vases are illustrated in William Turner's pottery biography of the Adams family in Plate No. XVIII.

The quality of Adams jasper is characteristically excellent, finely levigated clays which produced smooth surfaces in both jasper and in the other stonewares. Occasionally a piece seems variable or more clumsily executed but these are often wares which are attributed and not marked, such as the tripod vase in Figure 122.

Adams caneware is exceedingly rare, but pie dishes are known to have been made in caneware (Fig. 126), as well as a mustard pot with a 'dark chocolate glazed neck', listed as No. 45 'caneware' in the Turner book. Impressed marks on jasper of *ADAMS & CO.* early, and marks of *W. ADAMS & CO.* are known. A cameo in the former Rakow collection bears the mark of *ADAMS & CO* (Fig. 112).

lamps (Fig. 115), resembling those made by Wedgwood based on Attic pottery prototypes, and candlesticks. Like Wedgwood, Adams made jasper bases for girandoles (Fig. 119) and figures (Colour Plate 34). There is a bulbous pot for four roots, marked *ADAMS* in the Bowes Museum,

Fig. 123 **Three small jugs**, white smear-glazed stonewares with Sheffield plate covers. Marks (l-r): ADAMS, SPODE, DAVENPORT, all early 19th c., all around 4 inches high. (Fisk collection.)

Fig. 124 *Jug*, white smear-glazed stoneware with brown enamel neck, foot and top of handle and Sheffield plate cover. Mark: ADAMS, early 19th c., 7¼ inches high. (Collection of Olive Talbot.)

Fig. 125 *Jug*, white smear-glazed stoneware with brown enamel neck, foot and upper handle and sprig relief of Silenus and boys, Sheffield plate rim. Mark: ADAMS, early 19th c. (Burgin collection.)

Although it has been shown that William Adams of Tunstall was involved in factories at both Burslem and Tunstall in the 1780s, the directories of that period do not mention Adams at Tunstall. This may be due to oversight (only one potter, Anthony Keeling, is listed at Tunstall) or because the directory compiler chose to give only the major, 'office' address for Adams. Thus, the partnership of William Adams and Co. may have operated both Burslem and Tunstall factories in the 1780s, and produced ware marked '& CO.' at either or both.

There is very little documentary evidence of the production of jasper and dry bodies by Adams at Tunstall. In 1790, at a time when Josiah Wedgwood I complained to his son, Josiah Wedgwood II, that 'in the cameo and bas relief line' they had 'scarcely orders for one days work',[48] his agent in Birmingham, Mr Burley, was urged to get some orders 'on account of the new rivals that are starting up'.[49] A year later, Burley wrote to Etruria that 'Our demands for Cameos are lessen'd much owing to being undersold by Adams at least 20 P. Ct.'.[50]

In 1865, a Mrs Boott of Derby wrote her recollections of visiting the Adams family at Tunstall between 1802 and 1808 for Eliza Meteyard.[51] She included, 'in each room ... "Jasper Ware" abounded ... stored with vases, tea services, placques (*sic*) & every possible description of this beautiful fabric [jasper]' and later mentioned the 'smelling bottles

Fig. 126 *Pie dish*, caneware. The Adams produced little caneware. Mark: ADAMS, early 19th c., 3 inches high. (Polikoff collection.)

Fig. 127 *Jug*, white smear-glazed stoneware with brown enamel and sprigged relief. Mark: B. ADAMS (*Benjamin Adams*), c. 1805-21, 4 inches high. (Rakow collection.)

Fig. 128 **Spill vase and pot-pourri basket**, *caneware with sprig reliefs; engine-turned basket. Mark on vase:* EASTWOOD; *basket unmarked, c. 1802-22; vase 4½ inches high, basket 4¼ inches high. (Burgin collection.)*

and other pretty mementoes' given to her. She said that William Adams had the privilege of manufacturing this ware which would expire when he died.

The recorded impressed mark of 'B. ADAMS' (Fig. 127) on stoneware jugs[52] and the mention of 'figure and other

Fig. 129 **Vase**, *caneware with sprig reliefs. Unmarked, attributed to William Baddeley of Eastwood, c. 1802-22. (Royal Ontario Museum, 944.17.14.)*

ornamental moulds' to be auctioned in December 1821[53] help to confirm that stoneware was made at Greengates after 1805 and before 1822. William Turner wrote that Adams bought sprig moulds at the close of the Turner potteries at Lane End in 1802 (although no sale is known then), as a justification for the same figures appearing on both Turner and Adams stoneware.[54] Bevis Hillier stated that both Spode and Adams bought quantities of the Turner moulds at the Turner sale of 1829.[55] (Adams of Tunstall was out of business by then, of course.) There is no real evidence for either assertion. One sprig mould, impressed B ADAMS, has been found at the Spode works.[56]

Joseph Mongenot, a Swiss artist, engraver and modeller, died at Tunstall in 1814.[57] He came to England in 1788 and worked in various towns, spending his last two years in the Potteries. He is said to have designed bas-reliefs of the *Sacrifices to Apollo, Diana and Pomona*, emblems of the *Arts and Sciences, Females and Cupid Conversing, Nymphs Dancing, Aphrodite in her car drawn by swans on clouds*, etc., for Adams.

ASTBURY

'Astbury' is included in this study of dry-bodied ware because two unglazed engine-turned red stoneware pieces marked ASTBURY are in the Fitzwilliam Museum, Cambridge.[1] A teapot and a covered jug are so marked, and are said to be *en suite* with an un-marked covered sugar-box and a cream jug with a Chinese seal mark.

The engine-turned decoration dates their production to the 1760s at the earliest, so that the Astbury reputed to have stolen secrets from the Elers and from Dwight, the Astbury who made redware figures and white-sprigged redware, the

Fig. 130 **Pot-pourri basket**, caneware with black sprig reliefs and swan finial, a 'D'-shaped central basket of a garniture of three. Mark: EASTWOOD, William Baddeley, c. 1802-22. (Rakow collection.)

near Congleton in Cheshire. Astbury is a very common surname in Staffordshire.

Joshua Astbury, 1764–80;
Ann Astbury, 1781– ;
John Astbury and Richard Meir Astbury, c.1790–95;
Richard Meir Astbury, 1795–97;
Lane Delph, Staffordshire.

Richard Meir of Lane Delph died 24 October 1762, and left his potworks to his unmarried daughter, Sarah Meir.[2] Surviving invoices in the Wedgwood papers neatly document the change of ownership: from Sarah Meir signing a bill for her father on 4 June 1762, to Sarah Meir herself billing Wedgwood between 5 February 1763 and 1 December 1763.[3] Sarah Meir married Thomas Smith of London, a widower, at Stoke on 11 December 1763;[4] and again the Wedgwood accounts indicate a change of ownership, this time to Joshua Astbury, who issued bills to Wedgwood between 24 February and 11 October 1764.[5] Bills from all three suppliers, Richard Meir, Sarah Meir and Joshua Astbury, are for tortoiseshell ware and 'red china' (red stoneware).

Joshua Astbury had already married Anne, another daughter of Richard Meir, when her father made his will on 12 October 1761; and he signed a bill to Wedgwood on behalf of his sister-in-law, Sarah Meir, on 9 June 1763,

Astbury who discovered the use of Bideford clay and flint, the Astbury who painted at Chelsea and the Astbury whose methods were pirated by Ralph Shaw are not candidates for making these pieces. Two possible makers are described below. Though probably derived from Astbury Newbold

Fig. 131 **Urn** (minus cover), rosso antico. Mark: EASTWOOD, William Baddeley, c. 1805-10, 4 inches high. (Royal Ontario Museum, gift of Mrs G. Edgerton Brown, 1984.18.31.)

Fig. 132 *Spill vase*, drab-coloured stoneware with black sprigging. Mark: EASTWOOD, *William Baddeley, c. 1802–22, 4½ inches high. (Fisk collection.)*
Fig. 133 *Mark on Figure 132.*

Fig. 134 *Two vases*, *(left) drab brown stoneware with black sprig figures; (right) red stoneware with black figures. Marks: both EASTWOOD, William Baddeley, c. 1802–22, 5¼ and 4⅝ inches high. (Rakow collection.)*

obviously working for her then.[6] Earlier writers have identified this Joshua Astbury with Joshua Astbury, the son of John Astbury of Shelton, baptised at Stoke 18 November 1727.[7] Their evidence is an inscription on a tombstone at Stoke churchyard, recording the death on 25 April 1780 of Joshua Astbury, late of the Folley (*sic*), aged 52, son of John Astbury the elder, of Shelton, potter. There is a discrepancy of location between Lane Delph and 'Folley' (Foley), which are distinct areas, about half-a-mile apart. That might be explained by the tombstone having been carved at a later date from the imprecise recollections of a descendant.

After 1764, there is no further evidence extant of Joshua Astbury as a pottery manufacturer, but Anne Astbury, presumably his widow, insured a house, pothouse, brewhouse and stables at Lane Delph on 27 March 1781.[8] The evidence for Joshua Astbury of Lane Delph being the

maker of engine-turned redware is only circumstantial: he was the descendant of a redware maker at Shelton; his father-in-law, sister-in-law and he were all redware makers at Lane Delph in 1762–64; and he probably continued as a master potter until his death in 1780. Engine-turning began to be used in the Potteries in the 1760s, and so Joshua Astbury and his widow, Ann Astbury, *could* have made engine-turned redware between the 1760s and the 1780s, and marked it ASTBURY.

The name of Astbury did not occur in local directories of 1781, 1783 or 1784, but they are less than comprehensive. Joshua and his wife Ann had a son, Richard Astbury, baptised at Stoke on 27 April 1764,[9] who would be aged about sixteen when his father died. Richard Meir Astbury ('Meir' is not given in the baptismal record, but obviously refers to his mother's maiden name) was a master potter by 1790. John Astbury and Richard Meir Astbury of Lane Delf (*sic*), potters and co-partners in trade, became partners with fifteen other potters in Fenton Park coalmines, in August 1790.[10] In November of the same year, Richard Meir Astbury, Valentine Close and Robert Barber Wolf, Staffordshire Earthenwaremen, insured their utensils and stock at 151 Drury Lane, London, and in a warehouse in Lincolns Inn Fields.[11] The insurance policy also covered Astbury's household goods and wearing apparel at 151 Drury Lane, suggesting that he was resident there at that time. In April 1791, Richard and John Astbury were amongst seventeen master potters who signed a notice about their workers' dinner-hour.[12]

John Astbury of Lane Delph, potter, died 18 March 1795,[13] and Richard Astbury of Lane Delph, manufacturer, appeared alone in directories of *c*.1795 and *c*.1796.[14] A series of newspaper notices in 1797 and 1798 show that

Richard Meir Astbury of Lane Delph, potter, was bankrupt then.[15] He went on to a second, much more successful career, in cotton, at Manchester, and died in 1834.[16]

White earthenware 'Fair Hebe' jugs survive, signed by John Voyez the modeller in 1788, with RMA in the moulding and ASTBURY impressed below,[17] suggesting that Richard Meir Astbury had bought the model from Voyez in or after 1788. The mark ASTBURY, albeit impressed in moulded white earthenware, make John and Richard Astbury also candidates for making the engine-turned redware so marked, though their known active period of 1790 to 1795/1797 make them less likely. An engine-turned black basalt teapot marked ASTBURY has been attributed to Richard Meir Astbury, by reason of its c.1790 shape.[18]

The actual site of Joshua, Ann, John and Richard Astbury's potworks at Lane Delph is not known.

Thomas Astbury, c.1788; Lane Delph, Staffordshire.

Thomas Astbury of Lane Delph is known as a master potter only by dying in debt, by 1788.[19] A dividend was paid to his creditors in 1795, and possibly it was his affairs that were still being settled in 1802.[20] It may be he who was hired by Thomas Whieldon in 1751 for six shillings a week.[21] A black basalt teapot and cover, naturalistically moulded as a tree stump, marked ASTBURY, has been attributed to Thomas Astbury because of its 1770s shape,[22] but could also have been made by the Astbury family described above. Equally, the engine-turned redware pieces could have been made by this potter. The site of his works is not known.

BADDELEY:
William Baddeley, 1802–22, Eastwood, Hanley, Staffordshire.

William Baddeley owned and operated a potworks at Eastwood, on the north-west side of the Caldon Canal, Hanley, No. 85 on the 1802 map (see Appendix 1),[1] from c.1802 to 1822.[2] 1805 and 1809 Directories noted him as producing 'Egyptian Black'[3] and an 1822 Directory listed him for 'Fancy and Ornamental' ware.[4] His works were offered for auction in 1822, a small potworks and house at Eastwood, and land connecting to the canal, used as a wharf, now occupied by William Baddeley and used for some years by him as a Black and Caul (Cane?) manufactory, applications to William Baddeley or Ward, solicitor, Newcastle-under-Lyme, copyhold of Newcastle Manor.[5] The rate record extracts show that William Baddeley's property was afterwards occupied by Herbert Baddeley in 1824, Hanson Moreton 1824–25, and Thomas Moreton from 1825 to 1828.[6]

Jewitt wrote in 1878 that a William Baddeley made brown ware at Eastwood in 1720 and invented an engine lathe in 1740. One son, John, continued to make lathes whilst the other, William, improved the ware and imitated Wedgwood. He died at Eastwood and the works were sold.[7] The dates at least are wrong, but a descendant was alive when Jewitt was researching and may have told him this garbled story. Shaw wrote fifty years earlier that the noted lathe maker, John Baddeley of Eastwood, made engine lathes about 1765.[8] He certainly sold a (simple) lathe to Josiah Wedgwood in 1763.[9] When a John Baddeley died in Shelton in 1841, his obituary stated that his father invented the engine lathe and he himself had made them.[10] An 1800 Directory listed John Baddeley as a lathe maker at Fields, Hanley.[11]

There appears to be no connection with the family of John Baddeley of Shelton, pottery and porcelain makers, who were 'gentrified' by 1800.[12] Baddeley's Eastwood works was not the factory occupied by William Hackwood, q.v.

Although there was a not inconsiderable manufacture of black basalt wares emanating from the Eastwood factory, little else seems to have been produced apart from some few caneware examples which are of a peculiarly dense fine dry caneware, both in light and in a darker cane colour (Figs. 128–130). Shapes include D-shaped garnitures of bough pots for chimney pieces (Fig. 130) as well as the more common spill vases (Figs. 128,129). Red stoneware of the rosso antico type was also made at Eastwood (Fig. 131) and appears to be of high quality, but it is very infrequently found. Another unusual drab-coloured stoneware vase (Figs. 132, 133) increases the range of stoneware produced by the factory. A fine white jasper vase with blue jasper handles is in the Schreiber collection in the Victoria and Albert Museum (Sch.570–A). Regrettably, the cost of reproduction of the photograph prohibited its publication here.

BARKER
Thomas Barker, c.1781–1786;
Elizabeth and Samuel Barker, 1786–1796;
Samuel Barker, 1796–1804;
Lane Delph, Staffordshire.

The name of Barker occurs several times as a manufacturer of pottery: at Lane Delph and Lane End in Staffordshire and at Rawmarsh and Mexborough in South Yorkshire. As early as 1762, Jos. Barker was a partner in Robert Garner & Co. at Fenton, Staffs., when that firm supplied Josiah Wedgwood with 'brown china', i.e., red stoneware: tea pots, tortoiseshell teapots, black teapots, Landskips (sic), [printed or painted with landscapes] teapots and pineapple jars'.[1]

There is a lack of documentation on the Lane Delph Barkers until 1781, when Thomas Barker was listed as a master potter at Lane Delf (sic).[2] A 1784 Directory omits Thomas Barker,[3] and in fact he died in 1786, leaving his potworks etc. to his wife, Elizabeth, for her life, with their son Samuel as her partner.[4] Elizabeth Barker died in 1796, and willed her half of the potworks business equally to her descendants, except her sons Charles and Thomas.[5] Samuel thus had over half the business, and continued to run it until he was bankrupt in 1804.[6] His potworks (the Upper Bank) and other property was offered for auction in 1799,[7] but the potworks at least remained unsold, and was offered again in 1804.[8] A map of 1802 (Appendix 1) shows two adjoining potworks occupied by Samuel Baker (sic),[9] and Samuel Barker's two potworks were offered for auction on 6 April 1804.[10] The contents of the potworks were also offered for sale,[11] but gave no indication that stoneware was produced.

John Barker, 1784; **William Barker**, 1784;
Richard Barker I, 1784–1809;
Richard II, John and James Barker, 1809–1818;
Richard Barker II, 1820–1822 and 1832–1835;
Thomas Barker, 1834–1841;
John and Joseph Barker, 1818–1831;
Longton, Staffordshire.

John Barker was listed as a master potter at Longton in 1784, making cream colour, china glaze and blue wares.[12] William Barker was also listed as a master potter at Longton in 1784, without any description of his products.[13]

Richard Barker I was a master potter at Longton from 1784 until 1809,[14] at what became known as the Crown Works, Flint Street. He died in 1810 and his will shows that his sons, Richard II, John and James, had already taken over the potworks, the ownership being left to them on the death of his wife Mary.[15] James Barker was an earthenware dealer in Oxford, and all three brothers were bankrupt in 1818.[16] Richard Barker was again in business in Flint Street from 1820 to 1822, and also 1832–35.[17] There is no indication of what these successive businesses produced, other than 'earthenware'.

There were also later Barkers, who were master potters in Longton. Richard Barker I bequeathed another small potworks, probably adjoining the Crown Works, to a fourth son, Thomas Barker, in 1810, but he did not appear as a master potter until 1834–41, making china, enamel, lustre and gilt ware.[18]

John and Joseph Barker were in business from 1818 at High Street, Longton.[19] A partnership between James, John and Joseph Barker and John Myatt was dissolved on 25 March 1821,[20] leaving John and Joseph Barker to continue making china and earthenware until 1831.[21] Their relationship with the other Barkers is not known.

Barker and Co., 1790s–c.1810;
Rawmarsh, South Yorkshire.

John Wainwright and Peter Barker rented Low Pottery, Rawmarsh, in the 1790s, and remained in partnership as Barker and Co., earthenware manufacturers, until Wainwright bought the works in 1810 and Peter Barker joined his brother at Mexborough c.1812.[22]

Jesse and Peter Barker, 1809–1820s;
Samuel Barker, 1820s–1840s;
Mexborough, South Yorkshire.

Jesse Barker rented Mexborough Pottery in 1809 (previously Sowter & Co., q.v.), and bought it in 1811,

Fig. 135 *Teapot, white felspathic stoneware with enamel painted landscape panel. A similar teapot with the same mark is illustrated in Miller and Berthoud,* An Anthology of British Teapots, *Plate 858. Mark:* BARKER, *c. 1810, probably Yorkshire, 6⁵⁄₁₆ inches high. (1996 Sotheby's Inc.)*

jointly with his brother Peter, who moved from Low Pottery, Rawmarsh in 1812. They ran the works until the late 1820s, handing over to Jesse's son, Samuel Barker, who owned the works by 1838. He continued in business at Mexborough until the 1840s, also owning the Don Pottery (q.v.) from 1839. Shards found on the site are of earthenware rather than stoneware.[23]

The basalt and white felspathic stoneware pieces impressed *BARKER* present a problem of attribution. Some of the Barker businesses detailed above could be discounted as makers on grounds of date or product. There is evidence of felspathic stoneware production as some teapots exist marked *BARKER* (Fig. 135). The existence of another teapot in the Yorkshire Museum as well as the general conformation of gallery, hinged lid and finial argue for a Yorkshire rather than Staffordshire manufacture. In general, however, both Yorkshire and Staffordshire researchers have been equally careful not to claim these *BARKER*-marked pieces as products of one county or the other.[24]

It has been suggested that Sowters, Barkers' predecessors at Mexborough, made the felspathic stoneware marked 'S. & Co.', and, if so, it would be reasonable to suppose that Barkers continued production under their own name from 1811. However, we suggest elsewhere that 'S. & Co.' marked ware could have been made by Sheridan of Longton, Staffs., q.v.

Although there is no documentation for Thomas Barker as a potter at Lane Delph before 1781, David Barker has argued persuasively that a group of seal-marked red stoneware pieces were made by him between 1765 and 1775.[25] If David Barker is correct, the Lane Delph Barkers had a tradition of making fine red stoneware, which they might have continued into basalt and felspathic stoneware up to 1804.

Alternatively, Richard Barker and his sons at Longton from 1784 to 1818 were operating in close proximity to

Chethams, Turners and Cyples, firms known to have made fine stonewares, and it *might* be extrapolated that these Barkers made similar wares.

The very rare *BARKER*-marked felspathic stonewares (Fig. 135) bear no specific resemblance to those marked *S. & Co.* wares (see Figs. 253, 256), discussed above. That does not exclude the possibility of the odd *BARKER*-marked stoneware having been made by the same manufacturer who produced the *S. & Co.* teawares, but it does suggest that there are no answers. The one marked teapot illustrated (Fig. 135) has a competently painted landscape in the central panel and a hinged lid with a swan finial, all common attributes of Yorkshire white stoneware teawares, although not a positive identification to the county. Another almost identical marked teapot without the landscape painted panel is in the Yorkshire Museum.

All this suggests that until further wares are discovered it is not possible to make an identification to manufacturer, or manufacturers.

BIRCH:
Birch & Whitehead, 1796–98;
E.J. Birch, 1798–99;
E.J. Birch & Co., 1800–10; Shelton, Staffordshire.

Edmund John Birch, (*c*.1776–1829)[1] and Christopher Whitehead (*c*.1774–1818)[2] were partners manufacturing pottery in Shelton from *c*.1796[3] until they dissolved partnership at the end of 1798.[4] E.J. Birch continued in business, and the firm was described as 'E.J. Birch & Co.' from 1800.[5] His partner(s) are not known. Birch attempted to let his works in 1806[6] because he was retiring, but, according to the rate book extracts, seems to have continued in business until late 1810.[7] In 1811, Birch again offered his works to be let,[8] and went to live at Fradswell Hall, near Stafford.[9] He had previously lived at Bank House, Etruria, the house built by Josiah Wedgwood I for his partner, Thomas Bentley. Birch sub-let Bank House to R. Stevenson in 1811.[10]

The land tax records suggest that Birch's works was owned and occupied by Joshua Heath until 1796, leased by Heath to Birch until 1800, then bought by Birch.[11] The factory was No. 66 on the 1802 map (Appendix 1), a pottery later occupied by Dimmocks and now the site of a departmental store, C & A Modes, Stafford Street, and a bingo hall in Albion Square, both in Hanley. When Birch's works was finally offered for sale in 1814, it was proposed to be split it into two works, each with 'two hovels' (detached ovens).[12]

E.J. Birch married Mary, youngest daughter of Josiah Spode II, in 1821,[13] and died in 1829.[14] He had probably been married previously, as he had a son, also named Edmund John, born *c*.1802.[15] In early 1810 Birch wrote to Josiah Wedgwood II of 'the very grievous loss I have so lately experienced in my family', suggesting that his first wife had recently died.[16] E J. Birch may have been a partner in Birch and Moore, bankers, Stone and Stoke-upon-Trent, and Birch, Yates and Moore, bankers, Stafford, in 1818;[17] and Birch, Yates and Co., bankers, Stafford in 1828.[18] His son, also Edmund John Birch, was described as manager of the Stafford branch of the Manchester and Liverpool District Bank at his death in 1835.[19]

Although Birch and Whitehead and E.J. Birch made basalts there are few recorded wares in other bodies. There is a caneware milk jug in the Schreiber collection at the Victoria and Albert Museum (Sch.II.569). To the regret of the authors the cost of reproduction for this object in this publication was prohibitive. An identical unmarked example is illustrated on page 10.

BRADLEY:
Bradley and Co., *c*.1796–*c*.1799, Coalport, Shropshire.

Bradley and Co. were in business making earthenware and stoneware at Coalport from *c*.1796 to *c*.1799.[1] The Bradley was Walter Bradley, who joined the Quaker Coalbrookdale Monthly Meeting in December 1787. He was a clerk in William Reynolds's ironworks then. William Reynolds leased land adjoining the River Severn in 1793, which probably included the Coalport Pottery site, and he may have been the '& Co.' of the partnership, investing in his erstwhile clerk's pottery venture. Sales recorded in the Horsehay Company's daybook in 1796 confirm that Walter Bradley was a potter by then: 'ground clay' was sold successively to Walter Bradley, Walter Bradley & Co., Coalport Delftwork and Coalport Pottery.

A traveller visited 'Mr Reynolds' Pottery lately established here [Coalport]' in November 1796, supporting the suggestion that Reynolds had financed the works. Bradley and Co. opened a wholesale earthenware warehouse in nearby Shrewsbury in April 1797; and the last documentary references to Bradley as a potter are in the Horsehay Company's day book: straw was lent (sent?) to 'Walter Bradley from the Pottery' and 'Walter Bradley & Co.' in August and September 1797.

Walter Bradley had gone to London by January 1799, when the Shrewsbury Quakers certified his removal thereto.[2] A partnership of William Reynolds, William Horton and Thomas Rose was formed in June 1800, and it is assumed that they took over the pottery works to make porcelain. Bradley returned to Shropshire in 1804 and died there at the end of 1809.[3]

The works site was on a narrow strip of land between the River Severn and the canal, opposite the Coalport porcelain works.

L. Jewitt published an engraving in 1862, showing both factories in a 'view of the Coalport China Works ... copied from an interesting painting by Muss [1779–1824], who, before his successful artistic career in London, was employed as one of the painters at this establishment'.[4] In view of some discussion about the source of this engraving, it is worth noting that Jewitt, who was himself a trained engraver, visited Coalport in January 1862, and noted in his diary for 27 January that he had 'Sent the drawing of the Old Coalport Works to S.C. Hall [editor of the *Art Journal*] to have engraved'.[5] Jewitt stayed at W.F. Rose's house, and when W.F. Rose's effects were offered for sale in 1863, the

Fig. 136 *Jug, buff-coloured unglazed stoneware with brown enamel neck and scenes of the hunt. Mark: BULKELEY & BENT, c. 1790-97, 5¼ inches high. (Borough Museum and Art Gallery, Newcastle-under-Lyme, on loan from Martin Pulver.)*

Fig. 137 *Mark on Figure 136.*

notice included 'high-class OIL PAINTINGS and ENGRAVINGS, in rich gilt frames';[6] possibly including Muss's original painting of the Coalport China Works. The conclusion must be that Jewitt saw a pre–1824 painting by Muss whilst at Coalport and made a drawing of it for Hall's engraver.

Until now there is no evidence that Bradley and Company made any stonewares except for a few basalts so marked. However, there are ongoing excavations which have uncovered earthenware shards[7] and may include some stonewares. These are being undertaken by the Ironbridge Gorge Trust with the help of a grant from English Heritage, with a condition that no-one is allowed to publish details before the official report.[8]

BULKELEY:
Bulkeley and Bent, 1790–1797;
Newcastle-under-Lyme, Staffordshire.

William Bent of Newcastle-under-Lyme, surgeon, and James Bulkeley, said to be of Huntley Hall, Cheadle, Staffs., a professional soldier,[1] had a pottery at Newcastle-under-Lyme by December 1790.[2] William Bent, Barrow and Co. also had a brewery there by January 1794, when they insured it for £600.[3]

Bulkeley and Bent took an apprentice, John Rowley c.1791,[4] and another, Samuel Scarlett, in 1794, who was to learn on-glaze and blue painting.[5] A c.1795 Directory lists 'William Bent & Co., potters & brewers',[6] and one of 1796 lists 'Buckley (*sic*) & Bent, manufacturers, Newcastle'.[7] James Bulkeley and William Bent, manufacturers and co-partners,

signed a bond in the Potters Clay Company on 4 May 1797, together with Josiah Wedgwood II and other potters.[8]

Bulkeley and Bent ended their partnership on 11 November of that year,[9] and William Bent continued as a brewer.[10] The works was on the site of the Borough Arms Hotel, King Street, Newcastle.

William Bent had been a surgeon, brother to the James Bent who undertook the amputation of Josiah Wedgwood's leg in 1768, attended Mrs Wedgwood in her confinements and was in attendance when Josiah died in 1795. Both William and James Bent were doctors for the Etruria Works sick club.[11] Thomas Bentley told Josiah Wedgwood II that William Bent had tried to tempt William Greatbatch (q.v.) away from Wedgwoods, with the offer of higher wages.[12]

A sprigged buff stoneware jug (Figs. 136, 137), impressed *BULKELEY AND BENT*, very much in the Turner style, is in Newcastle-under-Lyme Museum,[13] and a black basalt shard, the base of a sucrier or small teapot, impressed 'Bulkeley & Bent', was excavated at Broseley, Shropshire c.1988.[14] No other marked pieces are yet known.

CASTLEFORD POTTERY see DUNDERDALE

CHATTERLEY:
Charles Chatterley, fl.1765–70;
Charles and Ephraim Chatterley, fl.1783–86;
Chatterley and Whiteheads, 1787–93;
Hanley, Staffordshire.

The Chatterley family achieved mention in 1829 by the

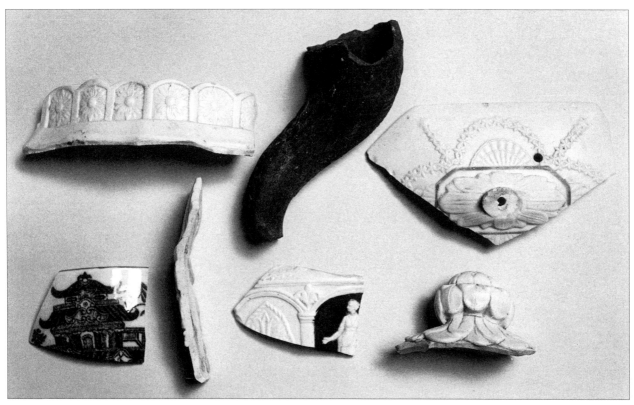

Fig. 138 *Shards from the Chetham & Woolley site c. 1800-20. Shards match teapots in the Blake collection (figs. 139, 140) as well as a* Mist London *marked teapot in the Liverpool Museum (fig. 221). (City Museum and Art Gallery, Stoke-on-Trent.)*

Potteries historian, Simeon Shaw,[1] who wrote that Charles Chatterley (1732–86) had two engine lathes made by John Baddeley of Eastwood around 1765; and went on to affirm that Charles Chatterley, like Humphrey Palmer, q.v., made cream colour and dry bodied pottery about 1770. If true, it betokens that Charles Chatterley was a sophisticated potter by then. Samuel Chatterley signed a salt-glaze potters' price agreement in 1770.[2]

Charles and his brother Ephraim Chatterley (1745–1811) were listed as potters at Hanley in directories of 1783 and 1784,[3] when they had already built themselves a mansion at Shelton, 'eminent and opulent manufacturers'.[4] Charles Chatterley died in 1786,[5] and Ephraim took into partnership his nephews James, Charles and John Whitehead. Chatterley and Whitehead supplied 'milk pots' to Wedgwood in 1787[6] and insured their potworks and contents in Hanley for a total of £1,000 in December 1792.[7] Ephraim Chatterley left the partnership in 1793.[8] See Whitehead for continuation of the business.

Ephraim and Charles Chatterley were said to be exporters to Europe, with Elijah Mayer (q.v.) as their agent.[9] Ephraim Chatterley was in a partnership to buy Dorset clay in 1791,[10] and in another partnership with John Yeates (*sic*) (probably Yates) and Charles Chatterley, as china, glass and earthenware dealers at 31 St Paul's Churchyard, London in 1791, when they insured a modest £50 worth of utensils and stock.[11] Charles Chatterley had died in 1786, and presumably this partnership existed prior

to 1786 and had been continued in his name by his executors.

In the absence of firm evidence, it is assumed that the works occupied by Charles and Ephraim Chatterley is that occupied later by James and Charles Whitehead, No. 82 on the 1802 map (Appendix 1). Ephraim Chatterley died 7 May 1811, aged 66,[12] leaving his half of the potworks in trust for his widow and then to the daughters of his brother, Charles Chatterley.[13]

A Samuel Chaterley (*sic*) is named as a (pottery) manufacturer in a directory of c.1795;[14] and a *William* Chatterley in a locally-compiled directory of 1796.[15]

Apart from one marked basalt creamer, no dry-bodied stonewares have been identified with the Chatterleys.

CHETHAM:
Chetham & Woolley, c.1794–1807;
(Mrs Ann) Chetham & Woolley, 1807–09;
Mrs Ann Chetham, 1809–14;
Chetham & Son, 1814–21;
Chetham and Robinson (and Son), 1822–40;
Chethams, 1841–71;
Commerce Street, Longton, Staffordshire.

James Chetham and Richard Woolley were in partnership at Commerce Street, Longton, from c.1794[1] until James Chetham's death in 1807. James Chetham's widow, Ann, continued the partnership until Richard Woolley (see

Fig. 139 **Teapot**, *white felspathic stoneware with enamel lines picked out in blue. Unmarked, attributed to Chetham and Woolley by shards, c. 1800-20, 5⅛ inches high. (Blake collection.)*

Fig. 140 **Teapot**, *white felspathic stoneware, smear-glazed and with sprig relief and hinged metal lid. Iron-red inscription reads:* N & H Macclesfield Devonport 1810 *(doubtless a marriage commemorative), Unmarked, attributed to Chetham and Woolley by shards, c. 1810, 5½ inches high. (Blake collection.)*

below) left in 1809. Ann Chetham took her son Jonathan Lowe Chetham into partnership from 1814 until her death in 1821. J.L. Chetham took John Robinson as a partner in 1822, and Robinson's son joined them in 1834. John Robinson died in 1840 and his son left the business then. J.L. Chetham was the sole proprietor from 1841 to his death in 1861. His sons, John, Robert and Frederick Chetham, took over the business then. Frederick Chetham & Co. was insolvent in 1871, due to partnership differences.[2]

Chethams' works, No. 134 on the 1802 map (Appendix 1), was at the junction of Commerce Street and Chancery Lane, a site now occupied by two preserved ovens, the remains of the Empire Theatre and Kwiksave grocery stores.

Surviving marked examples of stonewares produced by either Chetham or Woolley are limited to white dry-bodied and wares of the smear-glazed felspathic type. The few existing wares and a number of shards excavated at the factory site (Fig. 138) seem to support Simeon Shaw's description that 'about 1795, a new kind of Pottery, a *dry* body, or without glaze or smear, was introduced into the market by Messrs Chetham and Woolley, of Lane End'.[3] Only a handful of marked examples have survived and they include an impressive range of shapes, from candlesticks (Fig. 141) to planters (Fig. 143) as well as teapots (Colour Plate 41; Figs. 139, 140) and jugs (Fig. 142), mostly impressed *CHETHAM & WOOLLEY* or very rarely, as in the case of a felspathic covered milk jug and lid in the

Fig. 141 **Candlestick**, *fine white smear-glazed stoneware with enamel painting. Mark:* CHETHAM & WOOLLEY, *c. 1800, 5 inches high. (Newark Museum, New Jersey.)*

Fig. 142 **Jug**, *white smear-glazed stoneware with brown enamel neck and upper handle and relief scenes of the hunt. Mark:* CHETHAM & WOOLLEY *(at base of handle), c. 1800-20, 12 inches high. (Weldon collection.)*

Victoria and Albert Museum simply *CHETHAM*. Apparently the Chethams were manufacturing wares to be sold in London by James Mist, as a teapot in the Liverpool Museum marked *MIST LONDON* (Fig. 221) conforms to shards excavated at the factory site.

Richard Woolley, 1809–11,
Market Street, Longton, Staffordshire.

Richard Woolley (*c*.1764–1825) was in a partnership with Chethams from *c*.1794 to 11 November 1809,[4] and then started in business alone, in a works on the north side of Market Street, Longton.[5] He leased sixteen houses, this works, fixtures and utensils from John Smith,[6] a relative by marriage of William Turner and John Turner junior (q.v.), who had operated the factory until their bankruptcy in 1806. Woolley's independent business only lasted some sixteen months: he was bankrupt by March 1811[7] and appears to have repaid only 10% of his debts.[8] Part of Woolley's debt was for some of Turners' stock-in-trade which he had taken over.[9] He was succeeded in the works by Harley and Seckerson.

A set of five flower vases in white stoneware, partly dipped in blue, and ornamented in white, impressed WOOLLEY,[10] and one other marked vase,[11] are the only known marked pieces. Similar shapes in stoneware (Fig. 143)[12] and porcelain,[13] unmarked, are known.

CHURCH GRESLEY see GRESLEY

Fig. 143 ***Bulb pot*** *(two of three tiers), fine white stoneware enamel painted in blue. Unmarked, attributed to Richard Woolley (an example marked Woolley is in the Fitzwilliam Museum, Cambridge) c. 1809-11, 8½ inches high. (Rakow collection.)*

CHRYSANTHEMUM PAD

This name refers to stoneware vessels, bearing underneath only a flower-shaped pad, with a number impressed. Dr R.K. Henrywood wrote about them in detail in *Northern Ceramic Society Newsletter 83*,[1] stating that he had then recorded sixteen different numbers, between 5 and 97. He gave the name of 'Chrysanthemum Factory' to the unknown manufacturer.

The vessels noted include jugs (Figs. 144, 145), mugs and flower pots, in unglazed brown, white, cane or blue stoneware, with brown or white sprigged decoration, or self-coloured moulded designs. A range of dates from 1815 to 1835 is suggested for production of this ware. Responses to his article did not increase the range of numbers, but did produce a variation in the style of the actual chrysanthemum.[2]

R. Hildyard has recently aired the name of Dudson in connection with this and other mystery marks,[3] but no evidence has yet come to light about the maker of this ware.

CLEWS:
Ralph & James Clews, 1813–1827, Bleak Hill Works; 1817–1834, 'Globe' Works and 'Brownfield' Works; all in Cobridge, Staffordshire.

The brothers Ralph and James Clews became master potters at the Bleak Hill Works, Cobridge in 1813.[1] By 1817 they were able to lease a second works at Cobridge, later called the Globe Works.[2] They were bankrupt in 1827, and gave up the Bleak Hill Works.[3] Undaunted, they then rented a larger works at Cobridge, and ran this and the 'Globe' works until 1834, when they were again bankrupt.[4]

James Clews, who had gained pottery experience under Andrew Stevenson in 1811,[5] then went to the United States to found the Indiana Pottery at Louisville, Kentucky.[6] He moved to New York in 1842[7] and was back in England in 1849.[8] Ralph Clews stayed in England and managed a flint mill and a colliery which the brothers had formerly controlled.[9]

The Bleak Hill Works, probably indicated by † on the 1802 map (Appendix 1), was owned by the Warburton family (q.v.),[10] and stood between Warburton Street and Elder Road, Cobridge. The site is now built over as Camoys Court.

The Globe Works site, No. 60 on the 1802 map, stood at the junction of Waterloo Road and Cobridge Road, a site occupied by Drayton of Stoke Ltd.'s garage in 1996. Clews's third works, No. 59 on the 1802 map, was occupied by Brownfield partnerships from 1836 to 1900, when it was largely demolished.[11] Douglas Street and Crane Street now occupy the site, apart from a small portion of the old works which is within Churchill China's Alexander Works.

Extant stonewares identified with the Clews factory are extremely rare and seem to consist of smear-glazed jugs with sprig relief, and occasionally other wares such as drab grey or brown dipped and glazed white stonewares (Fig. 146). The sprig relief decoration often appears to be

Fig. 144 *Covered jug, drab-coloured stoneware with reliefs of the hunt in white and white serpent handles entwined to extend to make a spout. Mark: Chrysanthemum pad with "15", c. 1825, 8¼ inches high. (Richardson collection, ex Nina Fletcher Little collection.)*

Fig. 145 *Jug, buff stoneware with white sprig relief. Mark: Chrysanthemum pad with "16", c. 1825, 5 inches high. (Blakey collection.)*

crudely produced, frequently with crazing and staining. However, it is interesting to note that Felix Joseph, the Nottingham Museum benefactor, was collecting Clews stoneware in the nineteenth century, bequeathing his collection in 1892.

CLOWES:
William Clowes and Co., c.1778–1783;
Clowes and Williamson, fl.1784;
Henshall, Williamson and Clowes, c.1792–1800;
Henshall and Williamson(s), 1800–c.1830;
Longport, Staffordshire.

William Clowes and Co.'s advertisement in May 1778 that Staffordshire Ware was for sale at 112 The Minories, London and at the manufactory at Longport, is the earliest

Fig. 146 *Jug and spill vase, jug, drab-grey stoneware with white sprig decoration; spill, white stoneware with brown slip and white sprig floral reliefs. Marks: both CLEWS, c. 1815-25, jug. 5½ inches high, spill 3⅞ inches. (Blakey collection.)*

mention of this firm. Three months after his better-known contemporary, Josiah Spode II, William Clowes joined the Spectacle Makers Company of London on 11 June 1778.[1]

John Ward wrote in 1843 that three manufactories were erected at Longport around 1773 (after the Trent and Mersey Canal had reached that point), one of them by Robert Williamson;[2] and he was one of William Clowes's partners. Clowes insured his own household goods at Longport in 1781,[3] probably living in the house at the works at that time. The firm was William Clowes and Co. in Directories of 1781 and 1783;[4] Clowes and Williamson in 1784,[5] but (Hugh) Kenshall (*sic*) (surely Henshall), (Robert) Williamson and (William) Clowes when they insured their potworks and contents at Longport for £1,500 in 1792;[6] and in Directories c.1795 and 1796.[7] The change in the order of names in the partnership may indicate that William Clowes senior (died in 1782)[8] was the founder of the firm, and that his son, also William Clowes, succeeded him.

William Clowes junior inherited a fortune from his Uncle, Josiah Clowes, canal engineer, who died in 1795,[9] and this may have been the reason why he retired from the partnership in 1800. William Clowes of Porthill, gentleman, was associated with the New Hall China firm between at least 1803 and 1810.[10] Born c.1745, he died on 29 December 1822.[11]

The firm continued as Henshall and Williamson(s) from 1800 to 1831.[12] Robert Williamson left the partnership in May 1826[13] but his mother, Anne Williamson, and his brother, Hugh Henshall Williamson, carried on until Anne died on 26 September of the same year.[14] Possibly Robert Williamson inherited his mother's stake as he again ended a partnership with Hugh Henshall Williamson as Henshall and Williamsons on 31 December 1830, leaving his brother

Robert to continue the family firm.[15] The firm does not appear in directories after 1830, and Ward stated in 1843 that the factory was disposed of to Davenports.[16]

The works had six ovens in 1832, a large works.[17] Shown as No. 20 on the 1802 map (Appendix 1), the main building still stands as part of Arthur Wood's Price and Kensington Works, Trubshaw Cross.

Henshalls, Williamsons and Clowes were all related: Hugh Henshall was the brother of Mrs Anne Williamson, and William Clowes junior was her nephew. Robert and Hugh Henshall Williamson were two of her children, and Hugh Henshall Williamson married Anne, daughter of William Clowes junior. Mrs Williamson was formerly the young wife of James Brindley, canal engineer;[18] and both Hugh Henshall and Josiah Clowes were canal carriers and canal engineers.[19] To compound confusion, there was a distinct pottery firm of Williamson and Henshall,[20] with its factory at site No. 21 on the 1802 map, literally across the road from Clowes's works, a site now occupied by a boat-yard.

Apart from a very few marked basalt teawares, no dry bodies have been identified with the firm.

CLULOW:
Robert Clulow & Co., 1800–1802;
Lower Lane, Fenton, Staffordshire.

Robert Clulow and Co., Lower Lane, Fenton is known from the 1802 map (Appendix 1),[1] a dissolution of partnership notice,[2] and one marked piece of white felspathic stoneware.[3] The 1802 map marks their works by . on the south side of what is now City Road, Fenton, a site occupied by Jack Ashley Court in 1996. The partners were Robert Clulow, Joseph Rogers, John Hampson and Daniel Morris, and their partnership was dissolved 5 February 1802, Clulow paying their debts.

A Robert Clulow was a grocer in Longton from 1796 to 1802.[4] Probably he had financed the partnership. His grocery stock was sold for his creditors in December 1802.[5]

Joseph Rogers may have been the potter who was in Bovey Tracey in 1805, born at Newcastle-under-Lyme in 1773, apprenticed at fourteen to John Harrison of Stoke, and in business himself for two years, presumably in the Clulow partnership.[6] A John Hampson was an enameller in Longton 1800–02;[7] whilst a Daniel Morris was a potter in Burslem until his bankruptcies in 1793 and 1797.[8]

Clulow wares have for years been defined by a single fine white felspathic stoneware teapot in the Newark Museum, New Jersey (Fig. 147). A symbol of the superb possibilities of a small pottery, this teapot, most unusually signed on the face of the pedestal of the sprig relief *CLULOW & Co. FENTON*, remains the flagship of this scarcely recognized firm.

CYPLES:
Joseph Cyples I *c*.1780; **Joseph Cyples II** 1781–89;
Mary Cyples, 1790–1802; **Jesse Cyples**, 1803–10;
Lydia Cyples, 1811–32;
William & Richard Cyples, 1833–40;
Cyples, Barlow & Cyples, 1841–44;
Cyples & Robey, 1845;
Cyples & Barker 1846–47;
Market Street, Longton, Staffordshire.

A potworks at Market Street, Longton was run by the Cyples family from around 1780 to 1847, making earthenware, particularly Egyptian Black; and also china from 1828. The site of the works, No. 132 on Allbut's 1802 map (Appendix 1), is now occupied by a shop, with 'Cyples Old Pottery' in terracotta on the gable.[1]

Richard Cyples (1807–58)[2] was in various other pottery businesses in Longton between *c*.1839 and 1855.[3]

The Cyples family were probably making a fairly wide range of the popular earthen/stonewares of the period, but they are rarely marked and therefore, difficult to identify. There are examples of white felspathic stoneware teawares bearing the impressed factory name (Fig. 148) which are well potted and appealingly conceived.

Fig. 147 *Teapot, white felspathic stoneware with blue enamel lines picked out. Mark: CLULOW & Co. FENTON (on base of pedestal in relief), c. 1800-02, 6 inches high. (Newark Museum, New Jersey, Morris collection.)*

Fig. 148 *Covered sugar, white felspathic stoneware with lines picked out in blue enamel and a spaniel finial. Mark: CYPLES, probably Jesse or Lydia Cyples, c. 1810-15, 5¼ inches high. (Robertshaw collection.)*

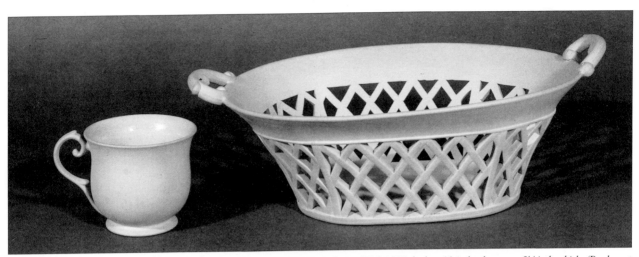

Fig. 149 **Basket and cup**, *caneware undecorated. Mark:* Davenport *above an anchor, c. 1795-1815, basket, 10 inches long; cup, 2¼ inches high. (Pendergast collection.)*

DAVENPORT:
John Davenport, 1794–97;
John & James Davenport, 1797–1822;
John Davenport, Son & Co., 1822–*c*.34;
William & Henry Davenport & Co., 1834–35;
William Davenport & Co., 1835–69;
Henry Davenport & Co., 1869–81;
Davenports Ltd., 1881–87;
Longport, Staffordshire.

John Davenport began his pottery manufacturing business at Longport in 1794, and it was continued there by his descendants until 1887.[1] During those ninety-three years, the firm expanded to have at best four pottery factories, a glass works, and warehouses in Liverpool, London, Brussels, Lubeck, Hamburg and New York.

John Davenport (1765–1848) may have had a small pottery in Burslem between 1789 and 1791.[2] He was certainly a pottery merchant in Liverpool from 1790, before he began manufacturing earthenware and later porcelain and glass at the 'Unicorn Works' on the canal-side at Longport, Staffordshire in 1794.[3] He took his cousin James Davenport (1776–1822) into partnership in 1797, and, in another partnership, started a glass works next to his 'Unicorn Works' in 1801.

Davenports took over Walter Daniel's nearby Newport Pottery in 1806,[4] and had a London showroom by 1807. In 1818, Davenports changed their London address to 82 Fleet Street, formerly Mist's showroom, and earlier Turner and Abbott's.

John Davenport became Member of Parliament for Stoke-upon-Trent in 1832, and the firm was in the names

Fig. 150 **Teapots and covered sugar**, *caneware with enamel lines picked out in blue or brown. Marks on teapots,* Davenport *over an anchor* "WARRANTED", *sugar unmarked, c. 1805-15, all around 4 inches high. (Lockett collection.)*

Fig. 151 *Jug*, caneware with blue enamel and pencil painted cartouche of galleons and a cart moving a bathing hut with the motto "Trifle from Lowestoft". The scene is one seen in Lowestoft porcelain, illustrated in a flask in S. Smith, Lowestoft Porcelain in Norwich Castle Museum, *Volume 2, Pl. 21a. Mark: Davenport over an anchor, c. 1800-10, 5 inches high. (Lockett collection.)*

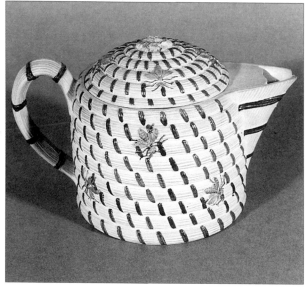

Fig. 152 *Syrup jug*, caneware in honeycomb form moulded with bees, brown enamel painting. Mark: Davenport *over an anchor, c. 1798-1815, 3¼ inches high. (Royal Ontario Museum, gift of Mrs G. Edgerton Brown, 984.18.22.1&2.)*

of his sons, Henry and William Davenport, when they took over the adjoining Top Bridge Pottery from Robert Williamson & Co. in 1834. With three factories, Davenports was the biggest pottery firm in the Potteries, having thirty ovens and employing 1,400 workers in 1836. Henry Davenport was killed whilst out hunting in 1835, and the firm was William Davenport & Co. from then until 1869.

A measure of the firm's success is shown in orders fulfilled for the Coronation Banquets of George IV and William IV, and a City of London banquet for Queen Victoria, together with appointments as glass makers to the

Prince of Wales in 1806, and porcelain manufacturers to William IV and Adelaide in 1831. In 1849 Davenports acquired the Bottom (or New) Bridge Works, Longport, formerly Phillips's. The firm had reached its peak.

The Liverpool warehouse was offered for sale in 1856, and the Newport Works was sold in 1857. William Davenport died in 1869, and his son Henry took over, inheriting a mortgaged business.

In 1879 the London showroom was changed from 82 Fleet Street to more modest premises at 32 Ely Place. The Bottom Bridge Works was sold in 1876 and the Top Bridge

Fig. 153 *Plate*, reticulated caneware with vermicelli border in green. Mark: Davenport *over an anchor, c. 1800-10, 7½ inches diameter. (Burgin collection.)*

Fig. 154 *Cream jug*, caneware with enamel border in blue green and black floral arabesque. Mark: Davenport *over an anchor, c. 1810, 2¹¹⁄₁₆ inches high. (Zeitlin collection.)*

Fig. 155 **Wine cooler**, *caneware with sprig reliefs of the 'Jolly topers' and brown enamel Greek key border. Mark: Davenport over an anchor., c. 1810, 8¼ inches high. (Darlington collection.)*

Fig. 156 **Wine cooler**, *pale red stoneware with bold Greek key band in black enamel and dolphin head lug handles. Mark: Davenport above an anchor, c. 1810. (Royal Ontario Museum, gift of Mrs G. Edgerton Brown, 984.18.23.)*

Works in 1881. In the same year the business was formed into a limited company, Davenports Ltd., only to be wound up in 1887 and all its assets sold.

Davenports produced some of the finest caneware of any of the manufacturers. Often enamel painted or moulded and painted, the decoration further embellished a superb cane body. Even the shapes, which in most factories were restricted to tea wares, were more imaginative and included candlesticks, wine coolers, honey pots, egg stands and pie dishes as well as a wide variety of tea wares. A cake plate of reticulated creamware form with a green enamel border

(Fig. 153) is an example of flawless caneware production in a shape rarely seen in a dry body. A rare jug (Colour Plate 43 right) with enamel Greek key border and pencil painted Egyptian motifs illustrates the skill and imagination Davenports used in addressing a universally popular theme. A wine cooler with similar decoration is in the collection of the Merseyside Museums.

The factory also produced some white stoneware mugs and jugs (Fig. 157, see also Fig. 355, page 205) and, most unusually, a wine cooler in fine red stoneware (Fig. 156) in a shape produced more frequently in caneware (Fig. 155).

Fig. 157 **Two mugs**, *white stoneware with brown enamel and gilding (left) and brown enamel ground (right). Marks: both Davenport above an anchor, c. 1810, 5 inches and 3¼ inches high. (Darlington collection.)*

Fig. 158 *Teapot*, white felspathic stoneware with moulded and applied relief outline painted in blue. Mark: D.D. & Co CASTLEFORD *c. 1805-10, 5⅛ inches high. (Private collection.)*

Fig. 159 *Teapot*, white felspathic stoneware with a moulded body and sprig relief, sliding lid. Mark: D.D. & Co., CASTLEFORD POTTERY, *c. 1805-10, 5 inches high. (Turnbull collection.)*

DON POTTERY:
John Green, 1801–03;
Greens, Clark & Co., 1803–*c*.1816;
John & William Green and Co, 1816–23;
John & William Green, 1823–34;
Samuel Barker (& Son), 1837–93;
Don Pottery, Swinton, South Yorkshire.

John Green built a potworks on the Don Canal, in South Yorkshire in 1801 and it continued in business in various hands until 1893.[1]

John Green (*c*.1743–1805) had been a partner in both the Leeds and Swinton Potteries until he was personally bankrupt in 1800. Two of his former partners in the Swinton Pottery, John and William Brameld, and a Leeds rope manufacturer, Richard Clark, joined him at the Don works. By 1803 more partners had been taken including Green's son, John, and the firm traded as Greens, Clark and Co. John Green died in 1805, and another son, William, joined the partnership.

With varying partners until 1823, John Green junior and William Green ran the business until they were bankrupt in 1834. Samuel Barker of Mexborough Old Pottery bought the Don works in 1839, and was joined by his three sons, Henry, Edward and Peter Jesse Barker, as Samuel Barker and Sons. Father and all three sons had left the firm or died by 1882, but the firm continued under the same name until final failure in 1893.

The works was extensive, built in circular form, and the adjoining Don Canal enabled raw materials to be received and finished goods to be despatched conveniently. 600 workers were employed in the early years and 500 in the 1880s.

A shape book, issued in 1807,[2] illustrated the range of creamwares produced by the factory but there were also some few dry-bodied stonewares produced. There is a caneware tea canister and cover with brown stoneware relief sprig decoration marked *SWINTON, DON POTTERY* in the Victoria and Albert Museum.[3]

DUNDERDALE:
David Dunderdale & Co., 1790–1821;
Castleford Pottery, Castleford, West Yorkshire.

A fine-ware pottery was established near Castleford in 1784, and David Dunderdale (1740–99) and John Plowes, both Leeds textile merchants, took it over in 1790. Dunderdale died in 1799 and was replaced by his son, also David (1772–1824). Plowes was bankrupt in his textile business in 1803, and left the pottery partnership. Dunderdale continued with various partners through the difficult period of the Napoleonic wars, but the firm went into liquidation in 1821.[1]

The Castleford Works was built on a meander of the navigable River Calder, very well placed for the import of clay and flint, and distribution of finished wares over the Yorkshire canal network. Dunderdales traded with France,

Fig. 160 *Hot milk jug*, white felspathic stoneware moulded and with relief sprigging. Mark: D.D. & Co. CASTLEFORD *c. 1800-15, 5⅛ inches high. (Private collection.)*

Fig. 161 *Teapot, white felspathic stoneware with moulded and applied reliefs, outline painted in blue. Mark:* D. D. & Co. CASTLEFORD *c. 1800-10, 6½ inches high. (Private collection.)*

Fig. 162 *Teapot (minus cover), white felspathic stoneware with moulded and applied reliefs. Mark:* D.D. & Co. CASTLEFORD POTTERY *c. 1800-15, 4½ inches high (without cover). (Private collection.)*

Spain and America via Hull. After closure in 1821, the works was re-opened by three distinct pottery firms, and continued in use as a pottery until 1960.

The dry-bodied wares produced at Castleford under the Dunderdales appear to have been primarily restricted to production of white felspathic stonewares and a few basalt teawares. The felspathic wares were smear-glazed, occasionally embellished with enamel painting, and rather narrow in range of shapes. Limited to tea wares and mugs and jugs, the forms were not numerous. Only three or four teapot shapes have been recorded (Figs. 158, 161, 162), the principal shape being the classical form in Figure 158. Dunderdale wares are rare but are identified by impressed marks including D.D. & Co. CASTLEFORD or CASTLEFORD POTTERY.

Fig. 163 *Mug, fine white stoneware with brown enamel rim and applied reliefs. Mark:* D.D. & Co. CASTLEFORD *c. 1810, 6½ inches high. (Claude D. Pike collection.)*

Fig. 164 *Jug, white stoneware with applied reliefs of the hunt. Mark:* D.D. & Co. CASTLEFORD POTTERY *c. 1800-10, 6¼ inches high. (Yorkshire Museum.)*

Fig. 165 *Jug, white stoneware with reliefs of the hunt. Mark:* D.D. & Co. CASTLEFORD POTTERY *c. 1800-10. (Yorkshire Museum, Hurst collection.)*

EASTWOOD see BADDELEY

GLASS:
John Glass, *c*.1784–*c*.1796, High Street;
Glass and Taylor, *c*.1798–1801, High Street
and Market Street;
John Glass, 1802–*c*.1817; **Glass and Sons**, *c*.1818–1821;
John Glass,1821–1834, Market Street,
all in Hanley, Staffordshire.

John Glass (*c*.1757–1840)[1] was first listed as a master potter in Hanley in 1824.[2] He continued in business there until 1821 and either he or his son of the same name went on until 1834. John Glass married Sarah Dean (*c*.1765–1829)[3] Stoke-upon-Trent on 31 May 1785 and they had four children, all baptised at Hanley: Thomison [*sic* - Thomasina?], a girl, on 30 June 1789; John on 14 December 1790; Richard Dean on 29 January 1793 and Sarah, on 29 June 1795.[4]

John Glass attended meetings of the local Committee of Commerce from 30 November 1784 to 16 July 1790.[5] This last meeting, chaired by Josiah Wedgwood, agreed to examine and translate the spy Ljungberg's book; and discussed letters from Baltimore, attempting to recruit a turner, a modeller and a superintendent for Mr Wilson of New York, to make white and cream-coloured ware.

John Glass was in business alone from *c*.1784 to *c*.1796,[6] and then was in partnership with John Taylor in Hanley from *c*.1798 to 1801.[7] John Taylor is not otherwise known, but was possibly a son of George Taylor (q.v.), a nearby master potter.[8] John Glass resumed business alone in 1802, but by 1818 the firm was Glass and Sons, Market Street, Hanley,[9] a partnership of John Glass the elder, John Glass the younger and Richard Dean Glass, which was dissolved on 9 January 1821.[10] By then John Glass the elder was aged sixty-four, and it may be his son, John Glass the younger, then aged thirty-one, who continued the business in the same name until 1834,[11] when John Glass the elder would have been seventy-seven.

John Glass of Hanley, gentleman, insured his house in Hanley for £50, his potworks for £200 and his stock and utensils for £150 on 27 May 1790, with the Sun Fire Office.[12] Two years later, 20 June 1792, he changed his insurer to the more local Salop Fire Office, who described him as a potter, and insured his house and stables for £100, his household goods for £150, his potworks for £250 and his stock of earthenware, blocks and moulds for £500.[13] A memo of 12 September 1794 on this policy record notes that his stock of earthenware, blocks and moulds, which had been removed to Mr Richard Mare's potworks, continue to be insured. Richard Mare had insured his potworks for £300 with the Salop Fire Office on 20 June 1792,[14] so that they were familiar with his premises.

John Glass renewed his insurance with Salop on 10 October 1795, with similar cover to that of 1792, except that he increased the value of his potworks from £200 to £400, and covered a second set of potworks for £250.[15] It seems likely that he had taken over Richard Mare's potworks

by October 1795 and insured them for £400, and that the second set of potworks was Glass's earlier works.

Richard Mare had died by June 1797,[16] and a memo dated 30 October 1797 on Glass's 1795 policy record states that his household goods, being removed to Mr Glass's new dwelling-house, late in the occupation of Mr Richard Mare, continue to be insured. The inference is that John Glass took over Richard Mare's house in 1797, substantiated by the 1807 rate records and an 1807 advertisement.[17]

The 1802 map (Appendix 1) shows John Glass's works as No. 78, on the north side of Market Street (now Huntbach Street), Hanley, opposite the side of Boots The Chemists. The rate records start in 1807 and list John Glass owning and occupying one works, rated at £1.3s.4d, and owning another works, then occupied by Leigh and Breeze, rated at £2.1s.8d;[18] confirming that Glass had bought a larger works (Mare's) and retained his first works.

In 1831, John Glass advertised his Market Street works, with two biscuit and three glost ovens, to be let, together with a flint and colour mill;[19] and Hackwood and Keeling were his tenants from 1834 to 1836,[20] followed by Samuel Keeling and Co. from 1838 to 1849.[21] The extensive earthenware manufactory lately occupied by Samuel Keeling and Co. was offered to be let with vacant possession 20 October 1849;[22] and Keeling's partnership was dissolved a year later.[23] J. and G. Meakin were the occupants from 1852 to 1859,[24] followed by Taylor Brothers.[25] The works, named as 'Opaque Porcelain Manufactory' in 1865, were demolished by 1875.[26]

John Glass died 27 April 1840, aged eighty-three, the oldest earthenware manufacturer in the Potteries,[27] two years older than Enoch Wood who died in the same year.

The location of John Glass's first works can be identified retrospectively. In 1802, 'Joseph Lees' occupied potworks no. 70, on the east side of Hanley High Street (now Town Road) – (see Appendix 1), a site now (1997) at the entrance to *Glass* Street. Lees's name is probably a misspelling for Joseph Leigh, who was John Glass's tenant in 1807.[28] If this is correct, potworks no. 70 was John Glass's first works, and the rear parts of Glass's two factories would adjoin each other. When they were demolished between 1865 and 1875, the new street and adjacent buildings would all be constructed on Glass's former land, and the street was certainly named after him.

As shown above, Leigh and Breeze were Glass's tenants in 1807. Joseph Leigh and William Breeze ended their partnership in December 1808,[29] to be followed in Glass's works by Wilson and Breeze to 1811 and Breeze and Wilson until 1814 (see Neale). Later tenants were William Booth and Isaac Bentley in 1815, a partnership dissolved 5 March 1816;[30] the Peover family 1818 to 1822; next John Mayer/Mare from 1823 to 1825; and Barlow, Ellis and Hulme 1825–27.[31] John Glass advertised his china or earthenware manufactory in High Street, Hanley to be let again in November 1828,[32] and his last known tenants were Thomas Gray and Henry Jones from 1830 to 1836.[33] The works, a three-oven 'China Manufactory', were still standing in 1865, but demolished by 1875.[34]

The range of bodies produced by John Glass is not known. They certainly made basalt and appear to have made translucent white smear-glazed teawares (Fig. 356, page 205), forms of which are identical to marked basalt examples.

GREATBATCH:
William Greatbatch, 1762–1782, Fenton, Staffordshire.

The work of earlier writers on William Greatbatch was eclipsed by David Barker's seminal monograph;[1] only additional information will be referenced. William Greatbatch was born c.1736 and worked in some capacity for Whieldon & Wedgwood at Fenton in the 1750s, probably as a modeller. Josiah Wedgwood and Thomas Whieldon ended their partnership in 1759 and Greatbatch had some involvement with Wedgwood in his new factory at Burslem in 1760.

In 1762 William Greatbatch rented a newly erected potworks at Lower Lane, Fenton, and *inter alia* supplied Wedgwood with both block moulds and ware. Greatbatch continued in business at Lower Lane until he was bankrupt in 1782. His factory was No. 107 on the 1802 map (Appendix 1), then occupied by Chelenor and Adams. It was later known as the Sutherland Pottery (occupied between 1902 and 1916 by Arnold Bennett's nephew, Frank Beardmore)[2] and was demolished in 1975 or later.[3] The site is now occupied by Fenton Open Market ground. Archaeological excavation on Greatbatch's factory waste tip has provided evidence of the manufacture by him of a wide variety of earthenwares and stonewares.

Josiah Wedgwood helped to settle Greatbatch's bankruptcy, lending or giving £254 and possibly £600 more in 1783.[4] In 1786, Greatbatch had 'delivered up all his effects' and most of his creditors agreed to release him at a meeting on 15 February. Josiah Wedgwood wrote to the remainder, asking for their agreement so that Greatbatch could 'provide for his wife and family'.[5] By August, Greatbatch was working for Wedgwood at Etruria, and he continued in employment there until he was about seventy-one, in 1807. After Thomas Wedgwood's death in 1788, Greatbatch probably took his place as general manager of Wedgwood's 'useful' works. Greatbatch was said to have worked for Turner before going to Wedgwood's in 1786; for Child of Newfield, Tunstall c.1786; and to have been unsuccessfully 'head-hunted' by Bulkeley and Bent in the 1790s: clearly a desirable employee.

A William Greatbatch junior rented a potworks in Stoke-upon-Trent from Rachel Wolfe in 1828[6] but he was bankrupt by March of that year.[7] The description of him as 'junior' and 'the younger' suggests that he was the son or grandson of William Greatbatch (1736–1813). He manufactured blue-printed china and earthenware.[8] A blue-printed mark 'W.G.' has been recorded, not associated with any manufacturer.[9]

In dry-bodied stoneware, Greatbatch wares appear to have been confined principally to red stoneware (Fig. 9) and (deduced from a few excavated shards) a buff-coloured stoneware used for teapots.[10] Excavations revealed that the pseudo Chinese-seal marks were used on teapots in both buff and red stonewares. However, William Greatbatch did make a unique and very fine caneware which was not identified until the factory site was excavated (Fig. 10). The recorded vessels were all teapots in the boat-shaped form, some of which had parapet collars and enamel-painted outline embellishment. They were all moulded in cane patterns.

Red stoneware from the Greatbatch site can be positively identified and appears to date, for the most part, to the period of its greatest popularity, from 1765 to 1770. The wares from the earlier phase (Phase I) tend to have basketweave handles and spouts, or straight spouts with basketweave handles. Sprigged reliefs are few with the most prominent being a figure of Minerva and a pair of Oriental ladies. No mould-applied reliefs have been found on Greatbatch stonewares. Earlier phase examples bear few marks, even Chinese seal marks, whereas, later phase shards are seen to be consistently marked with seal impressions. In the last phase of production, sprigged wares seem to be replaced by engine-turned decoration of the wavy reeded type which make a Greatbatch identification of those wares particularly difficult.[11]

GRESLEY:
Church Gresley Pottery, 1794–c.1808;
Gresley, Derbyshire.

Sir Nigel Gresley and C.B. Adderley started a pottery at Gresley in 1794, 'with also a place at Burton[-on-Trent]',[1] some four miles away. W. Coffee, a modeller, formerly at the Derby china works, was employed there for about three months in 1795.[2] The works at Church Gresley, together with a flint mill with colour and glaze pans nearby, 'the whole now at work' was offered to be let in 1798.[3] A further offer to let in 1799 offered immediate possession, with lathes, moulds, a printing press etc., to be taken at a fair valuation.[4]

Jewitt stated that the works was run by William Nadin from about 1800 for four or five years, by a Mr Burton for a few years and then closed.[5] A partnership dissolution of 1808 may well signify the end of pottery manufacturing at this site.[6]

Jewitt also wrote of another pottery at Church Gresley that W. Bourne bought in about 1816, enlarged it, and commenced the manufacture of 'Derbyshire ironstone cane ware'.[7] Jewitt was referring to glazed buff-bodied kitchen ware, production of which continued on this site until the 1980s,[8] and not to *dry-bodied* cane ware.

Very few marked examples of Church Gresley production are known, but those few illustrate a variety of techniques used there: a cream-coloured earthenware tureen, enamelled, impressed 'C. Greasley', and two matching but unmarked plates;[9] an earthenware plate printed in blue underglaze with a Chinese scene, marked 'Gresely (*sic*)';[10] an unglazed drab-coloured stoneware jug, impressed 'C.GREASLEY'(Fig. 166);[11] and an earthenware teapot, moulded, painted in 'Pratt' colours, marked 'Church Gresley'.[12] There is also a suggestion of an attempt to make porcelain at Church Gresley.[13]

Fig. 166 **Milk jug**, *brown-drab stoneware with satin stripes, glazed interior. Mark: C. GREASLEY, c. 1794-1808, 6 inches high. (Nottingham Museum, 1882-407.)*

Fig. 167 **Mark** *on jug in Figure 166.*

HACKWOOD:
Hackwood, Dimmock & Co., 1807–27,
Eastwood, Hanley, Staffordshire;
William Hackwood, 1827–43;
Hackwood & Son, 1843–55;
New Hall, Shelton, Staffordshire.

William Hackwood (1777–1849), son of Wedgwood's famous modeller of the same name,[1] was a pottery manufacturer from *c.*1807 to 1849. His partnership with Thomas Dimmock and James Keeling was dissolved in 1827,[2] and he continued at the Eastwood works until *c.*1843. He and his son Thomas then moved to the New Hall Works at Shelton, and his son carried on business there alone after William died in 1849,[3] until *c.*1855.

Although Timothy Dimmock signed a letter to Wedgwood on behalf of Hackwood, Dimmock & Co. in 1813,[4] it was *Thomas* Dimmock who was the partner in 1827. As Thomas Dimmock senior (1751–1827), a pottery manufacturer at Cheapside, Hanley, died 17 August 1827,[5] it seems likely that it was his death which precipitated the dissolution of the partnership.

James Keeling (1762–1837) was an earthenware manufacturer in New Street, Hanley between *c.*1795 and *c.*1830,[6] and his second wife was Sarah Dimmock (1777–1854) probably a daughter of Thomas Dimmock.[7] This James Keeling should not be confused with James Keeling, a factor in Shelton and partner of an Elijah Mayer (q.v.), both bankrupt in 1821.[8]

William Hackwood's son Thomas was described as an earthenware manufacturer when he married in 1830,[9] and it is likely that Thomas had been actively engaged in the Eastwood Works, long before he was acknowledged as a

Fig. 168 **Spill vase with flower pot stand and teapot**, *white stoneware with blue sprig floral band and enamel lines. Unmarked, Hackwood, c. 1810-20, 2¼ and 5½ inches high. (Fisk collection.)*

Fig. 169 **Pot-pourri basket and spill vase,** *white stoneware with sprig relief in shades of blue. Mark: spill HACKWOOD & C, c. 1810-25, 4 and 5½ inches high. (Rakow collection.)*

partner when Hackwoods moved to New Hall in 1843. A Thomas Hackwood was in partnership with Samuel Keeling as earthenware manufacturers in a five-oven works at Hanley from *c.*1835 to 1837.[10]

The Eastwood Works was not built when the 1802 map (Appendix 1) was prepared, and the only surviving original rate book, that of 4 August 1807, shows 'Hackwood & Co. in hand Potwork 4677 £– 13s.4d.' amongst 'additions 1807/8', suggesting that the Eastwood Works was new in 1807.[11] Hackwood's works was of modest size then; in the same book, Wedgwoods' Etruria works was rated at £13.15s.0d., twenty times the value. A fire at Hackwood's works in 1830 damaged a printing shop, painting shops and a biscuit warehouse, in three-storeyed buildings,

uninsured;[12] and an 1832 map shows a three-sided layout, with five ovens; clearly a substantial factory by then.[13]

Hackwoods' Eastwood Works later became Sherwin and Cotton's Tile Works on the north-east side of Eastwood Road, between Derby Street and Stubbs Lane. It should not be confused with other Eastwood Works.

William and Thomas Hackwood leased the New Hall Works in Shelton for fourteen years from 7 January 1843,[14] but had been succeeded by Cockson and Harding by 1856.[15]

A *Josiah* Hackwood was a figure manufacturer in Upper High Street, Hanley *c.*1844.[16] Another *William* Hackwood was a toy and ornamental china manufacturer in Hope Street, Shelton in 1853,[17] and it is probably the auction of

Fig. 169a **Teapot,** *octagonal drab-grey glazed stoneware with blue scroll sprig relief. Mark: HACKWOOD 22, c. 1820, 5½ inches high. (Richardson collection.)*

Fig. 170 **Teapot,** *glazed caneware with white sprig relief. Mark: HACKWOOD, c. 1827-35, 5¼ inches high. (Blake collection.)*

Fig. 171 *Pot-pourri basket*, *white felspathic stoneware with brown slip and white reliefs. Mark:* J. & W. HANDLEY, *c. 1820, 5 inches high. (Rakow collection.)*

Fig. 172 *Flower pot*, *drab green stoneware smear-glazed with white relief. Mark:* J. & W. HANDLEY, *c.1825-30, 3⅛ inches high. (Hosking collection.)*

his utensils and stock which has been mistakenly quoted as that of William Hackwood and Son.[18]

In the main, Hackwood dry bodies consist of a few distinctive fine white stonewares with characteristic bands of teal-coloured daisy chain sprigging and dark blue enamel lines (Colour Plate 44, Figs. 168, 169). The occasional caneware pot with similar decoration appears, and there are two examples of other wares, in glazed caneware (Fig. 170) and in drab-glazed stoneware which differ from the perceived notion of Hackwood-type wares.

HANDLEY:
James & William Handley, 1819–1828,
Burslem, Staffordshire; 1822–24, Shelton, Staffordshire.

James Handley (1796–1873) and William Handley (1800–83) made china and earthenware at Burslem and Shelton between 1819 and 1828.[1] They were brothers, sons of Sampson Handley (1768–1819), flint and corn miller at Sandon, a few miles south of the Potteries.

Handleys leased the Kilncroft Works at Burslem from 1819; No. 46 on the 1802 map (Appendix 1), previously occupied by John Brettell from *c.*1815 to 1817.[2] They were in business there until 1828, when they were bankrupt.

Handleys also leased a china works at Shelton between 1822 and 1824, No. 88 on the 1802 map, formerly occupied by William Breeze.[3] The next occupant was John Mare, himself bankrupt in 1826. Besides their manufacturing businesses in Burslem and Shelton, the Handley brothers had warehouses and shops in London, and possibly also a warehouse in Bristol.

Some few marked smear-glazed stonewares were produced by the factory. A handled flower basket and pierced cover of white stoneware with a drab green dip was formerly in the Rakow Collection (Fig. 171). Five inches high, the shape was identical to shape No. 134 in the Spode shape book and very similar to some made by David Wilson (see Fig. 247). The firm also made another shape of flower pot in solid drab green stoneware (Fig. 172) with

boldly applied foliage relief decoration in white. In time other wares may surface with the Handley *imprimatur*, but at the moment these are the sole examples of their stoneware manufacture.

HARTLEY, GREENS:
Hartley, Greens & Co., *c.*1781–1830,
Jack Lane, Leeds, West Yorkshire.

The Leeds Pottery or Leeds Old Pottery commenced in 1770 and continued, with fluctuating fortunes, until 1881.[1]

It has been suggested that because there was a substantial pottery decorating business in Leeds in the 1760s (Robinson and Rhodes), the Leeds Pottery must have started earlier,[2] but there were other potworks in Leeds, and Robinson and Rhodes dealt with Wedgwood[3] and possibly other potters in Staffordshire. Leeds was a substantial town and would provide business for a 'chinaman'.

The first partnership, Humble, Green and Co., built a potworks at Jack Lane, Leeds in 1770, and insured it for £1,000 in 1771, the same value as the Worcester porcelain works then. Other partners joined, and the firm was Humble, Hartley, Greens and Co. from 1776 to 1781. Utensils and stock, insured for £500 in 1771,[4] were covered for £2,000 by 1778, when the firm had also acquired a windmill worth £1,000.[5] Humble left in 1781 and the firm became Hartley, Greens and Co.[6]

The Leeds Pottery was linked with the Swinton Pottery (q.v.) from 1785. In the 1790s the firm was valued at £53,861, with a London warehouse, and an export business as far afield as Russia.[7] By 1800, John Green, a principal partner, was bankrupt; the connection with Swinton ended in 1806 and the Leeds works closed down for periods in 1806 and 1808. Receivers were appointed in 1813, but the factory continued in production.

Thomas Lakin (q.v.), from Staffordshire was appointed manager in 1818, followed at his death in 1821 by his son, also Thomas, until 1824.[8] The surviving partners of Hartley,

Fig. 173 *Sugar and cover, fine white stoneware. Mark: HARTLEY GREENS & CO. LEEDS ★ POTTERY c. 1790-1800, 5⅛ inches high. (Rakow collection.)*

Fig. 174 *Sugar and cover, white felspathic stoneware with moulded body and applied reliefs commemorating admirals Nelson (d. 1805) and Howe (d. 1799). Nelson died at Trafalgar and Howe, hero of both the Seven Years' War and commander of the British fleet during the American Revolution, was best known for his defeat of the French in 1794. Nelson and Howe are rarely seen together on a commemorative. Mark: '23', c. 1805-10, 5⅛ inches high, possibly Leeds Pottery. (Private collection.)*

Greens and Co. sold the business in 1830, and it passed through various owners: Leeds Pottery Co., S. and J. Chappel, Warburton and Britton, and Britton and Sons, who were bankrupt in 1878. It was taken over in 1881 by Taylor and Sons, who owned several Leeds potteries, but closed finally in the same year.

'Leeds Pottery' has been produced more recently, by Seniors c.1895–1949 and Morton from c.1909 to 1950s.[9] A new Hartley, Greens and Co. has produced cream-coloured earthenware from c.1992 to the present day, albeit in Staffordshire.[10]

Fig. 175 *Teapot, white felspathic stoneware, outline painted in blue, with the completely moulded body often distinguishing wares made by Heath Mark: HEATH & SON, c. 1805-10, 5⅜ inches high. (Monmouth County Historical Society, New Jersey.)*

Fig. 176 **Teapot, sugar and cream jug,** *white felspathic stoneware with outline painting in blue and moulded decoration. Marks: all* HEATH & SON, *c. 1805-10, teapot, 6¼ inches high. (Rakow collection.)*

Stoneware production from the Hartley, Greens era must have either been virtually non-existent or, more probably, the majority of wares were unmarked. Two marked pieces illustrated here constitute most of the known wares, one is smear glazed (Fig. 173), the other unglazed (Fig. 174). Both are of high quality, suggesting that they were neither trial pieces nor single examples.

HEATH:
Heath & Son, *c.*1796–99, Burslem, Staffordshire.

There were several master potters in North Staffordshire named Heath, but the only 'Heath and Son' business occurs at Burslem in 1796, 1797 and 1799.

Heath and Son, Burslem are listed as earthenware manufacturers in *The Staffordshire Pottery Directory,* published by Chester and Mort at Hanley in 1796.[1] Walter Daniel insured a house at Burslem in tenure of Nathen (*sic*) Heath and Son for £100 and a set of potworks nearby for £300 on 11 February 1797. A few days later, Nathan Heath and Son of Burslem themselves insured their household goods in their house for £50 and their stock and utensils in a set of potworks for £400.[2] In November 1799, Daniel offered by auction a potworks near the Newcastle turnpike, held under lease by Nathan Heath and Son.[3]

When the 1802 map (Appendix 1) was compiled, the firm of Nathan and John Heath occupied works No. 30, shown as near the Newcastle turnpike, and presumably the same works. John Heath moved in 1802 to the Hill Works.[4] He was insolvent in 1810, and his earthenware stock was sold, including printed, painted, edged and dipped ware.[5]

Stonewares marked *HEATH & SON* are rare indeed and limited to a few white felspathic smear-glazed examples in

teawares. They seem to be often embellished with enamel lines picked out in blue. In producing the white stoneware teawares, Heath and Son frequently moulded the entire body (Figs. 175, 176) and rarely added the characteristic sprig decoration. One jug has surfaced with added sprig relief (Fig. 177), but the other known examples made by Heath are entirely moulded. The result was less definition in the relief and a limited range of decoration, perhaps offset by the economic advantages of simpler production.

Fig. 177 **Cream jug,** *white felspathic stoneware with sprigged decoration and blue enamel lines. Mark:* HEATH & SON, *c. 1805-10, 4½ inches high. (Fisk collection.)*

Fig. 178 *Sugar box and cover, fine white stoneware with moulded body and applied relief. Mark: HERCULANEUM, c. 1805-10, 6 inches high. (City Museum and Art Gallery, Stoke-on-Trent.)*

Fig. 179 *Jug, fine white stoneware with moulded body and applied relief decoration. Cream jug, fine white stoneware with moulded body. Marks: both HERCULANEUM, jug. 8½ inches high. (Rakow collection.)*

HERCULANEUM POTTERY:
S. Worthington and Co., 1796–1806;
Herculaneum China and Earthenware Manufactory, 1806–33;
Case, Mort and Co., 1833–36;
Mort and Simpson, 1836–40;
Herculaneum Pottery, Liverpool, Merseyside.

The Herculaneum Pottery was in operation on the east bank of the River Mersey, near Liverpool, from 1796 to 1840.[1]

Although porcelain and tin-glazed earthenware had been made at Liverpool previously, the Herculaneum Pottery was an entirely new enterprise, the majority of its workers coming straight from Staffordshire to start the works on the traditional hiring day of 11 November. The pottery was founded by Samuel Worthington, a merchant from North Wales, on the site of an old copper works, with its own dock, well-placed for the importation of coal and clay, and for exporting finished ware. Herculaneum had a warehouse in Liverpool, which also bought from Staffordshire and Scottish potters, and sold locally and overseas.

Initially with a staff of sixty, Herculaneum expanded to have some three hundred workers by 1827. A new partnership was formed in 1806, increasing the capital to £25,000, thus enabling the company to invest in new works buildings, more workers' cottages, new warehouses, etc. Business continued through the vicissitudes of the Napoleonic Wars, with embargoes and blockades interfering with exports.

Fig. 180 *Cream jug, fine white stoneware with brown enamel decoration. Mark: HERCULANEUM, c. 1810, 4 inches high. (Polikoff collection.)*

Fig. 181 *Coffee pot, teapot and pot-pourri vase, white stoneware with chocolate-brown ground and white reliefs. Marks: all HERCULANEUM, c. 1805, coffee pot 10½ inches high. (Liverpool Museum, Museums & Galleries on Merseyside, 1012B11, 1970 204A, 1994-100.)*

Fig. 182 *Jug*, large drab-brown stoneware with reliefs of the 'Jolly topers' and a brown enamel neck. Mark: HERCULANEUM, c. 1805-15, 7½ inches high. (Rakow collection.)

Fig. 183 *Tobacco jar and mug*, fine white stoneware with smear-glaze and buff-coloured sprigs, enamel lines. Marks: both HERCULANEUM, jar 7½ inches high. (Liverpool Museum, Museums & Galleries on Merseyside, 1967.131, 13.5.27.3.)

In 1833 the business was offered for sale, and taken by a new partnership, Case, Mort and Co. Case left in 1836 and James Mort and John Simpson became the final proprietors. The pottery closed in 1840 and was demolished, the site occupied by a gas holder in 1993.[2] James Mort, formerly of Herculaneum Pottery, Liverpool, died in Melbourne, Australia on 30 October 1864, aged 61.[3]

Herculaneum provided a fairly wide range of fine white stonewares, dipped (Fig. 181), marbled (Fig. 186), drab (Figs. 182, 185), blue coloured (Fig. 187 right) and landscape painted (Colour Plate 45) white dry-bodied and smear-glazed wares. The variety included coffee and tea wares, mugs and jugs, plaques and medals (Fig. 187) and small busts (Fig. 188), as well as oddments such as humidors (Fig. 183). The quality was usually high and frequently superb, with finely levigated clays and interesting decoration. Marbling of hunt jugs (Fig. 186) was probably unique to the Herculaneum Pottery and the effect was electrifying. Their drab ware mugs with gilded rims were equally effective (Fig. 185). In a market where diversity would accelerate the cost the Herculaneum Pottery took some initiative in diversification.

Fig. 184 *Sugar bowl and cover*, white stoneware with drab-brown sprig relief and slip painted mauve cross hatching. Mark: HERCULANEUM, c. 1805, 3¹¹⁄₁₆ inches high. (Zeitlin collection.)

Fig. 185 *Mug,* drab-coloured stoneware with gilt rim and sprig relief. Mark: HERCULANEUM, c. 1805-10, 5 inches high. (Hyland collection.)

Fig. 186 **Jug,** *solid marbled stoneware of ovoid shape and brown enamel neck. Sprig relief decoration includes 'The Red Hot Marriage'. Unmarked, attributed to Herculaneum, c. 1805-10, 8½ inches high. (Hyland collection.)*

Fig. 187 **Plaque,** *white stoneware with brown ground and relief depicting France and England, 2¼ x 1¼ inches;* **Medal,** *blue stoneware simulated frame with white smear-glazed stoneware medal of George IV as a Roman emperor, 2⅞ inches diameter. Marks: both HERCULANEUM, c. 1805-25. (Rakow collection.)*

Fig. 188 **Busts of Naval heroes,** *(left) Vincent and Abercromby, buff stoneware. Vincent marked HERCULANEUM. (Right) Nelson and Duncan, white stoneware, unmarked attributed to Herculaneum, c. 1805. (Liverpool Museum, Museums & Galleries on Merseyside, 17.1114.1, 17.11.14.2, 8.3.12.18, 42.1.29.)*

Fig. 189 **Teapot**, *drab-blue stoneware with blue enamel painting. The finial, associated with both Samuel Hollins and with Chetham and Woolley, is* Venus and Cupid. *A teapot in this unusual shape was also made by J. Glass, Hanley in basalt. Unmarked, Samuel Hollins, c. 1790-1800, 5 inches high. (Rakow collection.)*

Fig. 190 **Cream jug**, *drab-blue stoneware with blue enamel painting. Mark: S. HOLLINS, c. 1790-1800, 4 inches high. (Rakow collection.)*

HOLLINS, SAMUEL:
Samuel Hollins, *c.*1773–*c.*1806;
Thomas Hollins junior & Co., *c.*1808–c 1814;
Vale Pleasant, Shelton, Staffordshire.

Samuel Hollins was born *c.*1749,[1] the sixth of nine children of Richard Hollins (1702–1780) and Mary, née Adams (1707–1779) of Far Green, Hanley.[2] He appears to have succeeded his brother Thomas Hollins senior (*c.*1743–1772) in a potworks at Vale Pleasant, Shelton, in the mid–1770s.[3] Samuel Hollins's son, Thomas junior, followed him in the same works *c.*1808;[4] and his son-in-law, Matthew Mare took over *c.*1815.[5] Samuel Hollins died 5 November 1820 aged 71.[6]

Samuel Hollins's daughter Anne married Herbert Minton at Hanley 1 September 1819.[7] Her brother, Thomas Hollins junior's son, Michael Daintry Hollins, born in Manchester in 1815, became a partner in Minton[8] The separate firm of T. and J. Hollins, later T., J. and R. Hollins (q.v.), was at the family home, Far Green, Hanley.

The likelihood that Samuel Hollins succeeded his brother in a potworks at Vale Pleasant depends on a reference in Samuel Hollins's own will of 19 July 1819 to 'potworks at Shelton late the estate of my late brother Thomas Hollins',[9] which Samuel left to his daughter Sarah, wife of the Matthew Mare who was then operating the Vale Pleasant works.

Thomas Hollins died in 1772,[10] so that his works was established before the Caldon Canal was promoted in 1776.[11] This branch canal from the Trent and Mersey canal passed so near Samuel Hollins's works that a short arm was provided to connect the works to the canal system, a convenience also enjoyed by Wedgwood at the nearby Etruria Works. The site is shown on Allbut's map of 1802 (Appendix 1) as No. 95, Hollins, Samuel.[12]

Samuel Hollins, the 'Red China Potter',[13] continued in business from the mid–1770s until *c.*1806, and was followed from at least 1808 by his son, Thomas Hollins, as Thomas Hollins Junior and Co.[14] Rate records from 1809 to 1815 list Mayer (*sic*) and Hollins as occupants, Mayer surely an error for Mare.[15] Samuel Hollins's daughter Sarah married Matthew Mare, so presumably he was a partner of Thomas Hollins Junior. Matthew and John Mare ran the works from *c.*1815 to *c.*1827.[16]

In 1790 Samuel Hollins insured his house for £500, a large quadrangular range of workshops and warehouses, and second and third ranges, for £800, and his stock for

Fig. 191 **Saucer**, *drab stoneware with metallic resist in a running triangle and pale green enamel ground border. Mark: S. HOLLINS, c. 1800, 5 inches diameter. (Zeitlin collection.)*

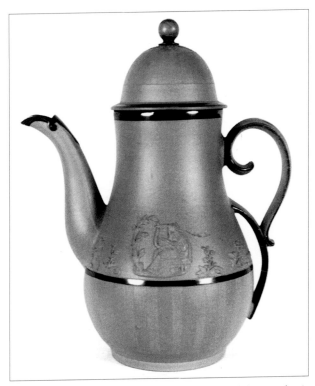

Fig. 192 *Coffee pot, drab stoneware with silver line embellishment and sprig reliefs. Unmarked, Samuel Hollins, c. 1800, 9½ inches high. (Rakow collection.)*

£850.[17] In 1808 he insured the same property for the same values, occupied by Thomas Hollins the Younger and Co., who insured their stock for £1650.[18]

Samuel Hollins came from a family of means. Already well established, he received £500 on his mother's death in 1779, and property, shares in mines and money on his father's death in 1782.[19] His interest in the raw materials of his trade is shown by his purchase of a water mill at Bucknall in 1786,[20] his membership of one partnership for buying Dorset clay in 1791,[21] and another for china clay in 1799.[22] Samuel Hollins was a partner in the New Hall

company by 1803,[23] and he owned numerous properties (over forty houses) in 1807.[24]

Samuel Hollins supplied Wedgwoods with round, octagonal and oval ware, presumably cream-coloured, in 1777;[25] 'goods' from 1777 to 1780,[26] and red china teapots, bowls, sugar boxes and cream ewers in 1801.[27] He supplied Wyllies in London with unspecified ware in 1805 and 1806.[28] His son's firm, T. Hollins junior and Co., sent blue-printed, black, green, yellow and green-edged ware and imaged jugs to Wyllies between 1809 and 1813.[29] A Scottish dealer, Walter Lamont of Paisley, owed them £174 in 1811, and they owed him £14 for Paisley shawls.[30]

S. Hollins dry-bodies are among the most interesting and innovative of all the manufacturers. The quality of the potting was always superb combining unique shapes and colours ranging from teal, green and blue (Colour Plate 47; Figs. 194, 195) to rich dark red (Colour Plate 48; Figs. 196–198) and a variety of drab colours (Colour Plate 46; Figs. 189–193, 201). Imaginative forms and colours were frequently further embellished with enamel or silver additions or a combination of enamel and silver decoration. The forms were usually tea and coffee wares and mugs and jugs. Along with the better-known coloured body wares Samuel Hollins produced some rare, but very fine, white stonewares (Fig. 200).

HOLLINS, THOMAS & JOHN:
Thomas & John Hollins, 1789–1809;
Thomas, John & Richard Hollins, 1809–20;
John & Richard Hollins, 1821–22;
Far Green, Hanley, Staffordshire.

The Hollins brothers operated a pottery at Far Green, Hanley, from c.1789 to 1822. They seem to be the sons of John Hollins senior (1736–1804) of Newcastle-under-Lyme, mercer, who was a member of the New Hall partnership, Hollins, Warburton and Co.[1] They should not be confused with their uncle, Samuel Hollins (q.v.),[2] who had a pottery at Vale Pleasant, Shelton, between c.1773 and 1806, nor with his son, Thomas Hollins junior, who

Fig. 193 *Bowl and mug, drab stoneware with silver line decoration and sprig reliefs. Marks; both S. HOLLINS, c. 1800, mug. 5 inches high. (Rakow collection.)*

Fig. 194 *Cream jug, teal blue stoneware with moulded body and blue enamel trim. Unmarked, Samuel Hollins, c. 1800, 3¾ inches high. (Blakey collection.)*

Fig. 195 **Jugs,** *left, slate-blue stoneware with silver, right, drab stoneware with silver triangular border and green ground, both with sprig decoration. Marks: left unmarked, 6¼ inches high; right Mark:* S. HOLLINS, *c. 1800-05. (Blakey collection.)*

Fig. 196 **Teapot,** *deep-red stoneware with silver decoration. The finial is a Venus and Cupid. Unmarked, Samuel Hollins, c. 1790, 6½ inches high. (Rakow collection.)*

Fig. 198(above) **Salt,** *deep-red stoneware with silver decoration. Unmarked, Samuel Hollins, c. 1800, 1⅝ inches high. (Fisk collection.)*

Fig. 197(left) **Creamer and jug,** *deep-red stoneware with silver decoration and sprig relief. Marks: both* S. HOLLINS, *c. 1800-05, jug. 6⅛ inches high. (collection of Olive Talbot.)*

Fig. 199 **Teapot and milk jug**, *dark red stoneware, engine-turned and sprig relief. Unmarked, possibly Samuel Hollins, c. 1800, teapot, 4¼ inches high, jug, 4½ inches high. (Rakow collection.)*

Fig. 200 **Jug**, *fine white stoneware with enamel border in copper-red, blue and green. Mark:* S. HOLLINS, *c. 1800, 7⅛ inches high. (Private collection, ex Nina Fletcher Little.)*

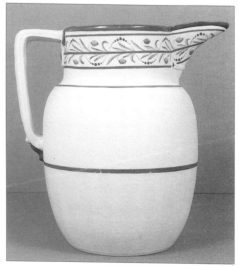

Fig. 201 *Teapot*, drab stoneware with fluted body and silver trim. Unmarked, attributed to Samuel Hollins, c. 1790-1800, 5⅛ inches high. (Liverpool Museum, Museums & Galleries on Merseyside, M 1155.)

Fig. 202 *Jug*, white stoneware with moulded body and applied reliefs scenes of the hunt. Upper third brown enamel painted. Mark: T. & J. HOLLINS, c. 1800-10, 7¼ inches high. (Rakow collection.)

continued the Shelton business until c.1814.

The firm of T. and J. Hollins is first recorded in 1789.[3] They joined a partnership to buy Dorset clay in 1791,[4] and, as Hollins and Sons, insured their works, stock, house and contents for £1,600 in 1792.[5] Their works was No. 74 on the 1802 map, north of the junction of Keelings Road and Turner Street in 1996 terms. John Hollins senior died in 1804,[6] and the house and potworks 'in possession of T. and J. Hollins' was offered for sale by auction in 1805, probably clearing up his estate.[7]

By 1809, a younger brother Richard had joined the firm, now T., J. and R. Hollins.[8] Rate and land tax records from

1821 show only J. and R. Hollins,[9] and the partnership between John and Richard Hollins was dissolved in 1822.[10] Zachariah Boyle, who had warehouses in Leeds and Bradford, took over the works in 1823.[11] He moved to Stoke in 1828.[12] John and Richard Hollins sold their utensils in 1830,[13] and by 1832 their land was laid out in streets and part of their buildings converted to houses.[14]

Marked *T & J HOLLINS* wares are very rare, suggesting that very few were marked. Creamware was certainly made by T. and J. Hollins, and probably basalt; and a handful of stonewares survive to document the factory production. White stoneware hunt jugs of very good quality were produced (Fig. 202) as well as fine white stoneware unglazed teawares (Colour Plate 49) with blue sprig relief of excellent quality. When looking at these pieces it is tantalising to consider the unmarked wares of similar distinction which must have been made.

ISLEWORTH:
Joseph Shore, 1757–66;
Joseph Shore, William Shore and
Benjamin Quarman, 1766–69;
Ann Shore and two remaining partners, 1769–77;
Edward Shore, 1777–94;
Ann Quarman, 1794–1813;
Edward Shore and Robert Balmain, 1813–16;
Joanna and Ann Goulding, 1816–29;
Joanna Goulding, 1829–31.

Although recent information on the Isleworth pottery has made it one of the most salient subjects in English pottery, knowledge of the pottery has long been a subject of ceramic lore, if only from speculated objects. In 1926 *The Burlington Magazine* published an account[1] illustrating some objects marked with the highly speculative signature of *S & G*, presumed to be the signature from the Shore/Goulding

Fig. 203 *Jug*, fine white stoneware with moulded body and rare Chinoiserie applied reliefs. The upper third of the jug is enamel painted in brown with a gilded rim. Mark: LAKIN & POOLE, c. 1795, 6½ inches high. (Private collection, ex Rakow.)

Fig. 204 *Teapot, sugar box and cream jug,* buff-coloured stoneware with blue enamel decoration and sprig relief. Unmarked, Lakin & Poole, c. 1795, 4¼ inches high. (Blakey collection.)

interests. This is not confirmed. For another aspect please consult Chapter IX for Schiller and Gerber.

The Isleworth pottery remained in one family almost exclusively from beginning to end. The rate books show that a Joseph Shore, reputedly from Worcester, was listed as the principal in the pottery from 1757 to 1768. His son William Shore, operating as William Shore and Company, was listed from 1769 to 1813, followed by the executors of William Shore from 1813 to 1817. A niece of the Shore's, Miss Goulding, was thereafter listed from 1817 to 1831. By August 1831 the pottery was empty.[2]

Excavations of the pottery site by Ray Howard and Norman Bayliss indicate that combed slipware may have been the major production, although the pottery produced a wide range of wares, from porcelain and creamware to red stoneware and lead-glazed redware and blackware. There is at least one example of basalt marked *Shore,* but no basalt shards or wasters have been excavated on the site to date.[3] In red stoneware the shapes excavated include teapots, jugs and bowls.

LAKIN:
Lakin & Poole, 1791–95;
Poole, Lakin & Shrigley, 1795– 96;
Hadderidge, Burslem;
Thomas Lakin, 1797–99; Bourne's Bank, Burslem;
Thomas Lakin & Co./ & Son, 1810–17,
Stoke- upon-Trent, all Staffordshire.

Thomas Lakin (1769–1821) was a practical potter and chemist. He was in several businesses, as a master potter, as an enameller, and as a pottery manager.[1]

Lakin was in partnership with Thomas Ellison Poole at a modest pottery in the Hadderidge, Burslem, from November 1791. They were joined by Thomas Shrigley in 1795, and Lakin left the partnership in 1796. Poole and Shrigley were bankrupt by the next year. Thomas Lakin was in another pottery at Bourne's Bank, Burslem by 1797, but he had left by the end of 1799, when the works was offered for sale by auction.

Thomas Lakin worked as a manager for John Davenport for some years until 1810, and had a partnership with Harveys of Longton as makers of litharge (lead monoxide, used in glass, enamels and glazes), which also ended in 1810.

Lakin then became a master potter again, first in a short-lived partnership at Stoke with John Arrowsmith of Prescot, dissolved in December 1810. He was in Wolfe's works at Stoke as Lakin and Co. or Lakin and Son from 1810 to 1817, as a manufacturer; and from 1815 to 1817 in premises in Stoke owned by Spode, probably as an enameller. Finally, Thomas Lakin went to the Leeds Pottery as a manager, and died there in 1821.

Thomas Lakin's 'receipts [recipes]' for bodies, glazes and colours were published after his death by his widow. Perhaps it was he who advertised for a partner in 1814:[2]

> A person who understands the manufacturing of blue, brown, purple and olive, printed, yellow and orange, mditto, painted in colours, blue and green edge, blue and brown line, Egyptian Black, cane, stone, China chalk, drab yellow and green ware, blue, brown, yellow and orange toping [*sic,* topping] colours; and enamel colours in all their stages, not only in receipt [recipe], but practical and has several hundred pounds to advance, would be glad to meet with a partner. Letters to AB. Mr Chesters, Newcastle-under-Lyme, Staffs.

His son, also Thomas, succeeded him at Leeds until his own death in 1824.

Although very few stonewares have been documented from the Lakin partnerships, the ones which survive distinguish themselves by their fine potting and unique shapes and decoration. Besides some few basalts, Lakin produced some caneware and white felspathic stoneware teawares and jugs. The teawares (Fig. 204) are the characteristic boat-shape seen in basalt usually with the addition of blue enamel around the neck or shoulder. The one documented white jug (Fig. 203) has beautifully executed and unusual chinoiserie figures sprigged onto the fine body of the jug. Lakin wares are not always impressed with the factory mark and are frequently identified by shape alone.

LEEDS POTTERY see HARTLEY, GREENS

LOCKETT:
Lockett & Shaw, 1796–1804;
George Lockett & Co., 1804–16;
Lockett, Robinson & Hulme, 1816–18;
Lockett & Hulme, 1818–26;
John Lockett & Son, 1826–35;
John and Thomas Lockett, 1835–55;
John Lockett, 1855–77;
John Lockett & Co., 1877–1960;
Longton, Staffordshire.

The Lockett family was in business in various partnerships in Longton, from 1796 to 1959, and the business name is still owned by Burgess and Leigh, Middleport, Burslem, Staffordshire.[1] The Longton Lockett firm should not be confused with Timothy and John Lockett of Burslem, potters, who were in business in 1785[2] and dissolved partnership in 1800.[3]

George Lockett, John Lockett I and George Shaw were in partnership from 1796 to 1804. Shaw left and the firm was George Lockett and Co. until John Lockett I died in 1816. John Robinson and John Hulme joined John Lockett II in a new partnership, Robinson leaving in 1818 and Hulme in 1826. The firm became John Lockett (II) and Son, until the death of John Lockett II in 1835.

The sons of John Lockett II continued the firm as John and Thomas Lockett from 1835 until the death of Thomas in 1854. John Lockett III continued the firm alone until 1877, when he died and left the business to his nephews, John W. Hancock and Robert Lockett Hancock. The Hancock family continued to own the firm until 1960, when the factory was closed and the business sold to Burgess and Leigh.[4]

Locketts had three factories in Longton. Their works at King Street, No. 133 on the 1802 map (Appendix 1), was their principal factory. They probably occupied it from 1796, and continued there until it was closed and demolished c.1959. (The address became Kingcross street in 1955.) A second small factory in Chancery Lane (Transport Lane from 1955) was occupied between 1822 and 1858. Locketts had a third works on Market Street from 1842 to 1876,[5] referred to as a china and lustreware manufactory in 1856. Locketts employed 205 workers in 1851.

The stonewares which exist documenting the Lockett manufacture are restricted to some large white wine casks, elaborately modelled (Colour Plates 50, 51), probably made during the John Lockett II period and impressed *J. LOCKETT*.

MASON:
Mason, Wolfe and Lucock 1796–1800,
Islington, Liverpool, Merseyside;
Mason and Wolfe, 1796–1800;
Miles Mason, 1800–07; Lane Delph, Staffordshire;
Mason and Son(s), 1807–17;
Park Street, Fenton, Staffordshire;

Mason and Sons, 1811–24;
G. and C. Mason and Faraday, 1824–30;
Mason and Faraday, 1830–44;
C.J. Mason, 1844–48;
Fenton Stone Works, Fenton, Staffordshire;
C.J. Mason, 1849–53, Longton, Staffordshire.

The history of the Mason businesses has been researched in detail, and published by several historians.[1]

Miles Mason (1752–1822) was a London 'china-man' in the late eighteenth century. In 1796 he entered into three partnerships: one in London, to sell pottery; one in Liverpool with Thomas Wolfe and John Lucock to make porcelain at the Islington China Manufactory; and a third at Lane Delph, Staffordshire, to make earthenware with George Wolfe. The Liverpool and Lane Delph partnerships ended in 1800, whilst the London one endured until 1802. Miles Mason continued in business at Lane Delph, making 'Mason's China' in 1804.

The works of 'Mason and Co.' was No. 111 on the 1802 map (Appendix 1), on the site of the later Victoria Works (now demolished), between China Street and Canning Street, on the south-west side of King Street, Fenton. Mason left this works by 1807 and it was then occupied by Samuel Ginders.

From 1807, Miles Mason was in a works owned by the Broad family, with his son, William, from 1809. This works was No. 109 on the 1802 map (Appendix 1), then occupied by Mason's former Liverpool partner, John Lucock. Miles Mason's second son, George Mason, was shown as the occupier of Broads' works in 1816 and 1817, when it was taken over by Felix Pratt. It became the Minerva Works, Park Street, Fenton, and is now occupied by the Coalport China division of the Wedgwood Group. Miles Mason later moved to Liverpool and lived there in 1816 and 1818, but died at Lane Delph in 1822.

Miles Mason had three sons. The eldest, William (1785–1856) was in partnership with his father between 1809 and 1811. He appears to have been in business alone from 1813 to 1818, but possibly his father remained a 'sleeping' partner, whilst in Liverpool (see below).

After his father's death in 1822, the trustees of Miles Mason deceased and William Mason, earthenware manufacturers, offered for private sale a freehold estate, trade and business of earthenware manufactory, stock, utensils etc., carried on many years by Miles Mason,[2] and suggesting that Miles Mason and his eldest son had continued in partnership. Premises owned by the executors of Miles Mason were void (empty) in 1825.

William Mason's creditors were called together in 1828 for a statement of affairs,[3] and a week later, the creditors of Miles Mason (*sic*), William Mason and William Hammersley, all late of Lane Delph, earthenware manufacturers, were invited to consider the general state of their affairs,[4] another suggestion of a continuing partnership. William Mason may have been in London between 1830 and 1835. He died at Fenton on 6 June 1856, aged 71.[5]

Fig. 205 **Teapot**, caneware with moulded body and sprig relief. Unmarked, attributed to Elijah Mayer, c. 1790-1800, 4½ inches high. (Burgin collection.)

Fig. 206 **Cream jug**, caneware with relief decoration. Unmarked, attributed to Elijah Mayer, c. 1790-1800, 5 inches high. (Royal Ontario Museum, 934.7.2.)

The second son, George Miles Mason (1789–1859) was in partnership with his younger brother, Charles, between 1813 and 1830. A works owned by Bagnall was shown in the rate list extracts as being occupied variously by Miles Mason, Miles Mason & Son, the executors of Miles Mason and William Mason from 1811 to 1825. On the 1802 map (Appendix 1), Bagnall's works was No. 108, between Park Street, Park Place, Challinor's Square and and King Street. William, George and Charles Mason are said to have bought a house, potworks and land from Sampson Bagnall in 1813, then occupied by Josiah Spode, taking possession in 1815. Possibly Masons already occupied the works, Spode's tenancy being only the land, later to become the site of the Fenton Stone Works, which did adjoin Bagnall's No. 108 works. This works stood on the north-east side of the junction of King Street and Victoria Road, Fenton.

The third son, Charles James Mason (1791–1856), was an extraordinary entrepreneur. He patented 'Ironstone China' in 1813, and conducted much of his sales by mammoth auctions, alienating both fellow manufacturers and local china dealers in the process. Samuel Bayliss Faraday joined the partnership of George and Charles Mason in 1824. George Mason left the business in 1830[6] and Faraday died in 1844.

In 1846, Charles Mason intimated that he was retiring,[7] but he was gazetted bankrupt in 1848. His moulds and engravings are thought to have been bought by Francis Morley of Shelton in 1848, the basis of the Mason's Ironstone business which continues today (1996) as part of the Wedgwood Group. Richard Daniel occupied Mason's Fenton Stone Works briefly from 1846 to 1847,[8] followed by Samuel Boyle in 1849. C.J. Mason also had a works at Terrace Buildings, Fenton, south-west of Old Tramway, Fenton, offered for sale in 1848[9] and no longer extant.

C.J. Mason resumed business in 1849 at Longton, and continued until 1853. He died in 1856.

Some glazed felspathic stoneware hunt jugs and bacchanalian jugs were produced during the C.J. Mason

tenure, from about 1813 and through the remainder of the life of the factory. These constituted a tiny portion of the factory's output, which is much better known for porcelain and ironstone china.

MAYER:
Elijah Mayer, *c.*1787–*c.*1800;
Elijah Mayer & Son, *c.*1800–*c.*1831;
Hanley, Staffordshire.

Elijah Mayer (1749–1813),[1] merchant, married his cousin Jane Mayer at Bagnall, near Stoke-on-Trent, 5 March 1773.[2] Their son, Joseph, was baptised in Amsterdam on 29

Fig. 207 **Punch pot**, caneware with sprig relief decoration and a widow finial. Unmarked, attributed to Elijah Mayer, c. 1790-1800, 8 inches high. (Liverpool Museum, Museums & Galleries on Merseyside, 804 M.)

Fig. 208 **Teapot**, *caneware of oval form with moulded body and scalloped gallery, widow finial. Mark: E. Mayer, c. 1810, 5½ inches high. (Rakow collection.)*

Fig. 209 **Teapot**, *caneware drum-shaped with moulded body, sprig relief and a widow finial. Mark: E. Mayer, c. 1800, 7¼ inches high. (Rakow collection.)*

Fig. 210 **Sugar bowl**, *caneware with sprig relief and blue line decoration. Mark: E. Mayer on base and inside cover, c. 1800, 4½ inches high. (Polikoff collection.)*

January 1775.[3] Elijah Mayer resided in Hanley from *c.*1781[4] and was named as an enameller when he insured property in 1783,[5] and in a Directory of 1784.[6] By 1787 his insurance policy included a potwork and wareroom in a quadrangle;[7] he supplied Wedgwood with earthenware in 1789;[8] and he was listed as a manufacturer in Directories from 1795 to 1802.[9] By 1800, accounts to Wedgwood are from Elijah Mayer *and Son*,[10] and from 1805 to 1834, Directories and other records show the firm's title as Elijah Mayer and Son,[11] although Elijah Mayer had died 9 January 1813, after 'a lingering illness'.[12] Presumably Joseph Mayer was his father's partner from *c.*1800, and continued to use the same style after his father's death in 1813. Extracts from rate records suggest that Joseph Mayer ceased production *c.*1831.[13]

Joseph Mayer never married, and when he died aged 85, on 28 June 1860, at his residence at High Street, Hanley,[14] he left an estate valued at £200,000. Without descendants, his ambiguous will was productive of several lawsuits.[15]

Elijah Mayer (1749–1813) should not be confused with Elijah Mayer (1778–1842) of Hanley and Shelton, variously commission agent, china manufacturer, ironmonger and potter; a factor with James Keeling in Shelton until their bankruptcy in 1821.[16] Likewise, Joseph Mayer (1775–1860) should not be confounded with Joseph Mayer (1803–1886) the Liverpool antiquarian.[17]

Elijah Mayer's factory is No. 72 on the 1802 map (see Appendix 1),[18] in Hanley, on the east side of 'the road to Congleton' (a road later called variously High Street, Upper High Street, Old Church Street and Town Road, but now Old Town Road). In 1996 the site was within J.H. Weatherby and Sons Ltd.'s Falcon Pottery. Joseph Mayer is said to have ceased business *c.*1833 and leased part of his works to his cousin William Ridgway.[19] The extracts from the rate records suggest that this occurred between 1830 and 1832.[20] Mayer's connection with Ridgway may explain a single 1841 Directory reference to 'Joseph Mayer and Co.'.[21] After his death in 1860, Joseph Mayer's '5 hovel [oven]' works was bought by Herbert Keeling of Longton in 1864.[22]

Fig. 211 **Teapot and bulb pot and stand,** *caneware with vertical striped engine turning and blue enamel line painting; sprig relief on bulb pot. Unmarked, attributed to Elijah Mayer, c. 1800, bulb pot 5¼ inches high. (City Museum and Art Gallery, Stoke-on-Trent, 1956, 1958.)*

Potteries historian Simeon Shaw stated that Elijah Mayer was agent in Holland for Ephraim Chatterley (1745–1811).[23] A letter of 28 July 1773 has been quoted, addressed to him as 'Pot Coopman, De Haarlemerdyke, Amsterdam', written by Sampson Bagnall of Hanley, referring to a shipment of cream colour and black ware.[24] A 1776 letter in the Wedgwood papers is from E. Mayer in Amsterdam to William Taylor at The Hill, Burslem, ordering many crates of white (salt-glazed) ware, to be sent to him via Gainsborough and Hull.[25] An 1806 letter from Leipzig to Wedgwood includes payment of an account from Elijah Mayer and Son,[26] suggesting that the Continental connections had been maintained.

Elijah Mayer was a member of the Potters Clay Company in 1797,[27] and Elijah Mayer and Son supplied flint and building bricks to Wedgwood and Byerley in 1806.[28] Joseph Mayer is said to have bought the Church Works opposite in 1828 or later, and leased it to William Ridgway and Co.[29] After Joseph Mayer's death, the family fortune (£6.6 million in 1991 figures) was said to have been founded by his father, Elijah Mayer, and continued and improved by Joseph through other mercantile pursuits.[30] Joseph was said to be reticent and parsimonious yet secretly benevolent.

Joseph Mayer employed Leonard James Abington (1785–1867), the well-known designer and modeller, from c.1822 to 1831, when Abington went into business with William Ridgway.[31] Abington was said to have designed exclusively for the Continental market in his early years.

Joseph Mayer had retained a warehouse when he leased

Fig. 212 **Mugs,** *caneware, engine-turned with enamel line painting. Marks: left, Davenport over an anchor, 3½ inches high, middle, E. Mayer, right, unmarked. All c. 1800-10. (Burgin collection.)*

Fig. 213 *Teapot*, caneware with moulded body and sprig relief. Mark: E. Mayer, c. 1805, 4 inches high. (Rakow collection.)

Fig. 214 *Cream jug,* caneware with moulded decoration. Mark: E. Mayer, c. 1805, 3¾ inches high. (Rakow collection.)

his works to William Ridgway, and on his death it was found to contain a tremendous stock of antique black, drab, lustre, enamelled and other wares, cream colour table and tea wares for the Continental markets, potters' materials, colours, fixtures and sundries.[32] In 1868, some of Abington's early specimens were said to have been recently brought to light, no doubt when Mayer's warehouse was cleared.

The manufacture of 'Drab China' was attributed to Elijah Mayer and Son in Directories of 1828–29 and 1830–31,[33] and the auction notice for 17 December 1860 included 'a quantity of glazed drab Tea Ware, jugs, Mugs &c.', together with 'Drab Stone dessert ware, vases, candle sticks, Toilets, Teapots, Boxes and Creams, Lamp Pillars etc'.[34] A later auction included 'Blocks and moulds of the Antique ware, with Bas-relievo moulds, [and] a large lot of Drab Stone Ware in the biscuit state'.[35]

It is interesting that the surviving marked *E. Mayer* pieces do not seem to include the drab stoneware listed in the 1828–31 Directories and in the 1860 auction notice. The principal marked wares, in addition to a great deal of basalt, are canewares of superb quality and some few examples of white stoneware (Fig. 216, see also Fig. 357, page 205).

The caneware output consisted mostly of tewares of great variety following styles of the period (Figs. 205–214). Judging from the shapes caneware was produced throughout the factory history as both eighteenth and early nineteenth century forms survive. Elijah Mayer, along with Davenport and Wedgwood, was one of the few manufacturers to include honeypots in the repertoire (Fig. 215). Sprig mouldings frequently included scenes from Aesop's 'Fables' as well as Lady Templetown scenes from 'Domestic Employment'.

Fig. 215 *Honey pot and stand*, caneware in the form of a beehive. Mark: E. Mayer, c. 1810, 3½ inches high. (Burgin collection.)

Fig. 216 *Jug*, white stoneware with sprig relief and brown enamel upper third. Mark: E. Mayer, c. 1800, 4½ inches high. (City Museum and Art Gallery, Stoke-on-Trent.)

MINTON;

Mintons (various titles, always including Minton)
*c.*1796–present, Stoke-upon-Trent, Staffordshire.

The successive Minton businesses have been extensively researched, and only a summary is given here.[1] Thomas Minton (1765–1836) was born in Shrewsbury and apprenticed as an engraver at Caughley, following that trade there, in London, and at Stoke-upon-Trent. In 1793 he bought land in Stoke, and built a pottery works. Joseph Poulson, a skilled potter, also bought land in Stoke, in 1792, and built a pottery works nearly opposite that of Minton. Minton and Poulson had become partners by 1796, producing earthenware in Minton's works and, from 1797, porcelain in Poulson's works. A Liverpool merchant, William Pownall, was a third partner.

Joseph Poulson died in 1808, but his executors leased his 'China Works' to Minton until *c.*1817.[2] (From 1823, these works were occupied by Henry Daniel.) Thomas Minton is said to have replaced Poulson's skills by employing John Turner II q.v. (bankrupt in 1806), but Turner was back in a business of his own by 1814. By then Thomas Minton's sons Thomas Webb (1791–1870) and Herbert (1793–1858) were in their early twenties and probably capable of replacing Turner. Thomas Minton took both sons into partnership in 1817. Thomas Webb Minton went into the church and left the partnership in 1823,[3] his father and Herbert Minton continuing the firm until Thomas Minton's death in 1836.

When Thomas Minton died in 1836, he left most of the business to his older son, Thomas Webb Minton, who redressed the unfairness of his father's will by surrendering £23,000, enabling Herbert Minton to continue. From 1836 to 1841, John Boyle was his partner. Herbert Minton's nephew, Michael Daintry Hollins, became a partner in 1845, and Colin Minton Campbell, another nephew, also became a partner in 1849.

Under Herbert Minton's dynamic leadership, the firm expanded greatly from making earthenware, stoneware and china, into the manufacture of tiles, hard porcelain, parian and majolica, winning many prizes at international exhibitions and becoming a world leader in ceramic production. Herbert Minton died in 1858 and Campbell took over running the firm.

French ceramicists and artists were recruited, and the firm had its heyday from the 1840s to the 1880s, becoming a limited company in 1883. Minton continued as an independent concern until 1968, when it became part of the Royal Doulton group.

The works buildings on Minton's original 1793 site, No. 104 on the 1802 map (Appendix 1), were demolished in the 1950s and the site is now occupied by a large office block, London House. Herbert Minton built a new china works on the opposite side of London Road in 1823, and this site still holds some older factory buildings, together with a 1950s building, including Minton House, Royal Doulton's headquarters. Minton china is now produced elsewhere in the group, but some specialised decorating processes continue on Thomas and Herbert Minton's china works site.

Mintons produced very little in the way of dry-bodied stonewares in the period we are considering. Although the Minton inventories of 1817 include stoneware mugs and jugs in brown (Fig. 358, page 205), plain, coloured or 'china figured'; examples from this period are rare and difficult to identify. By 1824 the production had increased to include garden seats and 'filters',[4] but the principal stoneware forms were produced after 1830 when hunt jugs and mugs and related drinking-theme Bacchanalian jugs were made. Examples of these wares are illustrated in accounts of the pottery by Geoffrey Godden and by Joan Jones (cf., note 1).

MIST:

James Mist, 1809–1815, 82 Fleet Street, London.

James Underhill Mist became the partner of Andrew Abbott on 25 March 1806,[1] in a pottery and glass merchants' business at 82 Fleet Street, London. They dissolved partnership on 25 March 1809[2] and James Mist continued in business alone until he was bankrupt in April 1815.[3] That was the end of a series of businesses which began with John Turner (q.v.) at 10 Bennetts Hill in 1768, moving to Old Fish Street in 1774; and continued through Turner and Abbott (*c.*1780–1788), first at Old Fish Street and then at 81 Fleet Street from 1782. The firm became Turner, Abbott and Newbury at 82 Fleet Street between 1788 and 1792, when Turners withdrew, Abbott and Newbury 1792–1802, then Andrew Abbott alone until Mist joined him in 1806.[4]

Recent scholarship has shed a little light on the origins of James Underhill Mist. He was baptised at St Martin-in-the-Fields, London, on 20 May 1783, son of James and Mary Mist.[5] So much is fact; beyond that, James Mist, who

Fig. 217 **Flower pot and stand**, *white stoneware with relief decoration on a dark brown ground: Jupiter and the eagle, Sportive love, Britannia and Fame with a tablet inscribed Howe and Nelson. Mark: J. MIST LONDON, c. 1810-18, pot 3¼ inches high. (Victoria & Albert Museum, Schreiber collection, 564.)*

Fig. 218 **Vases,** *white stoneware with chocolate-brown slip and white relief sprigs of* Britannia and Fame with a tablet of inscribed Howe and Nelson. *All unmarked, possible attribution to manufacturer who supplied James Mist in London, c. 1810, 4 inches high. (Blakey collection.)*

could have been his father, was also baptised at St Martin's on 14 July 1746; one of the six children of Thomas and Mary Mist, who were all baptised at St Martin's between 1744 and 1757.[6] Add to that the fact that a Thomas Mist of London sold brown ware to the 4th Duke of Gordon in 1764,[7] and there begins to appear a possibility that James Underhill Mist was a member of a family of London pottery suppliers. Mist brought £4,159 into the partnership with Abbott in 1806–07,[8] say £137,000 in present-day terms, no mean sum for a young man, probably aged only twenty-three. The partnership ended in 1809 because of 'differences and disputes' between the sixty-six year old Abbott and Mist, aged about twenty-six.[9]

Mist would then have to pay to Abbott his share of the business, £4,867, and commence paying £108 a year rent to Abbott for his lease of the premises.[10] As early as 1812, Minton accepted five shillings in the pound from Mist in settlement of a debt[11] and he was gazetted bankrupt on 29 April 1815.[12] His entire trading period between 1806 and 1815 was in the difficult times of the Napoleonic Wars, added to by the American war of 1812–15. This must have contributed to Mist's failure, ironically only weeks before the Battle of Waterloo signalled the start of an economic boom. Trading indices for 1810 to 1816 show the biggest slump since the catastrophic fall of 1793–1798.[13] Abbott's warehouse at 82 Fleet Street was destroyed by fire in 1817,[14] but re-built and leased by Davenports (q.v.) from 1818 to 1879.[15]

Fig. 219 **Vases,** *white stoneware with chocolate-brown slip and relief sprig including inscriptions (left)* 'Trafalgar, Howe [and] Nelson' *and (right)* 'Patriots Howe [and] Nelson'. *Left unmarked, attributed to supplier to James Mist, 7½ inches high; right marked* J. MIST LONDON, *c. 1810, 5½ inches high. (Blakey collection.)*

Fig. 220 *Vase and mug,* white stoneware with chocolate-brown slip and white relief sprigs. Marks: both J. MIST 82, FLEET STREET, LONDON, c. 1810, 6¼ and 3¼ inches high. (Polikoff collection.)

Account books now in Dorset Record Office list twelve pottery manufacturers with whom Abbott and Mist were trading in 1806, and it is likely that these businesses continued to supply Mist. They are: W. and T. Bathwell; R. Billington and Sons; Jos. Boon; Bourne, Baker and Co.; J. Davenport; Hicks and Meigh; Keeling, Toft and Co.; Miles Mason (and Son); Elijah Mayer jun.; Minton, Poulson and Co.; John Rose and Co.; and David Wilson.[16] That Mist-marked wares were made by other manufacturers has been understood for some time. However, they do seem to be confined to a narrow scope of ceramic production, that is,

fine white stoneware, usually with brown slip, and to utilitarian mortar wares (Fig. 222). Shapes are usually confined to tea wares, flower containers and inkwells in the white stoneware although many basalts are also found with the Mist mark.

Mist marked white stonewares are often found with the *Britannia* and *Fame* symbols commemorating the Howe and Nelson victory (Figs. 217–219) as well as other commemorative symbols of the Battle of Trafalgar (Fig. 219). One teapot in the Liverpool Museum marked *MIST LONDON* (Fig. 221) matches shards excavated at the

Fig. 221 *Teapot,* white felspathic stoneware with chocolate-brown panel and white sprigs. Shards from the Chetham and Woolley site match this teapot indicating that Chetham and Woolley among other manufacturers were supplying James Mist. Mark: J. MIST LONDON, probably manufactured by Chetham and Woolley, c. 1810, 5¼ inches high. (Liverpool Museum, Museums & Galleries on Merseyside, 18.11.25.3.)

Fig. 222 *Three mortars, mortar ware. Marks: left,* TURNER, *3½ inches high, middle,* Spode, *right* MIST 82, FLEET STREET, LONDON 2, *all early 19th c. (Fisk collection.)*

Chetham & Woolley site (Fig. 138), adding Chetham & Woolley's name to the list of manufacturers linked with the Mist-marked ceramics.

English collectors have given the name of 'Spur-handled Group' to jugs and mugs with the distinctive handle shown on the mug in figure 220 (right), the name derived from the pronounced inward spur on the handle. Bowls and other forms appear to be related, but the handle is definitive. The body is often creamy stoneware, orange-translucent under a strong light, unglazed outside, and usually decorated with bands of blue or brown glazed slip and a variety of applied ornamental sprigs in the same unglazed creamy body. These jugs and mugs are frequently seen, but no piece with a maker's mark has been reported. Other spur-handled pieces marked 'Mist' (a mustard pot[17] and a jug[18]) are known, but these 'marked' pieces of spur-handled ware do not help to identify the actual maker.

Many guesses have been made about the manufacturer of these high quality wares, including Spode,[19] Turner,[20] Chetham,[21] Chetham and Woolley,[22] Woolley, Barnes, Lockett,[23] Herculaneum[24] and Newbigging in Scotland.[25] With nine manufacturers already suggested in connection with these spur-handled pieces, positive evidence is still awaited to identify the real maker.

MYATT:

Richard Myatt *c.*1781–1796; **Joseph Myatt** 1796–*c.*1802;
Foley works, Fenton, Tollgate works and Lower
Market Place works, Longton;
Benjamin and Joseph Myatt, 1818–1827,
High Street, Longton;
John Myatt, 1822;
Church Street, Longton, all Staffordshire.

Richard Myatt (*c.*1739–1796)[1] owned three potworks: one at Foley, Fenton; one near the Tollgate and one at the Lower Market Place, both these at Lane End (Longton).[2] He was in business from before 1781[3] until his death in 1796, and was succeeded by his eldest son, Joseph. Joseph Myatt was out of business by 1802.[4] Forrester and Mayer rented the Lower Market Place Works in 1802,[5] and William Turner (q.v.) occupied the Foley works from 1806 to 1813.[6]

The Foley works was No. 117 on the 1802 map (Appendix 1), a site now occupied by Hadida Fine Bone China Ltd., on the south side of King Street, Fenton. The Lower Market Place works (No. 119 in 1802) was approximately on the site of Longton railway station. The 'tollgate' was in King Street, nearby, but the Tollgate works site has not been identified.

Members of the Myatt family were again in business as potters in Longton. Benjamin, Joseph, William, and James Myatt, trading as Benjamin and Joseph Myatt made china and earthenware in High Street from 1822 to 1827.[7] John Myatt left that partnership in 1818 and was recorded in business alone in Church Street in 1822, making earthenware.[8]

The Myatts produced both basalt and red stonewares, but few appear to have been marked. Limited to tea wares, the shape of the stonewares suggest they were made in the 1780s and 1790s. The few known red stoneware examples (Fig. 223) are glazed, engine-turned cylindrical teapots.

NEALE:

Humphrey Palmer, 1750s–78;
James Neale & Co., 1778- 82;
Neale & Wilson, 1783–92;
Robert Wilson, 1792–1801; **David Wilson**, 1801–09;
David Wilson & Sons, *c.*1809–14;
David Wilson & Son, 1814–17;
Assignees of David Wilson & Sons, 1817–18;
Church Works, Hanley, Staffordshire.

There is no firm evidence to indicate when Humphrey Palmer started business as a potter at the Church Works, Hanley.[1] A salvage excavation on this site in 1985 revealed wares dating from as early as 1755-60.[2] Humphrey Palmer married Mrs Ann Adams at Burslem in 1750,[3] and it is said that he acquired the Church Works site from her family,[4] so it might be assumed that he was a master potter in this area from around the mid-century. Palmer's second wife, Mary,

Fig. 223 *Teapot, red stoneware with engine-turned decoration. Mark:* MYATT, *probably Richard Myatt, Foley, Fenton, c. 1780-96, 4⅛ inches high. (Royal Ontario Museum, 983.236.25.1 & 2.)*

Fig. 224 *Part tea set*, blue jasper with white relief and moulded body. This is part of a complete tea set, other pieces of this pattern are in the City Museum, Stoke-on-Trent, and in Kansas City at the Nelson-Atkins Museum. All marked (except tea cups) NEALE & Co., c. 1785-90, teapot 4⅛ inches high. (Rakow collection.)

whom he married in 1751, was a daughter of Thomas Heath of Fenton.[5] Mary's sister, Hannah, married James Neale of Wapping, London, merchant, at Stoke-upon-Trent church 31 August 1762.[6] Neale dealt in pottery, and his acquaintance with Palmer must date from this period.

Neale was certainly involved with Palmer in 1770 when Wedgwood accused them of infringing his patent for encaustic painting.[7] By 1778, Neale and Palmer were equal partners. Wedgwood wrote on 14 March 1778 that Palmer was in distress and that 'Mr Neale is come down to settle the affairs of the latter [Mr Palmer] who it is said owes £10,000 – £5,000 of which sum Mr Neale is in for'.[8]

From 1781 to 1783, the business at the Church Works was referred to as 'James Neale & Co.',[9] but from 1783 onward to 1792, the partnership was Neale and Wilson.[10] When David Wilson the elder died in 1816, it was said that he had succeeded his brother Robert (who died in 1801) and together they had manufactured on the premises near fifty years,[11] taking Robert Wilson's involvement back to c.1766. Robert Wilson's date of birth is not known, but his brother David was born c.1758, and Robert must have been quite a young man in 1766. It is tempting to associate these Wilsons with Joseph Wilson of Limehouse, who is thought to have moved to Newcastle-under-Lyme in c.1747[12] and made porcelain there,[13] but no evidence has been found for a relationship.

Fig. 225 *Coffee cup and saucer*, solid blue jasper with white rim and relief sprigs. Unmarked, attributed to Neale & Co., c. 1785-90, cup 2⅞ inches high. (Burgin collection.)

Fig. 226 *Teapot*, solid blue jasper with applied relief figures of Cupid and Psyche. *Mark:* NEALE & Co., c.1785-90, 6 inches high. (City Museum and Art Gallery, Stoke-on-Trent.)

Fig. 227 *Figures of Apollo and Venus, white jasper on blue jasper pedestals. Mark: Apollo unmarked, Venus, NEALE & Co., c. 1785-90, 7 inches high. (National Museum of American History, Smithsonian Institution, Washington, D.C., 65.99A,B.)*

Fig. 228 *Pair of cameos, blue jasper figures of* Andromache and Antonia. *Mark: both NEALE & C0., c. 1785, 1⅛ inches high. (Rakow collection.)*

Fig. 229 *Candlestick vase, blue jasper with applied relief depicting* Sportive Love. *Mark: NEALE & Co., c. 1780-90, 9½ inches high. (City Museum, and Art Gallery, Stoke-on-Trent.)*

Robert Wilson was Neale's partner at Church Works, Hanley from 1783 until their partnership was dissolved on 24 April 1792.[14] From then onward, Robert Wilson was the sole proprietor until his death on 19 January 1801.[15] His brother, David Wilson the elder, succeeded him, and was also in sole charge until about 1809.[16]

By then, David Wilson's sons were old enough to become partners in David Wilson and *Sons*: John (Jack) born c.1784[17] and James born 1788.[18] (Robert, the eldest son, died in 1807; and another son, David Wilson the younger, born 1790,[19] seems to have not been in the family business. He died 15 January 1817.)[20] James Wilson died in 1814,[21] leaving only David Wilson the elder and John Wilson in the business, and the firm became David Wilson and *Son*.[22]

John (Jack) Wilson was a wild character, of whom his father despaired. John's eldest brother Robert and his child were accidentally killed in 1807, when John was setting off three cannon in Robert's garden.[23] On another matter, Jack fled when a warrant was issued for him in 1815,[24] and in 1816 he was said to have 'flogged his wife down the street'.[25]

In January 1816 David Wilson the elder wrote to Josiah Wedgwood II, complaining of John's behaviour, and said he was determined to dissolve his partnership with him 'and all my family will be ruined'.[26] A month later, David Wilson

Fig. 231 **Bulbous root vase**, *blue jasper with white relief decoration on four panels of* Art, Industry, Commerce *and the* Anglo-French Commercial Treaty *of 1786. Unmarked (other examples marked Neale & Co exist in the Victoria and Albert Museum and in a former collection of a Neale descendant), c. 1786-7, 5¼ inches high. (Laver collection.)*

Fig. 230 **Vase**, *blue jasper with white relief of* Andromache *and dolphin handles*. *Mark:* NEALE & Co., *c. 1785-90, 8¼ inches high. (National Museum of American History, Smithsonian Institution, Washington, D. C., gift of Dr Lloyd E. Hawes, 65.100.)*

the elder gave notice that workmen hired for next Martinmas (November 1816) would be hired to John Wilson only, as he intended to end the partnership on 11 November 1816.[27] However, David Wilson the elder died on 21 June 1816,[28] and John Wilson immediately sought another partner, apparently without success.[29]

By July 1817, John Wilson, surviving partner of David Wilson, was bankrupt,[30] and the firm was run on behalf of the assignees by John Hatherley, David Wilson's son-in-law.[31] During 1817-18, the stock of earthenware, David Wilson's extensive real estate (including the potworks, John Wilson's house, and Botteslow Mill, occupied by John Hatherley), and John Wilson's furniture were all offered for sale by auction.[32]

All the creditors of David Wilson and John Wilson were paid in full in 1819, probably out of the proceeds of David Wilson's real estate.[33] John Wilson died on 8 April 1835, aged 51, 'formerly an extensive manufacturer'.[34]

Palmer, Neale and Wilsons were successively in the Church Works, Town Road, Hanley, north of St John's

Fig. 232 **Bulbous root pot**, *blue jasper with white relief of theatrical figures. Unmarked, attributed to Neale & Co., c. 1785-90, 7¼ inches high. (Victoria and Albert Museum Crown copyright, No. 93-1870.)*

Fig. 234 **Bulb pot**, *blue jasper with basket weave-moulded base and white sprig relief. No mark, attributed to Neale & Co., c. 1785-90, 4⅞ inches high. (Former collection descendant.)*

Fig. 233 **Bulbous root pot**, *drab-coloured jasper with white reliefs. Mark: NEALE & Co., c. 1790, 6½ inches high. (Former collection descendant, sold at Phillips, London, March, 1984.)*

Church, No. 71 on the 1802 map (Appendix 1). Later occupants included Jacob Phillips, Phillips & Bagster, Bagster, Ridgway, Powell & Bishop and Bishop & Stonier.[35] The works was demolished between 1948 and 1960, and the site now lies under Quadrant Road.

James Neale always maintained his glass and china business in St Paul's Church Yard, London, in partnership with Maidment and Bailey 1783-88; with Bailey alone from 1789 to 1808; and then as Neale, Bailey and Neale from 1809 when Neale's son Benjamin joined the firm. James Neale died in 1814, and Benjamin Neale died in 1816.[36] Thomas Bailey, a native of Newcastle-under-Lyme, then became sole proprietor and continued the business as Neale and Bailey until his own death in 1828.[37] Directories suggest that the firm continued until 1834.[38]

David Wilson the younger (1790–1817), does not appear to have been a partner in the family business. Joseph Leigh and William Breeze were in partnership as earthenware manufacturers in John Glass's smaller works, Hanley, from c.1805 to 1808.[39] David Wilson the younger took Leigh's place until 1811, in the same works.[40] He was then replaced

Fig. 235 **Teapot** (left), *caneware with moulded body, blue, green and white enamel painting. Mark: SPODE, C. 1790, 5¼ inches high. And (right)* **teapot** *identically moulded caneware with blue enamel painting and gilding. Mark: NEALE & Co., c. 1790, 6 inches high. (Norwich Castle Museum, ex Philip Miller.)*

Fig. 236 **Sugar boxes and covers**, *caneware moulded and painted in turquoise (left) and in blue, carmine and gilded (right). Marks: both* NEALE & Co., *(left incised N31, right incised N60, N67), 4¼ inches high. (Burgin collection.)*

by his father, David Wilson the elder, and the partnership became Breeze and Wilson.

Breeze and Wilson continued making earthenware in Glass's works until c.1814;[41] and also manufactured pottery in a works owned by Chatterleys, from 1811 to 1817.[42] William Breeze, surviving partner of David Wilson the elder in this business, was bankrupt in 1817.[43] His creditors were paid in full in 1819,[44] and he went on to a short-lived china making business in Shelton, failing again in 1820.[45] William Breeze died in 1828, aged 64.[46]

David Wilson the elder advertised a glass, china and earthenware shop for sale in an unspecified 'large midland town' in 1816.[47] His oldest daughter, Charlotte, married Elijah Cotton in 1805,[48] who became a glass and china merchant in Edinburgh. Cotton was bankrupt in 1810, and

in 1813-14, his firm was known as Cotton and Wilson, Picardy Place, Edinburgh, suggesting that David Wilson had invested in his son-in-law's business.[49] Neither of the Hanley David Wilsons were involved in David Wilson & Co., potters, West Pans. They were both dead by 1817, whilst David Wilson of West Pans was still alive in 1824.[50]

The variety and quality of Neale stoneware production was considerable. The firm made fine white stoneware, manufacturing small busts (Figs. 237, 238) to rival anything produced by Wedgwood or Enoch Wood. Other stoneware included copies of the Barberini vase in both the form produced by Wedgwood, an example of which is in the Victoria and Albert Museum and another version (Fig. 239) which seems to have as its source an engraving by Piranesi.

Fig. 237 **Small busts of Louis XVI and Necker**, *unglazed buff-coloured stoneware. Mark on bust of Necker:* NEALE & Co., *c. 1790, 7⅞ inches high (Louis XVI). (Grigsby collection.)*

Fig. 238 **Small bust of Lafayette**, *unglazed buff-coloured stoneware. Mark:* NEALE & Co., *c. 1790, 8¼ inches high. (Colonial Williamsburg.)*

161

Fig. 239 **Vase**, white stoneware version of the Barberini or Portland vase. Although it might be thought of as a copy of Wedgwood's famous vase, the Neale versions are closer to a vase depicted in the Piranesi print Le Antichita Romane than to the Wedgwood Portland. Mark: NEALE & Co., c. 1792, 11½ inches high. (Photograph courtesy Christie's, New York.)

Fig. 240 **Jug**, caneware with moulded body and enamel painting in blue, Sheffield plate cover. Mark: NEALE & Co., c. 1790, 7⅞ inches high (without cover). (Private collection.)

Fig. 241 **Mugs and jug**, white smear-glazed stoneware, moulded and relief decoration and enamel painting. Marks: all NEALE & Co., c. 1800-10, left mug 3⅞ inches, middle mug 6 inches and jug 12 inches high. (Former collection of descendant.)

Fig. 242 **Teapot**, *deep red stoneware in commode shape with relief decoration. Mark: NEALE & Co., 4¼ inches high. (Norwich Castle museum, ex Philip Miller collection.)*

Fig. 243 **Teapot**, *caneware, engine-turned and with sprig relief decoration of Aesop's fables. Unmarked, possibly Robert and David Wilson, c. 1800, 6¼ inches high. (Royal Ontario Museum, 084.18.20.1 & 2.)*

Caneware was among the finest of the Neale dry bodies. Although little seems to have been made, a trophy cup (Colour Plates 54, 55), 'Success to the Royal British Bowmen' stands, in the opinion of the authors, as the single finest example of caneware produced by any manufacturer.

Jasper produced by the factory was of excellent quality, the body being dense and buttery smooth, imparting an almost grey-blue hue. The forms were varied and included tewares, as well as flower containers, vases and figures. Neale produced some few cameos (Fig. 228) and medallions which were not as successful as those made by Wedgwood and others. There is a little evidence that Humphrey Palmer was producing jasper before his bankruptcy in 1778. There is a jasper seal in the Victoria &

Albert Museum, marked *H. PALMER* (acc.#245-1901). No other pieces are known in jasper. Neither the quantity nor variety of Neale jasper was large. Only a few teapot forms have been identified (Figs. 224, 226) and tea cups are frequently distinguished by their heart-shaped handles.

Both jasper and felspathic stonewares owe debts to larger manufacturers for certain designs, particularly Spode (Fig. 235) and Wedgwood (Figs. 231, 239). However, the quality of these replacements (or copies) is typically and superbly Neale.

Like Hollins, Neale dipped into the production of fine red stoneware and the existing few pieces (Fig. 242) are fine examples of the possibilities presented by an archaic body in currently popular forms. Judging from the few survivors they

Fig. 244 **Teapot and sugar box**, *red-bodied stoneware with brown slip ground of a matt finish, white sprigs. Marks: both WILSON, c. 1800-10. (Rakow collection.)*

Fig. 245 *Jugs,* white stoneware with drab-brown slip (left) and chocolate-brown slip (right), both with fanciful Cupid *sprig decoration. Marks: both* WILSON, *C. 1800-17, 5¼ inches high (left). (Rakow collection.)*
Figs 246 *Covered jug,* red stoneware with chocolate-brown slip and white fanciful Cupid *relief decoration. Mark:* WILSON, *c. 1805-17, 7¼ inches high. (Polikoff collection.)*

Fig. 247 *Pot-pourri basket,* white stoneware with chocolate-brown slip and white sprig relief. Mark: WILSON, *c. 1805-17. (Newark Museum, New Jersey.)*
Fig. 248 *Vase and mug,* red stoneware with drab-brown slip, vase with green enamel handles and mug with white floral relief. Marks: both WILSON, *c. 1800-17, vase, 6¼ inches high. (Blake collection.)*

were not successful with the purchasing public.

The Wilson output was substantially less imaginative and varied, specialising in brown dipped jugs and teawares (Figs. 245-247). No jaspers have been associated with the Wilson tenure; however, there is one possible caneware teapot (Fig. 243) which is similar to a basalt example marked *WILSON,* suggesting the possibility of a small caneware business. Fine red stoneware was also made in limited quantities. Although the quality of the wares was generally maintained, it was not as consistently so as by the predecessor ownership of James Neale.

PRATT

The Pratt family were pottery manufacturers in the Fenton area from *c.*1781 to *c.*1916, on several sites and in various partnerships and companies. A fuller account of their activities has been published by John and Griselda Lewis.[1]

They operated factories in two areas of Fenton: at Lane Delph, also called Fenton Vivian, on the Longton side of Fenton and at Fenton Culvert, near to Stoke-upon-Trent. Their activities are most easily explained under three headings: the founder, William Pratt and his widow Ellen, his second son Felix and his third son John. William Pratt's will provided that half of his potworks should be sold when his youngest child became twenty-one, c.1812.[2] Ellen Pratt's will, effective in 1815, called for her half to be shared amongst all her children. These testamentary provisions, and the enterprise of Felix and John Pratt, may explain some of the complications described below.[3]

William Pratt c.1781-1799,
Ellen Pratt 1799-c.1806;
Lane Delph, Fenton, Staffordshire.

William Pratt (1753-1799) was a master potter at Lane Delph from at least 1781[4] until his death in 1799.[5] His works was on a site on the north of King Street, bounded by Vivian Road, Wallis Street, St Matthew Street and Fenpark Road, No. 110 on the 1802 map (Appendix 1).[6] His widow, Ellen Pratt (1760-1815) continued the business until c.1806.[7] She died 3 January 1815.[8]

Felix Pratt & William Coomer, c.1806-1809;
Felix Pratt, 1809-1816; Pratt & Gardner, 1810;
Pratt, Weston & Co., 1817-1821;
Pratt, Hassall & Gerrard, 1821-c.1834;
all at sites in Lane Delph;
Felix Pratt, 1816-1817;
Felix & Richard Pratt, 1818-c.1840;
F. & R. Pratt & Co., c.1840-c.1916,
Fenton Potteries, Fenton; part of Cauldon Potteries, c.1916-1962, Shelton, all Staffordshire.

Felix Pratt (1780-1859),[9] second son of William and Ellen Pratt, succeeded his mother in the works at Lane Delph, in partnership with William Coomer until 1809.[10] Felix Pratt continued alone in that factory until 1816.[11] In 1813, 1814 and 1815, there were attempts to sell a house and potworks at Lane Delph, occupied by Felix Pratt.[12] In March 1816, Felix Pratt's potworks at Lane Delph was offered to be let, on a 'long unexpired lease', applications to be made to Felix Pratt.[13] This suggests that Felix Pratt had the works on a long lease, but now wished to leave.

Felix Pratt in fact took over a factory at Fenton Culvert in 1816.[14] It was on the north side of City Road, No. 105 on the 1802 map (Appendix 1),[15] then occupied by Harrison and Hyatt. They left in 1806,[16] and Josiah Byerley, son of Wedgwood's partner, Thomas Byerley, moved in. He failed in 1810,[17] and was followed by Charles Bourne, until 1816.[18] By 1818, Felix Pratt had taken a younger brother, Richard into partnership.[19] In 1841 the business was Felix and Richard Pratt and Co.,[20] and it continued into the twentieth century, vacating the Fenton Potteries site c.1916[21] when the firm became part of Cauldon Potteries, Shelton, until that firm closed in 1962.[22] The Fenton Potteries factory, later called the Rialto Works, had been demolished by 1934 and replaced by the Workshops for the Blind.[23]

Reverting to the early nineteenth century, Felix Pratt was also in a partnership with John Gardner at Lane Delph as enamellers of china and earthenware, which ended in 1810.[24] Felix Pratt was in yet another business at Lane

Delph, from 1817 to c.1834: first as Pratt, Weston & Co. until 1821,[25] and then Pratt, Hassall and Gerrard until c.1834;[26] in what became known as the Minerva Works, previously occupied by George Mason, q.v.

John Pratt, 1807-1817, Fenton Culvert;
John Pratt, c.1814-1830s;
John & William Pratt, 1830s-1840s;
John Pratt the younger & William Pratt, 1847;
John Pratt & Co., 1847-1878;
Pratt & Simpson, 1878-1883;
Lane Delph, all Staffordshire.

John Pratt (c.1782-1840s?) was the third son of William and Ellen Pratt. He occupied a works at Fenton Culvert between 1807 and 1817,[27] followed by Thomas Hughes. The location of the site is not known.

Directories of 1805 and 1809 show John Pratt at Lane Delph, but these entries may refer to his residence rather than his works, which appear to have been at Fenton Culvert.[28] His mother's will of December 1814 mentions 'all these potworks ... at Lane Delph ... in the occupation of my son John Pratt',[29] whilst the Land Tax lists and rate extracts show him at Lane Delph from 2 April 1816 onward, in a works which he appears to have taken over from his brother, Felix Pratt.[30] John Pratt remained at Lane Delph, and in 1836 was in partnership with a younger brother, William.[31] In November 1847, his son, John Pratt the younger, and William Pratt assigned their business for the benefit of their creditors.[32] The firm continued to be called John Pratt and Co. until c.1878,[33] when it became Pratt and Simpson. The Pratt name was finally extinguished at Lane Delph in 1883, when the works was taken over by Wallis and Gimson.[34]

Pratt stoneware seems confined to one or two shapes of marked drab-grey smear glazed stoneware, probably intended for burning incense or containing pot-pourri, which would appear by form and function to date to the early nineteenth century (Colour Plate 56).

RIDGWAY:
Ridgway, Smith and Ridgway c.1796-1798;
Job and George Ridgway, 1798-1802;
George Ridgway, 1802-14;
John Ridgway & Co., 1814-30;
William Ridgway (& Son/& Co.), 1830-54;
Bell Works, High Street, Shelton;
Job Ridgway (& Sons) 1802-14;
John and William Ridgway 1814-30;
John Ridgway (& Co.), 1830-58;
Cauldon Place Works, Shelton, Staffordshire.

Generations of the Ridgway family made pottery in Staffordshire.[1] George Ridgway (1758-1823)[2] and his brother Job (1761-1814)[3] began business as earthenware manufacturers about 1791,[4] at the Bell Works, Shelton (No. 86 on the 1802 map, see Appendix 1), now the site of the City Museum and Art Gallery; for a time with a with a third partner, William Smith. Smith died in 1799,[5] and Job

Fig. 249 *Vase, buff-coloured stoneware with applied relief sprigging in white. Mark: RIDGWAY, c. 1815-25, 10¼ inches high. (City Museum and Art Gallery, Stoke-on-Trent, 842.)*

Fig. 250 *Small pastille burner, buff-coloured stoneware with smear glaze and white sprig reliefs. Mark: RIDGWAY, c. 1835, 2¾ inches high. (Blakey collection.)*

left in 1802 to start his own business at Cauldon Place.[6]

George Ridgway continued at the Bell Works. Two of his sons died young: Ralph in 1809 and George junior in 1812. A third son, Job Ridgway junior, who married in 1821,[7] died in 1833,[8] but it is not known if he was ever a partner. George Ridgway retired in 1814, at the time of his brother Job's death, and his nephews John and William took over both Cauldon and Bell Works. In 1830 the two

brothers separated, William keeping the Bell and John having the Cauldon Works.

William Ridgway (1788-1864)[9] and his son, Edward John, continued in partnership until 1854. At times they operated several other works, including those of Elijah Mayer (q.v.) and of Bagster (see Neale and Wilson), as Ridgway and Abington.[10] William Ridgway was also in another partnership, Ridgway, Morley, Wear and Co., earthenware manufacturers, Shelton, dissolved in 1842;[11] and had business interests in the United States.[12] He was bankrupt in 1848 for over £50,000,[13] and his various properties, works and contents were for auction.[14] William Ridgway's Bell Works was taken by Joseph Clementson.[15] When William Ridgway died in 1864 he was said to have been 'enterprising but lacked caution'.[16]

In 1864-66, his son, Edward John Ridgway, built a model factory at Bedford Place, Hanley, and gave up the 'Mayer' and 'Bagster' High Street Works.[17] That business continued under the name of Ridgway until the late 1970s, latterly as part of Royal Doulton.

When Job Ridgway left his brother in 1802, he built the Cauldon Works, at Shelton,[18] on a potworks site now occupied by the Cauldon Site of Stoke-on-Trent College. He took his two sons John and William Ridgway into partnership in 1808.[19] At his death in 1814,[20] his brother George at the Bell Works retired, and Job's sons took over both their father's Cauldon Works and their uncle's Bell Works.

John and William Ridgway separated in 1830, John remaining at the Cauldon Works and William at the Bell Works. John Ridgway (1786-1860) continued to run the Cauldon Works, in partnership with Bates and Brown-Westhead from 1856.[21] His sister, Anna, had married

Fig. 251 *Small pie? dish, red stoneware with relief sprig decoration. Mark: J. RIDGWAY, c. 1830, 5 x 6 inches. (Rakow collection.)*

Fig. 252 *Pair of vases,* dark blue jasper dip with white classical reliefs. Mark: E. J. RIDGWAY, *c. 1866, 10 inches high. (Rakow collection.)*

Thomas Bates, a barrister of the Middle Temple,[22] and Bates may have been her son, joining his uncle in Ridgway, Bates & Co. John Ridgway formally retired in 1858,[23] and died in 1860, aged 74.[24] The business continued as Bates, Brown-Westhead, Moore and Co. until 1861, then as T.C. Brown-Westhead, Moore & Co. until *c.*1905, then becoming Cauldon Ltd.[25]

Several of the Ridgways produced both dry- and glazed-bodied stoneware. It is not always easy to attribute the individual pieces to a particular partnership or factory, and the marks vary. Most of the marked *RIDGWAY* examples (Colour Plate 57; Figs. 249, 250) are glazed caneware, often with white sprig relief. The extant wares are well executed and were probably made by William Ridgway and Son.

Another pie dish in unglazed caneware with the mark *J. RIDGWAY* (Fig. 251) was probably made by Job Ridgway in the first few years of the nineteenth century.

Although somewhat outside the time period considered here, it is worth mentioning that Edward John Ridgway made fine jasper at the Bedford Works from 1866 (Fig. 252).

SHERIDAN:
Coomer, Sheridan & Hewitt, 1802-05;
Sheridan & Hewitt, 1805-08,
Green Dock, Longton;
Sheridan & Hyatt, 1807-11; **J.H. Sheridan,** 1812-15,
High Street, Longton;
J. H. Sheridan, 1808-21,
Union Market Place, Longton, Staffordshire.

John Hendley Sheridan (1780–1859), son of a London lawyer, was in several businesses in Longton, between 1802 and 1821.[1] All made earthenware, and the High Street works (now the Gladstone Pottery Museum) yielded basalt waster shards which may well have been made during Sheridan's period there, 1807-15.

Sheridan & Hyatt, and J.H. Sheridan supplied Wyllies, London pottery merchants, with teapots and creamers, between 1808 and 1811.[2] The teapots were described as: pressed, Dutch, satin, round Dutch, bellied oval, diamond, oval, prest oblong [with] key border, bellied oblong, Regency, and new siver (*sic*) shape, but it should be noted that the bodies of these pots were <u>not</u> specified. Basalt waster shards with Greek key borders were found at the High Street works site.[3]

Sheridan and partners are possible manufacturers of the white felspathic stoneware items marked 'S & Co', although his firms have not been found referred to as Sheridan & Co., nor were felspathic stoneware shards found at the High Street works. Both Sheridan's Union Market Place works and High Street works were in the vicinity of both Chetham's and Cyples's works, where white felspathic stoneware was actually made.

SHORTHOSE:
Shorthose and Heath, Juniors, *c.*1794-1818, Slack Lane;
Shorthose and Co., 1818-1823, Tontine Street;
both at Hanley, Staffordshire.

John Shorthose (1768-1828,[1] sometimes Shor*thouse*) was in partnership with Lewis Heath (fl.1785-1804),[2] grandson of John Simpson the younger, Hanley, earth potter.[3] The first documentary reference found for them as partners is an insurance policy of 3 April 1794 for John Shorthose and Lewis Heath's utensils and stock in warehouses and a hovel at Hanley.[4] Directories of *c.*1795 and 1796[5] mention Shorthose and Heath, manufacturers, Hanley.

There are references to an adult John Shorthose in 1771[6] and 1783,[7] presumably of an earlier generation. John Shorthose of Hanley, packer and dealer in Staffordshire ware, appeared in a *c.*1795 Directory,[8] and a John Shorthose was also noted as a merchant in High Street, Hanley in Directories of 1800 and 1802.[9] These references might also be to the older man.

Shorthose and Heath, Juniors, issued a price-list in Dutch in 1797,[10] consistent with their description in 1805 and 1809 Directories as manufacturers of earthenware for exportation,[11] and with recorded plates marked Shorthose which have Dutch decoration.[12] Another facet of their business was the supply of cobalt: Shorthose and Heath supplied large quantities to Thomas Daniel, colour maker, about 1808;[13] to the Herculaneum Pottery at Liverpool in 1808;[14] and to Minton in 1810.[15] They also bought from Minton in 1810.[16]

The 1805 and 1809 Directory entries are for Shorthose and Heath*s, junrs.*, and as a Lewis Heath died in 1811,[17] this suggests that he had been succeeded by two or more sons. The 1809 Directory also listed another partnership, Heath and Shorthose, Hanley, earthenware manufacturers.

The Shorthose and Heath partnership is shown at potworks site No. 67 on the 1802 map (Appendix 1). This works, probably at Slack Lane (now Bryan Street), may

have been where Christopher Charles Whitehead (q.v.) was in business in 1776. Lewis Heath was a grandson of John Simpson, who left his potworks to his Simpson grandchildren;[18] and the rate records show that Shorthose and Heath occupied a potworks owned by 'Simpsons', from 1807 until 1818.[19] A works in Slack Lane could well be the one described as 'near New Hall', occupied by Shorthose and Heath, which was offered for sale or to be let in 1815, 1816 and 1817.[20]

John Shorthose moved to two potworks in Hanley in 1818, owned by Mrs Chatterley, until his bankruptcy in 1823.[21] Directories for 1818 and 1822[22] refer to John Shorthose *and Co.*, Tontine Street, Hanley, earthenware manufacturers, but when John Shorthose was bankrupt in 1823, the formal notices referred to him alone, trading as 'Shorthose and Co.'. His bankruptcy dragged on to a final dividend in 1840,[23] although John Shorthose had died at Brussels in 1828.[24]

Both Shorthose and Heath and Shorthose and Company produced basalts and may have produced other stonewares, such as caneware, but no extant examples are known to illustrate at this time.

SOWTER:
R. Sowter & Co., 1800-09,
Mexborough, South Yorkshire.

Robert Sowter and William Bromley established a pottery at Mexborough in 1800, trading as 'R. Sowter & Co.' in 1804.[1] In 1809, the partners were Robert Sowter, a merchant at Hull; Joseph Sowter, a corn factor at Castle Donnington, Derbyshire; and John Hopkinson, a corn factor at Derby. In the same year the pottery was leased to Jesse Barker, who took his brother Peter Barker into partnership at Mexborough in 1812. Peter Barker had been a master potter at Rawmarsh, nearby, from the 1790s. The Barker family continued to manufacture earthenware at Mexborough until the 1840s.

Fig. 253 *Teapot with hinged cover, white felspathic stoneware moulded and with sprig relief, blue outline painting. Mark:* S & Co. No. 1, *possibly Sowter and Co., Mexborough, Yorkshire, c. 1800-10, 7⁷⁄₁₆ inches high. (Historic Deerfield, Inc., Massachusetts.)*

Fig. 254 *Teapot, white felspathic stoneware with moulded body and applied reliefs, outline painted in blue. An American market teapot, the sprig relief included the American Eagle and thirteen stars and a Figure of Liberty on the reverse. Unmarked, possibly Sowter and Company, Mexborough, Yorkshire, c. 1800-15. (Private collection.)*

Fig. 255 *Teapot, white felspathic stoneware with moulded body and applied reliefs, sliding cover. Mark: 22, attributed to Sowter and Company, Mexborough, Yorkshire, c. 1800-10, 5½ inches high. (Dunderdale collection.)*

It has been suggested that white felspathic ware (Figs. 253, 256), basalt ware and polished redware, all marked 'S & Co', were made by Sowter and Co.,[2] but see also *Sheridan*. Superficial excavation on the site did not produce felspathic shards. Latterly, Alwyn and Angela Cox have stated 'that to the writers' knowledge there is absolutely no evidence, neither archaeological nor documentary, to associate such pieces [marked 'S & Co' or 'S & oC'] with this firm [Sowter and Co]. In the absence of conclusive evidence, such attributions, at best, can only be conjectural'.[3] More recently, Geoffrey Godden has also evinced doubt about 'the traditional attribution to Sowters & Co. [of wares marked S & Co]', and suggested several Staffordshire makers with appropriate initials: Shirley & Co., Slack & Co., and Shorthose & Co.[4]

SPODE:

Spode & Tomlinson, *c.*1767-74, Stoke-upon-Trent;
Mountford & Spode, 1772-*c.*1779, Shelton;
Josiah Spode I, 1776-97; **Josiah Spode II**, 1797-1827;
Josiah Spode III & Trustees, 1827-33;
Copeland & Garrett, 1833-47;
W.T. Copeland and successors, 1847-present;
Stoke-upon-Trent, all Staffordshire.

The Spode family and its manufacture of pottery has been written about extensively, and only a summary is given here.[1]

Josiah Spode I was born at Lane Delph in the parish of Stoke-upon-Trent in 1733,[2] and was apprenticed to Thomas Whieldon of Fenton, a leading mid-eighteenth century potter, for three years from 1749.[3] As Spode was then aged sixteen, it is likely that he had been previously employed in the pottery trade as a boy labourer. Whieldon employed Spode at a man's wage in 1752 and 1754.[4] Simeon Shaw, the Potteries historian, stated that Spode was afterwards employed by Mr Banks, who lived at Stoke and made white stoneware and cream coloured earthen-ware.[5]

Fig. 256 *Teapot, white felspathic stoneware with moulded body and sprig reliefs. Mark: S. & Co., No. 5, c. 1800-10, 6¼ inches high. (Blake collection.)*

Josiah Spode I married Ellen Finley in 1754, and they had several children, including two sons, Josiah II born in 1755 and Samuel born 1757.[6] Spode bought a cottage in Stoke in 1758,[7] and later his wife had a haberdashery business,[8] both evidence of some modest accumulation of capital.

From 1767 to 1775, Spode I rented a potworks, later called the Bridge Bank Works, approximately on the site of Woolworths' store in London Road, Stoke-upon-Trent in 1996.[9] In 1772, he entered into a partnership to manufacture pottery with Thomas Mountford, in Mountford's mother's potworks at Shelton.[10] In the agreement with Mountford, there was provision for Spode to complete the outstanding two years of an existing partnership with William Tomlinson. It is likely that this partnership with Tomlinson had been for seven years at the 'Bridge Bank' works, starting in 1767, soon after Spode had rented that factory.[11]

The partnership agreement with Mountford was to run

Fig. 257 **Teapot**, caneware with moulded body and sprig relief, enamel painted in white, green/blue and carmine. The moulded shape is identical to teapots made by Neale & Co. (see fig.235). Unmarked, probably Spode, c. 1790-1800, 5¼ inches high. (Burgin collection.)

Fig. 258 **Teapot**, caneware painted in white and blue enamel with Chinoiserie moulded body. Similar examples are known by Neale & Co. Mark: SPODE, c. 1785-1800, 5½ inches high. (Jacobs collection.)

until 1779, and it precluded Spode from starting any other business. However, in 1776, he purchased the potworks and land in Church Street, Stoke,[12] which is still the site of Spode Ltd.'s works in 1996. By 1776, Spode's eldest son Josiah Spode II was aged twenty-one, and it seems feasible that he was nominally in charge of the newly purchased works, thus avoiding infringement of the partnership stipulation.

Josiah Spode II had already married in 1775,[13] and by 1778 he was in London, establishing a pottery warehouse in Fore Street.[14] Josiah II remained there until his father's

death in 1797, when he took over the Spode works in Stoke.[15]

When Josiah II went to London in 1778, his brother Samuel was almost twenty-one, and could likewise have been nominally in charge of the 'Spode' works until his father's agreement with Mountford expired in 1779. Samuel married in 1783,[16] and had his own factory at Foley, Fenton, until shortly before his death in 1817.[17]

Josiah Spode II remained in charge of the Spode Works until his death in 1827.[18] His son, Josiah Spode III, was in the business, but retired about the time of his marriage in

Fig. 259 **Teapot and jug**, caneware with cane moulded body and enamel painting, sprig relief and interior white slip on jug. Marks: both SPODE, c. 1790-1800, jug 7 inches high. (Fisk collection.)

Fig. 260 **Teapot and honeypot and stand**, teapot, caneware with cane moulded body and blue, black and white enamel painting, boy finial; honeypot, glazed cane moulded caneware. Marks: both SPODE, c. 1795-1810, 4 and 4½ inches high. (Fisk collection.)

1815.[19] He returned in 1827, until his own death only two years later, in 1829.[20] The factory was run by trustees until 1833.[21]

William Taylor Copeland, who had been a partner in the London warehouse since 1824,[22] took over both the Stoke factory and London warehouse in 1833,[23] and brought in a new partner, Thomas Garrett. Copeland and Garrett owned the entire business until 1847, when Garrett left.[24] The Copeland family then owned the business until 1966,[25] when it was sold to Carborundum Ltd. After various changes in ownership the business (known as Spode Ltd. since 1970) is now (1996) owned by Exeter International.[26]

Josiah Spode I's first factory was the 'Bridge Bank' works in Stoke, from 1767 to 1775, probably in partnership with William Tomlinson. This was followed and overlapped by a works at Shelton, from 1772 to 1779, owned by the family of his partner there, Thomas Mountford. This Shelton works, No. 94 on the 1802 map (Appendix 1),[27] was on the site of what is now The Elms, Howard Place, part of Stoke-on-Trent College.

In 1776 Josiah Spode I purchased the 'Spode' works in Church Street, Stoke, occupied since then by the successive Spode, Copeland and Spode firms until the present day.

Josiah Spode II commenced a London warehouse at Fore Street, Cripplegate, in 1778.[28] After moves within Fore Street, by 1796 the showrooms were in Portugal Street[29] managed after Spode II's return to Stoke in 1797 by his son William Spode and William Copeland.[30] William Copeland became a partner in the London warehouse in 1805, and

Fig. 261 **Pair of spill vases**, caneware with transfer-printed Chinoiserie flowers infilled with pink, yellow, green, iron-red and matt black with gilding. Marks: both SPODE and painters' number 3405, c. 1805-15, 4⅛ inches high. (Burgin collection.)

Fig. 262 **Wine cooler**, caneware with sprigged grape and vine relief, satyr mask lug handles. The Sheffield plate rim is marked GAINSFORD, 1806 Sheffield. Another wine cooler in the Sheffield Museum has a rim marked by the same maker. Mark: SPODE, c. 1806, 4¼ inches high. (Burgin collection.)

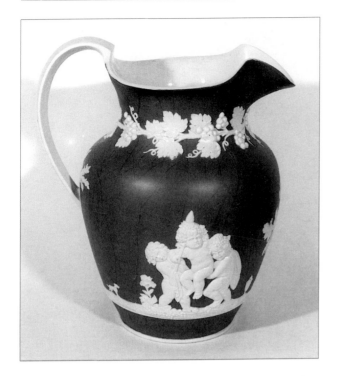

Fig. 264 ***Covered jug,*** *blue jasper dip with white interior slip and white relief decoration. Mark: Spode, c. 1800-10, 6¼ inches high. (Fisk collection.)*

Fig. 263 ***Jug,*** *blue jasper dip with white slip interior and white sprig decoration. Mark: SPODE, c. 1800, 10 inches high. (Fisk collection.)*

his son William Taylor Copeland joined the London partnership in 1824.[31] William Copeland died in 1826, and a new partnership for seven years was made between William Taylor Copeland and Josiah Spode II.[32] This was continued by Spode's trustees until 1833 when W.T. Copeland and Thomas Garrett took over both the Stoke works and London warehouse.[33]

Spode joined several partnerships for raw materials; the two first being Fenton Park Colliery in 1790 for coal[34] and

a partnership to get china clay in 1799.[35]

Josiah Spode I is credited with the perfection of blue under-glaze printing in Staffordshire in the 1780s[36] and he or his son with the first reliable bone china body by 1800.[37] Josiah Spode II made stone china by 1813,[38] and was early in the field with felspar porcelain in 1821.[39]

The range and variety of dry-bodied and smear glazed stonewares produced at Spode was considerable. Although consisting almost entirely of useful wares, Spode made very

Fig. 265 ***Flower container (minus lid) custard cup (minus cover) and spill vase,*** *all blue jasper dip with white sprig relief. Marks: left, SPODE 8, centre and right, Spode, c. 1790-1810, spill 4¼ inches high. (Fisk collection.)*

Fig. 266 **Cream jug**, blue jasper dip with white sprig relief. Mark: Spode, c. 1790-1800, 5½ inches high. (Fisk collection.)

Fig. 267 **Covered bowl**, solid drab ware with glazed exterior and white slipped interior, relief decoration in white. Mark: SPODE, c. 1800-10, 3¼ inches high. **Pot-pourri vase**, dark green jasper dip with smear glaze and white relief decoration. Mark: Spode 6, c. 1800-10, 3½ inches high. (Fisk collection.)

Fig. 268 **Covered jug**, white stoneware with chocolate and blue dip dice work, and white sprig relief. Mark: Spode, c. 1795-1805, 4½ inches high. (Fisk collection.)

Fig. 269 **Teapot**, white stoneware with chocolate-brown slip and white reliefs. Mark: SPODE, c. 1805-10, 4¼ inches high. (Liverpool Museum, Museums & Galleries on Merseyside, 852M.)

Fig. 270 **Vases (minus liners)**, left, glazed caneware with black sprigging; right, drab-dipped smear-glazed white stoneware with white reliefs. Marks: both SPODE, c. 1810, both 3¾ inches high. (Fisk collection.)

Fig. 271 **Small coffee pot**, white stoneware with drab-green ground and white daisy chain sprigging. Unmarked, attributed to Spode, c. 1810. (Fisk collection.)

Fig. 272 **Jug**, white stoneware with brown ground and sprigged decoration. Mark: SPODE, c. 1810, 3½ inches high. (Polikoff collection.)

fine caneware, jasper dipped wares, fine red stone and *rosso antico* wares, and many types of white and drab-bodied smear and dipped-glazed stonewares.

Spode excelled in caneware. The finely textured body was usually moulded, with additional enamel embellishment, and wares such as teawares (Figs. 257-260), jugs (Fig. 259) and spill vases (Fig. 261), as well as honey

pots (Fig. 260 right), wine coolers (Fig. 262), and pie dishes were among the offerings. The ice pails or wine coolers often had silver mounts which provide hallmark dates.

Jasper production was somewhat limited in quantity and was usually jasper dipped wares in medium blue (Colour Plate 58; Figs. 263-266) or occasionally in green (Fig. 267 right). The shapes followed the range of other Spode

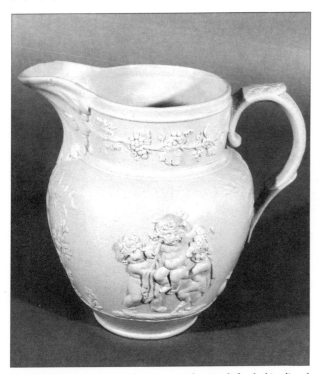

Fig. 273 **Jug**, smear-glazed drab stoneware with sprig relief and white slipped interior. Mark: SPODE, c. 1800-10, 4⅛ inches high. (Blake collection.)

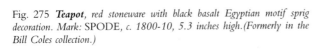

Fig. 275 **Teapot**, red stoneware with black basalt Egyptian motif sprig decoration. Mark: SPODE, c. 1800-10, 5.3 inches high. (Formerly in the Bill Coles collection.)

Fig. 274 **Travelling font**, mortarware, tripod decorated with trinity cross, the Host, and Hebrew inscription. Mark: SPODE, 19th century, 6½ inches high. (Fisk collection.)

Fig. 275 **Teapot**, *red stoneware with black basalt Egyptian motif sprig decoration. Mark: SPODE, c. 1800-10, 5.3 inches high. (Formerly in the Bill Coles collection.)*

Fig. 276 **Base of a pot-pourri vase**, *red stoneware with black basalt sprig relief and double Greek key band. Mark: SPODE, c. 1800-10, 7¼ inches high. (Fisk collection.)*

stoneware pieces, that is, teawares and jugs with occasional flower containers and other ornamental wares. There is a pair of jasper dipped candlesticks in the Spode Museum.

White stoneware and other coloured drab stone wares were made in considerable quantity, and they too were often decorated with coloured ground dips with white sprig relief decoration. Spode produced dipped diced wares (Fig. 268) which had been so popular in the Wedgwood

oeuvre. Some of the brown dipped white stonewares remind one of those produced by the Turners and the manufacturers who provided Abbott, Mist etc. in London with their wares. Spode also made objects in the so-called mortar ware body, such as travelling baptismal fonts (Fig. 274) as well as the usual mortars and pestles (Fig. 222).

It is probable that Spode was producing the fine red stonewares from the factory's inception but few of those

Fig. 278 **Teapot**, *dark red stoneware of low round shape decorated with opaque enamel flowers. Mark: SPODE, 4½ inches high. (Fisk collection.)*

Fig. 277 **Base of a pot-pourri vase**, *red stoneware with black relief on a round base with tripod Egyptian figures. Mark: Spode, c. 1800-05, 6¼ inches high. (Fisk collection.)*

Fig. 279 **Jug**, *dark red stoneware of octagonal form and white relief decoration. The serpent handle appears to be biting off the head of one of the female relief figures around the neck. Mark: SPODE, c. 1810-20, 5 inches high. (Fisk collection.)*

down-market wares seem to have been marked by almost any factory. However, during the red stoneware revival of the early nineteenth century, Spode, like Wedgwood, produced very fine red stonewares, frequently embellished with Egyptian relief decoration in black (Figs. 275, 277) or occasionally with Chinese opaque enamel flowers (Fig. 278). One marvellous redware teapot in the Coles collection is an exuberant reproduction of an Yixing seventeenth century prototype (Colour Plate 59). Some of the red stone manufacture was less successfully conceived and executed than the previously mentioned examples, such as the jug (Fig. 279), which had a handle added after the sprig decoration was applied, making the snake appear to be biting off the head of one of the relief figures.

STEEL, DANIEL:

Daniel Steel (& Son), *c.*1796-98, Burslem; *c.*1802-09, 'Red Lion' Works, Burslem; 1818-22, Hole House Works, Nile Street, Burslem; 1828-30, Bourne's Bank, Burslem, Staffordshire.

Earlier accounts of this potter give his dates in operation variously as 1766-1824,[1] 1780-1824[2] and 1790-1824,[3] but no firm evidence has been found for such early starting years. An 11 November 1790 entry in a Wedgwood Commonplace Book may be relevant.[4] It is to the effect that Moses Steel had care of cameo moulds but a certain connection rendered him ineligible, so he was to be transferred to the useful works. Three boys named Moses Steel, baptised in Burslem in 1757, 1763 and 1772 respectively, had brothers named Daniel, baptised 1757,

1760 and 1771, the 1757 brothers being twins.[5] Thus, the Moses Steel employed by Wedgwood could have been the brother of Daniel Steel, jasper manufacturer. If Daniel Steel had commenced business making jasper in 1790, and it was his brother Moses who had care of cameo moulds, that could be the 'certain connection' which would make Moses ineligible to continue looking after cameo moulds.

The same book shows that two sons of Daniel Steel of Etruria were apprenticed to Wedgwood as painters: Moses in 1783 and Thomas in 1787. In 1790, Moses Steel *senior* was a presser and finisher in Wedgwood's Ornamental Works, and 'Mountford' had applied to him for jasper recipes. Altogether, a Steel family was much involved in Wedgwood's Ornamental Works in the late eighteenth century.

What is certain is that Daniel Steel was listed as a potter in Burslem in 1796,[6] and supplied unspecified types of ware to John Wyllie in London in 1797 and 1798.[7] From *c.*1802 to 1809, he occupied a potworks on a site in Burslem, owned by John Gilbert,[8] next east of the 'Red Lion' public house, Moorland Road (Appendix 1).[9] This site has been erroneously identified as the Scotia Works,[10] which did not exist in 1802.[11]

After J. and R. Riley had finally vacated the Hole House Works, Nile Street, Burslem in 1817,[12] Daniel Steel and Son, jasper and ornamental stoneware manufacturers occupied it from about 1818 until *c.*1822.[13] This was quite

Fig. 280 **Smelling bottle**, *pale blue jasper with white reliefs of* Flora *and* Ganymede *and the Eagle. Mark: STEEL around tip of base, c. 1796-1800, (Daniel Steel, Burslem) 3½ inches high. (Rakow collection.)*

a large works, with five ovens, and was next occupied by Thomas Swettenham from 1824.[14] The site is now within Royal Doulton's Nile Street Works.

Lastly, Daniel Steel and Son were at Bourne's Bank, Burslem from 1828 to 1830, making 'jasper and stone'.[15] The suggestion that Daniel Steel was at St James Street from 1790 to 1818[16] may have arisen from his address being given as St John's Street in 1818.[17] A St James street is not known in Burslem, and there is no other evidence to support Steel occupying a works in St John's Street. Daniel Steel was buried in Burslem Churchyard on 20 May 1831, aged 71.[18]

Daniel Steel appears to have only made jasper dry bodies and the jasper is often distinctive in appearance. The range of shapes was considerable, tending to the ornamental rather than the utilitarian. Watch holders (Colour Plate 60), spill vases (Colour Plate 61), and smelling bottles (Fig. 280) were among the products of a firm which exhibited a scope of blue colour from light to steely-dark blue, the latter being the colour most often associated with the firm. In the main the jaspers, which were generally dipped, can be characterised as bold in appearance with a dark jasper body contrasted with a prominent white relief. Impressed marks from the factory are *STEEL* and *STEEL BURSLEM*, the latter being the most commonly found on the dark blue jaspers. It is possible that the lighter blue jaspers were made by Henry Steele, who is the next manufacturer discussed.

STEELE, HENRY:

Henry Steele, jasper manufacturer, no date or place;
Adams & Steele, n.d., Shelton;
Henry Steele, 1837, Burslem; 1841, Marsh Street, Shelton, all Staffordshire.

Henry Steele of Burslem, manufacturer of jasper and stoneware, late of Shelton, was insolvent in 1837.[1] He had been employed by John Ridgway as a journeyman in the manufacture of jasper and stoneware, afterwards in business on his own, then with James Adams as manufacturers of stone and jasper ware at Shelton. Despite his insolvency in 1837, Henry Steele was again listed as ornamental jasper manufacturer at Marsh Street, Shelton, in 1841.[2]

A Henry Steel (*sic*) potter, Burslem, was insolvent in 1822,[3] and this may relate to the end of Daniel Steel and Son's business in Nile Street, Burslem (q.v.). Henry Steel, son of Daniel and Ann Steel, was baptised at Burslem Church on 29 March 1789;[4] and it seems possible that this was the Henry Steel who made jasper, following in his father's footsteps.

Jasper ornaments were made by Henry Steele at Marsh Street, Shelton.[5] The jasper smelling bottle (Fig. 280) marked *STEEL* may be a product from this factory.

SWANSEA:

Cambrian Pottery, 1764-1870, Swansea, Glamorgan.

The potteries at Swansea are well documented.[1] The Glamorgan Pottery, 1814-38, did not make dry-bodied ware,[2] but the Cambrian Pottery made cane-coloured ware, amongst many other types, during its century or so of history. It is first recorded in 1764, when William Coles was allowed to pull down the old copper works and build a stoneware or earthenware manufactory on the west bank of the River Tawe.[3] From then on there was a series of occupiers until the pottery's closure in 1870:[4]

Year	Occupier(s)
1764	William Coles
1784	Coles and Cave
1790	Coles and Haynes
1802	Haynes, Dillwyn and Co.
1811	Dillwyn and Bevingtons
1817	T. & J. Bevington and Co.
1821	T. & J. Bevington
1824	L.W. Dillwyn
1831	L.L. Dillwyn
c.1850	Evans and Glasson
c.1861	D.J. Evans
1870	Pottery closed

Jewitt stated that Haynes, who was at the Cambrian Pottery from 1790 to 1810, introduced 'a very passable kind of biscuit ware'.[5] Nance argued that this was caneware,[6] which was certainly made at Swansea, and illustrated a caneware teapot, impressed SWANSEA[7] and two game pie dishes, also impressed SWANSEA.[8] He also referred[9] to a caneware cream-jug in the Victoria and Albert Museum (#3484-1901). The Royal Ontario Museum recently acquired a cream jug marked *SWANSEA* (Colour Plate 62 right) which is indeed caneware, but in a form more often associated with the felspathic stoneware body. Although not a subject in this work, basalt was also made in small quantities.

SWINTON:

Greens, Bingley & Co., 1785-1806;
Brameld & Co., 1806-1842; Swinton, South Yorkshire.

The Swinton Pottery in South Yorkshire has been the subject of research since at least 1855, when the catalogue of the Museum of Practical Geology included a substantially correct account of its history, for which the writers were 'indebted to the kindness of the Earl Fitzwilliam, K.G.'[1] The following summary is made from more recent works on the subject.[2]

The site was owned by the Marquess of Rockingham, and Joseph Flint was the first known potter, making bricks from 1745 and having a 'Pot House' by 1753. Edward Butler took over the pot house c.1755. He died in 1763, and William Malpass replaced him in 1765. These potters had made rough country slipware, but Malpass took William Fenney as a partner by 1768. At Swinton, Fenney made use of his previous experience of making fine ware at Rotherham, to produce white salt-glaze stoneware, tortoiseshell ware and cream-coloured ware, until 1776. Malpass left in 1778 and was succeeded by Bingley and Wood.

Fig. 281 *Mug*, glazed caneware with white reliefs. Mark: BRAMELD 7, *c. 1820-30, 3 inches high. (Rakow collection.)*

It is likely that John Brameld was the practical overseer of Swinton Pottery from 1778, and he and his son William became partners in 1785, when John Green and others of the Leeds Pottery joined Bingley as Greens, Bingley and Co. That partnership endured until 1806, making cream-coloured earthenware, pearlware, basalt, and red and brown stoneware.

Aided by a loan from the second Earl Fitzwilliam (the owner of the Swinton Pottery site), John Brameld took over the Swinton works in 1806, joined by his sons William, Thomas, George and John Wager. William Brameld died in 1813, John Brameld senior died in 1819 and the remaining brothers were bankrupt in 1825. By then they had a large works with seven ovens and had ventured into porcelain manufacture.

The second Earl Fitzwilliam rescued the concern, and the Bramelds continued in business from 1826 as the Rockingham works, making earthenware and high-class porcelain. By 1842 they were again heavily indebted to the then third Earl, and the works was closed down.

Stoneware made at Swinton was confined to two principal categories: red stonewares both glazed and unglazed and fine brown stoneware.[3] Redware is only known from excavated shards. However, there was a small *oeuvre* in glazed caneware produced at Swinton, some of which is of fine quality. Rice illustrated a number of examples including an unusual cup with a hoof-and-mane handle in the Victoria and Albert Museum.[4] Most of the glazed caneware bears the mark *BRAMELD + 7* (Fig. 281); occasionally the wares are marked with an oval pad mark impressed with the name and a letter mark, such as the jug (Colour Plate 63) impressed with *BRAMELD H.*

TAYLOR, GEORGE:
George Taylor (senior) *c.*1784-1809;
Thomas and James Taylor 1809-1819;
Thomas Taylor 1819-1830, High Street, Hanley;
George Taylor (junior), 1807-1811, Broad Street, Shelton; all in Staffordshire.

George Taylor senior was a master potter at High Street, Hanley, from *c.*1784[1] to his death in 1809.[2] He was succeeded by his younger sons, Thomas and James Taylor,[3] until James left the partnership in July 1819.[4] Thomas Taylor continued in business until 1830, when the works was taken over by William Ratcliffe.[5] The works was No. 73 on the 1802 map (Appendix 1), on the site of what is now H. & E. Smith's Britannic Works, Broom Street, Hanley.

In 1807, George Taylor senior bought a works in Shelton from Baddeleys,[6] and his eldest son, George Taylor junior, ran it. After his father died in 1809, he sought a young partner with capital;[7] probably unsuccessfully, as his family bought him out in 1811.[8] Hicks and Meigh were their first tenants, and the factory remained Taylors' property until sold to Joseph Clementson in 1844, partly to pay Thomas Taylor's debts.[9] The works was No. 88 on the 1802 map (Appendix 1), later known as the Phoenix Works, now replaced by ABC Cinemas, Broad Street, Hanley.

George Taylor junior was a 'potter' at the Don Pottery, Yorkshire (q.v.) by 1815.[10] He may have been back in Shelton in 1822 as a potter or warehouseman,[11] and in a short-lived 'stoneware' partnership with Joseph Locker and Edward and John Poulson at Hanley between 1824 and 1825.[12] In 1844, Thomas Taylor was a land agent at Clayton, Staffordshire, and James Taylor was a maltster in Hanley.[13]

Caneware is suggested as being made by Taylors, Hanley and Shelton, but none has been positively identified.

TAYLOR, JOHN:
Burslem, Staffordshire.

John Taylor of Burslem is suggested as a maker of dry-bodied ware. His name occurs as a master potter in at least six businesses in Burslem, Longport and Cobridge, between 1798 and 1828, as follows:

Bagshaw, Taylor and Meir, *c.*1796-1802, Burslem.

Bagshaw, Taylor and Meir were manufacturers at Burslem by 1796,[1] and a newly erected potworks in Burslem occupied by them was offered by auction in 1798.[2] Presumably they bought it, as later in the same year Bagshaw, Taylor and Co. insured 'Till Croft' (*sic*), probably Kiln Croft) works for £600; and they insured the same works and stock for £600 in 1801.[3] A year later, John Taylor left a partnership with James Bagshaw and John Meir as earthenware manufacturers at Burslem.[4] The works was shown as No. 46 on the 1802 map (Appendix 1); and the site now lies within Royal Doulton's Nile Street Works, Burslem.

John Taylor and Co., fl. 1802, Burslem.

This firm is shown at a potworks indicated by an asterisk on the 1802 map (Appendix 1); in the vicinity of the present Portland House, south of Newcastle Street. Nothing more is known of this firm, but the site could be that of Mellor and Taylor, see below.

Mellor and Taylor, fl.1804-09, Burslem.

The Upper Potworks and house, Newcastle Street, Burslem, was offered to let or sell in 1804,[5] then occupied by – Mellor and – Taylor. They remained in business until c.1809, but perhaps Taylor left him then, as Thomas Mellor alone was still trying to let or sell a potworks in 1810, and he alone was bankrupt in 1811.[6]

Stubbs and Taylor, 1817, Longport.

Joseph Stubbs and John Taylor ended a partnership as earthenware manufacturers at Longport in 1817,[7] Stubbs continuing until 1834 in Dale Hall Works,[8] a works occupied in 1809 by John and George Rogers,[9] and now part of Steelite International's works at Longport. A John Taylor, perhaps the same man, was the superintendant (*sic*) of Davenports' works in 1822.[10]

Fig. 282 **Vase**, *blue jasper dip with white relief sprig decoration on an octagonal polished basalt plinth. Unmarked, attributed to John Turner, c. 1790, 8 inches high. (Liverpool Museum, Museums & Galleries on Merseyside, 2819M).*

Taylor and Wildblood, fl.1810, Cobridge.

In 1810, John Taylor and James Wildblood dissolved a partnership as earthenware manufacturers at Cobridge. Wildblood was bankrupt in 1811,[11] and in 1814 Adams offered the factory to be let, formerly occupied by Thomas Godwin (No. 55 on the 1802 map, see Appendix 1) and lately by Taylor and Wildblood.[12] The site is now occupied by houses on the north side of Sneyd Street, Cobridge.

Cowap, Hughes and Co., 1822-28, Cobridge.

Cowap, Hughes and Co. were earthenware manufacturers in Cobridge in 1822[13] and John Taylor was one of three partners remaining when Edward Meigh left in 1823.[14] This John Taylor is probably the earthenware manufacturer of Cobridge who died aged 49 in 1828 whilst 'inspecting accounts prior to paying wages'.[15] The works site is not known.

It has been suggested that caneware was made by one or other of the John Taylor partnerships, but none have been positively identified.

TURNER:
Turner and Banks, c.1760, Stoke-upon-Trent;
John Turner, 1762-81; **Turner and Abbott**, 1781-87;
Turners, Abbott and Newbury, 1788-92;
William and John Turner, 1792-1803;
Turners, Glover and Simpson, 1803-04;
Turner, Glover and Simpson, 1804-06;
Lane End (Longton), Staffordshire;
William Turner, 1807-12, Fenton;
John Turner, c.1814, Lane End;
William Turner, 1824-29, Lane End,
all in Staffordshire.

This multiplicity of titles covers the pottery manufacturing activities of John Turner and his two sons, William and John, for seventy years between 1760 and 1829, mostly in Lane End (Longton).[1] John Turner I was an energetic and innovative master potter, making all kinds of earthenware and stoneware, and attempting to make porcelain, until his early death at the age of forty-nine in 1787.

At John Turner's death, his two sons, then aged twenty-five and twenty respectively, continued the business until 1803, when they took Glover and Simpson as partners. The brothers were bankrupt in 1806. William Turner then had a smaller factory in Fenton from 1807 to 1812; and resumed business in Longton from 1824 to 1829. John Turner II was briefly in business again in 1814.

John Turner I was born in 1738,[2] and apprenticed to Daniel Bird, a potter at Stoke, in 1753.[3] Before moving to Lane End in 1762, Turner was in partnership with William Banks at the potworks which became Spode's factory from 1776.[4] At Lane End, he had two works. By 1768 Turner had his own warehouse in London,[5] and, as Turner and Abbott, the firm styled itself Potters to the Prince of Wales in 1784.[6]

In 1775 John Turner supported Josiah Wedgwood in

Fig. 283 **Small plaque**, blue jasper dip with white relief. **Belt buckle**, white jasper with blue, pale yellow and dark yellow dip and white sprig reliefs. Marks: both TURNER, c. 1795, both 2 x 3 inches. (Rakow collection.)

London in opposing renewal of Champion's patent, and afterwards travelled to Cornwall with Wedgwood to lease china clay ground.[7] Turner experimented with some form of steam engine,[8] and in 1781 he was one of the partners who bought Champion's patent to make porcelain.[9] Shortly before his death in 1787, John Turner I agreed to support the French arcanist Gerverot in making porcelain at Lane End, an unsuccessful venture.[10]

William Turner and John Turner II continued the business, in partnership with Andrew Abbott and another London dealer, Benjamin Newbury, until 1792.[11] In 1800 they obtained a patent for the use of a locally mined 'rock'

to make 'Turner's Patent' ware in both porcelain and earthenware.[12] The brothers took their brother-in-law, John Glover, and their chief clerk, Charles Simpson, into partnership in 1803.[13]

John Turner II left the business in 1804,[14] and Glover and Simpson left in 1806.[15] Both Turner brothers were then bankrupt,[16] but William continued to manufacture at Fenton until 1812,[17] whilst John Turner is said to have managed Minton's works at Stoke for a time.[18] He appears to have briefly resumed potting in Lane End in 1814,[19] was insolvent again in 1815,[20] and then moved to Brewood, Staffordshire. John Turner II died there in 1824.[21]

William Turner was again in business in Lane End from 1824 to 1829,[22] and he died there in 1835.[23]

The first factory occupied by John Turner Senior as a master potter seems to have been in his c.1760 partnership with William Banks, at a potworks in Stoke which had existed since at least 1751,[24] and which was bought by Josiah Spode I in 1776;[25] still part of the Spode Works site in 1996. John Turner had left both Banks and the Stoke works by 1764.[26]

John Turner's Upper Works (or Near Bank) was on the north-east side of Market Street/Uttoxeter Road, Longton, opposite the end of Commerce Street, No. 136 on the 1802 map (Appendix 1).[27] His Lower Works (or Far Bank), which he bought in 1779,[28] was opposite his Upper Works, between Market Street and Kingcross Street. Neither was standing in 1996.

Fig. 284 **Necklaces**, one blue jasper and two black and white jasper beads. Unmarked, attributed to Turner by family provenance, c. 1790-1800, left 28 inches long. (City Museum and Art Gallery, Stoke-on-Trent, 126 P1966.)

Fig. 285 **Cup and saucer**, solid blue jasper with white relief decoration. Mark: TURNER, c. 1795-1800, 2½ inches high. (Polikoff collection.)

Fig. 286 **Sugar bowl**, solid blue jasper with white reliefs. Mark: TURNER, c. 1800, 5¼ inches high. (Royal Ontario Museum, 984.18.30.1&2.)

After his bankruptcy in 1806, William Turner resumed business in a works at Foley, Fenton, from 1807 to 1812,[29] owned by Joseph Myatt, probably No. 117 on the 1802 map (Appendix 1).[30] The site is now (1996) cleared, next east of the Wedgwood factory shop, King Street, Fenton. From 1824 to 1829, William Turner was back in a small new works in High Street (now Uttoxeter Road), Longton, owned by William Waller.[31]

John Turner II was mentioned as occupying a small

potworks near Longton Town Hall, when it was offered for sale in 1814.[32]

Like his great contemporary and friend, Josiah Wedgwood I, John Turner had a warehouse in London: at 10 Bennetts Hill by 1768,[33] and at 9 Old Fish Street from 1774.[34] He had taken Andrew Abbott as his partner there by 1781, and they moved to 81 Fleet Street in 1782.[35] They were billed as 'Potters to the Prince of Wales' from 1784.[36] After the death of John Turner I in 1787, Benjamin

Fig. 287 **Group of three teawares**, solid blue jasper with white relief decoration. Marks: sugar, TURNER & CO., probably 1803-06, 4¼ inches high; Coffee pot and cup and saucer, TURNER, c. 1790-1800, coffee pot 9¼ inches high. (Nottingham Museum, 1892-321, 1892-311, 1892-322.)

Fig. 288 *Mug*, solid blue jasper with white relief decoration. Mark: TURNER, c. 1800, 3½ inches high. (Newark Museum, Newark, New Jersey)

Fig. 289 ***Teapot, milk jug and tea canister***, solid blue jasper with white relief decoration. Teapot and milk jug unmarked, tea canister, TURNER, c.1795-1800, milk jug, 5⅛ inches high. (Liverpool Museum, Museum & Galleries on Merseyside, 1167M, 18.11.25.2.)

Newbury joined Abbott and Turner's sons in a new partnership, which ended in 1792.[37]

On their exploratory journey to Cornwall in 1775, John Turner I and Josiah Wedgwood agreed to get china clay and china stone from Gonnamarros for twenty-one years[38] and William Turner and John Turner II joined a partnership to buy Dorset clay in 1791.[39] Turners occupied mills for grinding potters' materials, at Anchor Ground, Longton, and at Fenton.[40]

Items of transfer-printed pottery have been noted marked 'Turner/Mist/Sole Agent'.[41] James Mist was

Andrew Abbott's partner in London from 1806 to 1809. From 1809 to 1815, James Mist was in business there alone,[42] and any wares marked 'Turner/Mist/Sole Agent' must have been made by either William Turner at Foley between 1807 and 1812, or just conceivably by John Turner II at Lane End in 1814. Letters of January 1813 quoted by Hillier suggest that Mist dealt with William Turner.[43]

At the sale of all types of Turners' stocks in 1807, it was stated that 'purchasers will also have the opportunity of matching, and continuing the patterns, at Mr WILLIAM TURNER'S present Manufactory, in Lane End', suggesting that William Turner had retained moulds and engravings.[44]

If one finds stoneware impressed 'Turner-Mist-Sole Agent' this would suggest dates between 1809-12 or possibly as late as 1814.

The Turner production of dry-bodied stonewares was

Fig. 290 ***Pair of candlesticks of figures of Ceres***, caneware. Marks: both TURNER, c. 1790-1800, 9⅜ inches high. (Royal Ontario Museum, 984.18.8.1&2.)

Fig. 291 ***Double bulbous root pot***, caneware with rococo scroll moulded body of a central three garniture group of pots, sprig reliefs, outline painted in blue. Mark: TURNER, c. 1790-1800, 6¾ inches high. (Rakow collection.)

Fig. 292 **Pot-pourri vase**, caneware with cane moulded body and blue enamel painting. Mark: TURNER, c. 1795, 6¼ inches high. (Zeitlin collection (c.f. Colour Plate 65).)

Fig. 293 **Large bulbous root pot**, caneware with moulded body and sprig relief, Clodion-type babies frolicking, outline painted in blue. Mark: TURNER, c. 1790-1800, 7½ x 18¼ inches. (Lady Lever Art Gallery, Museum & Galleries on Merseyside, LL1617.)

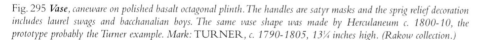

Fig. 294 **Mug and sugar bowl**, caneware with moulded floral body, outline painted in blue. Marks: both TURNER, c. 1795-1800, mug 3⅛ inches high. (Rakow collection.)

Fig. 295 **Vase**, caneware on polished basalt octagonal plinth. The handles are satyr masks and the sprig relief decoration includes laurel swags and bacchanalian boys. The same vase shape was made by Herculaneum c. 1800-10, the prototype probably the Turner example. Mark: TURNER, c. 1790-1805, 13¼ inches high. (Rakow collection.)

Fig. 296 **Vase**, white stoneware of octagon shape, handles formed of two mouth-to-mouth dragons and sprig relief, glazed interior. Unmarked, attributed to John Turner, c. 1795-1800, 12 inches high. (Blake collection.)

Fig. 297 **Pair of bulbous root pots** (minus liners), white jasper with relief sprig decoration on polished basalt plinths. These were popular shapes in the Turner oeuvre with variations in decoration. The Royal Ontario Museum has an example in caneware with chocolate ground and others were made in blue jasper (Colour Plate 64) and in basalt. Mark: TURNER, 8 inches high. (Blake collection.)

Fig. 298 **Teapot**, *cane moulded caneware.Mark: TURNER, c. 1786-90, 5¼ inches high. (Blake collection.)*

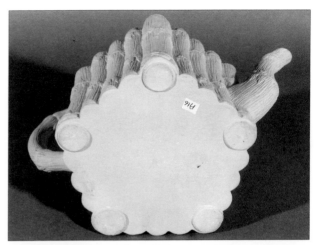

Fig. 299 **Base of teapot** *in figure 298.*

Fig. 300 **Milk jug**, *caneware with moulded bamboo lower body. Mark: TURNER, c. 1787-1800, 4¼ inches high. (Pendergast collection.)*

Fig. 302 **Kettle**, *caneware with moulded ribbed lower body and sibyl finial. Mark: TURNER, c. 1790-1800, 10 inches high. (Rakow collection.)*

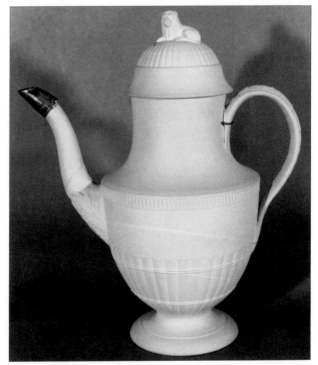

Fig. 301 **Coffee pot**, *caneware with moulded body and lion finial. Mark: TURNER, c. 1790-1800, 9½ inches high.(Collection of Olive Talbot.)*

the largest of any manufacturer apart from Wedgwood. The range included nearly all the bodies produced by the other potteries with the exception of the coloured-bodied stonewares in the Samuel Hollins fashion. Jasper, cane and felspathic stonewares were made in a wide diversity of shapes, none of which resembled the wares of any other manufacturer. It is clear that the Turners were sufficiently admired for their own products to command a clientele which sought them out, and not one that was seeking a less expensive version of Wedgwood.

In jasper the wares were not particularly numerous compared to Adams or Wedgwood but the forms were individual and, judging from the shapes, jasper appears to have been produced by both John Turner I and his sons,

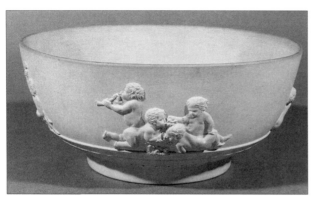

Fig. 303 **Bowl**, caneware with high relief sprigged bacchanalian boys. Mark: TURNER, c. 1787-1800, 2¾ x 6¾ inches. (Liverpool Museum, Museums & Galleries on Merseyside, 54.135.106.)

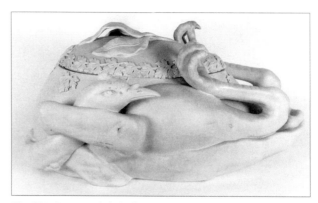

Fig. 304 **Game pie dish**, buff-coloured stoneware moulded in the form of a fowl, sprig embellishment. Mark: TURNER, c. 1820s, 6½ x 13½ inches. (Rakow collection.)

Fig. 305 **Pork pie dish**, buff-coloured stoneware washed with naturalistic colours, some enamel decoration. This realistically modelled pie dish, like the one in figure 304 has a surface which resembles a pastry crust. Mark: TURNER, c. 1820s, 4 x 14½ inches. (Liverpool Museum, Museums & Galleries on Merseyside, 759M.)

Fig. 306 **Small pie dish**, caneware with sprigged floral relief. Mark: TURNER, c. 1810-25, 2⅛ inches high. (Lockett collection.)

John and William. The body is always tight and dense but not as smooth as the jasper produced by Neale. The Turner body has texture as does Wedgwood jasper. Turner jasper is a variable blue, sometimes tending to a grey-blue hue. With the exception of some cameos and medallions which were jasper dip, the hollow wares were generally solid jasper. Although the wares were mainly tea and coffee wares, some very fine ornamental pieces (Colour Plates 64, 65, 70; Fig. 282) were produced as well as cameos, medallions and plaques (Fig. 283 left) and jewellery in the form of jasper beads (Fig. 284). Very little coloured jasper was made but a tri-colour belt buckle marked *TURNER* (Fig. 283 right) indicates that they were proficient at a technology not often practised. The marks on jasper varied little from the usual impressed *TURNER*. However, there is a vase in the Victoria and Albert Museum (c.285-1913) marked *TURNER & Co.*

Caneware was one of the factory's strongest suits. Ornamental figural candlesticks (Fig. 290), tripod pastille burners (Colour Plate 67), flower vases (Colour Plate 70; Fig. 295), and ornamental root pots (Figs. 291, 293), as well as garnitures of bulb pots for mantelpieces were produced in caneware along with the more utilitarian tewares. A number of naturalistic pie dishes (Figs. 304, 305) in the form of the animal from which the pie was to be made were produced, as

Fig. 307 **Stirrup cup**, caneware with white slipped interior and a band of enamel decoration at the rim, on a modern wooden mount. Mark: TURNER, c. 1800, 6⅛ inches long. (Laver collection.)

Fig. 308 **Mug**, *caneware with dimpled body and sprig relief with silver rim and interior white slip with a floral/vermicelli border. Mark: TURNER, c. 1800, 4 inches high. (Polikoff collection.)*

Fig. 309 **Mug**, *caneware with cane moulded body and interior white slip with band of floral/vermicelli enamel painting. Mark: TURNER, 4⅛ inches high. (Laver collection.)*

Fig. 310 **Satyr mugs**, *white stoneware, the left example with enamel painting, glazed interiors. Marks: left TURNER, right TURNER & CO., c. 1800-06, 4½ inches high. (Blake collection.)*

well as the more common pie dish form (Fig. 306). The former were generally produced in a smooth surfaced white or stone-coloured body, not actually the cane body. Sometimes the covered dishes were enamel painted in life-like colours, such as the pork pie dish in Figure 305. Turner caneware also included stirrup cups (Fig. 307) and satyr mugs (Colour Plate 66 left) as well as a variety of beautiful mugs with painted borders on the inside rim and white interior slip (Figs. 308, 309).

Caneware cane teapots were produced which had five cane pads on the base (Figs. 298, 299) distinguishing them

from those made by some other manufacturers, such as Wedgwood, who in basalt often had only three.[45]

Perhaps the largest and most distinguished group of dry-bodies made by the Turners was in the white and felspathic stoneware category. Both smear-glazed and unglazed wares abounded in ornamental forms such as garnitures of vases (Figs. 311, 312) and flower containers (Figs. 314, 324), as well as more practical but unusual shapes like egg stands (Fig. 318), pie dishes (Fig. 315) and double wine coolers (Fig. 316). A large bust of Voltaire (Fig. 317) speaks to the

Fig. 311 **Garniture of three vases** (minus two covers), fine white stoneware with blue and white relief on octagonal polished basalt bases. Marks: all TURNER, c. 1790-1800, central vase 11½ inches high. (Rakow collection.)

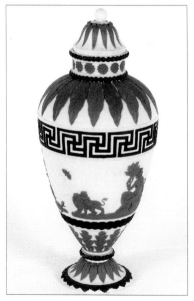

Fig. 312 **Vase**, fine white stoneware with blue and black relief. Unmarked, attributed to Turner, c. 1790-1800, 7 inches high. (Rakow collection.)

Fig. 313 **Pot-pourri vase and teapot**, white stoneware with brown ground and white reliefs. Marks: TURNER, vase 8½ inches high. (Polikoff collection.)

Fig. 314 **Flower pot and stand**, *white stoneware with brown and black bead rims. Marks: both* TURNER, *4⁵⁄₁₆ inches high. (Grigsby collection.)*

Fig. 315 **Pie dish**, *white stoneware with brown slip and white reliefs. Mark:* TURNER, *c. 1815-25, 5¼ x 9½ inches. (Rakow collection.)*

Fig. 316 **Double wine cooler** *(tub with two attached cylindrical jars inside), white stoneware with bands of brown simulating barrel staves, sprig relief decoration and metal ring handles (later additions). Relief decoration includes the* Marriage of Cupid and Psyche *and* Boys and Goat. *Mark:* TURNER, *c. 1800-20, 6¼ x 14¼ inches. (Liverpool Museum, Museums & Galleries on Merseyside.)*

Fig. 317 **Bust of Voltaire**, *white stoneware on a polished basalt pedestal. Mark:* TURNER, *c. 1790-1800, 11⅜ inches high. (Laver collection.)*

Fig. 318 **Egg stand**, *white stoneware with blue enamel decoration and sprigging on rim. Mark:* TURNER, *c. 1790-1800, 2⅝ inches high. (Burgin collection.)*

Fig. 319 **Three teapots**, *left, caneware with moulded and sprig reliefs; centre and right, white stoneware, moulded with sprig reliefs and brown embellishments. Marks: all TURNER, c. 1800, centre teapot 6 inches high. (Blake collection.)*

Fig. 320 **Teapot**, *white stoneware with moulded floral scroll body, outline painted in brown. Mark: TURNER, c. 1790-1800. (Monmouth County Historical Society, New Jersey.)*

Fig. 321 **Teapot and cream jug,** *white felspathic stoneware with smear-glazed exterior and glazed interior. Brown inset panel with white sprig reliefs, additional brown enamel embellishments. Marks: both TURNER, c. 1800-05, teapot 5¼ inches high. (Blake collection.)*

Fig. 322 **Part tea set**, white felspathic stoneware , smear-glazed with brown cartouche and white sprig reliefs, outline painted in blue. Marks: all TURNER, all 4¼ inches high. (Newark Museum, Newark, New Jersey.)

Fig. 323 **Teapot** (minus sliding lid), white felspathic stoneware with sepia painted landscape in an oval cartouche, outline painted in blue. Mark: TURNER, c.1800-05, 5 inches high. (Royal Ontario Museum, 984.18.28.)

Fig. 324 **Vase,** fine white stoneware with moulded panels and oval cartouche of landscape painting, blue enamel outline painting. Mark beneath handle: TURNER, c. 1790-1800, 8 inches high. (Robertshaw collection.)

Fig. 325 **Jug**, white, smear-glazed stoneware with relief decoration and brown enamel neck with a Sheffield plate rim impressed with Thoˢ Law & Cº. Mark: ADAMS, c. 1796, 5½ inches high; **Sugar box**, white stoneware with smear glaze and blue enamel trim. Mark: TURNER, c. 1800-10, 4⅝ inches high. (Blakey collection.)

Fig, 326 **Sugar bowl**, white felspathic stoneware, smear-glazed with oval painted cartouche, outline painted in blue. Mark: TURNER, c. 1800-05, 5¼ inches high. (Rakow collection.)

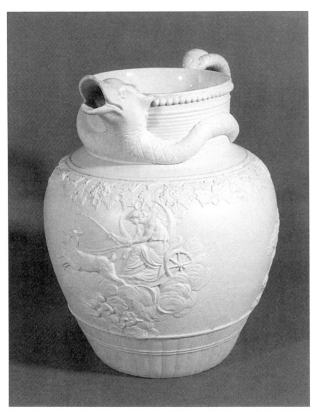

Fig. 327 **Jug**, *white stoneware, smear-glazed, with white relief of Diana driving her cart pulled by two gazelles. A pair of entwined serpents form the handle. Mark:*TURNER, *c. 1800-05, 8 inches high. (Burgin collection.)*

Fig. 328 **Jug,** reverse photograph of jug in figure 327.

Fig. 329 **Jug**, *white stoneware with moulded body and relief decoration, brown neck, mounted with a pewter lid. Mark:* TURNER, *c. 1790-1800, 5¼ inches high. (Rakow collection.)*

Fig. 330 **Mug and jug,** *white stoneware with moulded body, sprig relief decoration of* The Archery Lesson *(left) and* The Audience of a Cock Fight *(right), brown neck and silver rim dated 1790. Marks: both* TURNER, *1790 (jug) to 1800, mug 3¾ inches high; jug 7⅛ inches high. (Blakey collection.)*

Fig. 331 **Mug**, *white stoneware with smear glaze and sprig relief of* The Drunken Silenus *and brown band beneath Sheffield plate rim. Mark : TURNER, c. 1790-1800, 5 inches high. (Collection of Olive Talbot.)*

Fig, 332 **Mark** *on figure 331.*

Fig. 333 **Jug**, *white stoneware with moulded body, relief decoration and enamelled band in blue. Mark: TURNER, c. 1800, 4½ inches high. (Rakow collection.)*

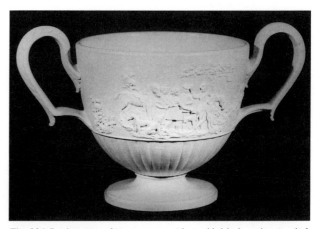

Fig. 334 **Loving cup**, *white stoneware with moulded body and sprig reliefs of drinking and hunting scenes. Mark: TURNER, c. 1790-1800, 6½ inches high. (Kanter collection.)*

Fig. 335 **Jug**, *white stoneware with moulded body and applied reliefs of bacchanalian boys. Mark: TURNER, c. 1800-05, 5¼ inches high. (Rakow collection.)* See also Fig. 359, page 206.

TWEMLOW:
George and Thomas Twemlow 1760-88;
Twemlow and Weston, 1789-94;
John Twemlow, 1794-99; Cannon Street,
Shelton, Staffordshire.

The brothers George (1736-1808) and Thomas Twemlow (1738-1801) bought an old works and land at Shelton in 1760, the works formerly occupied by Warner Edwards.[1] They were potters there until 1788.[2] The Twemlows were sons of Cheshire gentry, who subscribed to shares in the Trent and Mersey Canal in 1766-70; and they built a substantial house on their land, later known as Cannon House.[3] Josiah Wedgwood noted in 1769 that they were employing Ralph Willcox, earlier a painter at Liverpool and Worcester and soon to be employed by Wedgwood, together with Willcox's more competent wife, daughter of Thomas Frye of Bow.[4]

The brothers returned to Cheshire in 1788, and were succeeded by their nephew, John Twemlow,[5] probably in a partnership with John Weston which was dissolved in 1794.[6] Both continued in business separately as potters in Shelton, and Weston was bankrupt in 1797.[7] John Twemlow insured his potworks, houses, stock, utensils etc. for £1,000 in 1795.[8] He retired in 1799,[9] and Simpson and Wright were the next potters on the site, No. 90 on the 1802 map (Appendix 1). The house and re-built works were on the south-east side of Cannon Street, Hanley, and both were demolished in the 1980s.

It has been suggested that Twemlows made dry-bodied ware, but marked examples have not been noted.

W(★★★)

Pottery and porcelain marked W(★★★) has puzzled ceramic historians and collectors for many years. In 1884, Lady Schreiber included a pair of earthenware candlesticks, one marked W(★★★), in the catalogue of her collection, without comment.[1] When Bernard Rackham re-catalogued this collection in 1929, he was able to refer to the same mark being found on porcelain and on figures, and to state that it was believed to come from the Wood factory at Burslem.[2]

Suggestions are not wanting for the maker of these wares, amongst them Wood, Wolfe, Whitehead, Warburton[3] and Herculaneum;[4] and there have been three detailed and reasoned studies.[5] The different types of ware bearing this mark include:

hybrid hard-paste porcelain (one piece decorated c.1800)[6]
bone china (London shape teacup)
cream-coloured earthenware
green-glazed earthenware
basalt, including shapes up to 1813

Marked pieces in other bodies continue to come to light.

Decorative techniques noted include on-glaze black printing, on-glaze enamel painting, on-glaze gilding and on-glaze platinum lustre. The impressed mark must have been applied at the factory/ies of origin, before the pieces had their first firing, but these surface decorations may have been applied outside the factory/ies of origin, and so are not necessarily a reliable guide to the maker/s.

Variations in marking include a piece marked with W and *five* asterisks but no parentheses: W★★★★★;[7] and a jug impressed both W(★★★) and also WS.[8] A green-glazed earthenware dish marked only WS is in a private collection. The mark WS could be attributed to several potters, amongst them William Shelley, William Shirley, William Stanley and William Stevenson. These four potters are studied briefly below.

William Shelley (1786-1841) was in business at Longton from 1812 to 1821 as William Shelley and Co., earthenware manufacturers, and then from 1822 to 1824 as Shelley and Shaw.[9] As the firms were 'Shelley and Co'. or 'Shelley and Shaw', it seems unlikely that their wares would be marked 'WS'.

Shirley and Co. are listed at Shelton in the sole surviving original 1807 rate book, and variously 'Shirley and Co.' or 'W. Shirley' in later transcripts up to c.1818.[10] The firm was named as solely William Shirley in an 1809 Directory.[11] In 1811 Wm. & Jesse Shirley contributed to a subscription list,[12] and were noted as also occupying the Old Hall Works, Hanley.[13] William and Jesse Shirley, Shelton, potters and partners, were bankrupt in 1816 (as were also John and Benjamin Shirley of Worship Street, London, earthenware dealers).[14] These bankruptcies were also referred to together in 1821 and as late as 1835,[15] suggesting that the two firms were connected. The varying styles of the firm suggest that its products could have been marked 'WS', 'S & Co' or 'W&JS', and therefore it is a possible contender for making wares marked 'WS', between 1807 and 1816.

William Stanley was in partnership with John Stanley at Hanley, as Stanley & Co., from c.1796 to 1798.[16] He was at the Knowl Works, Burslem by 1802,[17] when John Stanley left a partnership with William Stanley and William Stanley the younger.[18] William Stanley junior also left later that year,[19] but William Stanley senior continued making earthenware for nineteen years at the Knowl Works until late 1821 when the works was advertised to be sold or to be let, 'late occupied by William Stanley'.[20] He is listed alone as William Stanley, earthenware manufacturer, in Directories of 1805, 1809 and 1818,[21] and must be considered a leading candidate for the manufacture of earthenware marked 'WS', between 1802 and 1821.

Stevenson. A Jasper-type pedestal with figures of *Ganymede* etc. in the Victoria and Albert Museum is marked W. STEVENSON/HANLEY/MAY 2/1802.[22] The only other reference to a W. Stevenson in this period which has been found is 'Stevenson, William, potter, Well Street,

Old Hall Street [Hanley]' in an 1818 Directory,[23] and the mark may well refer to a working potter rather than a manufacturer. It seems unlikely that this W. Stevenson would be the maker of wares marked 'WS'. The potential makers of earthenware marked 'WS' are therefore:

William Stanley, between 1802 and 1821, or
William and John Shirley, between 1807 and 1816.

However, there is no evidence to suggest that either Shirley or Stanley made hard-paste hybrid porcelain or bone china, and so neither is likely to have been the maker of *all* the pieces marked (W★★★). The inference must be that a 'middleman' was ordering pots from various makers, and having them marked (W★★★). The real question remains unanswered – who instructed Shirley or Stanley and other potters to impress their wares with the mark (W★★★)?

The purpose of a mark is to identify the maker/supplier so that he can receive further orders. Some retailers had their own names put upon ware, but it had to be their actual names, so that casual individual customers would return to them; a code would defeat the intention. Therefore it must be a manufacturer or a wholesaler who used the code. Why would either a manufacturer or a wholesaler wish to conceal his identity under a code?

Speculation could continue endlessly, but proof would be a contemporary document which clearly linked pots marked (W★★★) with a maker or wholesaler, and that document has not yet been found.

WARBURTON

The Warburtons were engaged in several pottery businesses, chiefly in Cobridge but also in other parts of the Staffordshire Potteries, Leeds, North-East England and France. Detailed information is only given about three Warburton businesses which might have made dry-bodied ware.

Jacob Warburton, *c.*1769–*c.*1796;
Jacob and John Warburton, 1800;
John Warburton, 1800–1827;
Hot Lane, Burslem, Staffordshire.

Josiah Wedgwood noted in 1769 that Mr Warburton had taken R. Daniel's works,[1] and 'Mr Warburton' is thought to be Jacob Warburton (*c.*1742–1826), who signed the 1770 salt glaze price agreement.[2] He was listed in Directories from 1783 to 1796,[3] and insured his works in Hot Lane, utensils and stock, for £300 in 1789.[4] Jacob Warburton retired from a partnership with his son, John Warburton, in 1800;[5] and John continued to manufacture earthenware in Hot Lane until 1827.[6] Jacob Warburton was also a partner in the New Hall china works, often called Hollins, Warburton and Co.[7]

John Warburton is shown on the 1802 map (Appendix 1) as occupying two works, both numbered 54, east and west of Elder Road. The works west of Elder Road was

occupied by William Cope in 1832,[8] and was later known as the Villa Pottery, the site being at the north-east end of Rushton Road. The works on the east of Elder Road would lie in what is now Cobridge Park.

Peter and Francis Warburton, 1801–1802;
Peter Warburton, 1802–1813;
Bleak Hill Works, Cobridge, Staffordshire.

Jacob Warburton bought land at Cobridge from Ralph Wedgwood in 1795, named the Upper and Lower Brief Longs, and in 1802 sold part of it to his son Peter Warburton (*c.*1773–1813), to build a house.[9] It is likely that Peter and his brother Francis Warburton had already bought another part, which formed the site of the Bleak Hill works, insured by them in December 1801.[10] Peter and Francis Warburton dissolved partnership in March 1802,[11] Francis going to France to start a pottery at La Charité sur Loire, Nièvre (see below) and Peter Warburton continuing at Bleak Hill works until his death in 1813.[12] He was succeeded by Ralph and James Clews (q.v.) whilst his house was leased by Robert Blackwell until *c.*1818 and later by Enoch Wood junior.[13] A potworks existed on the Bleak Hill site until the 1970s, a site now occupied by Camoys Court, between Warburton Street and Elder Road.

The works is not positively identified on the 1802 map (Appendix 1). A potworks indicated by † is in the approximate position of Bleak Hill works, but the symbol is not allocated to a manufacturer in the key. Two other symbols, ★ and ‡ are also used for new potworks on this map, for John Taylor (q.v.), and Robert Clulow and Co. (q.v.), perhaps an indication that these were additions when the 1802 map was revised from an 1800 version, which has not been traced.

Like his father Jacob, Peter Warburton was a partner in the New Hall china works and in 1810 he patented a process for decorating china etc., with gold, silver, platina, etc.[14]

Warburtons and Moseley, 1815,
probably Churchyard Works, Burslem, Staffordshire.

This partnership is only known by its dissolution: John and Benjamin Warburton and John Moseley ended their partnership in 1815.[15] John and Benjamin Warburton were probably two sons of Jacob Warburton;[16] and Mary Warburton, his daughter, was referred to as the relict (widow) of John Moseley when she died in 1855.[17] John Moseley made Egyptian Black and earthenware at the Churchyard Works until his death in 1824.[18]

Other Warburton pottery businesses included:

Edward Warburton, 1752–*c.*1761,
Fenton Low, Staffordshire.[19]
Joseph Warburton, –1752;
John Warburton, 1752–1761;

Ann Warburton and Son, 1761–*c*.1771,
Hot Lane, Burslem, Staffordshire.[20]
Joseph Warburton, *c*.1763–1769,
Sneyd Street, Cobridge, Staffordshire.[21]
Isaac and Jacob Warburton, fl.1765,
Cobridge, Staffordshire.[22]
Thomas Warburton and Joseph Stone, 1770–71,
Burslem, Staffordshire.[23]
Joseph Warburton, *c*.1781–1788,
Cliff Bank, Stoke-upon-Trent, Staffordshire.[24]
James Warburton, *c*.1810–1827,
Mary Warburton, 1827–*c*.1830;
Hot Lane, Burslem, and Cobridge, Staffordshire.[25]
Joseph Warburton *c*.1757;
John Warburton, 1770–1795;
Isaac Warburton, *c*.1795–*c*.1801;
Ellen Warburton *c*.1801–1817; and **Joseph Warburton**
c.1833 were all pottery manufacturers in the vicinity of
Newcastle-upon-Tyne, Northumbria.[26]
Samuel Warburton *c*.1852–1863, and **William Henry
Warburton**, 1863, were partners in the Leeds Pottery,
Leeds, Yorkshire.[27]
Francis Warburton, 1802–03,
La Charité sur Loire, Nièvre, France.[28]

Although there are some basalts associated with the
Warburton potteries, no other stonewares have been
positively identified with their manufacture, although it is
likely they were produced and sold without factory
imprimaturs.

WEDGWOOD & CO:

Wedgwood & Co., 1788–97, Burslem, Staffordshire;
Wedgwood & Co., 1798–1800,
Ferrybridge, West Yorkshire.

Ralph Wedgwood and Co. made pottery at the Hill House
Works, Burslem, from 1788 to 1797. Ralph Wedgwood
then joined a partnership at the Knottingley Pottery,
Ferrybridge, Yorkshire, which used the mark 'Wedgwood &
Co.', until he left at the end of 1800.

Ralph Wedgwood was baptised on 8 May 1766, eldest
son of 'Useful Thomas', Josiah Wedgwood's partner in
making useful ware at Burslem and later at Etruria.[1] By
1783, then aged seventeen, Ralph Wedgwood showed
interest in enamels used by Wedgwood,[2] and from 1786 to
1788 he supplied colours, paints, pencils (paint-brushes)
and borax to Wedgwood.[3] Much later, in 1826, Ralph
Wedgwood told Enoch Wood that he had made about
£500 from making and selling colours, which he had used
to set up his youngest brother, John Taylor Wedgwood, as
an engraver.[4]

On 3 March 1788, Josiah Wedgwood II wrote to his
father with great concern because he had heard that 'you
and TW [Thomas Wedgwood] are going to part at
Martlemas [Martinmas, 11 November]' and that TW was
hiring men to work for himself or his son Ralph 'which is
much the same thing'. In another letter of 7 March, Josiah's

son was happier because 'Mr Swift tells me that Mr TW has
written to you which I am very glad of'.[5] Thomas
Wedgwood was going to start business in his family
property, the Hill House Works, Burslem, earlier occupied
by William Adams of Tunstall (q.v.). However, Thomas
Wedgwood died on 10 October 1788,[6] and family
tradition states that Ralph Wedgwood provided money to
start his younger brother, Samuel, and Peter Swift, Josiah
Wedgwood's accountant, in business as Wedgwood & Co.
at the Hill House Works.[7]

Both Burslem and Ferrybridge firms were known as
Wedgwood & Co., and there are many pieces of pottery so
marked.[8] The Burslem firm is referred to in two 1790s
Directories: 'Burslem, Wedgwood, Ralph and Co.' in the
nationally compiled *c*.1795 *Universal British Directory;* and
'Wedgwood & Co.' in Chester and Mort's locally compiled
The Pottery Directory of 1796.

Samuel Wedgwood was in Paris in 1788, studying
languages, visiting the Sèvres works and learning the
methods of French potters but he died at Whitworth,
Lancashire on 15 January 1790, aged only twenty-two.[9] He
is only mentioned as a master potter by J.C. Wedgwood and
subsequent writers, and could have spent fourteen months
at most in the business.

Peter Swift had left Etruria in 1777 and tried to set up as
a potter at Burslem, but returned to Josiah Wedgwood
within a year, promising to 'sit quietly at his desk, & think
of nothing further'. Josiah Wedgwood then lent Swift
money to pay off his debts.[10] A study of relevant Wedgwood
papers shows that letters before 5 November 1788 were
written by Peter Swift in the first person, but letters for the
next month refer to him in the third person, suggesting
that Peter Swift had ended his employment with the
Etruria firm but was willingly advising Wedgwood on
unresolved matters.[11] On 20 February 1789, Josiah
Wedgwood and Peter Swift made an agreement for Swift
to lease the former parsonage house in Burslem for eight
years. On 9 November 1789, Peter Swift wrote from 'Hill,
Burslem' to Josiah Wedgwood about a workman 'here'
paying off a debt to Josiah Wedgwood.[12] Clearly, Peter Swift
did leave Josiah Wedgwood amicably in November 1788
and join Ralph and Samuel Wedgwood at Hill House
Works.

Ralph Wedgwood attended meetings of master potters
from March 1789[13] and insured with the Sun Company his
house and adjoining potworks, utensils and stock in June
1789, together with two other potworks held by tenants.[14]
Ralph Wedgwood alone was bankrupt in 1797. He was
obviously the leading light in the Wedgwood and Co.
concern. It is not clear how long Swift stayed with him. In
1813, Swift's daughter told Josiah Wedgwood II that in
1810 her father was living in Cheshire, 'afflicted'.[15]

In November 1791, Ralph Wedgwood and Co. opened a
London warehouse.[16] When Ralph Wedgwood changed his
insurers to the Salop Fire Office in January 1793, the third
potworks was no longer mentioned,[17] perhaps the first sign
of decline. In April 1793, Josiah Wedgwood wrote that
Ralph Wedgwood was 'tottering',[18] and Ralph's London

Fig. 336 *Cameos and medallions, white jasper with blue jasper dip and reliefs of:* Peace, A Sacrifice, Louis XVI, George III *and* Queen Charlotte. *Marks:* Wedgwood & Co., *c. 1788-1800,* Peace, *2⅝ inches high. (Private collection, ex Rakow collection.)*

warehouse was closed in September 1794.[19] In February 1797, Ralph Wedgwood consulted Boulton and Watt about a steam engine he wanted for a proposed new earthenware factory near Glasgow.[20] Two months later, he was bankrupt.[21] According to Jewitt,[22] writing eighty years later, Ralph Wedgwood was ruined through losses during the (Napoleonic) war.

His house, potworks, sliphouse and land were offered by auction in June 1797, with immediate possession of the house and manufactory if desired.[23] Utensils and fixtures were for sale at a fair valuation. Ralph had evidently continued his colour business: 'a large assortment of colours for Enamelling upon and under the Glaze' (and 'several compleat (*sic*) Sets of Valuable Engravings') were also in the auction. A year later, a further auction was advertised, covering Ralph's house at the Hill, the adjoining potworks, the sliphouse, land, furniture and materials, including 'a large lot of Jasper Stone in boxes'.[24] By then, Ralph Wedgwood was at Ferrybridge in Yorkshire. The 1797 colours and engravings were not included in 1798 as some

of them had already gone to Ferrybridge. The 1802 map (Appendix 1) shows that Ralph Wood III later occupied the Hill House works, No. 27.

In 1797 Ralph Wedgwood became interested in the Knottingley Pottery at Ferrybridge, Yorkshire where he went in the September to 'review the state of the works' and bought some of his moulds, colours and engravings from his assignees in Burslem,[25] for his new partners: John Foster, John Thompson, John Seaton and William Tomlinson.[26] Ralph Wedgwood joined the partnership from January 1798 and the firm became known as 'Tomlinson, Foster, Wedgwood & Company'. Ralph Wedgwood was to manage the works, make known his secrets to the other partners, and produce ware equal to that made by him at Burslem and specimens provided by him. The other partners became dissatisfied with Ralph Wedgwood, and he was paid £1,025 to leave completely by 1 January 1801. Ralph Wedgwood's own cash book shows that he was paid £50 a quarter from 1 January 1798 to 31 October 1800 for managing the business.[27] He had been a master potter at Burslem for a little under ten years, and at Knottingley Pottery for less than three. A final dividend on Ralph Wedgwood's Burslem bankruptcy was paid in 1804, making a total return to his creditors of 10s.2d. in the pound (51%).[28]

Ralph Wedgwood was inventive, and registered three pottery-related patents in 1796.[29] He made further inventions, including carbon-paper, but could not manage his financial affairs, and wrote pathetic begging letters to Josiah Wedgwood II, Enoch Wood and Joseph Mayer. As late as 1835, Joseph Mayer was moved to write that 'Ralph Wedgwood possesses a mind peculiarly constituted - that is his misfortune'.[30] Ralph Wedgwood died in penury in 1837.[31]

It does not appear that Wedgwood & Co. produced much in the way of dry-bodied stoneware. Some very fine basalt was made by the firm but very little has been identified. They also made some few jasper dip medallions and cameos (Fig. 336) of good quality.

WHITEHAVEN:
Bell and Jackson, fl.1834, Whitehaven, Cumbria.

On 25 July 1834, Bell and Jackson of the Ladypit Pottery, Whitehaven advertised that they intended to commence manufacturing 'IRON-STONE-CANE-WARE' etc.[1] This is likely to have been a glazed yellow-ware, rather than a dry-body cane ware. There were several earthenware and coarseware potteries around Whitehaven,[2] and glazed yellow-ware shards have been found at various sites.[3]

WHITEHEAD:
Christopher Charles Whitehead, 1777-1792, Hanley;
Dorothy Whitehead, 1793-98,
Hanley, 1800-01, Shelton;
Christopher Whitehead, 1801-04 and 1817-18,
Shelton;
James and Charles Whitehead, 1793-1810,
Hanley; all Staffordshire.

No pieces of pottery marked Whitehead are known, and the firms are only included in this study because one made red stoneware and another offered to supply dry bodies. The members of the Whitehead family involved are Christopher Charles Whitehead (1737-c.1792), his wife Dorothy, three of their sons: Charles, Christopher and James; and nephew John.

Christopher Charles Whitehead of Hanley sold red china (red stoneware), cream-coloured ware and black ware to Wedgwood from 1777 to 1790.[1] C.C. Whitehead died about 1792, and his widow, Dorothy Whitehead, inherited his estate and carried on his business.[2] Dorothy Whitehead of Hanley continued to supply Wedgwood with red china from April 1793 to November 1798.[3] Shapes of redware supplied include teapots, stands, sugar dishes, ewers, milks, bowls, toy teasets, slop basins and coffee pots. Finishes included plain, engined, sprigged and glazed.

The site of Christopher Charles Whitehead's works in Hanley is uncertain. Shaw says that *Mr* Whitehead, father of James and Charles Whitehead, produced white stone ware salt glaze at the Old Hall Works, Hanley;[4] and certainly Christopher Charles Whitehead owned land in that area.[5] However, Christopher Charles Whitehead was given use of a potworks and other property at Slack Lane (now Bryan Street), Hanley in 1776,[6] and this date fits well with the commencement of his invoices to Wedgwood in 1777.

Bills for ware supplied to Wedgwood show that Dorothy Whitehead, widow of Christopher Charles Whitehead, had moved her business to Shelton by January 1800, and was supplying cream-coloured ware. That business continued in her name until May 1801.[7] Her son, Christopher Whitehead, took over in June 1801 and he supplied cream-coloured ware to Wedgwood until October 1801.[8] Mother and son occupied a works at Howard Place, Shelton, shown as No. 94, Dorothy (*sic*) Whitehead on the 1802 map (Appendix 1). The works occupied by Christopher Whitehead was offered for sale in April 1803, unsuccessfully, and offered to be let, vacant, at Martinmas (11 November) 1804.[9] Christopher Whitehead seems to have briefly resumed business at Howard Place, Shelton in 1817,[10] but he died of typhus on 6 January 1818.[11] Between 1796 and 1798, Christopher Whitehead was in a pottery partnership with E.J. Birch (q.v.).

Other Whiteheads were in partnership with Ephraim Chatterley by 1787, when they sold milk-pots to Wedgwood.[12] 'Chatterley and Whiteheads' insured a set of potworks in Hanley for £1,000 in 1792.[13] In 1793, Ephraim Chatterley left the partnership with his nephews; brothers James and Charles Whitehead and their cousin John Whitehead; potters at Hanley,[14] and the Whiteheads continued the business. By 1798, the partnership was only between James and Charles Whitehead, when they issued a catalogue of *Designs of ... Earthen-ware*.[15] On the title-page, they averred that 'At the same Manufactory may be had ... Dry Bodies, such as Egyptian, Black, Jasper, &c. &c.'. The 1802 map (Appendix 1) shows the brothers at No. 82, now the site of the General Post Office, Tontine Street, Hanley. James and Charles Whitehead were bankrupt in 1810.[16]

WILSON See NEALE

WOLFE:
Thomas Wolfe *c.*1781-1802,
Wolfe and Hamilton, 1802-1809,
Wolfe, Hamilton and Arrowsmith, 1809-1810,
Thomas Wolfe, 1810-1818,
Stoke-upon-Trent, Staffordshire;
Wolfe, Mason and Lucock, 1796-1800,
Liverpool, Lancashire.

Thomas Wolfe junior (1751-1818) was an established potter in Stoke-upon-Trent by 1781,[1] and a 1784 Directory gave his products as 'Queen's Ware in general, Blue, printed and Egyptian Black, Cane, &c.[2] His works, straddling what is now Kingsway, adjoined those of Josiah

Spode,[3] to be separated when the Newcastle branch from the Trent and Mersey Canal was built *c.*1796.

From the mid-1780s, Wolfe had warehouses in Liverpool and Dublin,[4] and he joined in the general interest in manufacturing porcelain by taking over an existing porcelain works in Upper Islington, Liverpool between 1790 and 1795.[5] In partnership with Miles Mason (q.v.) and John Luckock, he made porcelain there until 1800, when that agreement ended.[6] Obviously an enterprising businessman, Wolfe installed steam engines in both his Stoke and Liverpool works in the 1790s.[7] Thomas Wolfe also had interests in a clay partnership and collieries.[8]

By 1802 Wolfe had taken his son-in-law, Robert Hamilton, into partnership at Stoke[9] and they were making china there by 1805,[10] probably in an additional works on the opposite side of what is now Church Street. Another son-in-law, William Arrowsmith, insolvent as a brewer at Prescot, Lancs.,[11] was also a partner from 1809 to 1810, when both Hamilton and Arrowsmith left Wolfe.[12] Arrowsmith was then an independent earthenware manufacturer in Stoke until 1817, when he again became bankrupt.[13] Hamilton leased part of one works from Wolfe and Arrowsmith in 1810.[14]

Thomas Wolfe died 19 October 1818,[15] and both his works in Stoke were to be let, vacant, in July 1819.[16] Wolfe's stock of china and earthenware, moulds, raw materials, etc., was offered for auction in 1823.[17] A William Adams later leased both works.[18] Wolfe's affairs were the subject of court proceedings as late as 1857.[19]

Despite the reference to 'cane' in the 1784 Directory, no dry-bodied ware marked Wolfe has been noted.

WOOD:
Enoch Wood and Ralph Wood, 1783-84,
Enoch Wood, 1784-89,
Enoch Wood and Co., 1790-92,
Wood and Caldwell, 1793-1818,
Enoch Wood and Sons, 1818-1845,
Ralph Wood II, 1782-1795,
Ralph Wood III, 1795-1801;
various works, Burslem, Staffordshire.

The Wood family was the subject of a monograph as early as 1912, and there have been several partial studies since.[1] Enoch Wood, a prominent member of the family, was born 31 January 1759, son of Aaron Wood, a modeller.[2] About 1768, Enoch Wood worked as a boy of nine at Josiah Wedgwood's Bell Works, Burslem, and was sent to Liverpool about 1770 to learn drawing from his cousins, Richard and William Caddick. He was later apprenticed to Humphrey Palmer (q.v.), master potter at Hanley Green.[3] During the 1770s Enoch Wood modelled a plaque of the Wood family arms and other plaques, including a 'Crucifix', 'The Descent from the Cross' and 'Success to G.B. Rodney', examples of which survive in a jasper-type body.[4]

There is some doubt about how and when Enoch Wood commenced in business as a master potter, but there are two items of evidence which suggest that he was first in partnership with his cousin, Ralph Wood II (1748-95). Ralph Wood I died in 1771, and his sons, Ralph Wood II and John Wood, were briefly in business as a master potters at Burslem, but they failed in 1773.[5] Ralph Wood II was in Bristol between 1774 and 1781, but was back in Burslem by 14 August 1782, when he sent a bill to Wedgwood for figures.[6] Ralph Wood II bought bricks and clay from his brother John, and the account was settled with Enoch Wood in November 1783,[7] evidence that Ralph and Enoch Wood were connected in some way then.

Firmer evidence of a partnership is given on page 391 of *Bailey's ... British Directory ... for ... 1784, Volume the Second. The Western Directory* (W. Bailey, London, 1784), publication announced for July 1784:

> Wood, Enoch, and Ralph, *Manufacturers of all kinds of useful and ornamental Earthen Ware, Egyptian Black, Cane, and various other Colours, also Black Figures, Seals and Cyphers,* Burslem.

The linking of the names of Enoch and Ralph, the plural 'manufacturers', and the following text leaves no doubt that Bailey was given this information from a letter head, bill head or trade card provided by Enoch and Ralph Wood. The Directory compiler, William Bailey, issued his *Western & Midland Directory for ... 1783,* in 1783, printed in Birmingham.[8] In that directory he does not give the name

Fig. 337 *Large plaque, white stoneware depicting the* Descent from the Cross. *Mark:* ENOCH WOOD *Sculpsit, dated 1777, 20¼ inches high. (Birmingham Museums & Art Gallery, M13'53.)*

Fig. 338 **Medallions**, *solid blue jasper with white relief subjects:* Minerva *and* France? *Mark:* ENOCH WOOD *Sculpsit, c. 1784-89,* Minerva *4½ inches high. (Rakow collection.)*

Fig. 339 **Medallions**, *white jasper with blue jasper dip and reliefs of* Flora *and* Venus at Vulcan's forge, *the reverse of which reads:* 'Vulcan falls in Love with Venus when forging the Battle Axe for the Trojan War ...ENOCH WOOD Sculpsit', *c. 1784-89,* Flora *4½ inches high. (Rakow collection.)*

Fig. 340 **Medallions**, *solid blue jasper with white reliefs. Marks: left,* TURNER, *c. 1790, 4¼ x 5½ inches, right,* ENOCH WOOD *Sculpsit, c. 1784-89, 4½ x 3⅜ inches (Grigsby collection.)*

Fig. 341 *Sprig mould, unglazed white earthenware. Mark:* WOOD & CALDWELL 1818, 2½ x 3⅛ *inches. (Victoria & Albert Museum, C.158-1937.)*

of either Enoch or Ralph Wood as potters, so that Bailey acquired his information about Enoch and Ralph Wood between 1783 and July 1784, when he issued his 1784 Directory which included their names as partners. Bailey's 1784 entry for Enoch and Ralph Wood is repeated almost exactly in W. Tunnicliff's *A Topographical Survey of the Counties of Stafford, Chester and Lancaster* (Nantwich, 1787), but Tunnicliff repeats all Bailey's entries for potters, and so cannot be relied upon to substantiate any later date than 1784.[9]

On 14 August 1782, 26 July, 5 September and 16 November 1783, Ralph Wood alone billed Wedgwood for figures, ewers and flowerpots supplied.[10] A year later, 17 October 1784, Ralph Wood wrote in the singular, asking for payment of a bill and added 'hoping I may still be favord (*sic*) with your future orders'.[11] These factors suggest that Ralph Wood II was in business alone, and it is possible that Ralph Wood was operating his own business alongside a partnership with Enoch Wood. Even so, on the evidence available, Enoch and Ralph Wood were only partners for a short time between the purchase of bricks in late 1783 and the publication of Bailey's Directory in July 1784. No dissolution of a partnership between Enoch and Ralph Wood has been noted, and the Land Tax records do not help.[12]

Enoch Wood himself never referred to a partnership with Ralph Wood. Writing in 1814 or later, he stated that he modelled the Crucifix plaque when he was about fourteen years old (*c.*1773), and 'About ten years after this [making the Crucifix] [*c.*1783] I began to manufacture earthenware as a Master Potter and hired John Proudlove for 12/- [60 pence] per week, he was then said to be the best Tureen squeezer in the neighbourhood'.[13]

The locally based historian, Simeon Shaw, wrote in 1829 that 'In 1784, Mr E. Wood commenced business at Burslem, and continues to the present time. At that time, the best mould maker and tureen maker in that part, was John Proudlove, who was hired by Mr W. for *three* years, at *twelve* shillings per week [Shaw's italics]'.[14] The similarity of

this statement to that of Enoch Wood's, with the addition of 'three years', suggests that Shaw had his information personally from Enoch Wood, one of the master potters whom Shaw thanked for information in his preface, confirming that Enoch Wood commenced business in 1784.

Ralph Wood II continued in business alone in Burslem until his death in 1795, followed by his son, Ralph Wood III[15] (who succeeded Ralph Wedgwood (q.v.) at the Hill House Works) until he died 15 July 1801.[16]

Enoch Wood's first factory is not known. Many years later his large works at Fountain Place, Burslem was said to cover the sites of four or five old factories[17] and perhaps he originally occupied one of these. Between 1786 and 1796 Enoch Wood rented the Overhouse Works, Burslem, from the executors of the late Thomas Wedgwood; and bought some of his utensils in 1786.[18] From March 1787, Enoch Wood sold porphyry, French grey and 'grotto' ware to Josiah Wedgwood.[19]

Enoch Wood built what became known as Fountain Place Works in 1789.[20] In December of that year, he insured a brick and tiled potwork and thatched saggar house and warehouse for £255, and other miscellaneous buildings separately.[21] Two years later, in January 1792, Enoch Wood insured a set of potworks, all brick and tiled, for £600,[22] the increase suggesting that in the meantime he had cleared away the old thatched buildings, and extended his new brick-and-tiled Fountain Place works. In 1790 he bought cream-colour plates from Josiah Wedgwood,[23] and also borrowed £760 from him, probably repaid in 1799 to Josiah Wedgwood II and Thomas Wedgwood, when they were buying the Gunville estate in Dorset.[24]

Enoch Wood is said to have taken James Caldwell, a Newcastle-under-Lyme solicitor, into partnership in 1790.[25] Wood's firm is referred to as Enoch Wood and Co. in 1792 and 1793,[26] and Falkner illustrated a trade card of 'Enoch Wood & Co.', showing the Fountain Place Works and windmill, and an engine-turned urn with ram's-head handles,[27] possibly issued when the new factory was built. An official partnership agreement between Enoch Wood and James Caldwell was dated 1 January 1793;[28] perhaps there was an additional partner earlier. Wood and Caldwell supplied French grey and other ware to Wedgwood in 1798.[29]

In July 1800 Wood and Caldwell insured their set of potworks etc., for £1,300, more than double the 1792 figure, and also other properties including Enoch Wood's house.[30] They had the opportunity to buy two adjoining potworks in 1799, when Walter Daniel put them up for sale, leased to Leigh & Co. and Nathan Heath and Sons, 'near Newcastle turnpike'.[31] Perhaps the increased insurance value is indicative that they did so. Neither Leighs nor Heaths appeared in an 1805 Directory,[32] suggesting that both works had been absorbed into Fountain Place by then. In 1828, Enoch Wood bought the western part of Packhorse Lane, which ran between these works and his original factory.[33]

On 9 July 1818 Enoch Wood wrote to James Caldwell

Fig. 342 **Plaque**, *caneware with relief of a female figure in profile leaning on a column,. Mark:* ENOCH WOOD & SONS, *c. 1818-25, 7¼ inches high. (Burgin collection.)*

By 1833, Woods employed 1,100,[39] and in 1836 they had twenty-one ovens in their several works.[40] Another works in Burslem, the Knowl Works, was leased by Wood and Caldwell from c.1821 until 1835.[41] In the late 1830s, Woods also occupied yet another factory in Burslem, owned by John Brettell, site unknown.[42]

Joseph Wood left the partnership 1 January 1838,[43] and Enoch Wood senior died 17 August 1840, aged 81.[44] Enoch Wood junior and Edward Wood continued the business, but in August 1845 offered for sale the Furlong or Middle Works and the Lower Works, on Newcastle Street.[45] The entire business closed down on 6 December 1845, due to losses in the American trade and the death of the senior partner.[46] Attempts were made to sell the Hill Works (Fountain Place Works), Middle Works, Lower Works, Fountain Place House, a flint mill and the American Hotel on Waterloo Road, at various dates in 1846 and 1850.[47]

The local newspaper reported rejoicing when 'Enoch's bell pealed again' on 28 June 1851, upon Pinder, Bourne and Hope re-opening the Hill Works.[48] By March 1852, Peter Holdcroft had occupied the Lower Works and T., J. and J. Mayer the Middle Works, when the properties were yet again advertised, this time for sale as investments.[49] Enoch Wood junior died at Northwich, 11 June 1852.[50]

Enoch Wood produced more cameos, medallions and plaques than any other manufacturer outside Wedgwood. Medallions in blue and white jasper (Figs. 338, 339), tri-colour plaques (Colour Plate 71), and caneware plaques (Fig. 342) constituted some of the ornamental wares produced. Monumental plaques in a variety of ground colours were made, particularly the famous *Descent from the Cross* (Fig. 337) of which there are several known copies. Ralph Wood also manufactured caneware figures of good quality. *Apollo and Diana* (Colour Plate 72; Fig. 343) were among those produced by that factory.

Fig. 343 **Mark** on Colour Plate 72.

WOOLLEY See CHETHAM

offering to *buy* or *sell* the property of Wood and Caldwell.[34] The reply must have been speedy, because they had agreed to dissolve the partnership eight days later, on 17 July 1818.[35] A new partnership ensued from 1 January 1819, between Enoch Wood and three of his sons, Joseph, Enoch junior and Edward.[36] Hamlet Wood, relationship unknown, left Wedgwoods in 1819 to run a proposed establishment in Belfast for Enoch Wood and Sons,[37] in another partnership, which ended in 1827.[38]

Fig. 344 *Three vases*, white felspathic stoneware with classical reliefs and enamel sprigging, outline painted in blue. Unmarked, traditionally attributed to Herculaneum, c. 1790-1810, large vase 8½ inches high. (Liverpool Museum, Museums & Galleries on Merseyside.)

Fig. 345 *Teapot*, white felspathic stoneware smear-glazed with moulded and sprig relief decoration, outline painted in blue. A classical silver-shaped teapot, similar to some made by the Dunderdale at Castleford, these pots, nevertheless, defy attribution, c. 1800-10, 7½ inches high. (Private collection.)

Fig. 346 *Teapot*, white felspathic stoneware with smear-glaze in silver-shape with sprigged theatrical figures and blue enamel painting. Unmarked, c. 1800-10, 7 inches high. (Blake collection.)

Fig. 347 **Teapot,** *white felspathic stoneware, smear-glazed with vertical ribbing, green and blue enamel painting and dolphin finial. This unusual finial is also seen on a basalt teapot marked WEDGWOOD & Co. in the Hacking collection (see Edwards, Black Basalt, fig. 423). Unmarked, c. 1795-1800, 4½ inches high. (Blake collection.)*

Fig. 348 **Teapot**, *white felspathic stoneware, smear-glaze with horizontal ribbing in the form of a beehive, blue outline painting. These teapots were very popular from 1791, especially in basalt, particularly with the European markets, and the popularity continued well into the early nineteenth century. In basalt several potteries were making the wares which are rarely marked, including the Leeds Pottery of Hartley, Greens & Co, Spode, The Don Pottery, Keeling, Toft & Co., Spode and Wedgwood (see Edwards, Black Basalt, 92). Unmarked, c. 1795-1810, 5 inches high. (Blake collection.)*

See also Fig. 360, page 206.

Fig. 349 **Sugar bowl**, *white felspathic stoneware with applied relief and Venus and Cupid finial. Unmarked, c. 1800-1820, 5½ inches high. (Rakow collection.)*

Fig. 350 **Three jugs**, *drab-brown stoneware smear-glazed with Union Wreath sprig relief band at neck, Tudor Rose on each side of the spout, a George IV medallion under the spout and a floating angel along the side of the jugs, each with lion handles. Unmarked except for small jug which is impressed J 18, c. 1820-25, large jug 8½ inches high. (Blake collection.)*

Fig. 351 *Jug*, fine white translucent stoneware, smear-glazed with blue enamel bands and Duke of Wellington commemorative relief sprigging. Unmarked except for an impressed 5 over an impressed 6 and a N 1 painted underglaze, c. 1812, 6¼ inches high. (Lockett collection.)

Fig.352 *Jug*, white felspathic stoneware with moulded and relief sprigged decoration of Peace and Plenty, green and blue enamel embellishment. Unmarked, c. 1800-20, 7 inches high. (Richardson collection, ex Nina Fletcher Little.)

Fig. 353 *Small coffee pot*, brown stoneware, smear-glazed with pale blue sprigged figures and stylized floral bands, enamel blue outline painting. Unmarked, c. 1795, 6 inches high. (Hyland collection.)

Fig. 354 *Cribbage board*, solid light blue jasper with white reliefs of thistles, roses and shamrocks. Unmarked, c. 1801-1810, 8¼ x 3 inches. (Lady Lever Art Gallery, Museums & Galleries on Merseyside, LL1480.)

Fig. 355 **Jug**, *fine white translucent stoneware with moulded body and extraordinary S - shaped handle associated with the Davenport pottery. Unmarked, possibly Davenport, c. 1820-30, 6¼ inches high. (Spencer collection.)*
See also Fig. 157, page 130.

Fig. 356 **Teapot**, *white felspathic stoneware with hinged lid and blue enamel painting. Unmarked, attributed to John Glass, Hanley from marked examples in basalt, c. 1800-20, 6¼ inches high. (Spencer collection.)*
See also text reference page 134.

Fig. 357 **Sugar bowl**, *fine white stoneware with bamboo moulded body and enamel painted in blue. Unmarked, attributed to Elijah Mayer from marked examples in basalt from the same mould, 4¼ inches high. (Spencer collection.)*
See also Fig. 216, page 152.

Fig. 358 **Jug**, *glazed drab-brown stoneware with engine-turned body and satyr moulded spout. Although the impressed mark 'Minton' is reputedly mid-19th century, the shape and body of this jug suggests a much earlier date. Mark: MINTON, possibly c. 1820-30 or later, 6¹⁄₁₆ inches high. (Private collection.)*
See also text reference page 153.

Fig. 359 **Teapot**, *fine white stoneware with moulded body, sprig relief and enamel line and flower painting. Unmarked, attributed to Warburton, possibly John Warburton, Cobridge 1805-10, 6·8 inches high. (Spencer collection.)* See also Fig. 335, page 192.

Fig. 360 **Teapot**, *white felspathic stoneware with Greek key-moulded body and blue enamel painting. Cartouche has light blue enamel ground and bird relief associated with some Ridgway porcelains. Unmarked, 2⅝ inches high. (Spencer collection.)*
See also Fig. 348, page 203.

CHAPTER IX

Some Continental Manufacturers

NYON:
Dortu & Müller, 1781–83;
Müller, 1783–87;
Dortu, Bonnard & Veret, 1787–1813,
Nyon, Switzerland.

Jacques Dortu, a Frenchman formerly employed by a number of prestigious European factories (including Cassel, Ansbach, Berlin, Marseilles and Marieburg) and Ferdinand Müller, a German from Frankenthal, opened a porcelain manufactory in the town of Nyon near Bern in 1781. After a couple of years Dortu sold his share to Müller and returned to Berlin, while the latter continued to run the factory alone. In 1787, in an attempt by Müller to move the factory to Geneva, the town authorities intervened and Müller was expelled from the town and direction of the factory reverted to Dortu, who had returned, in association with Moyse Bonnard and Henri Veret. In 1789 the factory moved to the Rue de Porcelaine where they stayed until dissolution of the partnership in 1813 due to financial difficulties. After Nyon Dortu went on to Herpin in Geneva where he remained technical director until his death in 1819. It is to Dortu that Nyon owes its success.[1]

In addition to fine porcelain the factory produced basalt, fine red stoneware and buff-coloured stoneware (Colour Plate 73). The stoneware comes from the period 1807-1813 during the Dortu & Cie period. The wares were finely potted and very English in their conception and execution.

S & G: Schiller & Gerbing, fl.1829–50s, Bodenbach, Bohemia (now Podmokly, Czech Republic).

In 1945, W. B. Honey wrote:

> But how deceptively easy it was for some unknown connoisseur to fit the impressed mark 'S & G' to the Isleworth firm of Shore and Goulding, in spite of the fact that the wares so marked are such unlikely productions for a small Thames-side factory of the eighteenth century. That interpretation of S & G stood for long, but we now know that the initials stand for Schiller & Gerbing of Bodenbach in Bohemia, on wares of about 1840.[1]

Despite Honey's pronouncement over fifty years ago, it still seems necessary to repeat his statement. In 1878, Jewitt made no mention of 'S & G' marked ware being made at Isleworth or anywhere else,[2] but seven years later, when Lady Schreiber catalogued their wide-ranging collection, she had no hesitation in attributing her two pieces impressed 'S & G' to 'Isleworth'.[3] Re-catalogued by Bernard Rackham in 1929, the two pieces were placed in the foreign section as 'Perhaps made by Schiller & Gerbing, of BODENBACH, near TETSCHEN, BOHEMIA, about 1840', with a note about their former attribution in error

Fig. 361 *Cup and saucer*, *fine white stoneware with applied reliefs in black. Interior of cup unglazed. Mark: Sarguemines (France), c. 1810-20, 2½ inches high. (Rakow collection.)*

to 'Shore and Goulding' of Isleworth.[4]

A detailed article on 'Isleworth Pottery' by Henry Clay,[5] published in 1926, states that the British Museum catalogue of 1876 assumed that two 'S & G' pieces were made at Isleworth, and no doubt this was Lady Schreiber's authority. Clay went on to give detailed reasons why this class of ware was made in Bohemia, enough to convince Rackham.

Shore and Goulding at Isleworth (q.v.) did produce redware.

W.B. Honey wrote in 1952 that Schiller & Gerbing, F. Gerbing, and William Schiller & Sohn made 'a curious type of red, green and other coloured ware with varnished wax-like surface, in forms somewhat in the style of Wedgwood's stoneware' at Bodenbach in Bohemia from 1829, with impressed marks based on their initials.[6] Schiller & Gerbing exhibited at the 1851 London exhibition.[7]

Fig. 362 *Plaque*, *not strictly jasper but in the jasper métier, this plaque is hard paste biscuit porcelain, the ground washed with a blue slip and applied relief in white biscuit porcelain, mounted in a gilt metal frame. Mark: 36 Bi incised on reverse, Sèvres, France, c. 1786, 6 inches long. (British Museum, 1909, 12-1, 218, Falcke collection.)*

Fig. 363 *Spill vase, caneware with sprig reliefs of a classical woman placing* Cupid *in a basket. Mark:* S & G 2, *Schiller & Gerbing (Czech Republic), c. 1829-1850s. (Rakow collection.)*

Fig. 364 *Plate, caneware with chinoiserie relief border and central panel and moulded well. Mark:* S & G 41, *Schiller & Gerbing (Czech Republic), c. 1829-1850s, 7⅝ inches diameter. (Rakow collection.)*

Schiller and Gerbing wares included red stoneware and caneware in the English manner. The caneware often resembled wares produced by English factories with similar sprig relief decoration (Figs. 357, 358). On the other hand at times the potting and relief decoration deployed styles more commonly associated with Eastern Europe.

SARREGUEMINES: Jacobi, c.1790–99: Utzschneider et Cie; Fayenceries de Sarreguemines, Digoin et Vitry-le-François; 1799–1939; Villeroy and Boch, 1939–79; Lunéville-St-Clément, 1979–present, Sarreguemines, Moselle, France.

A factory for producing cream-coloured earthenware was established at Sarreguemines, Moselle, France by N.H. Jacobi in 1790.[1] Paul Utzschneider, who had studied ceramic techniques in England, took over in 1799 and the works made black, white, red (*carmélite*), marbled and lustred ware in the English style. Utzschneider left in 1836 but his family carried on the business, setting up branch factories at Digoin in 1877 and Vitry in 1881. By 1900, the firm was one of the largest in Europe, employing 3,000 workers. During the 1939–45 war, the factory was placed under the control of Villeroy and Boch, but was bought back in 1979 by Lunéville-St-Clément, tile-makers. From 1982 the factory has been known as Sarreguemines-Bâtiment, and makes only tiles.

Amongst many types of ware, the firm formerly made matt stoneware with relief decoration inspired by Wedgwood,[2] black basalt, cane, agate and marbled wares.[3] The examples of stoneware are not numerous but where found are distinctively in a French idiom in an English body. A case in point is the tea cup and saucer in white unglazed stoneware with black sprig relief (Fig. 355) formerly in the Rakow collection. Both the tea cup form and the decoration set it apart from its English counterparts.

SEVRES: Orry de Fulvy, 1738–45; Charles Adam, 1745–50; Manufacture Royale de Porcelaine, 1751–56; Vincennes, Paris; Manufacture Royale de Porcelaine, 1756–c.1790; Manufacture Nationale de Sèvres, c.1790–present; Sèvres, Paris, France.

This porcelain works, called Sèvres since c.1756, commenced at Vincennes in 1738, with the aid of skilled workers from an earlier French porcelain factory at Chantilly.[1] Vincennes was granted a monopoly of the manufacture of soft paste porcelain in 1745, and continued under royal patronage from 1751 until the French Revolution. A new works was built at Sèvres c.1756. In 1769, hard paste porcelain was made successfully, and production of both bodies continued until 1800.

In 1800 Napoleon Bonaparte brought in an engineer, Alexandre Brongniart, to reform the works. Brongniart abandoned soft paste and brought in many technical improvements in his forty-seven years at Sèvres. The works was moved to a factory at St Cloud, opened in 1876, and continues in operation as the National Manufactory. All three sites, Vincennes, Sèvres and St Cloud, are in the environs of Paris.

Some very fine blue and white biscuit porcelain tablets and medallions were manufactured by Sèvres (Fig. 356) in the mid 1780s. There is a rectangular blue-ground simulating jasper or biscuit porcelain plaque in Marie-Antoinette's jewel cabinet made by J.F. Schwerdfeger in 1787 and a circular version on a *secrétaire* stamped by Weisweiler in 1781, now in Bath, similar to another example made for the Empress, currently in the Schönbrunn Palace, Vienna.[2] Another plaque from the Kanter collection was sold at auction at Skinner's, Boston (Lot 206) in May 1997.

Allbut's 1802 Map of the Potteries

J. Allbut and Son, Hanley, issued *The Staffordshire Pottery Directory* in 1802. It contained the usual list of tradespeople, except pottery manufacturers, which were dealt with separately. The 'Earthenware Manufactories' were shown by symbols on a map, each symbol having a number which referred to a key list, the numbering starting at 1 at Green Lane in the north of the Potteries and ending at 144 at Longton in the south-east. Canal wharves, chapels, churches and market halls were also shown. (The term 'earthenware manufacturers' seems to include porcelain manufacturers: see for instance No. 63, Hollins, Warburton and Co., the 'New Hall company'.)

The map is of large format, and surviving copies are not suitable for reproduction. The Hanley section was re-drawn for J.C. Wedgwood's *Staffordshire Pottery and its History*, published by Sampson Low, London in 1912; and the entire map was reproduced by Wood, Mitchell & Co. Ltd., Hanley, for P.W.L. Adams in 1941, as part of the Second Supplement to his *A History of the Adams Family of North Staffordshire & of their connection with the Development of the Potteries*, published by The St Catherine Press, London, in 1914. We have very kindly been given permission by Mrs P.J. Adams to reproduce the Wood, Mitchell version, which appears to be a very accurate copy of the original.

Besides the 144 numbered sites, there are three manufactories marked with printing signs, respectively ★, † and ‡, two of them identified in the key list as ★ for John Taylor and Co., Burslem and † for Robert Clulow and Co., Lower-lane. The manufactory marked ‡ is not identified and we have speculated that it refers to Warburtons' Bleak Hill Works.

A very similar 'directory' was issued in 1800, compiled by T. Allbutt (*sic*) at Burslem, and printed for him by J. Tregortha, *A View of the Staffordshire Potteries*. Like the 1802 Directory, this also lists local tradespeople, but not earthenware manufacturers. It seems likely that a similar map and key were included, but the writers have found no copy which now contains such a map and list. The indication of three manufactories by printing signs on the 1802 map suggests that there was an 1800 map, and that these were additions for 1802, indicated by printing signs to avoid re-numbering the sites and key list. There is no textual reference to the map and key in either the 1800 or 1802 Directories.

The key list shows several firms with two sites: No. 17, A. and E. Keeling; No. 23, John and George Rogers; No. 54, John Warburton; and Nos. 114 and 115, Samuel Baker. Another firm, No. 60, William Adams of Cobridge is only listed as one site, but two sites are shown on the map.

NAMES & RESIDENCE of the EARTHENWARE MANUFACTURERS

1	JOHN LINDOP	Green-lane
2	John and Thomas Capper	Golden-hill
3	Thomas Tunstall	ditto
4	John Collinson	ditto
5	Abraham Baggaley	ditto
6	Moss and Henshall	Red-street
7	Riles and Bathwell	ditto
8	Samuel and Thomas Cartlich	Tunstall
9	Thomas Baggaley	ditto
10	Caleb Cole and Co.	New-field
11	William Adams	Tunstall
12	John Breeze	Smith-field
13	Unoccupied	Pits-hill
14	Jonathan Machin	Chell
15	John Horn	Brimleyford
16	Smith and Steel	Tunstall
17 17	A. and E. Keeling	ditto
18	John Wood	Brown-hills
19	John Davenport	Long-port
20	Henshall, Williamson and Co.	ditto
21	Williamson and Henshall	ditto
22	Shirley, Lindop and Co.	ditto
23 23	John and George Rogers	ditto
24	Walter Daniel	New-port
25	Holland and Co.	Burslem
26	John and Ralph Hall	ditto
27	Ralph Wood	ditto
28	Wood and Caldwell	ditto
29	Isaac Leigh	Burslem
30	Nathan and John Heath	ditto
*	John Taylor and Co.	ditto
31	William Dawson	ditto
32	Jacob Marsh	ditto
33	Robinson and Sons	ditto
34	Read and Goodfellow	ditto
35	Edward Bourne	ditto
36	Tellwright and Co.	ditto
37	Thomas Holland	ditto
38	Charles Davenport	ditto
39	Lewis Heath	ditto
40	Thomas Guest	ditto
41	John Gilbert	ditto
42	Thomas Wedgwood	ditto
43	Daniel Steel	ditto
44	Unoccupied	ditto
45	William and John Stanley	ditto
46	Bigshaw and Maier	ditto
47	J. and R. Riley	ditto
48	Mort Barker and Chester	ditto
49	Joseph Machin	ditto
50	Arkinstall and George	ditto
51	Richard Ball	ditto
52	William Wood and Co.	ditto
53	Thomas Green	ditto
54 54	John Warburton	Cobridge
55	Thomas Godwin	ditto
56	Benjamin Godwin	ditto
57	Smith and Billington	ditto
58	Stevenson and Dale	ditto
59	J. and A. Blackwell	ditto
60	William Adams	ditto
61	John Mozeley	ditto
62	Hewitt and Buckley	Booden Brook
63	Hollins, Warburton and Co.	Shelton
64	Booth and Marsh	ditto
65	Bourne and Co.	ditto
66	E. J. Birch	Hanley
67	Heath and Shorthose	ditto
68	John Mare	ditto
69	Yates and Shelley	ditto
70	Joseph Lees	ditto
71	David Wilson	ditto

72	Elijah Mayer	Hanley
73	George Taylor	ditto
74	T. and J. Hollins	ditto
75	Valentine Close	ditto
76	Joseph Keeling	ditto
77	Boon and Ridgway	ditto
78	John Glass	ditto
79	James Keeling	ditto
80	Meigh and Walthall	ditto
81	Billings and Hammersley	ditto
82	James and Charles Whitehead	ditto
83	Mrs. Mellor	ditto
84	John Stanley	ditto
85	William Baddeley	ditto
86	Job and George Ridgway	Shelton
87	John Hammersley	ditto
88	J. and E. Baddeley	ditto
89	Unoccupied	ditto
90	Simpson and Wright	ditto
91	John and William Yates	ditto
92	Thomas Pope	ditto
93	James Greatbach	ditto
94	Dorothy Whitehead	ditto
95	Samuel Hollins	Vale-pleasant
96	Wedgwood and Byerley	Etruria
97	Unoccupied	Stoke-lane
98	Mrs. Ratcliffe	ditto
99	John Harrison	Cliffgate-bank
100	Booth and Sons	ditto
101	Josiah Spode, Esq.	Stoke
102	Wolfe and Hamilton	ditto
103	Smith and Jarvis	ditto
104	Minton, Poulson and Co.	ditto
105	Harrison and Hyatt	Lower-lane
‡	Robert Clulow and Co.	ditto
106	Bourne and Baker	Fenton
107	Chelenor and Adams	ditto
108	Bagnall and Hull	Lane-delf
109	John Lucock	ditto
110	William Pratt	ditto
111	Mason and Co.	ditto
112	Thomas Forester	ditto
113	—— Shelley	Lower-lane
114 115	Samuel Baker	ditto
116	Samuel Spode	Folley
117	Joseph Myatt	ditto
118	Robert Garner	Lane-end
119	Charles Harvey	ditto
120	Hewit and Comer	ditto
121	John Aynesley	ditto
122	John Hewitt	ditto
123	W. and J. Phillips	ditto
124	Samuel Hughes	ditto
125	—— Dawson	ditto
126	Richard Barker	ditto
127	Booth and Co.	ditto
128	Thomas Stirrup	ditto
129	Charles Harvey	ditto
130	Samuel Bridgewood	ditto
131	Johnson and Brough	ditto
132	Mary Syples	ditto
133	J. and G. Locketts	ditto
134	Chetham and Woolley	ditto
135	J. and W. Berks	ditto
136	William and John Turner	ditto
137	George Barnes	ditto
138	William and John Turner	ditto
139	Thomas Jackson and Co.	ditto
140	Thomas Shelley	ditto
141	William Ward	ditto
142	—— Shaw	ditto
143	George Weston	ditto
144	Mark Walklete	ditto

WHARFS

on the CANAL, in the Neighbourhood of the Potteries,

AND NAMES OF THE AGENTS.

A. William Kenwright's, Long-port – Agent, Thomas Appleby.
B. Grand Trunk Canal Wharf, ditto – —— William Banks.
C. This Branch of the Canal is not completed.
D. Grand Trunk Canal Wharf, Etruria Agent, Moses Bates.
E. William Kenwright's, Shelton-lane — James Martin.

F. Smith and Sons, Shelton-lane – Agent, James Greaves.
G. Burton Boat Company's, Stoke — —— John Copland.
H. William Kenwright's, ditto – —— Stephen Spencer.
I. Grand Trunk Canal Wharf, ditto – —— John Hincks.
K. Cotton and Co's, ditto – —— John Brassington.

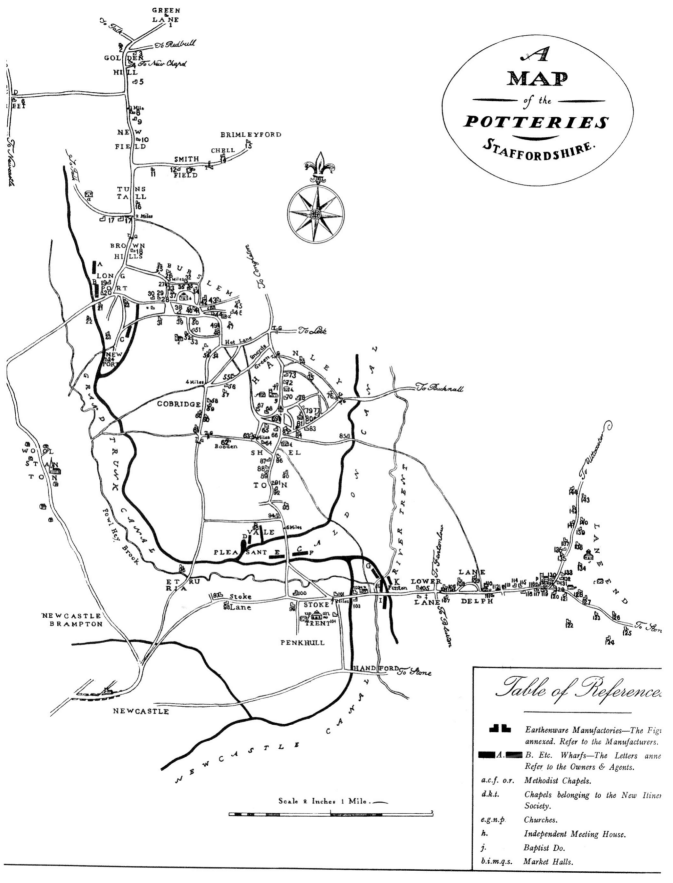

Terminology

The names which are used to describe different types of pottery cause a great deal of difficulty to historians, curators, collectors and dealers. As an example, one need only mention 'Jackfield', as a traditional collectors' name which appears to limit one class of pottery to being made at a particular place in Shropshire, but is well understood to mean an eighteenth century shiny black ware, wherever made.

A reference work of this kind has to use descriptive words in their current meanings. The authors cannot expect every reader to immediately turn to Appendix 2 for precise definitions, and so we have tried to use descriptions which will readily convey our meaning to more casual readers, rather than confuse them with pedantic or esoteric terminology. Here we discuss some of the terms used.

Drabware

Contemporary references to drabware can be read to mean any colour other than white. Dictionaries give alternative definitions of drab as an adjective – dull light brown, or dull, monotonous – and so we are left wondering if the contemporary writers meant only dull brown, or any dull shade.

A full transcription of John and Richard Riley's Recipe Book, held at the City Museum and Art Gallery, Stoke-on-Trent, was published in R. Pomfret 'John and Richard Riley China & Earthenware Manufacturers' in *Journal of Ceramic History Volume 13* (1988). The author has dated the Rileys' book as 'written almost wholly between 1821 and 1826'.

John and Richard Riley noted six recipes for drab bodies on pages 89 to 90, the colour given variously by iron stone, red clay, manganese, nickel, or under-glaze painting green, resulting in a 'fine delicate drab or ash', a 'pretty colour', a 'light drab', a 'handsome colour' or a 'delicate colour'. On page 91, under 'Drab Bodies', they give a seventh recipe which 'would form the basis of a body, to which may be added a variety of minerals in such proportion to the tints wanted', including zaffre, underglaze colours, ochre, manganese and dark red clays. It seems obvious from these recipes that Rileys' use of the term 'drab body' is capable of various interpretations. Thomas Lakin's recipes, published in 1824,[1] include the telling phrase 'various coloured Drabs', equally imprecise.

The manufacture of 'Drab China' was attributed to Elijah Mayer and Son in Directories of 1828–29 and 1830–31,[2] and an auction notice of 1860[3] included glazed drab ware and drab stoneware. Despite this availability of quantities of 'drabware' in 1860, when it was already becoming collectable, surviving marked *E. Mayer* pieces do not seem to include drab-coloured stoneware. The principal marked wares, in addition to a great deal of basalt, are canewares of superb quality and some few examples of felspathic stoneware. Altogether, this suggests that the Rileys, Lakin, the 1828–30 Directory compilers and the 1860 auctioneer, all used the term 'drab' very loosely.

Dry Bodies

The term Dry Bodies has a respectable pedigree, being used in our current sense by Simeon Shaw in 1829 and 1837[4] and also by the 1836 *Popular Encyclopedia*. Shaw used this term in his 1829 History when writing of seventeenth century or earlier wares, he stated that some were 'wholly without glaze, or in the vocabulary of our day *dry* bodies [Shaw's italics]'. On his page 160, he wrote again of salt-glazed ware, made by Thomas and John Wedgwood (fl. 1745–76); 'Those made from Clays without glazing, are called DRY BODIES [again, Shaw's emphasis]'. Thirdly, Shaw used the term 'a *dry* body' to describe a white ware made by Chetham and Woolley about 1795 (see White Felspathic Stoneware, below).

In his 1837 *Chemistry of Pottery*,[5] Shaw was even more specific:

> DRY BODIES. So named because without glaze are intermediate between porcelain and flint wares, partaking the properties of their biscuits. They are different in qualities and colours, and their value is enhanced by their employment to fabricate articles of taste and luxury rather than of general utility. They include the kinds: CHEMICAL UTENSILS, STONE, JASPER, PEARL, CANE, DRAB, RED, BLACK EGYPTIAN, FAWN, BROWN, SAGE, etc. …The *Jasper* and the *Pearl* have usually much embellishment; and the elegance of the decorations is preserved in the sharp, prominent outlines, which would suffer in the ratio of the thickness of glaze applied.

Shaw (462–63) gives recipes for all these bodies.[6]

In Volume II, part I of *The Popular Encyclopedia*, published by Blackie, Glasgow, in 1836, Dry Bodies are defined on page 192 as 'That class of wares which undergo incipient vitrescence, without any glaze on their surface'. The 'China ware' section of this encyclopaedia was re-published by William Evans in his *Art and History of the Potting business* at Shelton c.1846, as he explained on the first page of his preface: 'extracted from that most valuable, but expensive, work – the Popular Cyclopaedia (*sic*)'. Evans's *Art and History of the Potting Business* was itself re-published on pages 21 to 43 of *The Journal of Ceramic History No. 3* (1970). Evans did not give the date of the 'Popular Cyclopaedia', and the contents of his work are often quoted as being relevant to 1846, whereas in fact (except for the recipes in Evans's Appendix) the information is at least ten years older.

Sizes

In the chapter on 'Caneware', sizes of teapots in 1776 were quoted as 12s, 18s and 24s, and that was the usual way of referring to sizes of hollow-ware. This section is an attempt to show what those sizes meant. In theory, there was originally a standard of twelve pints to the dozen. The price per dozen bought a combined capacity of twelve pints, so that pint mugs were twelve to the dozen (12s); and half-pint mugs were twenty-four to the dozen (24s). In reality, the state of affairs revealed below suggests that it is now impossible to be sure what capacities were meant at particular periods by 12s, 18s, 24s, etc.

Prices and sizes go hand in hand. Eighteenth century pottery price lists show something of the difficulties of standardizing sizes, particularly of hollow-ware. Flatware (plates, dishes etc.) was easily described in inches of diameter, and jugs and mugs could be described by capacity (pint, quart); but other hollow-ware (tureens, sauceboats, butter-dishes for example) was described as large, middle, less, small, smaller, smallest, an extremely vague classification. Cups and matching saucers were described as Irish size or London size.

A proposal published by a committee of manufacturers in January 1796[7] makes it obvious that some makers were taking advantage of this vagueness to undercut their rivals. The notice recommended price increases for named sizes of flatware, cups and saucers. The size of mugs and jugs was to be strictly according to measure. More significantly, it remarked that 'loss is sustained on *Chamber-pots, Wash-hand Basons, Bowls & Tea-pots*, owing to the excess in the size' and went on to suggest maximum capacities for stated sizes, and to require that 'the number of each article shall be marked upon it, in order to denominate the size'. For teapots, 12s (to the dozen) were to contain 1½ pints, 18s 1 pint and 24s ¾ pints. Simple arithmetic shows that the standard proposed then was *eighteen* pints to the dozen.

However, that was only a recommendation to a general meeting of manufacturers, and the price list which emerged on 21 April 1796[8] was much more of a compromise: the 'Rules as to Sizes' included 'Mugs and Jugs are to be made strictly *according to Measure* [1796 italics]'; 'Chamber Pots, Bowls, Wash-hand Basons and Tea-Pots are not to exceed in Measure, *double their Denominations* [again, 1796 italics]'; and 'the number of each article is to be marked upon it, in order to denominate the size'. Some strong argument, probably the existing practices, had persuaded the assembled manufacturers to allow chambers, basins and teapots to be sold at prices agreed for half the actual capacity!

A study of this 1796 price list suggests that these rules as to sizes applied solely to earthenware: only one price per dozen (4s.6d.) is given for 'Covered Ware, as Tea-Pots, Coffee-Pots, Tea-Canisters, Sugar-Boxes, and Milk-Pots' so that the number of vessels per price–dozen must have varied with size. Dry-bodied ware as such is not specified, but prices are given for Egyptian Ware (basalt), with *different* prices for single large, second size, and third size teapots.

The January 1796 attempt to regulate sizes, and its immediate undermining in April of the same year, shows that there was already discontent amongst manufacturers about undercutting by selling large sizes at 'small' prices. Clearly, the April 1796 fudge would not solve the problem, and a *cri de coeur*, entitled *The Ruin of Potters, and the way to avoid it* was

published 'By a Manufacturer' in 1804.[9] The copy in Enoch Wood's scrapbook is endorsed 'Chas Simpson', and this seems likely to be the identity of the author, partner of John Turner II and William Turner at Lane End from 1803 to 1806.

Simpson wrote that the traditional standard for hollow-ware was twelve pints to the dozen (not the eighteen pints proposed in 1796), so that a six-pint vessel sold for two to the dozen (hence 2s), whilst a one-third pint coffee can sold at 36 to the dozen (therefore 36s). Forty years before, a three-dish teapot counted 12 to the dozen. By 1804, a 12s teapot held six cups, double the old quantity. Bowls and chamber-pots were sold similarly, double the capacity for the price. Jugs, sold by capacity measure, were being sold as 'double', meaning that quart jugs were being sold at pint prices. Flatware, too, was being made larger than the stated measurements.

Simpson's aim was to convince his fellow manufacturers that, although they cheated their workmen by paying smaller wage-prices for larger pieces, they cheated themselves more by selling the product of their clay, glaze, coal and oven space costs at half price. He instanced that 'Figured Stone Jugs' when first made were kept *nearly* (our emphasis) to their just size, and charged 24s a dozen, with sizes from gallon to pint. Now there were no gallon jugs charged for; merely up to three pints, because 'While a customer can have a 3 pint jug that will hold nearly a gallon, he will not order gallons' and so on. The practice continued.

An 1814 price list, chiefly for earthenware,[10] again does not name dry-bodied wares, but has a small section for Egyptian Black. For example, different prices per dozen for Egyptian Black oval teapots are given for 12s, 18s and 24s, with a proviso that 'none are to be counted more than 24 to a dozen'.

In what looks like an attempt to distance Wedgwood from the general confusion and deception, a Wedgwood price list of c.1815[11] gives prices for 'Egyptian Black, Cane, Red' by sizes, 'Per Dozen of twelve', the necessity to include this phrase showing that dozens of twelve were not usual. In fact, Wedgwood used size numbers from 1 to 10 for these bodies, translated in manuscript on the copy seen as from 2s to 36s. Thus size No. 4 (6s) plain teapots were 27 shillings per dozen of twelve; whilst size No. 4 bas-relief teapots were 90 shillings per dozen of twelve.

As Simpson had pointed out in 1804, the problem of size concerned both worker and manufacturer. When potters' trades unions were formed in 1824, one of the first concerns was the regulation of sizes of ware.[12] An example quoted was that of the nominally half-pint jug which would hold 'upwards of a wine quart [over a pint]'. The manufacturers were sufficiently concerned to meet nationally at Newcastle-upon-Tyne and at Hanley, and agreed to apply to Parliament for an act to regulate sizes and count of earthenware.[13] As occurred again later, with the employment of children in 1861, they had despaired of voluntary agreement, and sought legislation to enforce compliance. Nothing more is known of this application: a general election in July 1826 may have seen the end of it.

Stoneware

For a dependable account of the manufacture of stoneware,

including dry bodies, the reader is referred to G.W. Elliott 'Stoneware: some aspects of manufacturing technique and development' in *Stonewares & Stone chinas of Northern England to 1851* ed. T.A. Lockett and P.A. Halfpenny (City Museum and Art Gallery, Stoke-on-Trent, 1982) 9–13.

White Felspathic Stoneware

A recent alternative term to 'Castleford' has been 'white felspathic stoneware', and this is in no way misleading, when used for 'smear-glazed semi-translucent white stoneware'. The body is very white, and does contain felspar. *Coloured* dry bodies also contain felspar, and logic would dictate 'maroon etc. felspathic stoneware', but such terms have not heretofore been used, and we have not chosen to pioneer them.

Scientists in the laboratory of Winterthur Museum (Delaware, USA) are currently undertaking analyses of the felspathic body comparing an unmarked generic sugar box of the 'Castleford' type with a white stoneware marked *TURNER* example. Preliminary tests have not determined any difference in the two bodies. Further, more detailed, testing is expected to be undertaken which hopefully will aid and abet future clarification of this problematical body.

It seems likely that the contemporary name for 'smear-glazed semi-translucent white stoneware (erstwhile "Castleford" ware)' was 'Pearl'. That term has already been given by historians, collectors etc. to white earthenware with a bluey glaze, on the the authority of Josiah Wedgwood I and Thomas Bentley, who christened their new child 'Pearl White'.[14] The common contemporary name for this white earthenware was in fact 'China-glaze' (see the next paragraph), but this correct title has not gained common acceptance amongst collectors. Pearlware is accepted as white earthenware, and therefore the 'correct' use by us of 'Pearl' for what was once happily called 'Castleford' would only confuse readers.

When Turner and Co.'s wares were advertised for auction on 16 June 1807,[15] the auctioneer listed the types of ware as: 'Cream Colour, China-glazed blue edge, China-glaze printed and painted, Egyptian Black, Cane, Stone, Jasper, Pearl, and Patent China Goods; being the well known, and highly reputed manufacture of Messrs TURNER and Co. of Lane End'. The auctioneer made a clear distinction between China-glaze, Stone and Pearl goods.

John and Richard Riley noted another very specific reference to Pearl:[16]

Pearl Body
The first made by Messrs. Cheatham and Woolly (sic) and made by them for several years in Teapots &c Morters (sic) Jugs &c Mr Woolly gave it the Writer Jn⁰ Riley after he had given over business [*i.e.,* after March 1811].
   3   Composition ground.
   1   Blue Clay, or Brownish Blue Clay
To be placed in glost saggars, washed every time they are used in the biscuit oven, with Cream Colour Glaze. This is the best wash.– One side towards the saggar that is glazed the otherside of the Ware must have a glost bad (sic) to it made the shape of the Ware, and first glazed every time.

About the word 'bad', Pomfret noted that 'bat' or 'back'

would make more sense. Chethams' intention was that each piece of ware would have the newly-glazed wall of the saggar near one side, and a newly-glazed piece of clay (the 'bad') near the other side. Although the piece of ware was not dipped in glaze, it would receive a 'smear' from the glaze on the adjacent glazed surfaces, which would volatilise during firing. A similar process is described in S. Muspratt *Chemistry, Theoretical, Practical and Analytical* (Glasgow: Mackenzie, 1860) Div. VI, 818–19.

An early nineteenth century notebook kept by the Bramelds of Swinton, Yorkshire,[17] includes another recipe for 'Pearl body':

> 4 Cornish Stone
> 3 Blue Clay
> 1 Cornish Clay
> 1½ Flint Glass

Whilst other recipes are annotated 'this is too hard', 'Bad', 'useless' etc., no comment is noted against this recipe. Perhaps it was never tried by Bramelds.

In 1829 Simeon Shaw wrote:

About 1795, a new sort of Pottery, a *dry* body, or without glaze or smear, was introduced into the market by Messrs Cheatham (sic), (see Chetham) and Woolley, of Lane-End. It is to the white Pottery, what Jasper is to the coloured. Not being affected by change of temperature, but very fine in grain, durable in quality, and of a most beautiful and delicate whiteness, it received the name it still bears, of *Pearl* [Shaw's italics], from Mr J. Spode [II], at that time resident in London. It is used, like Jasper, for the finest description of ornaments; and is in general estimation among all ranks of society. Very few of the different attempts made to produce Pearl of equal excellence to the inventors, have been attended with any success.[18]

Pearl' recipes are also given in Blackie's 1836 *Popular Encyclopedia.*[19]

By 1871, the Museum of Practical Geology, London, had acquired a teapot of 'fine white ware', marked D.D. & Co., CASTLEFORD; and another teapot of similar ware, with the impressed mark obscure. The body of this piece was said to resemble that of 'Pearl Ware'.[20] It is notable that in 1871 the term 'Pearl Ware' was applied to what was later to be called 'Castleford' – would that the 1871 writer had been heeded!

The contemporary references to 'Pearl' in connection with Turner, Chetham and Woolley, Brameld and Spode all seem to confirm that it was the contemporary name for what collectors and dealers have for long termed 'Castleford ware'.

White Stoneware

The use made of the term 'White' can be a problem, as it has been used in recent years to describe stoneware of shades which might more accurately be called buff, fawn or stone.[21] Turners' 1807 auction advertisement[22] included 'Pearl' and 'Stone', clearly differentiating between *white* stoneware and *stone* coloured stoneware. 'Stoneware' has become a generic term which includes dry-bodied ware, and so we cannot expect our readers to understand 'stone stoneware' as meaning buff or fawn or cream or ivory stoneware. We have used 'white' to cover all these shades.

Selected Bibliography

The following bibliography is not intended to be comprehensive, but only a guide to works relating to dry-bodied ware, and to the *principal* histories of factories which made dry-bodied ware, where such exist.

Works relating to dry-bodied ware

Burton, William. *A History and Description of English Earthenware and Stoneware (to the beginning of the 19th century)*, London: Cassell, 1904.

Hollens, David. 'Some Researches into the Makers of Dry Bodies' in *English Ceramic Circle Transactions Volume 11, Part 3* (1983) 222–29, plates 112–22.

Lockett, Terence and Pat. Halfpenny *Stonewares & Stone Chinas of Northern England to 1851*, Stoke-on-Trent: City Museum and Art Gallery, 1982.

Price, Robin. 'Some Groups of English Redware of the Mid-Eighteenth Century' in *English Ceramic Circle Transactions Volume 4, Part 5* (1959) 1–9, plates 1–6; 'Part II' in *Volume 5, Part 3* (1962) 153–68, plates 150–61; 'Three Dragons Redware, Blackware, and Cane-coloured ware' in *Volume 7, Part 3* (1970) 246–47, plate 215.

Principal histories of factories which made dry-bodied ware

Adams

Furniss, David A. *An Account of William Adams,* Leeds: privately, n.d., *c.*1979.

Turner, William, (ed.). *William Adams: An Old English Potter with some account of his Family and their Productions*, London: Chapman and Hall, 1904; second edition 1923.

Barker

Barker, David. 'A group of Red Stonewares of the 18th Century' in *English Ceramic Circle Transactions Volume 14, Part 2* (1991), 177–98.

Lawrence, Heather. *Yorkshire Pots and Potteries,* Newton Abbot: David & Charles, 1974, 131–34.

Birch

Edwards, Diana. *Black Basalt: Wedgwood and Contemporary Manufacturers,* Woodbridge: Antique Collectors' Club, 1994, 122–27.

Bradley

Edmundson, Roger. 'Bradley & Co., Coalport Pottery 1796–1800' in *Northern Ceramic Society Journal Volume 4, 1980–81* (1984), 127–55; 'Walter Bradley and Co., Coalport 1796–1800' in *Northern Ceramic Society Newsletter No. 62,* June 1986, 31–35.

Chatterley

Gurnett, Robin. *Chatterley & Whitehead: Potters of Hanley & Shelton,* Bishop's Stortford: privately, 1996.

Chetham

Hampson, Rodney. 'Longton Potters 1700–1865' in *Journal of Ceramic History Volume 14* (1991), 46–48, 74–75.

Clews

F. Stefano. 'James and Ralph Clews, nineteenth century potters, Part I: The English experience' and 'James Clews, nineteenth century potter, Part II: The American experience' in Paul Atterbury (ed.) *English Pottery and Porcelain: an historical survey,* London: Peter Owen, 1980, 202–09.

Cyples

Hampson, Rodney 'Longton Potters 1700–1865' in *Journal of Ceramic History Volume 14* (1991), 56–58.

Davenport

Lockett, Terence A. *Davenport Pottery and Porcelain 1794–1887,* Newton Abbot: David & Charles, 1972.

Lockett, Terence A. and Geoffrey A. Godden *Davenport: China, Earthenware, Glass,* London: Barrie & Jenkins, 1989.

Don Pottery

Don Pottery Pattern Book 1807 Reprinted 1983, Doncaster: Doncaster Museums & Arts Service, 1983.

The Exhibition: Don Pottery 1801–1893, Doncaster: Museums and Arts Service, 1983.

Lawrence, Heather. *Yorkshire Pots and Potteries,* Newton Abbot: David & Charles, 1974, 95–104.

Mandby, T.G. 'Neglected Don Pottery', *Antique Collector,* September, 1986.

Dunderdale
Edwards (Roussel), Diana. *The Castleford Pottery 1790–1821,* Wakefield: Wakefield Historical Publications, 1982.

Dwight
Horne, Jonathan. *John Dwight Master Potter of Fulham 1672–1703,* London: Jonathan Horne, 1992.
Gaimster, David. *German Stoneware 1200-1900,* London: Trustees of the British Museum, 1997.

Greatbatch
Barker, David. *William Greatbatch: a Staffordshire Potter,* London: Jonathan Horne, 1991.

Gresley
Godden, Geoffrey. *Encyclopaedia of British Porcelain Manufacturers,* London: Barrie & Jenkins, 1988, 204.
Jewitt, Llewellynn. *The Ceramic Art of Great Britain: from Pre-Historic Times down to the Present Day ...,* 2 vol., London: Virtue and Co., 1878, II, 155.

Handley
Hosking, Mollie. 'James and William Handley: Staffordshire Potters 1819–1828' in *Journal of the Northern Ceramic Society Volume 11* (1994), 47–77.

Hartley, Greens
Jewitt, Llewellynn. *The Ceramic Art of Great Britain: from Pre-Historic Times down to the Present Day ...* 2 vol., London: Virtue and Co., 1878, II, 466–84.
Kidson, Joseph R. and Frank Kidson *Historical Notices of the Leeds Old Pottery,* Leeds: privately, 1892, republished East Ardsley: S.R. Publishers, and London: *The Connoisseur,* 1970.
Lawrence, Heather. *Yorkshire Pots and Potteries,* Newton Abbot: David & Charles, 1974, 17–40.
Morley, Ron. 'The Enigma of the Leeds Pottery's Co-partnership Shares' in *Journal of the Northern Ceramic Society Volume 6* (1987), 23–48; 'Mr Hartley of Hartley, Greens & Co.' in *Volume 8* (1991), 1–13.
Towner, Donald. *The Leeds Pottery,* London: Cory, Adams & Mackay, 1963.

Herculaneum Pottery
Brown, E. Myra and Terence A. Lockett (ed.). *Made in Liverpool: Liverpool Pottery & Porcelain 1700–1850,* Liverpool: National Museums & Galleries on Merseyside, 1993.
Smith, Alan. *The Illustrated Guide to Liverpool Herculaneum Pottery 1796–1840,* London: Barrie & Jenkins, 1970.

Hollins, Samuel
Holgate, David. *New Hall,* London, Faber, 1987.

Lakin
Blakey, Harold. 'Thomas Lakin: Staffordshire Potter 1769–1821' in *Northern Ceramic Society Journal Volume 5* (1984), 79–114; 'Thomas Lakin in Staffordshire and Yorkshire' in *Ars Ceramica No. 5* (1988), 18-21.

Lockett
Hampson, Rodney. 'Longton Potters 1700–1865' in *Journal of Ceramic History Volume 14* (1991), 106–12.

Mason
Godden, Geoffrey A. *Godden's Guide to Mason's China and the Ironstone Wares,* 3rd edition, London: Barrie & Jenkins, 1991.
Haggar, Reginald G. and Elizabeth Adams. *Mason Porcelain and Ironstone, 1796–1853* London: Faber, 1977.
Roberts, Gaye B. *Mason's: The first Two Hundred Years,* London: Merrell Holberton, n.d., 1996.

Mayer
Edwards, Diana. *Black Basalt: Wedgwood and Contemporary Manufacturers,* Woodbridge: Antique Collectors' Club, 1994, 195–204.

Minton
Atterbury, Paul and Maureen Batkin. *The Dictionary of Minton,* Woodbridge: Antique Collectors' Club, 1990, 9–22.
Cumming, Robert. 'Joseph Poulson 1749–1808: Bone China Pioneer: Minton and Poulson 1796–1808' in *Journal of the Northern Ceramic Society Volume 12* (1995), 59–91.
Godden, Geoffrey. *Minton Pottery & Porcelain of the First Period,* London: Barrie & Jenkins, 1968.
Jewitt, Llewellynn. *The Ceramic Art of Great Britain: from Pre-Historic Times down to the Present Day ...* 2 vol., London: Virtue and Co., 1878, II, 185–212.
Jones, Joan. *Minton: The First Two Hundred Years of Design and Production,* Shrewsbury: Swan Hill Press, 1993.

Mist

Howarth, Jack. 'Andrew Abbott and the Fleet Street Partnerships' in *Journal of the Northern Ceramic Society Volume 12* (1996), 75–117.

Neale

Edwards, Diana. *Neale Pottery and Porcelain: Its Predecessors and Successors 1763–1820,* London: Barrie & Jenkins, 1987.
Godden, Geoffrey. *Encyclopaedia of British Porcelain Manufacturers,* London: Barrie & Jenkins, 1988, 554–57.

Nyon

Bobbink-de Wilde, Hilde. *Porcelaines de Nyon,* Geneva: Christian Braillard, (n.d.)

Pratt

Lewis, John, and Griselda Lewis. *Pratt Ware: English and Scottish relief decorated and under-glaze coloured earthenware 1780–1840,* Woodbridge: Antique Collectors' Club, 1984. (Revised edition 1993)

Ridgway

Godden, Geoffrey A. *Ridgway Porcelains,* 2nd edition, Woodbridge: Antique Collectors' Club, 1985.

Sarreguemines

Bolender, C. 'Faïences imprimées de Sarreguemines.' *Les Cahiers lor rains,* No. 1, 1987; *Historie et Histoires, faïences de Sarreguemines,* Exposition Musée historique de Strasbourg, 1986.
Cameron, Elisabeth. *Encyclopedia of Pottery & Porcelain: The 19th & 20th Centuries,* London: Faber, 1986.
Decker, E. and Thévenin. *Faïences de Sarreguemines: les arts de la table,* Nancy, 1992.
Guillemé-Brulon, Dorothée. *La faïence fine française 1750–1867,* Paris: Massin Éditeur, (n.d.)
Kybalová, Jana. *European Creamware,* London: Hamlyn, 1989.

Schiller & Gerbing

Honey, William B. *European Ceramic Art fom the end of the Middle Ages to about 1815,* London: Faber, 1952, 79.

Sèvres

Svend, Eriksen and Geoffrey de Ballaigue. *Sèvres Porcelain: Vincennes and Sèvres 1740–1800,* London: Faber, 1987.

Sheridan

Edwards, Diana. *Black Basalt: Wedgwood and Contemporary Manufacturers,* Woodbridge: Antique Collectors' Club, 1994, 230.
Hampson, Rodney. 'Longton Potters 1700–1865' in *Journal of Ceramic History Volume 14* (1991), 91–92, 147–48.

Sowter

Lawrence, Heather *Yorkshire Pots and Potteries,* Newton Abbot: David & Charles, 1974, 114–16.

Spode

Copeland, Robert. *Spode & Copeland Marks, and other relevant Intelligence,* London: Studio Vista, 1993.
Roden, P.F.C. 'Josiah Spode (1733–1797) his formative influences and the various Potworks associated with him' in *Journal of the Northern Ceramic Society Volume 14* (1997).
Whiter, Leonard. *Spode: a History of the Family, Factory and Wares from 1733 to 1833,* London: Barrie & Jenkins, 1970.

Swansea

Nance, Ernest M. *The Pottery & Porcelain of Swansea and Nantgarw,* London: Batsford, 1942, reprinted 1985.
Hallesy, Helen L. *The Glamorgan Pottery Swansea 1814–38,* Llandysul: Gomer, 1995.

Swinton

Cox, Alwyn and Angela Cox. *Rockingham Pottery and Porcelain 1745–1842,* London: Faber, 1983.
Eaglestone, Arthur and Terence A. Lockett. *The Rockingham Pottery* new revised edition, Newton Abbot: David & Charles, 1973.
Jewitt, Llewellynn *The Ceramic Art of Great Britain: from Pre-Historic Times down to the Present Day ... 2 vol.,* London: Virtue and Co., 1878, I, 495–517.

Turner

Hampson, Rodney. 'Longton Potters 1700–1865' in *Journal of Ceramic History Volume 14* (1990), 157–66.
Hillier, Bevis. *Master Potters of the Industrial Revolution: The Turners of Lane End Cory,* London: Adams & Mackay, 1965.
Holgate, David and Geoffrey Godden. 'The Turner Porcelains' in G. Godden (ed.) *Staffordshire Porcelain,* London: Granada, 1983, 90–99.

W (★★★)

Godden, Geoffrey A. *Encyclopaedia of British Porcelain Manufacturers* London: Barrie & Jenkins, 1988, 743–47.

Wedgwood

Adams, Elizabeth B. *The Dwight and Lucille Beeson Wedgwood Collection at the Birmingham Museum of Art*, Birmingham Alabama: Birmingham Museum of Art, 1992.

Burman, Lionel. 'Joseph Mayer's Wedgwood Collection'. *Joseph Mayer of Liverpool,* London and Liverpool: The Society of Antiquaries in Association with the National Museums and Galleries on Merseyside, 1988.

Burton, William. *Josiah Wedgwood And His Pottery,* London: Cassell and Company, Ltd., 1922.

Buten, David. *18th-Century Wedgwood A Guide for Collectors & Connoisseurs,* New York: Methuen, Inc., 1980.

Church, A.H. *Josiah Wedgwood,* London: Seeley and Co., Limited; New York: Macmillan, 1903.

Dawson, Aileen. *Masterpieces of Wedgwood in the British Museum,* London: Published by the Trustees of the British Museum, 1984.

Des Fontaines, John. 'Wedgwood's Pyrophorous Vases', *English Ceramic Circle Transactions Vol. 14, Part 2, 1991.*

Farrar, Katherine Eufemia. *Letters of Josiah Wedgwood Vols. I, II, III.* Barlaston: The Wedgwood Museum, 1973 (originally published 1903).

Finer, Ann and Savage, George. *The Selected Letters of Josiah Wedgwood,* London: Cory, Adams & Mackay, 1965.

Hampson, Rodney. 'Josiah Wedgwood I Ceramic Historian'. *Ars Ceramica,* 1988.

Johnson, Harwood A. 'Books belonging to Wedgwood & Bentley the 10th of Aug't 1770'. *Ars Ceramica,* 1990.

Kelly, Alison. *Decorative Wedgwood in Architecture and Furniture,* London: Country Life Limited, 1965. *Wedgwood Ware.* London: Ward Lock Limited, 1970.

Macht, Carol. *Classical Wedgwood Designs,* New York: Gramercy Publishing Company, 1957.

Mankowitz, Wolf. *Wedgwood,* London: Hamlyn Publishing Group Limited, 1966 (originally published 1953).

Meteyard, Eliza. *The Life of Josiah Wedgwood,* 2 vol. London: Hurst and Blackett, 1865, 1866. *Wedgwood and His Works.* London: Bell and Daldy, 1873. *Memorials of Wedgwood,* London: George Bell and Sons, 1874. *Wedgwood Handbook.* London: George Bell and Sons, 1875. *Choice Examples of Wedgwood Art.,* London: George Bell and Sons, 1879.

Miller, Lynn and Des Fontaines, John. 'A Flash in the Pan Wedgwood's Pyrophorous Vase'. *Ceramics III,* May/June, 1986.

Reilly, Robin. *Wedgwood* 2 vol. London: Macmillan, 1989. *Wedgwood: The New Illustrated Dictionary,* Woodbridge: Antique Collectors' Club, 1995.

Reilly, Robin and Savage, George. *Wedgwood Portrait Medallions,* London: Barrie & Jenkins, 1973.

Roberts, Gaye Blake. 'Wedgwood in Russia'. *Ceramics Magazine,* July 1986.

Tait, Hugh. 'The Wedgwood Collection in the British Museum'. *Proceedings of the Wedgwood Society Vol. 5,* 1963.

The Wedgwood & Bentley Catalogue (1779), reprinted by the Wedgwood Society of New York, 1965.

The Wedgwood Catalogue (1787), reprinted by the Wedgwood Society of New York, 1980.

Wedgwood and Co.

Blakey, Harold. 'Ralph Wedgwood: Decline and Bankruptcy in Staffordshire and Arrival in Yorkshire' in *Northern Ceramic Society Newsletter No. 53* March 1984, 13–17.

Holdaway, Minnie. 'The Wares of Ralph Wedgwood' in *English Ceramic Circle Transactions Volume 12 Part 3* 1986, 255–64.

Lawrence, Heather. *Yorkshire Pots and Potteries,* David & Charles, Newton Abbot, 1974, 148–58.

Whitehaven

Sibson, Florence. *The History of the West Cumberland Potteries,* Hong Kong: Albert Chan Production, 1991.

Whitehead

Gurnett, Robin. *Chatterley & Whitehead: Potters of Hanley & Shelton,* Bishop's Stortford: privately, 1996.

Haggar, Reginald. (intro.) *James and Charles Whitehead Manufacturers Hanley Staffordshire,* Bletchley: Drakard, n.d., c.1973, originally published 1798.

Wolfe

Markin, Trevor. Articles on Thomas Wolfe and his enterprises in *Northern Ceramic Society Newsletters 48, 52, 55, 58* and *63*; and *Journal of the Northern Ceramic Society Volumes 7, 9 and 11.*

Wood

Falkner, Frank. *The Wood Family of Burslem,* London: Chapman & Hall, 1912, reprinted EP Publishing, East Ardsley, 1972.

Halfpenny, Pat. 'The Wood Family' in *Ceramics* Issue III May/June 1986, 118–26; *English Earthenware Figures 1740–1840,* Woodbridge: Antique Collectors' Club, 1991, 58–95.

References

(Dates are shown conforming to the current usage, i.e. day, month, year. In the eighteenth century, however, the date was expressed as month day, year.)

PREFACE

1. An excellent catalogue edited by T.A. Lockett and P.A. Halfpenny, *Stonewares & Stone chinas of Northern England to 1851*, was written to accompany The Fourth Exhibition from the Northern Ceramic Society (Stoke-on-Trent: City Museum & Art Gallery, 1982).
2. The copy of the *Wedgwood Shape Book Number 1* used in coordinating the vessel numbers in the sales lists with actual shapes includes the first 600 Wedgwood shapes, drawings of which were probably added to year by year. Thus, the first 179 shapes are the earlier ones which were principally basalt and variegated-glazed earthenware shapes, after which the jasper and other dry-bodied ornamental ware forms followed. It appears from the vessel forms that this particular book terminates around 1830, which, coincidentally, happens to be the end of the general period we determined to cover in the book. The copy of the shapes book used is in an American museum collection.
3. See Gaye Blake Roberts, Pat Halfpenny and Lynn Miller, 'Wedgwood & Bentley, The Art of Deception', *Ars Ceramica*, No. 11, 1994.

CHAPTER I
ANTECEDENTS OF ENGLISH DRY-BODIED STONEWARE

1. Margaret Medley, *The Chinese Potter* (New York: Charles Scribner's Sons, 1976), 263.
2. Geoffrey Godden, *Oriental Export Market Porcelain* (London: Granada Publishing Limited, 1979), 38.
3. S.J.Vainker, *Chinese Pottery and Porcelain* (New York: George Braziller, Inc., 1991), 157.
4. K.S. Lo, *The Stonewares of Yixing* (Hong Kong: Sotheby's Publications, 1986), 247.
5. Adrian Oswald, R.J.C. Hildyard & L.G. Hughes, *English Brown Stoneware 1670-1900* (London: Faber and Faber, 1982), 23.
6. Oswald et al., op. cit., 24.
7. Ibid.
8. Dwight's recipe books were accidentally found at the pottery in January 1870 when Lady Charlotte Schreiber visited the site. She transcribed the books and presented the transcriptions to Augustus Wollaston Franks, the Keeper of the Department of Medieval and Late Antiquities of the British Museum. Unfortunately, the recipe books themselves were later sold and their whereabouts is unknown. However, a complete copy of Lady Schreiber's transcription is published in the *Journal of Ceramic History* No. 11, edited by Dennis Haselgrove and John Murray (Stoke-on-Trent, 1979); Ai-xiii and Bi-vii.
9. Leslie B. Grigsby, *The Henry H. Weldon Collection of English Pottery 1650-1800* (London: Sotheby's Publications, 1990), 37.
10. Paul Bemrose, 'The Pomona Potworks, Newcastle, Staffs.' Part II, *English Ceramic Circle Transactions, Vol. 9, Part 3*, 1975, 298.
11. Ibid., 300.
12. See Robin Price, 'Some Groups of English Redware of the Mid-Eighteenth Century', *ECC Transactions Vol. 4, Part 5*, 1959), Plate 1d.
13. Ibid., 1-9.
14. Ibid., Plate 4c.
15. Ibid., 8.
16. 1962, 159-168.
17. David Barker & Pat Halfpenny, *Unearthing Staffordshire* (Stoke-on-Trent, City Museum and Art Gallery, 1990), 45-46, 49. David Barker, *William Greatbatch, A Staffordshire Potter* (London: Jonathan Horne, 1991), 83.
18. Ibid., Barker, 1991, 81.
19. Barker and Halfpenny, op. cit., 1990.
20. Barker, op. cit., 1991.
21. Ibid., 263.
22. Ibid., 265.
23. Ibid.
24. Brian Adams and Anthony Thomas, *A Potwork in Devonshire: The history and products of the Bovey Tracey potteries 1750-1836*. (Devon: Sayce Publishing, 1996), 51-3.
25. Alwyn Cox & Angela Cox, *Rockingham Pottery & Porcelain 1745-1842* (London: Faber & Faber, 1983), 50.

CHAPTER II
THE WEDGWOOD CONTRIBUTION

1. The Mosley Collection (W/M) takes its name from Mrs William E. Mosley (née Mary Wedgwood, 1880-1952), daughter of Godfrey Wedgwood and his second wife, Hope Elizabeth Wedgwood. The records that she and her father collected and preserved consist of family letters, business documents, and other ephemera related to the Wedgwood factory and family, many of which belong with records preserved in other parts of the collection. The Mosley Collection also includes material formerly at Leith Hill Place, near Dorking (LHP).
2. Rodney Hampson, 'Josiah Wedgwood I Ceramic Historian', *Ars Ceramica*, 1988, 22-25. Ceramic historian was one epithet for which Josiah Wedgwood was not known; however, in this article Hampson proves indisputably that Josiah was the author of an anonymous treatise written in 1788 or 1789 and sent to Mr John Walter, publisher of *The Times*.
3. There is a punch bowl in the British Museum with the initials E B and the date 1743 under the glaze on the base. This bowl and others with similar decoration have traditionally been ascribed to Enoch Booth of Tunstall. This is further confirmed by a letter in the Wedgwood archives (author unknown, W/M 1198) addressed to Mr Mayer, Esq., Silversmith, 68 Lord Street, Liverpool, 7 September 1852, saying that 'specimens of Queen's Ware [were] made by Enoch Booth of Tunstall first and improved by Josiah Wedgwood'.
4. See Diana Edwards, *Black Basalt – Wedgwood and Contemporary Manufacturers* (Woodbridge: Antique Collectors' Club, 1994), 26-7.
5. Wedgwood MS W/M 1449, 19 November, 1774.
6. Ibid., 26 November, 1774.
7. The first mention of Wedgwood's thermometer was a letter from Priestley to Wedgwood dated 21 March 1782 (Royal Society MSS V, No. 8) in which Priestley wrote that at a meeting of the 'Lunar Society' Wedgwood's 'curious and valuable thermometer' was mentioned by Matthew Boulton. Ann Finer and George Savage, *The Selected Letters of Josiah Wedgwood*, (London: Cory, Adams & Mackay, 1965), 265.
8. See Maurice H. Grant, *The Makers of Black Basaltes*, (London: Holland Press, 1967, originally published 1910) and Diana Edwards, *Black Basalt Wedgwood and Contemporary Manufacturers* (Woodbridge: Antique Collectors' Club, 1994).

CHAPTER III
WEDGWOOD RED STONEWARE AND BROWN STONEWARE

1. Agents' Letter Book, New York Public Library, 8 October, 1771. At this period Carroll's agents in Annapolis and London were Wallace, Davidson and Johnson.
2. Wedgwood MS 25/18355, 17 February, 1772.
3. Wedgwood MS 25/18421, 23 November, 1772.
4. Wedgwood MS W/M 1449, 26 November, 1774.
5. Wedgwood MS 25/18659, 3 March, 1776.
6. Wedgwood MS 25/18680, 5 July, 1776.

7. Wedgwood MS W/M 1449, 27 June, 1776.
8. Wedgwood MS W/M 1449.
9. Ibid.
10. Ibid.
11. Ibid., 2 November, 1776.
12. Ibid.
13. Ibid., 9 November, 1776. Before the English monetary system went on to the decimal system in 1971, the pound consisted of twenty shillings. In 1663 a gold coin, called a guinea, was struck. Originally worth 20s, after 1717 the guinea took on a 21s value. No more guineas were struck after 1813, but the term persisted and can still be occasionally heard today in pre-decimal generation conversation.
14. Wedgwood MS 25/18734, 25 January, 1777.
15. Wedgwood MSS 16/15211, 24 February, 1778; 16/15213, 11 March, 1778.
16. Wedgwood MS 16/15214, 20 March, 1778.
17. Ibid.
18. Wedgwood MSS 16/15209, 19 February, 1778; 16/15213, 9 March, 1778.
19. Wedgwood MSS 30/22572, 1777-81.
20. Wedgwood MS 16/15208, 4 February, 1778.
21. Wedgwood MS 16/15213, 11 March, 1778.
22. Wedgwood MS 16/15224, 10 June, 1778.
23. Wedgwood MS 16/15288, 10 August, 1779.
24. Ibid., 12 August, 1779.
25. Wedgwood MS 16/15281, 24 June, 1779.
26. Wedgwood MS 16/15294, 31 August, 1779.
27. Wedgwood MS 16/15263, 26 February, 1779.
28. Wedgwood MS 16/15274, 7 May, 1779.
29. Wedgwood MS 16/15288, 10 August, 1779.
30. Wedgwood MS 16/15283, 9 July, 1779.
31. Wedgwood MS 16/15302, 8 December, 1779.
32. Wedgwood MS 16/15280, 15 June, 1779.
33. Wedgwood MS 16/15272, 21 April, 1779.
34. Wedgwood MS 16/15302, 8 December, 1779.
35. Wedgwood MSS 16/15284, 12 July, 1779; 16/15291, 30 August, 1779.
36. Wedgwood MS 16/15217, 17 April, 1778.
37. Wedgwood MS 16/15226, 15 June, 1778.
38. Wedgwood MS 16/15321, 3 May, 1780.
39. Wedgwood MS 16/15331, 11 July, 1780.
40. Wedgwood MS 16/15332, 19 July, 1780.
41. Wedgwood MS 16/15325, 31 May, 1780.
42. Ibid., 29 May, 1780.
43. Wedgwood MS 16/15347, 13 November, 1780. The 1781 Wedgwood & Bentley sale at Christie & Ansell's Pall Mall Great Room included in lot 683 'six Pipe-heads for using with a Reed'.
44. Wedgwood MS W/M 1502, 13 August, 1781.
45. Wedgwood MS 16/15375, 30 July, 1786.
46. Wedgwood MS 16/15466, 27 September, 1788.
47. Wedgwood MS 16/15571, 28 November, 1791.
48. Wedgwood's agent Josiah Bateman's account book W/M 1602, 26 August, 1809.
49. Ibid., 10 September, 1809.
50. Ibid., 4 April, 1811.
51. Ibid., 21 February, 1818.
52. Ibid., 16 September, 1837; September [nd], 1838.
53. Ibid., 24 April, 1818.
54. Ibid., October [nd], 1821.
55. Ibid., November [nd], 1827.
56. Ibid., 2 July, 1835.

CHAPTER IV
WEDGWOOD CANEWARE

1. Wedgwood MS LHP 27 August, 1771.
2. Wedgwood MS 16/1502, 4 February, 1778.
3. Wedgwood MS 16/15267, 20 March, 1779; 16/15270, 9 April, 1779.
4. Wedgwood MS W/M 1449, 31 October, 1771.
5. Ibid., 3 October, 1776; 9 November, 1776.
6. Ibid., 23 November, 1776.
7. Ibid., 14 & 28 December, 1776.
8. Wedgwood MS 16/15233, 8 August, 1778.
9. Wedgwood MS 16/15244, 22 October, 1778.
10. Wedgwood MS 16/15249, 26 & 27 November, 1778.
11. Wedgwood MSS 16/15254 to 16/15305, 1779.
12. Wedgwood MS 16/15357, 28 February, 1781.
13. Christie and Ansell, Numb. 125 Pall-Mall, 3 December, 1781. New York Public Library GOF p.v.22.
14. Wedgwood MS W/M 1502, 13 August, 1781.
15. Wedgwood MS W/M 1460, 13 March, 1783.
16. Wedgwood MS 16/15367, 29 & 30 April, 1784.
17. Wedgwood MS 16/15368, May 4, 1786.
18. Wedgwood MS 16/15373, 15 June, 1786.
19. Wedgwood MS 16/15377, 14 July, 1786
20. Wedgwood MS 16/15392, 9 November, 1786.
21. Wedgwood MS 16/15380, 3 August, 1786.
22. Wedgwood MS 16/15377, 15 July, 1786.
23. Wedgwood MS 16/15381, 11 August, 1786.
24. Ibid., 12 August, 1786.
25. Wedgwood MS 16/15382, 14 August, 1786
26. Wedgwood MS 16/15385, 29 August, 1 September, 1786.
27. Ibid., 1 September, 1786.
28. Ibid., 29 August, 1786.
29. Ibid., 1 September, 1786.
30. Wedgwood MS 16/15389, 28 September, 1786.
31. Wedgwood MS 16/15396, 20 November, 1786.
32. Wedgwood MSS 16/15397, 29 November, 1786; 16/15423, 31 May, 1786.
33. 'Refraichisoir[s]' or 'rafraîchissoirs' as currently spelled are wine coolers.
34. Wedgwood MSS 16/15398 & a, 6 & 7 December, 1786.
35. Wedgwood MS 16/15408, 16 February, 1787.
36. Wedgwood MS 16/15423, 4 June, 1787.
37. Wedgwood MS 16/15424, 4 June, 1787.
38. Ibid., 6 June, 1787.
39. Wedgwood MS 16/15425, 12 June, 1787.
40. Ibid, 15 June, 1787.
41. Wedgwood MS 16/15432, week of 16-21 July, 1787.
42. Wedgwood MS 16/15436, 13 August, 1787.
43. Wedgwood MS 16/15462, 14 March, 1788.
44. Wedgwood MS 16/15466, 17 September, 1788.
45. Wedgwood MS W/M 1761, 8 May, 1788.
46. Wedgwood MS 16/15468, 7 January, 1790.
47. Wedgwood MS 16/15473, 11 February, 1790.
48. Wedgwood MS 16/15520, 29 November, 1790.
49. Wedgwood MS 16/15482, 29 March, 1790.
50. Wedgwood MS 16/15487, 3 May, 1790.
51. Wedgwood MS 16/15490, 21 May, 1790.
52. Wedgwood MS 16/15491, 29 May, 1790.
53. Wedgwood MS 16/15493, 8, 11 May, 1790.
54. Wedgwood MS 16/15499, 8 July, 1790
55. Wedgwood MS 16/15545, 1 May, 1791.
56. Wedgwood MS 16/15524, 3 January, 1791.
57. Wedgwood MS 16/15528, 4 February, 1791.
58. Wedgwood MS 16/15547, 10 June, 1791.
59. Wedgwood MS W/M 1761, 19 December, 1791.
60. Wedgwood MS 16/15554, 30 July, 1791.
61. Wedgwood MS 16/15577, 17 January, 1792.
62. Wedgwood MS 16/15620, 21 November, 1792.
63. Wedgwood MSS 16/15638, 28 March, 1793; 16/15657, 9 August, 1793.
64. Wedgwood MS W/M 1761, 13 May, 1793.
65. Wedgwood MS 16/15675, 6 August, 1793.
66. Wedgwood MS W/M 1600, [nd], c. 1806.
67. Wedgwood MS W/M 1602, 12 February, 1836.
68. Ibid., 26 August 1809.
69. Ibid., order for Mr John Dawson, York, 10 September 1809.
70. Ibid., 21 February 1818.
71. Ibid., 24 April 1818.
72. Ibid., [nd] September 1821.
73. Ibid., [nd], July 1827.

74. Ibid., 12 July 1830.
75. Ibid., 22 January 1831 and 11 October 1832.
76. Ibid., [nd], December 1837.

CHAPTER V
WEDGWOOD JASPER

1. Ruth Hayden, *Mrs Delany her life and her flowers* (London: British Museum Publications, 1980) 151.
2. Wedgwood MS 50/29994, 1773.
3. Wedgwood MS 25/18555, 30 August, 1774.
4. Wedgwood MS 25/18548, 21 July, 1774.
5. Wedgwood MS 25/18562, 6 November, 1774.
6. Wedgwood MS 25/18605, 3 July, 1775.
7. Wedgwood MS 25/18609, 11 July, 1775.
8. Wedgwood MS 25/18523, 13 March, 1774.
9. Wedgwood MS 25/18668, 12 May, 1776.
10. Wedgwood MS 25/18670, 20 May, 1776.
11. Wedgwood MS 25/18673, 6 June, 1776.
12. For more detail about Wedgwood's choice of clay see: J.P.M. Latham, 'Dorset Clay to Staffordshire Pot', *English Ceramic Circle Transactions* (hereafter referred to as *ECC*) No. 10 Part 2, 1976, 109-117.
13. Wedgwood MS W/M 1574 [nd]
14. Wedgwood MS W/M 1455, 23 November, 1777.
15. Wedgwood MS 25/18660, 10 March, 1776.
16. Ibid.
17. Ibid.
18. Ibid.
19. Ibid.
20. Ibid.
21. Wedgwood MS 25/18790, 3 November, 1777.
22. Wedgwood MS 25/18802, 15 December, 1777.
23. The inventories (W/M 1449), which are not complete, exist in part from November 1774 to June 1775; weekly inventories for 1776 are complete. One would assume that the prices quoted are suggested retail prices.
24. Wedgwood MS W/M 1449, 26 November, 1774.
25. Ibid, 20 March, 1775.
26. Wedgwood MSS 25/18612, 23 July; 25/18614, 6 August, 1775.
27. Wedgwood MS 25/18626, 27 November, 1775.
28. Ibid., 24 January, 1776.
29. Ibid., 27 January, 1776.
30. Wedgwood MS 25/18655, 21 February, 1776.
31. Wedgwood MS W/M 1449, 17 February, 1776.
32. Ibid., 14 February, 1776.
33. Wedgwood MS 25/18657, 24 February, 1776.
34. Wedgwood MS 25/18642, 14 January, 1776.
35. Wedgwood MS W/M 1449, 5 and 14 February, 1776.
36. Ibid., 16 March, 3 and 15 April, 1776.
37. Ibid., William Cox to Thomas Bentley, 22 April, 1776.
38. Ibid., 3, 11 and 27 May, 1776.
39. Ibid., 4 May, 1776.
40. Ibid., 31 May, 1776.
41. Ibid., 20 May, 1776.
42. Ibid., 8 and 15 June, 1776.
43. Ibid., 5 July, 1776.
44. Ibid., 26 September, 1776.
45. Ibid.
46. Ibid., 8 October, 1776.
47. Ibid., 19 October, 1776.
48. Ibid., 20 July, 1776.
49. Ibid., 28 June, 1776.
50. Ibid., 20 July, 1776.
51. Wedgwood MS 96/17677, 7 April, 1769.
52. Wedgwood MS W/M 1449, 10 August, 1776.
53. Wedgwood MS 25/18683, 10 July, 1776.
54. Wedgwood MS 1449, 6 and 18 November, 1776.
55. Wedgwood MS 25/18697, 18 September, 1776. It is interesting to note that Wedgwood sales in Dublin steadily declined from 1772 to 1775, from £1225.16.10 in 1772 to £926.5.12 in 1775. (W/M 1718) However, in 1775, the Dublin stock was still the largest of all the showrooms outside London, followed by Bath, Liverpool and Birmingham. (W/M1728)
56. Wedgwood MS W/M 1449, 12 October, 1776.
57. Wedgwood MS 25/18787, 22 October, 1777.
58. Wedgwood MS W/M 1449, 20 September, 1776.
59. Ibid., 8 November, 1776.
60. Wedgwood MSS 25/1878, 22 October; 25/18788, 27 October, 1777.
61. Ibid.
62. Ibid.
63. Ibid.
64. Wedgwood MS 16/15209, 11 February, 1778
65. Wedgwood MS 16/15211, 24 February, 1778.
66. Wedgwood MS 16/15209, 11 February, 1778.
67. For further discussion regarding the various classical versions of *Venus* see: Francis Haskell & Nicholas Penny, *Taste and the Antique* (New Haven and London: Yale University Press, 1981), 316-322.
68. Wedgwood MS 16/15213, 9 and 11 March, 1778.
69. Wedgwood MS 16/15214, 17 March, 1778.
70. Wedgwood MS 16/15229, 10 July, 1778.
71. Wedgwood MS 16/15243, 6 October, 1778.
72. Wedgwood MS 16/15216, 9 April, 1778.
73. Ibid., 11 April, 1778.
74. Wedgwood MS 16/15217. Gaye Blake Roberts also notes in her article 'Josiah Wedgwood and his associations with Arbury Hall, Warwickshire', *Ars Ceramica No. 5*, 32-34, that in a letter from Josiah Wedgwood to Thomas Bentley of 4 April 1778 that Sir Roger should have these free.
75. Wedgwood MS 16/15218, 1 May, 1778.
76. Wedgwood MS 16/15219, 5 May, 1778.
77. Wedgwood MS 16/15220, 13 May, 1778.
78. Wedgwood MS 16/15235, 19 August, 1778.
79. Wedgwood MS 16/15221, 18 May, 1778.
80. Wedgwood MS 16/15230, 15 July, 1778.
81. Wedgwood MS 16/15226, 15 June, 1778.
82. Wedgwood MS 16/15231, 24 July, 1778. Other jasper vases with gilding were cited in Wedgwood sales on 29 April, 1775 (W/M 1449) and 17 August, 1776 (Ibid.).
83. Wedgwood MS 16/15247, 13 November, 1778.
84. Wedgwood MS 16/15248, 16 November, 1778.
85. Wedgwood MS 16/15251, 7 December, 1778.
86. Wedgwood MS 16/15252, 15 December, 1778.
87. Wedgwood MS 16/15255, 2 January, 1779.
88. Wedgwood MS 16/15264.
89. Wedgwood MS 16/15291.
90. Wedgwood MS 16/15274, 7 May, 1779.
91. Wedgwood MS 16/15292, 8 September, 1779
92. Ibid.
93. Wedgwood MSS 16/15267, 16 March; 16/15265, 1 March; 16/15286, 26 July, 1779.
94. Wedgwood MS 16/15276, 5 May, 1779.
95. Wedgwood MS 16/15281, 23 June, 1779.
96. Wedgwood MS 16/15292, 8 September, 1779.
97. Wedgwood MSS 16/15290, 26 August; 16/15281, 23 June, 1779.
98. Wedgwood MS 16/15292, 8 September, 1779.
99. Wedgwood MSS 16/15268, 27 March; 16/15288, 10 August, 1779.
100. Wedgwood MS 16/15260, 3 February, 1779.
101. Ibid.
102. Wedgwood MS 16/15254, 2 January, 1779.
103. Wedgwood MS 16/15264, 6 March, 1779.
104. Wedgwood MS 16/15291, 2 September, 1779.
105. Wedgwood MS 16/15292, 8 September, 1779.
106. Wedgwood MSS 16/15257, 21 January; 16/15276, 17 May, 1779.
107. Wedgwood MS 16/15264, 6 March, 1779.
108. Wedgwood MS 16/15265, 10 March, 1779.
109. Ibid., 8 March, 1779.
110. Wedgwood MS 16/15274, 7 May, 1779.
111. Wedgwood MS 16/15254, 2 January, 1779.
112. Wedgwood MS 16/15292, 8 September, 1779.

113. Wedgwood MS 16/15274, 7 May, 1779.

114. Wedgwood MS 16/15280, 14 June, 1779.

115. Wedgwood MSS 16/15264, 5 March; 16/15273, 27 April, 1779.

116. Wedgwood MSS 16/15263, 23 February (1); 16/15264, 6 March (1); 16/15284, 13 July (1); 16/15290, 26 August, 1779 (2).

117. Wedgwood MS 16/15265, 10 March, 1779 (2).

118. Wedgwood MS 16/15268, 27 March, 1779 (1).

119. Wedgwood MS 16/15272, 23 April, 1779 (1).

120. Wedgwood MS 16/15292, 8 September, 1779 (2).

121. Wedgwood MS 16/15257, 20 January, 1779 (1).

122. Wedgwood MS 16/15274, 7 May, 1779 (1).

123. Wedgwood MS 16/15272, April 24, 1779 (1).

124. Wedgwood MS 16/15273, 26 April, 1779 (2).

125. Wedgwood MS 16/15274, 7 May, 1779 (2).

126. Ibid., 3 May, 1779 (1).

127. Wedgwood MS 16/15292, 8 September, 1779 (4).

128. Ibid (2).

129. Wedgwood MS 16/15275, 12 May, 1779 (2).

130. Wedgwood MS 16/15276, 17 May, 1779 (6).

131. Wedgwood MS 16/15281, 23 June, 1779 (2).

132. Wedgwood MSS 16/15275, 10 May, (6); 16/15283, 9 July, 1779 (10).

133. Wedgwood MS 16/15291, 3 September, 1779 (11 @ 5/- , 7 @ 10/6).

134. Wedgwood MSS 16/15283, 9 July (2 @ 10/6), 16/15293, 18 September (2 @ 10/6), 16/15260, 1 February (6 @ 7/6), 16/15272/3, 23 April, 26 (3 @ 5/-), 16/15289, 9 August (2 @ 5/-).

135. Wedgwood MSS 16/15260, 3 February (2 @ 10/6), 16/15262, 17 February (2 @ 10/6), 16/15263, 25 February (2 @ 10/6), 16/15260, 1 February (4 @ 7/6), 16/15263, 25 February (9 @ 7/6), 16/15286, 27 July (2 @ 5/6), 16/15295, 10 October (2 @ 5/-), 15 6/15286, July 30 (2 @ 4/-), 16/15259, January 29, 1779 (2 @ price illegible).

136. Wedgwood MSS 16/15300/1, 27 and 30 November, 1779 (2 @ 10/6).

137. Wedgwood MS 16/15263, 25 February, 1779 (1 @ 10/6).

138. Wedgwood MS 16/15256, 15 January (1 @ 10/6 with Chatham), 16/15262, 17 February (1 @ 10/6 with Cook), 16/15295, 22(?) October, 1779.

139. Wedgwood MS 16/15262, 17 February (2), 16/15274, 6 May, 1779 (1).

140. Wedgwood MS 16/15278, 5 June, 1779 (2 @ 10/6).

141. Wedgwood MSS 16/15280, June 15 (1 @ 10/6), 16/15286, July 31, 1779 (3 @ 10/6).

142. Wedgwood MS 16/15263, 25 February (2 Voltaire & Rousseau with gilt frames @ 7/6; 1 Rousseau w/o frame 5/-); 1 Rousseau (with Garrick) @ 5/-, 16/15262, 17 February; Rousseau and Voltaire 5/-, 16/15275, 15 May, 1779.

143. Wedgwood MSS 16/15267, 20 March (10); 16/15281, 23 June, 1779 (10).

144. Wedgwood MS 16/15265, 8 March, 1779.

145. Wedgwood MS 16/15279, 7 June, 1779.

146. Wedgwood MS 16/15292, 8 September, 1779.

147. Wedgwood MSS 16/15281, 23 June, 16/15295, 18 October, 16/15301, 30 November, 1779.

148. Wedgwood MSS 16/15249, 16/15250.

149. Wedgwood MS 16/15323, 20 May, 1780.

150. Wedgwood MS 16/15326, 9 June, 1780

151. Wedgwood MS 16/15321.

152. Wedgwood MS 16/15327.

153. Ibid.

154. Wedgwood MS 16/15340.

155. Wedgwood MS 16/15345.

156. Ibid.

157. Wedgwood MS 16/15367, 30 April, 1784.

158. Ibid., 28 April, 1784.

159. Ibid., 26 April, 1784.

160. Wedgwood MS 16/15368, 1 May, 1786.

161. Ibid., 27 April, 1784.

162. Ibid., 1 May, 1784.

163. Ibid., 26 April, 1784.

164. Ibid.

165. Ibid., 29 April, 1784.

166. Ibid., 1 May, 1786.

167. Wedgwood MS 16/15368.

168. Ibid. 1 - 6 May, 1786.

169. Wedgwood MS 16/15369.

170. Wedgwood MS 16/15372

171. Wedgwood MS 16/15370, 26 May, 1786.

172. It is probable that vases were in production in the early 1780s, although no sales records survive from the end of 1780 to April 1784. There is another hiatus of records from 1785 and the first five months of 1786, when, doubtless, many ornamental wares were being produced and sold. Oven books survive and Robin Emmerson, who is researching these, assured us vases were being produced in quantity through all those years.

173. Wedgwood MSS 16/15371, 31 May; 16/15372, 10, 13 and 14 June, 1786.

174. In a letter from Josiah Wedgwood to Sir William Hamilton of 24 June 1786 Wedgwood indicated the jasper items ordered by the King of Naples were placed though an unnamed merchant in Manchester (Finer & Savage, *The Wedgwood Letters* (London: Cory, Adams & Mackay, Ltd., 1965), 296.

175. Wedgwood MS 16/15374, 19 June, 1786.

176. Wedgwood MSS 16/15374, 24 June, 16/15375, 28 June, 1786.

177. Wedgwood MS 16/ 15375, 29 July, 1786.

178. Wedgwood MS 16/15374, 24 June, 1786.

179. Wedgwood MS 16/15375, 29 June, 1786.

180. Ibid., 30 June, 1786.

181. Wedgwood MS 16/15373, 15 June, 1786.

182. Wedgwood MS 16/ 15380, 3 August, 1786.

183. Ibid., 17 June, 1786.

184. Ibid.

185. Wedgwood MS 16/ 15376, 4 July, 1786.

186. Wedgwood MS 16/15378, 21 July, 1786.

187. Wedgwood MS 16/15380, 3 August, 1786.

188. Wedgwood MS 16/ 15378, 22 July, 1786.

189. Wedgwood MS 16/15379, 28 July, 1786

190. Wedgwood MS 16/15390, 13 October, 1786.

191. Wedgwood MS 16/15380.

192. Ibid., 1 August, 1786.

193. Wedgwood MS 16/15385, 1 September, 1786.

194. Ibid.

195. Wedgwood MS 16/15387, 19 September, 1786.

196. Wedgwood MS 16/15394, 8 November, 1786.

197. Wedgwood MS 16/15398, 7 December, 1786.

198. Ibid., 20 September, 1786.

199. Ibid., 21 September, 1786.

200. Wedgwood MSS 16/15383, 26 August, 1786; 16/15394, 1 November, 1786.

201. Wedgwood MS 16/15389, 28 September, 1786.

202. Wedgwood MS 16/15390, 4 October, 1786.

203. Wedgwood MS 16/15391, 10 October, 1786.

204. A green vase No. 266 sold for £5.5.0 on 6 December, 1786 (MS 16/15398).

205. Ibid., 9 October, 1786.

206. Wedgwood MS 16/15422, 21 May, 1787.

207. Wedgwood MS 17/15627, 2 January, 1793.

208. Wedgwood MS 16/15422, 21 May, 1787.

209. Wedgwood MS 16/15398.

210. Ibid.

211. Ibid.,7 December, 1786.

212. Wedgwood MS 16/15399B, 14 December, 1786.

213. Wedgwood MS 16/15409, 24 February, 1786.

214. Wedgwood MS 16/15420.

215. Wedgwood MS 16/15422, 21 May, 1787.

216. Ibid., 25 May, 1787.

217. Wedgwood MS 16/15425, 15 June, 1787.

218. Wedgwood MS 16/15427, 22 June, 1787.

219. Wedgwood MS 16/15428, 26 June, 1787.

220. Wedgwood MS 16/15429, 3 July, 1787.

221. Ibid., 2 and 6 July, 1787.

222. Wedgwood MS 16/15430, 13 July, 1787.
223. Wedgwood MS 16/15434, 10 August, 1787.
224. Wedgwood MS 16/15445, 8 October, 1787.
225. Wedgwood MS 16/15457, 14 February, 1788.
226. Wedgwood MS 16/15460, 7 February, 1788.
227. Ibid.
228. Wedgwood MS 16/15461, 3 March, 1788.
229. Ibid.
230. Ibid., 6 March, 1788.
231. Ibid.
232. Wedgwood MS 16/15462, 15 March, 1788.
233. Wedgwood MS 16/15464, 29 April, 1788.
234. Ibid., 2 May, 1788.
235. Wedgwood MS W/M 1761, May, 1788.
236. Wedgwood MS W/M 1460, 17 August, 1788.
237. Ibid., 11 September, 1788.
238. Ibid., 13 September, 1788.
239. Wedgwood MS 16/15467.
240. Ibid., December 30, 1788.
241. Wedgwood MS 17/15704, 7 February, 1789.
242. Ibid., 8 February, 1789.
243. Wedgwood MS 16/15715, 14 April, 1789.
244. Ibid.
245. Ibid., 29 May, 1789.
246. Wedgwood MS 16/15467, 1 January, 1790.
247. Ibid., 4 January, 1790.
248. Ibid., 5 January, 1790.
249. Ibid., 7 January, 1790.
250. Ibid., 8 January, 1790.
251. Wedgwood MS 16/15470, 18 and 21 January, 1790.
252. Ibid., 23 January, 1790.
253. Ibid., 29 January, 1790
254. Letter to Josiah Wedgwood II in Frankfurt from his father in Etruria W/M 1529, 12 September, 1790.
255. Ibid. Burley was Wedgwood's agent in Birmingham. The price of cameos was being undercut by Adams by 20% and this may account for Wedgwood's diminished sales.
256. Wedgwood MS 16/15473, 11 February, 1790.
257. Wedgwood MS 16/15373, 14 June, 1786.
258. Wedgwood MS 16/15474, 19 February, 1790.
259. Wedgwood MS 16/15480, 24 and 25 March, 1790.
260. Wedgwood MS 16/15482, 29 March, 1790.
261. Wedgwood MS 16/ 15483, week 6-10 April, 1790.
262. Wedgwood MS 16/15484, 12 April, 1790.
263. Ibid., 17 April, 1790.
264. Ibid.
265. Wedgwood MS 16/15485, 21 April, 1790.
266. Ibid., 24 April, 1790.
267. Wedgwood MS 16/15488, 12 May, 1790.
268. Wedgwood MS 16/15486, 26 April, 1790.
269. Wedgwood MS 16/15487, 3, 4 and 8 May, 1790. Another pair of tube flower pots in jasper sold 23 December, 1790 (16/155230).
270. Ibid., 6 May, 1790.
271. Wedgwood MS 16/15491, 24 May, 1790.
272. Wedgwood MS 16/15492, 31 May, 1 June, 1790.
273. Ibid., 3 June, 1790.
274. Wedgwood MS 16/15488,12 May, 1790.
275. Wedgwood MS 16/15493, 9 June, 1790.
276. Wedgwood MS 16/15497, 22 June, 1790.
277. Wedgwood MS 16/15498.
278. Wedgwood MS 16/15502, 28 July, 1790.
279. Wedgwood MS 16/15510, 13 September, 1790.
280. Wedgwood MS 16/15521, 6 December, 1790
281. Wedgwood MS 16/15518, 16 and 18 November, 1790.
282. Wedgwood MS 16/15574, 27 December, 1790.
283. Wedgwood MS 16/15518, 19 November, 1790. Another group of six medallions sold on 24 November (16/15519).
284. Wedgwood MS 16/15521, December 8, 1790.
285. Wedgwood MS 16/15524, 7 January, 1791.
286. Wedgwood MS 16/15529, 11 February, 1791. For further information on Thomas Hope see: Diana Edwards, 'Thomas Hope's Wedgwood Purchases', *Ars Ceramica*, 1996.
287. Wedgwood MS 16/15536, 25 March, 1791.
288. Wedgwood MS 16/15627, 1 February, 1793.
289. Wedgwood MS W/M 1460, 4 July, 1790.
290. Wedgwood MS 16/15537, 31 March, 1791.
291. Wedgwood MS 16/15541, 26 April, 1791.
292. Ibid., 29 April, 1791.
293. Wedgwood MS 16/15542, 3 and 6 May, 1791.
294. Wedgwood MS 16/15571, 28 November, 1791.
295. Wedgwood MS 16/15543, 14 May, 1791.
296. Wedgwood MS 16/15550, 27 and 28 June, 1791.
297. Ibid., 2 July, 1791.
298. Wedgwood MS 16/15559, 3 September, 1791.
299. Wedgwood MS 16/15561, 12 September, 1791
300. Wedgwood MS 16/15562, 23 September, 1791.
301. Wedgwood MS 16/15772, 9 December, 1791.
302. Wedgwood MS 16/15573, 13 December, 1791.
303. Wedgwood MS 16/15568, 4 November, 1791.
304. Wedgwood MS 16/15578, 28 January, 1792.
305. Wedgwood MS 16/15579, 2 February, 1792.
306. Wedgwood MS 16/15580, 7 February, 1792.
307. Ibid. The first recorded sale of a blue and white jasper flower pot No. 377 was on 21 February, 1792 (Wedgwood MS 16/15582).
308. Ibid.
309. Wedgwood MS 16/15607, 21 July, 1792.
310. Wedgwood MS 16/15602, 26 July, 1792.
311. Wedgwood MS 16/15603, 1 August, 1792.
312. Wolf Mankowitz, *The Portland Vase and the Wedgwood Copies* (London: Andre Deutsch, Ltd, 1952), 41.
313. Wedgwood MS 16/15605, 11 August, 1792.
314. Wedgwood MS 16/15611, 22 September, 1792.
315. Ibid
316. Wedgwood MS 16/15614, October 13, 1792.
317. Ibid.
318. Ibid.
319. Wedgwood MS 16/15620, 26 November, 1792.
320. Wedgwood MS 16/15625, 3 January, 1793.
321. Wedgwood MS 17/15635, 5 March, 1793.
322. Wedgwood MS 17/15637, 23 March, 1793.
323. Ibid.
324. Wedgwood MS 17/15640, 4 April, 1793.
325. Wedgwood MS 17/15642, 17 April, 1793.
326. Wedgwood MS 17/15643, 22 and 23 April, 1793.
327. Ibid., 26 April, 27, 1793.
328. Wedgwood MS W/M 1761, 15 and 17 May, 1793.
329. Wedgwood MS 17/15650, 19 June, 1793.
330. Ibid., 19 Jun,, 1793.
331. Wedgwood MS 17/15652, 2 July, 1793.
332. Wedgwood MS 17/15654, 19 July, 1793.
333. Ibid., 15 July, 1793.
334. Wedgwood MS 17/15661, 3 September, 1793.
335. Wedgwood MS 17/15673, 13 December, 1793.
336. Wedgwood MS 17/15678, January [nd], 1794.
337. Wedgwood MS 17/15679, 27 January, 1794.
338. Ibid., 29 January, 1794.
339. Wedgwood MS 17/15681, February [nd], 1794
340. Ibid.
341. Wedgwood MS 17/15687, 10 April, 1794.
342. Ibid.
343. Virginia Surtees, *The Grace of Friendship, Horace Walpole and the Misses Berry* (Norwich: Michael Russell, 1995), 223.
344. Wedgwood MS 17/15687, 12 April, 1794.
345. Wedgwood MS W/M 1773, 24 January, 1795.

CHAPTER VI
WEDGWOOD RETAILERS AT HOME

1. *Kents Directory* 1780, *Bailey's Directory* 1784, *Universal British Directory* 1790, *Andrews London Directory* 1793.
2. Wedgwood MS 16/15382, 17 August, 1786.
3. Wedgwood MS 16/15374.
4. Wedgwood MS 16/15383, 26 August, 1786.

5. Wedgwood MS 16/15389, 28 September, 1786.
6. Wedgwood MS 16/15465, 8 September, 1788.
7. Wedgwood MS 16/15445, 8 October, 1787.
8. *Kent's Directory* 1780.
9. *Universal British Directory* 1790.
10. Ibid., September 26, 1788.
11. Wedgwood MS 16/15461, 6 March, 1788.
12. Wedgwood MS 16/15462, 11 March, 1788.
13. Wedgwood MS W/M 1761, 8 May, 1788.
14. *Bailey's British Directory 1784; Universal British Directory* 1790.
15. Wedgwood MS 16/15461, 6 March, 1788.
16. *Chapman's Birmingham Directory of Merchants & Tradesmen*, 1800.
17. Wedgwood MS 16/15538, 4 April, 1791.
18. *Andrews London Directory* 1793; *Kent's Directory* 1795. The Strattons were listed at the same address, 3 Russia Court, Leadenhall Street, in earlier directories under other partnership names from 1780 onwards, but primarily with Charles Pieschell from 1784-90. The Gibson partnership name appears in the directories for the first time in 1793.
19. Wedgwood MS 16/15544, 21 May, 1791.
20. Wedgwood MS 16/15557, 16 August, 1791.
21. Wedgwood MS 16/15559, 31 August, 1791.
22. *Chapman's Birmingham Directory of Merchants & Tradesmen*, 1800.
23. Wedgwood MS 16/15597, 21 June, 1792.
24. Wedgwood MS W/M 1459, 19 May, 1792.
25. Wedgwood MS 17/15631, 6 February, 1793.
26. Wedgwood MS 17/15650, 17 June, 1793.
27. Wedgwood MS 17/15662, 12 September, 1793.
28. Wedgwood MS 17/15673, 11 December, 1793.

CHAPTER VII
WEDGWOOD SALES ABROAD:
PATRONS AND CONNOISSEURS

1. The volute-krater vase, *c.*325 BC, painted by the so-called Baltimore painter, was sold to the British Museum in Hamilton's first sale of vases in 1772 and remains in the collection (BM Cat. Vases F.284).
2. Wedgwood MS 25/18422, 23 November, 1772.
3. Wedgwood MSS 30/22426, 30/22427, 30/22428.
4. Wedgwood MS 112/21245, 31 July, 25 August, 1775.
5. Wedgwood MS 59/32486, 4 juillet 1772. This is also reproduced in: Quilitzsch *et al, 1775-1795 Wedgwood Englische Keramik in Wörlitz* (Wörlitz: E.A. Seemann Verlag, 1995), 18.
6. Wedgwood MS 53/9740, 21 November, 1779.
7. Ibid.,16 November, 1779.
8. Ibid., 5 October, 1779.
9. Wedgwood MS 53/9742, 17 October, 1780.
10. Ibid.
11. Wedgwood MS 53/9746, 15 May, 1787.
12. Ibid.
13. Wedgwood MS 53/9749, 27 March, 1788.
14. Wedgwood MS 53/9746 [nd].
15. Wedgwood MS 53/9750, 12 August, 1788.
16. Wedgwood MS 53/9751, 21 February, 1789.
17. Wedgwood MS 53/9756, 13 December, 1789.
18. Wedgwood MS 53/9757, 26 August, 1790.
19. Wedgwood MS 53/9754, 5 November, 1790.
20. Wedgwood MS 8/30382 [nd].
21. Wedgwood MS 16/15374, 18 June, 1786.
22. Wedgwood MS 16/15375, 27 June, 1786.
23. Wedgwood MS 16/15376, 3 July, 1786.
24. Wedgwood MS 16/15385, 28 August, 1786.
25. Wedgwood MS 16/15381, 9 August, 1786. This may be the first reference to 'basalt' in the surviving Wedgwood archives. Previous references were to 'black' or 'Egyptian black'.
26. Wedgwood MS 16/15383, 26 August, 1786.
27. Wedgwood MS 16/ 15385, 29 August, 1786.
28. Ibid., 30 August, 1786.
29. Ben Hawkesford apparently took over the Wedgwood representation in St Petersburg around 11 to 25 July 1786. His letters mentioned Baron Strognorth, Prince Potemkin, HRH the Grand Duchess (*sic*), Mr Fitzherbert, Mr Clay, Mr Parker

and Count Chermicoff (Wedgwood MS 120/23307-8).
30. Wedgwood MS 16/15385, 1 September, 1786.
31. Wedgwood MS 16/15387, 18 September, 1786.
32. Wedgwood MS 17/15627, 7 January, 1793.
33. Wedgwood MS 16/15387, 20 September, 1786.
34. Wedgwood MS 16/15389, 25 September, 1786.
35. Wedgwood MS 16/15422, 21 May, 1787.
36. Wedgwood MSS 16/15425, 15 June; 16/15426, 18 June, 1787.
37. Ibid.
38. Wedgwood MS 16/15432.
39. Wedgwood MS 16/15433, 28 July, 1787.
40. Wedgwood MS 16/15423, 20 May, 1787.
41. Wedgwood MS 16/15422, 26 May, 1787.
42. Wedgwood MS 16/15424, 6 June, 1787.
43. Ibid., 4 June, 1787.
44. Wedgwood MS 16/15457, 13 February, 1788.
45. Wedgwood MS 16/15455, 24 December, 1787.
46. Wedgwood MS 16/15458, 14 January, 1788.
47. Wedgwood MS W/M 1761, 9 September, 1788.
48. Wedgwood MS 16/15461, 5 March; 16/15462, 15 March, 1788.
49. Wedgwood MS 16/15464, 28 April, 1788.
50. Wedgwood MS 16/15462, 13 March, 1788.
51. Wedgwood MS 16/15466, 22 September, 1788.
52. Wedgwood MS 16/15471, 25 January, 1790.
53. Wedgwood MS 16/15480, 20 March, 1790.
54. Wedgwood MS W/M 1761, 8 May, 1788.
55. Ibid., 9 September, 1788.
56. Wedgwood MS 16/15466, 17 September, 1788.
57. Ibid., 10 September, 1788.
58. Wedgwood MS 16/15469, 11 January, 1790.
59. Wedgwood MS 16/15476, 4 March, 1790.
60. Wedgwood MS 16/15477, 12 March, 1790.
61. Ibid., 16 March, 1790.
62. Ibid., 17 March, 1790.
63. Wedgwood MS 16/15498, 28 June, 1790.
64. Ibid.
65. Wedgwood MS W/M 1761, 10 September, 1788.
66. Wedgwood MS 16/15498, 28 June, 1790.
67. Wedgwood MS 16/15511, 23 September, 1790.
68. Wedgwood MS 16/15522, 13 December, 1790.
69. Wedgwood MS 16/15545, 23 May, 1791.
70. Wedgwood MS 16/15568, 1 November, 1791.
71. Wedgwood MS W/M 1761, 19 December, 1791.
72. Wedgwood MS 16/15552, 11 July, 1791.
73. Wedgwood MS 16/15553, 20 July, 1791.
74. Wedgwood MS 16/15556, 9 August, 1791.
75. Wedgwood MS 16/ 15571, 28 November, 1791.
76. Wedgwood MS 16/15555, 1 August, 1791.
77. Wedgwood MS 16/15575, 6 January, 1792.
78. Wedgwood MS 16/15589, 17 April, 1792.
79. Wedgwood MS 16/15605, 8 August, 1792.
80. Ibid., 10 August, 1792.
81. Wedgwood MS 16/15614, 13 October, 1792.
82. Wedgwood MS 16/15416, 29 October, 1792.
83. Ibid., 27 October, 1792.
84. Wedgwood MS 16/15625, 3 January, 1793.
85. Wedgwood MSS 17/15627, 7 January; 16/15630, 31 January, 1793.
86. Wedgwood MS A440. For further information on John Bringhurst see Harwood Johnson and Diana Edwards, 'Ornamental Wedgwood in Philadelphia in 1793', *The Magazine Antiques*, January, 1994, 166-173.
87. Wedgwood MS 16/15387, 18 September, 1786.
88. Wedgwood MS 17/15635, 9 March, 1793.
89. Wedgwood MS 17/15636, 15 March, 1793.
90. Ibid., 11 March, 1793
91. Wedgwood MS 17/15648, 8 June, 1793.
92. Wedgwood MS 17/15687, 10 and 12 April, 1794.

CHAPTER VIII
CONTEMPORARY MANUFACTURERS
Adams
1. The ramifications of the Adams family of North Staffordshire were researched in great depth by P.W.L. Adams, a member of the family, in *A History of the Adams Family of North Staffordshire & of their Connection with the Development of the Potteries* (London: St Catherine Press, 1914).

    William Turner, writer of other ceramic histories, edited a book on the Adams family as potters, *William Adams an old English Potter with some account of his Family and their Productions*, first published in London by Chapman and Hall, in 1904. This book was based on a private work by P.W.L. Adams: see his *A History of the Adams Family ...* page 364, for an account of the circumstances. P.W.L. Adams also stated there that his collection of some one hundred specimens of eighteenth century Adams ware was presented to Tunstall Museum by 1906. Correspondence about the acquisition of this collection, and with the authors of the books on Adams, is held in the Wedgwood Museum, Barlaston. A second edition of Turner's book, obviously revised by P.W.L. Adams, was published in 1923.

    Robert Nicholls abridged Turner's work, and made some amendments, in *Ten Generations of a Potting Family* (London: Lund Humphries, n.d., *c.*1931); and Derek Peel wrote a popular work on Adams, *A Pride of Potters* (London: Barker, 1957). D.A. Furniss *An Account of William Adams* (Leeds, privately, n.d., *c.*1979) is the most recent summary. Dr Furniss edits a quarterly *Adams Notes* for an informal group of Adams collectors.
2. Adams, op. cit., 373.
3. Adams, op. cit., supplement J, 375.
4. Wedgwood MS 121/23479; R. Pomfret 'John & Richard Riley China & Earthenware Manufacturers' in *Journal of Ceramic History Volume 14* (1988) 1-36, 9.
5. R. Reilly *Wedgwood* 2 vol. (London: Macmillan, 1989) I, 77.
6. Adams, op. cit., 130.
7. Adams, op. cit., 126.
8. See note 6.
9. W. Mankowitz & R.G. Haggar *The Concise Encyclopedia of English Pottery and Porcelain* (London: Deutsch, 1957) 256, *Bailey's Northern Directory 1781*; and *Bailey's British Directory for 1784: Vol. II, The Western Directory* (London, 1784) 391. The list of 'Manufacturers of Pottery ware ...' in W. Tunnicliff *A Topographical Survey of the Counties of Stafford, Chester, and Lancaster* (Tunnicliff, Nantwich, 1787), repeats almost exactly the names in Bailey's 1784 Directory, and cannot be regarded as reliable for dating.
10. *The Staffordshire Pottery Directory* (Hanley: Chester and Mort, n.d., 1796).
11. Wedgwood MS 31/23101-23112.
12. Wedgwood MS 13/2423.
13. Wedgwood MS 121/23479.
14. L. Jewitt *The Ceramic Art of Great Britain from Pre-Historic Times down to the Present Day* 2 vol. (London: Virtue, 1878) II, 273.
15. J.C. Wedgwood and J.G E. Wedgwood *Wedgwood Pedigrees: being an Account of the Complete Family reconstructed from Contemporary Records* (Kendal: Titus Wilson, 1925) 139.
16. Wedgwood MS WM 1460, 3, 5 and 7 March, 1788.
17. *Manchester Mercury*, 21 October 1788.
18. H. Blakey 'Fire Insurances and Ceramic History - including extracts from the Sun Fire Office Policy Registers 1782-1793' in *Journal of the Northern Ceramic Society Volume 10* (1993) 161-97, 186. See also Wedgwood and Co. in this book.
19. *Staffordshire Advertiser*, 29 April 1797.
20. Ibid., 17 June 1797, 12 May 1798.
21. Ibid., 18 July 1801.
22. Ibid., 6 November 1802.
23. Stafford Record Office: QRPL/5/23A, Land Tax; *Staffordshire Advertiser* 26 May 1810, sale of John Heath's stock at the Hill Works.
24. Pomfret, op. cit. 9-10.
25. Adams, op. cit. 374.
26. Adams, op. cit. 375.
27. *Staffordshire Advertiser*, 19 January 1805.
28. Blakey op. cit., 186.
29. Wedgwood MS 11/9178-9199.
30. *The Staffordshire Pottery Directory* (Hanley: Allbut, 1802) map and key, No. 11.
31. Adams, op. cit. 375.
32. *Staffordshire Advertiser*, 18 May 1805.
33. Adams, *op. cit.* supplement J, 381.
34. Adams, *op. cit.* 381.
35. *Holden's Triennial Directory for 1809, 1810, 1811* (London, 1809) 367.
36. *Staffordshire Advertiser*, 9 October 1819.
37. Ibid., 15 January 1820.
38. Ibid., 4 August 1821.
39. Ibid., 8 December 1821.
40. Ibid., 16 February 1822.
41. Adams, op. cit. 382.
42. Ibid., 383.
43. Ibid., 382.
44. Allbut, op. cit. map and key, No. 10.
45. *Staffordshire Advertiser*, 19 June 1802.
46. Ibid., 30 October 1802.
47. Ibid., 2 March, 6 July 1805.
48. Wedgwood MS WM 1529.
49. Nicholls, op. cit. 66.
50. Ibid.
51. Adams, op. cit. supplement I, 379.
52. G. A. Godden *Encyclopaedia of British Pottery and Porcelain Marks* (London: Jenkins, 1964) 18.
53. *Staffordshire Advertiser*, 8 December 1821.
54. Turner, op. cit. 28.
55. B. Hillier *Master Potters of the Industrial Revolution: The Turners of Lane End* (London: Cory, Adams & Mackay, 1965) 75.
56. M.E. Leese 'Not Worth More than Sixpence' in *Northern Ceramic Society Newsletter No. 53* (March 1984), 19-22, 19.
57. *Staffordshire Advertiser*, 5 March 1814; Turner, op. cit. 25.

Astbury
1. B. Rackham *Catalogue of the Glaisher Collection of Pottery and Porcelain in the Fitzwilliam Museum Cambridge* 2 vol. (Cambridge, Cambridge University Press, 1935, reprinted Woodbridge: Antique Collectors' Club, 1987) I, 75, Nos. 468-71; II, plate 34 for the marked covered jug. All four pieces are illustrated in G.W. Rhead and F.A. Rhead *Staffordshire Pots & Potters* (London: Hutchinson, 1906, reprinted East Ardsley: EP Publishing, 1977) opposite p.162.
2. P.W.L. Adams *Notes on some North Staffordshire Families including those of Adams, Astbury, Breeze, Challinor, Heath, Warburton, &c.* (Tunstall: privately, 1930) 18-20.
3. Wedgwood MSS: 6/8475-80, 15/30913.
4. Adams, op. cit., 21.
5. Wedgwood MSS: 6/4902-05.
6. Wedgwood MS: 6/30915.
7. Adams, op. cit., 17; W. Mankowitz & R.G. Haggar *The Concise Encyclopaedia of English Pottery and Porcelain* (London: Deutsch, 1957) 10.
8. H. Blakey 'Sun Fire Insurance Records 1774-1782' in *Journal of the Northern Ceramic Society Vol. 9* 1992, 165-81, 179.
9. *Stoke-upon-Trent Parish Register* 4 vol. (Stafford; Staffordshire Parish Registers Society, 1925) III, 602.
10. Keele University, Spode MS: 851.
11. H. Blakey 'Fire Insurance and Ceramic History - including extracts from the Sun Fire Office Policy Registers: 182-1793' in *Journal of the Northern Ceramic Society Vol. 10* 1993, 161-97, 190.
12. *Staffordshire Pottery Industry: Local History Source Book No 4* ed. R.A. Lewis (Stafford: Staffordshire County Council Education Department, 1969) 33.
13. *Staffordshire Advertiser*, 28 March 1795.
14. *The Universal British Directory* (London: The Patentees, 1790-1798) (the Staffordshire section dated *c.*1795 by mention of the death of Josiah Wedgwood, 3 January 1795) 110; *The Staffordshire Pottery Directory ...* (Hanley: Chester and Mort, *c.*1796) 54.
15. *Staffordshire Advertiser* 20 May, 3 June, 2 September 1797; 1 December 1798.

16. Adams, op. cit., 21-22.
17. R.J. Charleston 'Jean Voyez' in *English Ceramic Circle Transactions Vol. 5, Part 1* 1960, 8-41, 24.
18. D. Edwards *Black Basalt: Wedgwood and Contemporary Manufacturers* (Woodbridge: Antique Collectors' Club, 1994) 110-11.
19. Ibid., 112.
20. *Staffordshire Advertiser*, 5 September 1795, 11 September 1802.
21. L. Jewitt *The Ceramic Art of Great Britain ...* 2 vol. (London: Virtue, 1878) II, 412.
22. Edwards, op. cit., 112.

Baddeley

1. *The Staffordshire Pottery Directory* (Hanley: Allbut, 1802) map and key, No. 85.
2. *Newcastle and Pottery Directory 1822-23* (Hanley: Allbut, 1822) 125.
3. *Holden's Triennial Directory for 1805, 1806, 1807* (London, 1805) 250; *Holden's Triennial Directory for 1809, 1810, 1811* (London, 1809) 367.
4. Allbut, 1822, op. cit. 125.
5. *Staffordshire Advertiser*, 22 June 1822.
6. A. Meigh *Manufacturers of Pottery in the Staffordshire Potteries ... 1807-1859 from the Rate Books* (privately, 1940) *passim*, 159-242.
7. L. Jewitt *The Ceramic Art of Great Britain from Pre-Historic Times down to the Present Day* 2 vol.(London: Virtue, 1878) II, 401-02.
8. S. Shaw *History of the Staffordshire Potteries; and the Rise and Progress of the Manufacture of Pottery and Porcelain; with references to Genuine Specimens, and notices of Eminent Potters* (Hanley: privately, 1829, rep. Newton Abbot, 1970) 174, 188.
9. Wedgwood MS 49/29829.
10. *Staffordshire Advertiser*, 7 August 1841.
11. *A View of the Staffordshire Potteries* (Burslem: Allbutt, 1800) 100.
12. J. Mallet 'John Baddeley of Shelton, an Early Staffordshire Maker of Pottery and Porcelain, Part II' in *English Ceramic Circle Transactions Vol. 6 Part 3* (1967) 181-247, 221: Appendix D, The Baddeley Family of Shelton.

Barker

1. D. Barker 'A Group of Red Stonewares of the 18th century' in *English Ceramic Circle Transactions Volume 14, Part 2 1991*, 177-98, 192.
2. W. Mankowitz & R. Haggar *The Concise Encyclopedia of English Pottery and Porcelain* (London: Deutsch, 1957) 268, quoting *Bailey's Northern Directory 1781*.
3. *Bailey's British Directory 1784*, multi-vol. (London, 1784) II, 392.
4. Information from Mr P. Roden: Thomas Barker was buried at Stoke-upon-Trent 28 July 1786; his will, made 19 July 1786, was proved at Lichfield 16 May 1787.
5. Information from Mr P. Roden: Elizabeth Barker was buried at Stoke-upon-Trent 26 February 1796; her will, made 30 March 1793, was proved at Lichfield 17 January 1797.
6. *Staffordshire Advertiser* 4 February 1804.
7. Ibid., 12 January 1799.
8. Ibid., 24 March 1804.
9. *The Staffordshire Pottery Directory* (Allbut, Hanley, 1802) map and key, Nos. 114 and 115.
10. *Staffordshire Advertiser*, 24 March 1804.
11. Ibid.
12. *Bailey's British Directory 1784,* multi-vol. (London, 1784) II, 392.
13. Ibid.
14. R. Hampson 'Longton Potters 1700-1865' in *Journal of Ceramic History Volume 14* (1990) i-viii, 1-236, 13-15.
15. Lichfield Joint Record Office: will of Richard Barker, Lane End, gentleman, made 20 November 1809, proved at Cheadle 3 May 1810.
16. Hampson, op. cit., 13-15.
17. Ibid.
18. Ibid.
19. Ibid.
20. D. Edwards *Black Basalt: Wedgwood and Contemporary Manufacturers* (Woodbridge: Antique Collectors' Club, 1994) 119.
21. Hampson, op. cit., 13-15.
22. H. Lawrence *Yorkshire Pots and Potteries* (Newton Abbot: David & Charles, 1974) 131-34.

23. Ibid., 114-16.
24. A. and A. Cox 'The Potteries of South Yorkshire' in *Antique Dealer and Collector's Guide* November 1970, 83-95, 92-93; Lawrence, op. cit., 116; Hampson, op. cit., 14; Edwards, op. cit., 120-21.
25. Barker, op. cit.,195.

Birch

1. Monumental inscription in Fradswell Church: Edmund John Birch of Fradswell Hall died 31 December 1829 aged 53.
2. *Staffordshire Advertiser*, 10 January 1818: died at Shelton Tuesday last (6th.), Christopher Whitehead aged 44.
3. *The Staffordshire Pottery Directory* (Hanley: Chester and Mort, n.d., c.1796). *The Staffordshire Advertiser* 26 March 1796 carried an advertisement by Chester and Mort which stated that 'the *Pottery Directory* is hoped to be published in a few weeks'.
4. D. Edwards *Black Basalt: Wedgwood and Contemporary Manufacturers* (Woodbridge: Antique Collectors' Club, 1994) 126, n.66.
5. Wedgwood MSS: 15/14509 (1800), 11/1987 (1806), 11/1988 (1808); *Holden's Triennial Directory for 1809, 1810, 1811* (London, 1809).
6. *Staffordshire Advertiser*, 5 July 1806.
7. A. Meigh *Manufacturers of Pottery in the Staffordshire Potteries ... 1807 to 1859 (inclusive) from the Rate Books* (privately, 1940) 52, 58.
8. *Staffordshire Advertiser*, 23 February 1811.
9. Wedgwood MS 15/14521; *Staffordshire Advertiser*, 2 March 1811: Birch's furniture for sale, changing his residence; Bank House, Etruria to be let.
10. Wedgwood MSS: 15/14510-30.
11. Stafford Record Office: QRPL/5/71 A, B, Land Tax, Shelton.
12. *Staffordshire Advertiser*, 4 June 1814.
13. L. Whiter *Spode: a History of the Family, Factory and Wares from 1733 to 1833* (London: Barrie & Jenkins, 1970) 205.
14. See note 1.
15. Wedgwood MSS: 15/14525-28; *Staffordshire Advertiser*, 25 July 1835: died 19th, Edmund John Birch aged 33.
16. Wedgwood MS: 15/14515.
17. *Staffordshire General and Commercial Directory* (Manchester: Parson & Bradshaw, 1818) 231, 89, 208.
18. *National Commercial Directory for 1828-9: Staffordshire* (London: Pigot, 1828) 732.
19. *Staffordshire Advertiser*, 25 July 1835.

Bradley

1. R. Edmundson 'Bradley & Co., Coalport Pottery 1796-1800' in *Northern Ceramic Society Journal Vol. 4 1980-81* (1984) 127-55 is the source of the following information, except where separately referenced.
2. H. John 'Thomas Rose at Coalport, continued' in *Northern Ceramic Society Newsletter No. 93*, March 1984 26-32, 28.
3. B. Trinder *The Industrial Revolution in Shropshire*, 2nd ed. (Chichester: Phillimore, 1981) 128.
4. L. Jewitt 'Salopian China. A History of the Coalport Porcelain Works' in *The Art Journal*, New Series Vol.I 1862, 65-68, 66.
5. W.H. Goss *The Life and Death of Llewellynn Jewitt FSA ...* (Hanley: Allbut and Daniels, 1887) 183.
6. *Staffordshire Advertiser*, 7 February 1863.
7. M. Messenger, *Coalport 1795-1926*. Woodbridge: Antique Collectors' Club, 1995, 51.
8. Conversation with Roger Edmundson.

Bulkeley

1. 'Letters to the Editor' in *Northern Ceramic Society Newsletter No. 70* (1970) 45-48, 46.
2. T. Pape *Newcastle-under-Lyme from the Restoration to 1760* (Newcastle-under-Lyme: Borough of Newcastle-under-Lyme, 1973) 186.
3. H. Blakey 'Sun Fire Insurance Policies from the Country Department Policy Registers' in *Northern Ceramic Society Journal Vol. 3 1978-1979* (1979) 101-48, 103.
4. Pape op. cit., 186.
5. P. Bemrose 'Hats, Pots and Clocks' in *Newcastle-under-Lyme*

1173-1973 ed. J. Briggs (Newcastle-under-Lyme: Newcastle-under-Lyme Borough Council, 1973) 85-96, 92.

6. *The Universal British Directory* (London: The Patentees, 1790-1798, Staffordshire section dated *c.*1795 by mention of the death of Josiah Wedgwood, 3 January 1795) 102.

7. *The Staffordshire Pottery Directory* (Chester and Mort, Hanley, n.d., 1796) 49.

8. Wedgwood MSS: 11/29504, W/M 1566.

9. W. Mankowitz & R.G. Haggar *The Concise Encyclopaedia of English Pottery and Porcelain* (London: Deutsch, 1957) 163.

10. J.J. Sanderson 'The Newcastle Canals: Historical Anomalies', Keele University, B.A. History Dissertation (1983) 32.

11. *The Selected Letters of Josiah Wedgwood*, ed. A. Finer and G. Savage (London: Cory, Adams & Mackay, 1965) 63, 87, 109, 131, 133, 223; R. Reilly *Josiah Wedgwood 1730-1795* (London: Macmillan, 1992) 69, 111, 143, 340.

12. D. Barker *William Greatbatch: a Staffordshire Potter* (London: Horne, 1991) 28.

13. P. Bemrose 'The Pomona Potworks, Newcastle, Staffs.' in *English Ceramic Circle Transactions Vol. 9* (1973) 1-18, 18 and plate 11; M. Pulver, 'Not *Another* Unique Factory Mark?' in *Antique Collecting Vol. 19, No. 9* (February 1985) 53, 53.

14. D. Darlington 'Three Bulb Pots in Search of a Factory' in *Northern Ceramic Society Newsletter No. 68* (1987) 32-33, 33, note by T. Lockett; T. Lockett 'Bulkely (*sic*) (not Beckett) & Bent' in *Northern Ceramic Society Newsletter No. 69* (1988) 33-34, 33.

Chatterley

1. S. Shaw *History of the Staffordshire Potteries; and the Rise and Progress of the Manufacture of Pottery and Porcelain; with References to Genuine Specimens, and Notices of Eminent Potters* (Hanley: privately, 1829, reprinted Newton Abbot: David and Charles, 1970) 188, 208.

2. Shaw, op. cit., 206.

3. *Bailey's Western & Midland Directory … for … 1783* (Birmingham, 1783); *Bailey's British Directory 1784* multi-vol, (London, 1784) II, 391.

4. J. Ward *The Borough of Stoke-upon-Trent …* (London: Lewis, 1843) 386.

5. R. Gurnett *Chatterley & Whitehead Potters of Hanley & Shelton* (Bishop's Stortford: privately, 1996) 11. This is the first attempt to collate information on these two pottery families.

6. Wedgwood MSS: 30/22596.

7. 13 R. Edmundson 'Staffordshire Potters insured with the Salop Fire Office 1780-1825' in *Journal of the Northern Ceramic Society Vol. 6* (1987) 81-93, 87.

8. G.A. Godden *Encyclopaedia of British Porcelain Manufacturers* (London: Barrie & Jenkins, 1988) 765.

9. Shaw, op. cit., 209.

10. J.P.M. Latham 'Dorset Clay to Staffordshire Pot' in *English Ceramic Circle Transactions Vol. 10* (1977) 109-17, 115.

11. H. Blakey 'Fire Insurance and Ceramic History - includng extracts from the Sun Fire Office Policy Registers: 1782-1793' in *Journal of the Northern Ceramic Society Vol. 10* (1993) 161-97, 193.

12. St John's Church, Hanley: monumental inscription.

13. P.W.L. Adams *A History of the Adams Family of North Staffordshire …* (London: St Catherine Press, 1914) 196.

14. *The Universal British Directory* (London: The Patentees, *c.*1795) 108.

15. *The Staffordshire Pottery Directory …* (Chester and Mort, Hanley, *c.*1796) 29.

Chetham

1. See R. Hampson 'Longton Potters 1700-1865', *Journal of Ceramic History Vol. 14* (1990) 46- 48 for a detailed summary of information about the Chetham businesses, 1796-1865. A. Eatwell and A. Werner 'A London Staffordshire Warehouse - 1794-1825', *Journal of the Northern Ceramic Society Vol. 8* (1991) 91-124, 100 show that Chetham and Woolley supplied unspecified pottery to Thomas Wyllie in London from 1794 to 1799.

2. *Staffordshire Advertiser*, 30 September, 28 October 1871.

3. S. Shaw *History of the Staffordshire Potteries; and the Rise and Progress of the Manufacture of Pottery and Porcelain; with References to Genuine Specimens, and Notices of Eminent Potters* (Hanley:

privately, 1829, reprinted Newton Abbot: David and Charles, 1970) 225. See also Appendix 2: White Felspathic Stoneware.

4. *Staffordshire Advertiser*, 16 December 1809.

5. For a fuller account of Woolley, see R. Hampson 'Longton Potters' in *Journal of Ceramic History Vol. 14* (1990) 174-75.

6. Staffordshire Record Office: D 3272/1/17/1/76.

7. *Staffordshire Advertiser*, 2 March 1811.

8. Ibid. 3 September 1814; Minton MSS: 1323, 1324.

9. *Staffordshire Advertiser*, 25 May 1816.

10. B. Rackham *Catalogue of The Glaisher Collection of Pottery & Porcelain in the Fitzwilliam Museum Cambridge* 2 vol. (Cambridge: Cambridge University Press, 1935, rep. Woodbridge: Antique Collectors' Club, 1987) I, 164, 1266-66d. Illustrated in J.E. Poole *English Pottery* (Cambridge: Cambridge University Press, 1995) 94-95.

11. Poole, op. cit. 94.

12. D.E. Roussel *The Castleford Pottery 1790-1821* (Wakefield: Wakefield Historical Publications, 1982) Plate 74.

13. *Staffordshire Porcelain*, ed. G. Godden (London: Granada, 1983) Plate 649A.

Chrysanthemum Pad

1. Dr R.K. Henrywood 'The Chrysanthemum Factory' in *Northern Ceramic Society Newsletter No. 83* September 1991, 48-49.

2. D. Beaton 'Chrysanthemums, Angels and Pad Marks' in *Northern Ceramic Society Newsletter No. 91* September 1993, 38; M. Ironside 'A Clutch of Pad Marks' in *Northern Ceramic Society Newsletter No. 92* December 1993, 19 (the chrysanthemum pad (C) appears to differ from that illustrated by Dr Henrywood); and R.K. Henrywood *An Illustrated Guide to British Jugs* (Shrewsbury: Swan Hill, 1997) 103, plates 288-98, 365.

3. R. Hildyard 'Country Classical' in *Antique Collecting Vol. 32, No. 4* September 1997, 12-17, 15.

Clews

1. The fullest account of the career of the Clews brothers is in two articles by F. Stefano: 'James and Ralph Clews, nineteenth century potters, Part I: The English experience' and 'James Clews, nineteenth century potter, Part II: The American experience' in *English Pottery and Porcelain: an historical survey* ed. P. Atterbury (London: Owen, 1980) 202-09. Additional information is given in G.A. Godden *Encyclopaedia of British Porcelain Manufacturers* (London: Barrie & Jenkins, 1988) 238-39. A summary is given in R.S. Hampson *Churchill China: Great British Potters since 1795* (Keele: Keele University, 1994) 124-25.

2. Stefano, op. cit, 202.

3. Ibid., 203; *Staffordshire Advertiser*, 19 April 1828.

4. *Staffordshire Advertiser*, 26 April 1834 *passim* to 12 September 1835.

5. Wedgwood MS 33/25182: an 1811 letter from Stevenson to Wedgwood, signed by James Clews.

6. Stefano, op. cit., 207.

7. Ibid., 208.

8. Ibid., 208.

9. *Staffordshire Advertiser*, 19 November 1836, 16 December 1837, 21 March 1857.

10. Wedgwood MS 30/22821, a letter from R. & J. Clews to Wedgwood, 7 September 1813.

11. R. and E. Hampson 'Brownfields, Victorian Potters' in *Northern Ceramic Society Journal Vol. 4* (1980-1981) 177-218.

Clowes

1. N. Valpy 'Extracts from 18th Century London Newspapers' in *English Ceramic Circle Transactions Vol. 12* (1985) 161-88, 172; and information from Peter Roden, quoting Guildhall Libary MS 5213/3.

2. J. Ward *The Borough of Stoke-upon-Trent …* (London: Lewis, 1843) 156.

3. R. Edmundson 'Staffordshire Potters insured with the Salop Fire Office 1780-1825' in *Journal of the Northern Ceramic Society Vol. 6* (1987) 81-93, 84.

4. *Bailey's Northern Directory 1781*; *Bailey's Western & Midland Directory … for … 1783* (Birmingham, 1783).

5. *Bailey's British Directory 1784* multi-vol, (London, 1784) II, 392.

6. Edmundson, op. cit., 85.
7. *The Universal British Directory* (London: The Patentees, c.1795) 105; *The Staffordshire Pottery Directory* (Chester and Mort, Hanley, c.1796) 47.
8. D. Holgate *New Hall* revised ed. (London: Faber, 1987) 22.
9. Ibid.
10. Ibid.
11. *Staffordshire Advertiser*, 4 January 1823.
12. Local Trade Directories, 1802, 1805, 1809, 1818, 1821, 1822, 1828, 1830.
13. *Staffordshire Advertiser*, 27 May 1826.
14. St James's Church, Newchapel, Staffordshire, monumental inscription.
15. *Staffordshire Advertiser*, 13 August 1831.
16. Ward, op. cit., 176.
17. *A Map of the Staffordshire Potteries and Newcastle-under-Lyme* (Burslem: Hargreaves, 1832).
18. Holgate, op. cit., 22; Ward, op. cit., 175-77.
19. Ibid. C. Hadfield *The Canals of the West Midlands* 1st ed. (Newton Abbot: David & Charles, 1966) 44, 79, 108, 138, 160-63, 171.
20. Edmundson, op. cit., 88.

Clulow
1. *The Staffordshire Pottery Directory* (Hanley: Allbut, 1802) map and key.
2. *Staffordshire Advertiser* 13 February 1802.
3. D.E. Roussel *The Castleford Pottery 1790-1821* (Wakefield: Wakefield Historical Publications, 1982) 37, plate 75.
4. *The Staffordshire Pottery Directory* (Hanley: Chester and Mort, n.d., 1796); *The Staffordshire Pottery Directory* (Hanley: Allbut, 1802) map and key.
5. *Staffordshire Advertiser*, 4 December 1802.
6. B. Adams and A. Thomas *A Potwork in Devonshire* (Bovey Tracey: Sayce, 1996) 39, 40; *Newcastle-under-Lyme Parish Register 1771-1812* (ed.) N.W. Tildesley, (Birmingham: Birmingham and Midland Society for Genealogy and Heraldry, 1981) 15: Joseph son of Thos. Rogers baptised 16 November 1773.
7. *A View of the Staffordshire Potteries* (Burslem: Allbutt, 1800); *The Staffordshire Pottery Directory* (Hanley: Allbut, 1802) map and key.
8. N. Valpy 'Extracts from the Daily Advertiser 1792-1795' in *English Ceramic Circle Transactions Vol. 14, Part 2* (1991) 228-34, 229; *Staffordshire Advertiser*, 22 April 1797.

Cyples
1. This information is summarized from R. Hampson 'Longton Potters 1700-1865' in *Journal of Ceramic History Vol. 14* (1990) 56-58.
2. *Staffordshire Advertiser*, 29 May 1858: Died 18th, Richard Cyples, formerly china manufacturer, aged 51.
3. G.A. Godden *Encyclopaedia of British Porcelain Manufacturers* (London: Barrie & Jenkins, 1988) 276-77.

Davenport
1. Except as otherwise referenced, all this information is summarized from two monographs: T.A. Lockett *Davenport Pottery and Porcelain 1794-1887* (Newton Abbot: David & Charles, 1972); and T.A. Lockett and G.A. Godden *Davenport: China, Earthenware, Glass* (London: Barrie & Jenkins, 1989).
2. A John Davenport (not necessarily the same one) insured a house, small potworks and stock in Burslem in 1791 (H. Blakey 'Fire Insurance and Ceramic History - including extracts from the Sun Fire Office Policy Registers: 1782-1793' in *Journal of the Northern Ceramic Society Vol. 10* (1993) 161-97, 193). A John Davenport owned and occupied a small property there from 1783 to post-1807, rented a smaller one from Anthony Keeling 1783-86, and a larger one (perhaps the potworks) from William Swinnerton between 1789 and 1791 (Stafford Record Office: Q RPL/5/23A, Burslem Land Tax Records, 1781-1809).
3. The respective works are all identified on J. Allbut & Sons's map in *The Staffordshire Directory* (Hanley: Allbut, 1802) (see Appendix 1): Unicorn Works, No. 19; Newport Pottery, No. 24; Top Bridge Works, No. 20; Bottom Bridge Works, No. 22.
4. Stafford Record Office: Q RPL/5/23A, Land Tax.

Don Pottery
1. The information given is summarized from the account by H. Lawrence in her comprehensive *Yorkshire Pots and Potteries* (Newton Abbot: David and Charles, 1974) 95-104. A monograph on the Don Pottery by John Griffin is awaited.
2. *The Don Pottery Design Book* of 1807 was reprinted in 1983 by the Doncaster Library Service, as *The Don Pottery Pattern Book*.
3. Victoria and Albert Museum: c.85+A-1966.

Dunderdale
1. This information is summarized from D.E. Roussel's monograph *The Castleford Pottery 1790-1821* (Wakefield: Wakefield Historical Publications, 1982). H. Lawrence *Yorkshire Pots and Potteries* (Newton Abbot: David and Charles, 1974) 163-82 describes this and several other potteries in the Castleford area.

Glass
1. *Staffordshire Advertiser* 2 May 1840: Died 27th, Market Street, Hanley, John Glass, oldest earthenware manufacturer in the Potteries, aged 83. Information about John Glass is also given in D. Edwards *Black Basalt: Wedgwood and Contemporary Manufacturers* (Woodbridge: Antique Collectors' Club, 1994) 157-59, plates 213-19.
2. *Bailey's British Directory for 1784* (London, 1784) 391.
3. *Staffordshire Advertiser* 24 January 1829; died 16th inst. aged 64, Mrs Glass, wife of Mr John Glass, earthenware manufacturer, Hanley.
4. *International Genealogical Index: Staffordshire* (1984): Glass.
5. Wedgwood MS 39/28404, Minute Book of the Committee of Commerce 1784-1790, p.7 *passim* to p.87.
6. *The Staffordshire Pottery Directory* (Chester and Mort, Hanley, n.d., 1706) 30.
7. A. Eatwell and A. Werner 'A London Staffordshire Warehouse – 1794-1825' in *Journal of the Northern Ceramic Society Volume 8* (1991) 91-124: Glass and Taylor dealt with Wyllie, London Staffordshire warehouseman, between 1798 and 1801, supplying black teapots in 1800; *London Gazette*, Nov 2, *15529* 1802: Partnership between John Glass and John Taylor as Potters at Hanley dissolved 4 January 1802 (information from Dr G.A. Godden).
8. Hanley Reference Library, EMT 11/815C.
9. *Staffordshire General & Commercial Directory* (Manchester: Parson and Bradshaw, 1818) 65, 81, 128.
10. *London Gazette 17669* 16 January 1821 (information from Dr G.A. Godden).
11. A. Meigh *Manufacturers of Pottery in the Staffordshire Potteries ... 1807-1859 from the Rate Books* (privately, 1940), p.7 *passim* to p.289; 1834 Glass, Jno. to Hackwood & Keeling.
12. H. Blakey 'Fire Insurance and Ceramic History – including extracts from the Sun Fire Office Policy Registers: 1782-1793' in *Journal of the Northern Ceramic Society Volume 10* (1993) 161-97, 190, policy no. 370/569996.
13. R. Edmundson 'Staffordshire Potters insured with the Salop Fire Office 1780-1825' in *Journal of the Northern Ceramic Society Volume 6* (1987) 81-93, 86, policy no. 1576.
14. Edmundson, op. cit., 86, policy no. 1577.
15. Edmundson, op. cit., 88, policy no. 1833.
16. *Staffordshire Advertiser* 17 June 1797.
17. Ibid., 7 March 1807: to be let or sold, large house facing Market Place, now occupied by J. Glass, apply John Mare junior.
18. Hanley Reference Library, SP 850.352: Stoke-upon-Trent Poor Law Union – West of Trent 2nd Book 1807-08, properties 3842, 3903.
19. *Staffordshire Advertiser* 12 February 1831.
20. Meigh, op. cit., 289, 291, 293.
21. Ibid., 298 *passim* to 338.
22. *Staffordshire Advertiser* 20 October 1849.
23. *Staffordshire Advertiser* 12 October 1850, partnership dissolved, S. Keeling and Co., earthenware makers.
24. B. Hollowood *The Story of J. and G. Meakin* (Derby: Bemrose, 1951) 12.
25. Jewitt *The Ceramic Art of Great Britain from Pre-Historic Times*

down to the Present Day 2 vol. (London: Virtue, 1878) II, 310.

26. Ordnance Survey 1:500 maps: *Staffordshire Hanley XI 16 17* 1866, surveyed 1865, which shows the works; *Staffordshire (The Potteries) Hanley XII 13 15* 1880, revised 1874–75, which shows the site rebuilt.

27. See note 1.

28. See note 18, Property 3903.

29. *Staffordshire Advertiser* 24 December 1808.

30. Ibid., 9 March 1816.

31. Meigh op. cit., *passim*.

32. *Staffordshire Advertiser* 8 November 1828.

33. Meigh, op. cit., 258 *passim* to 293; *Staffordshire Advertiser* 30 April 1836: Gray and Jones, Hanley, china manufacturers, dissolved partnership.

34. See note 26.

Greatbatch

1. D. Barker *William Greatbatch: a Staffordshire Potter* (London: Horne, 1991).

2. G.A. Godden *Encyclopaedia of British Pottery and Porcelain Marks* (London: Barrie & Jenkins, 1964) 64, 145; *Letters of Arnold Bennett* ed. J. Hepburn, multi-vol. (Oxford: Oxford University Press) IV (1986) 165, 179.

3. Author's notes, photographed January 1975.

4. Wedgwood MSS: 34/5908.

5. Wedgwood MSS: 26/19035-37.

6. A. Meigh *Manufacturers of Pottery in the Staffordshire Potteries … 1807 to 1859 (inclusive) from the Rate Books* (privately, 1940) 240, 248.

7. *Staffordshire Advertiser*, 22 March 1828, 13, 20 June, 7 November 1829, 2 January 1830.

8. Ibid., 7 November 1829: auction sale included 7 reams printing paper, 2 printing presses and copper plate engravings; *National Commercial Directory 1828-29: Staffordshire* (London: Pigot, 1828) 724, China Manufacturers ... Greatbach (*sic*) William, jun. Stoke.

9. A.W. Coysh and R.K. Henrywood *The Dictionary of Blue and White Printed Pottery 1780-1880* 2 vol. (Woodbridge: Antique Collectors' Club, 1989) II, 12, 'Albion'.

10. Barker, op cit., 263.

11. Ibid., 264-67.

Gresley

1. L. Jewitt *The Ceramic Art of Great Britain …* 2 vol. (London: Virtue, 1878) II, 155.

2. Jewitt op. cit., II, 98.

3. *Staffordshire Advertiser*, 17 March 1798.

4. Ibid., 4, 11 May 1799.

5. Jewitt, op. cit., II, 155.

6. G.A. Godden *Encyclopaedia of British Porcelain Manufacturers* (London: Barrie & Jenkins, 1988) 204.

7. Jewitt, op. cit., II, 159.

8. R.B. Brown 'Potteries of Derbyshire' in *Journal of the Northern Ceramic Society Vol. 11 1994* (1994) 95-153, 131-35; P. Atterbury *Cornish Ware; Kitchen and Domestic Pottery by T.G. Green of Church Gresley, Derbyshire* (Shepton Beauchamp: Richard Dennis, (1996) 9.

9. G.W. Rhead *The Earthenware Collector* (London: Jenkins, 1920) 272-75, plates 53, 54; now in Warrington, Cheshire, Museum.

10. 'Annual General Meeting 1986' in *Northern Ceramic Society Newsletter No. 63* (1986) 42-49, 49; and 'Two Unusual Marks' in *Northern Ceramic Society Newsletter No. 64* (1986) 43-44, 43 and Fig. 1.

11. Nottingham Museum.

12. 'A Church Gresley Teapot' in *Northern Ceramic Society Newsletter No. 78* (1990) 40.

13. Godden op. cit., 203-04.

Hackwood

1. *North Staffordshire Mercury* 26 March 1836: 'Deaths ... died at Newcastle on the 19th inst. Mr William Hackwood, father of Mr Hackwood sen. (*sic*), earthenware manufacturer in this town [Hanley], aged 84. He was considered the best modeller in the

Potteries, and had been in the employ of the Messrs Wedgwood, of Etruria, upwards of half a century'.

2. G.A. Godden *Encyclopaedia of British Porcelain Manufacturers* (London: Barrie & Jenkins,1988) 385.

3. *Staffordshire Advertiser* 9 June 1849: died 2 June, William Hackwood, aged 72.

4. Wedgwood MS 11/1970.

5. *Staffordshire Advertiser*, 8 September 1827: died 17 August, Thomas Dimmock, aged 76.

6. W. Mankowitz & R.G. Haggar *The Concise Encyclopaedia of English Pottery and Porcelain* (London: Deutsch, 1957) 120.

7. Newcastle Reference Library: TAB/2, Hanley Tabernacle Congregational Chapel Register, 3 October 1819, baptism of Catherine, daughter of James and Sarah Keeling, née Dimmock.

8. *Staffordshire Advertiser*, 6 January 1821.

9. Ibid., 6 November 1830.

10. A. Meigh *Manufacturers of Pottery in the Staffordshire Potteries … 1807-1859 from the Rate Books* (privately, 1940) 291, 293; *Staffordshire Advertiser* 4 March 1837.

11. Hanley Reference Library: West of Trent Rate Book, 4 August 1807, 118.

12. *Staffordshire Advertiser*, 2 October 1830.

13. *A Map of the Staffordshire Potteries and Newcastle-under-Lyme* (Hargreaves, Burslem, 1832).

14. D. Holgate *New Hall* revised edition (London: Faber, 1987) 234.

15. Meigh op. cit., 362, 365.

16. Mankowitz and Haggar, op. cit., 102.

17. Godden op. cit., 385.

18. Mankowitz and Haggar, op. cit., 102, quoting *Staffordshire Advertiser*, 10 December 1853. The 'Mr William Hackwood' of Hope Street mentioned in this advertisement was clearly alive at the time. William Hackwood of Eastwood and New Hall had died in 1849, and his son Thomas was in charge of the New Hall Works in New Hall Street.

Handley

1. Detailed research on this firm is given in a paper by M. Hosking 'James and William Handley: Staffordshire Potters 1819-1828' in *Journal of the Northern Ceramic Society Vol. 11* (1994) 47- 77.

2. Stafford Record Office: QRPL/5/23 B-D, Land Tax; *Staffordshire Advertiser* 30 August 1817; potworks late occupied by John Brettell to be let.

3. A. Meigh *Manufacturers of Pottery in the Staffordshire Potteries … 1807-1859 from the Rate Books* (privately, 1940) 131, 137, 150, 155.

Hartley, Greens

1. Leeds Pottery has been the subject of detailed research, from L.Jewitt *The Ceramic Art of Great Britain from Pre-Historic Times down to the Present Day* 2 vol. (London: Virtue, 1878) I, 466-84 to the monographs by J.R. Kidson and F. Kidson *Historical Notices of the Leeds Old Pottery* (Leeds: Kidson, 1892, reprinted East Ardsley: S.R. & Co., 1970) and *The Leeds Pottery* by D. Towner (London: Cory, Adams & Mackay, 1963). H. Lawrence *Yorkshire Pots and Potteries* (Newton Abbot, David & Charles, 1974) 17-40 gave a comprehensive summary.

2. Lawrence, op. cit., 18.

3. R. Reilly *Wedgwood* 2 vol. (London: Macmillan, 1989) I, 48-49, 155, 250-53.

4. E. Adams 'Ceramic Insurances in the Sun Company 1766-1774' in *English Ceramic Circle Transactions Vol. 10, Part I* (1976) 1-38, 11, 33.

5. H. Blakey 'Sun Fire Insurance Records 1774-1782' in *Journal of the Northern Ceramic Society Vol. 9* (1992) 165-81, 175.

6. R. Morley 'The Enigma of the Leeds Pottery's Co-partnership Shares' in *Journal of the Northern Ceramic Society Vol. 6* (1987) 23-48, 25-26.

7. Anon. *The Leeds Pottery, Hunslet, near Leeds 1770-1881* (Leeds: Leeds City Art Galleries and Leeds Art Collections Fund, 1983) [1]; Wedgwood MSS: 131/26336.

8. H. Blakey 'Thomas Lakin: Staffordshire Potter 1769-1821' in *Northern Ceramic Society Journal Vol. 5* (1984) 79-114, 107-08.

9. R. Morley 'The Leeds Pottery 'Revival' 1881-1949 Part 1' in

Northern Ceramic Society Newsletter No. 82 (June 1991) 8-13; Part II, Ibid. No. 83 (September 1991) 22-29.

10. *Yellow Pages Stoke-on-Trent 1995/96* (Reading: British Telecommunications, n.d.) 627.

Heath

1. The Directory is not dated, but *The Staffordshire Advertiser*, 26 March 1796 carried an advertisement by Chester and Mort which stated that 'the Pottery Directory is hoped to be published in a few weeks'.

2. H. Blakey 'Sun Fire Insurance Policies from the Country Department Policy Registers' in *Northern Ceramic Society Journal Vol. 3 1978-1979* (1979) 101-48, 110, 111.

3. *Staffordshire Advertiser*, 30 November 1799.

4. Stafford Record Office: QRPL/5/23 A & B, Land Tax; Wedgwood MS 121/23479. Earlier, the Hill works was occupied successively by William Adams; Ralph Wedgwood; and Ralph Wood (q.v.).

5. *Staffordshire Advertiser*, 26 May, 15 September 1810; 18 May 1811; 28 November 1812.

Herculaneum Pottery

1. The only monograph on Herculaneum Pottery is A. Smith *The Illustrated Guide to Liverpool Herculaneum Pottery 1796-1840* (London: Barrie & Jenkins, 1970). Warrington Museum and Art Gallery held an exhibition in 1983, and the catalogue, *Herculaneum the last Liverpool Pottery,* includes an essay by A. Smith. The catalogue of an exhibition held in 1993 at the Walker Art Gallery, Liverpool, *Made in Liverpool: Liverpool Pottery & Porcelain 1700-1850* ed. E.M. Brown and T A. Lockett (Liverpool: National Museums & Galleries on Merseyside, 1993), includes essays on 'Herculaneum Porcelains' by G.A. Godden and 'Herculaneum' by A. Smith.

2. *The Herculaneum Echo No. 6* ed. P. Hyland (January 1994) 3. This is one of a series of occasional bulletins for collectors, published by the editor, 5 Beckets Square, Berkhamsted, Herts., HP4 1BZ, England.

3. *Staffordshire Advertiser* 14 January 1865.

Hollins, Samuel

1. Brief accounts of Samuel Hollins are given in P.W.L. Adams *A History of the Adams Family of North Staffordshire & of their Connection with the Development of the Potteries* (London: St Catherine Press, 1914) 193-94; and more accessibly in D. Holgate *New Hall* revised edition (London: Faber, 1987) 17-18. Samuel Hollins's death was reported in the *Staffordshire Advertiser* 11 November 1820: 'died Sunday last [5th] aged 71, Samuel Hollins Esq. of Shelton'. A tombstone in St John's Churchyard, Hanley, confirms Samuel Hollins's date of death as 5 November 1820, but gives his age as 70.

2. Holgate, op. cit., 17.

3. Adams, op. cit. 193.

4. R. Edmundson 'Staffordshire Potters insured with the Salop Fire Office 1780-1825' in *Journal of the Northern Ceramic Society Volume 6* (1987) 81-93, 90, policies nos.5621 and 5622.

5. A. Meigh *Manufacturers of Pottery in the Staffordshire Potteries ... 1807-1859 from the Rate Books* (privately, 1940) 95.

6. See note 1; also *Staffordshire Advertiser*, 1 June 1822 for sale of part of Samuel Hollins's effects.

7. Holgate, op. cit. 17.

8. Adams, op. cit., 194.

9. See note 3.

10. A tombstone inscription in St John's Churchyard, Hanley, includes: Thomas Hollins died 23 February 1772 aged 29.

11. *A History of the County of Stafford* ed. J.G. Jenkins multi-vol. (London: Oxford University Press, 1963) VIII, 147, n.43.

12. *The Staffordshire Pottery Directory*, (Allbut, Hanley, 1802) map and key, No. 95.

13. S. Shaw *History of the Staffordshire Potteries; and the Rise and Progress of the Manufacture of Pottery and Porcelain; with references to Genuine Specimens, and notices of Eminent Potters* (Hanley: privately,1829, rep. Newton Abbot: David & Charles, 1970) 201.

14. Edmundson, op. cit., 90, policies Nos. 5621 and 5622.

15. Meigh, op. cit., 38-88, *passim*.

16. Meigh, op. cit., 38-212, *passim; The Newcastle and Pottery General*

and Commercial Directory for 1822-23 (Hanley: Allbut, n.d.). 82; and see W. Mankowitz & R.G. Haggar *The Concise Encyclopedia of English Pottery and Porcelain* (London: Deutsch, 1957) 111 and *Staffordshire Advertiser* 29 July 1826, 13 October 1827 for sale notices for the factory 1825-27.

17. Edmundson, op. cit., 85, policy 1438.

18. See note 14.

19. Adams, op. cit., 189-92.

20. Adams, op. cit., 245.

21. Holgate, op. cit., 30.

22. R. Nicholls, *Ten Generations of a Potting Family* (London: Lund Humphries, c.1931) 50.

23. Holgate, op. cit., 232-33.

24. Hanley Reference Library: West of Trent Rate Book, 4 August 1807, 70, 74-76.

25. Wedgwood MS 30/22429-22431.

26. Wedgwood MS WM 1459.

27. Wedgwood MS 12/2157-2163.

28. A. Eatwell and A. Werner 'A London Staffordshire Warehouse - 1794-1825' in *Journal of the Northern Ceramic Society Volume 8* (1991) 91-124, 101.

29. Eatwell and Werner, op. cit., 102-22, *passim*.

30. J. Turnbull 'Staffordshire Potters and Scottish Merchants' in *Journal of the Northern Ceramic Society Volume 9* (1992) 115-22, 121.

Hollins, Thomas & John

1. *Staffordshire Advertiser*, 31 March 1804: 'Died a few days ago, at his son's house at Hanley, John Hollins, gent of Newcastle, Alderman of that borough, and one of the partners in the New Hall china-manufactory'; 7 April 1808: debtors or creditors of late John Hollins to send their account to Thomas, John or Richard Hollins of Hanley, executors.

2. D. Holgate *New Hall* revised edition (London: Faber, 1987) 17.

3. Stafford Record Office: QRPL/5/43 A, Land Tax.

4. J.P.M. Latham 'Dorset Clay to Staffordshire Pot' in *English Ceramic Circle Transactions Vol. 10, part 2* (1977) 109-17, 115.

5. R. Edmundson 'Staffordshire Potters insured with the Salop Fire Office 1780-1825' in *Journal of the Northern Ceramic Society Vol. 6* (1987) 81-93, 86.

6. See note 1.

7. *Staffordshire Advertiser*, 26 October, 14 December 1805, 1 March 1806.

8. A. Eatwell and A. Werner 'A London Staffordshire Warehouse - 1794-1825' in *Journal of the Northern Ceramic Society Vol. 8* (1991) 91-124, 102.

9. A. Meigh *Manufacturers of Pottery in the Staffordshire Potteries ... 1807-1859 from the Rate Books* (privately, 1940) 141; Stafford Record Office: QRPL/5/43 B, Land Tax.

10. G.A. Godden *Encyclopaedia of British Porcelain Manufacturers* (London: Barrie & Jenkins, 1988) 562.

11. R. Morley 'Zacharia (*sic*) Boyle in Yorkshire' in *Northern Ceramic Society Newsletter No 88* (December 1992) 29, 29; Meigh, op. cit., 149.

12. T. Markin 'Thomas Wolfe: Man of Property - Part III' in *Northern Ceramic Society Newsletter No. 58* (June 1985) 6-15, 13; *Staffordshire Advertiser* 27 September 1828, 2 January 1830.

13. *Staffordshire Advertiser*, 16 January 1830.

14. Ibid., 18 February, 14 April, 13 October 1832.

Isleworth

1. Henry Clay, 'Isleworth Pottery', *The Burlington Magazine*, July–December 1926, 83–85.

2. Frank Britton, *London Delftware* (London: Jonathan Horne, 1987), 77–79.

3. Op. cit., Edwards, *Black Basalt*, 1994, fig. 357.

Lakin

1. Thomas Lakin has been thoroughly researched by H. Blakey, see his 'Thomas Lakin: Staffordshire Potter 1769-1821' in *Northern Ceramic Society Journal Vol. 5* (1984) 79-114.

2. *Staffordshire Advertiser*, 7 May 1814.

Lockett

1. A detailed summary of information about Locketts is given in R. Hampson 'Longton Potters 1700-1865' in *Journal of Ceramic History Vol. 14* (1990) 106-12.
2. Wedgwood MS 39/28404.
3. *Staffordshire Advertiser*, 15 November 1800, dissolution of partnership.
4. *Pottery Gazette and Glass Trade Review*, February 1962, 245, 280.
5. *Staffordshire Advertiser*, 24 June 1876; Hanley Reference Library: EM 26/876a, sale particulars.

Mason

1. The standard works are: R. Haggar and E. Adams *Mason Porcelain and Ironstone 1796-1853* (London: Faber, 1977); and G.A. Godden *Godden's Guide to Mason's China and the Ironstone Wares* 3rd edition (London: Barrie & Jenkins, 1991). G.B. Roberts *Mason's The first Two Hundred Years* (London: Merrell Holberton, n. d., 1996) is the most recent summary and has a good bibliography.
2. *Staffordshire Advertiser*, 6 July 1822.
3. Ibid., 15 November 1828.
4. Ibid., 22 November 1828.
5. Ibid., 14 June 1856.
6. Ibid., 4 August 1832: partnership between George Miles Mason, Charles James Mason and Samuel Bayliss Faraday as China and Earthenware Manufacturers at Lane Delph dissolved by mutual consent 11 November so far as regards George Miles Mason. 22 November 1830 (*sic*). (The notice was published almost two years later.)
7. Ibid., 19 September 1846: auction of first portion of finished stock, C.J. Mason retiring.
8. Ibid., 31 October 1846: (Sale at Daniels' works at Stoke) 'Messrs. Daniel having taken the extensive manufactory of Mr Mason at Fenton, with the entire Fixtures and Fittings'; ibid., 1 May 1847, auction by order of the assignees of Richard Daniel, his stock on the premises at Fenton.
9. Ibid., 18 March, 8 April 1848.

Mayer

1. Summaries of Elijah and Joseph Mayer as potters are published in L. Jewitt *The Ceramic Art of Great Britain from Pre-Historic Times down to the Present Day*, 2 vol. (London: Virtue, 1878) II, 302, 339; M.H. Grant *The Makers of Black Basaltes* (Edinburgh: Blackwood, 1911, reprinted London: Holland Press, 1967), 254-62; W. Mankowitz & R.G. Haggar *The Concise Encyclopedia of English Pottery and Porcelain* (London: Deutsch, 1957) 145; and D. Edwards *Black Basalt: Wedgwood and Contemporary Manufacturers* (Woodbridge: Antique Collectors' Club, 1994) 195-204. Mayer family history is recorded in a bound typescript in Hanley Reference Library: S 192, 'The Mayer Story 1575-1929' compiled by F.K. Mayer, assisted by W. Mayer.
2. *Bucknall-cum-Bagnall Parish Register 1762-1812* (Stafford: Staffordshire Parish Registers Society, 1920) 38.
3. Hanley Reference Library: SP 192 MAY, copy of baptismal certificate.
4. Stafford Record Office: QRPL/5/43A, Land Tax.
5. R. Edmundson 'Staffordshire Potters insured with the Salop Fire Office 1780-1825' in *Journal of the Northern Ceramic Society Volume 6* (1987) 81-93, 84, policy No. 737.
6. *Bailey's British Directory for 1784* (London, 1784) 391.
7. Edmundson, op. cit. 84, policy No. 737.
8. Wedgwood MS 75/12826.
9. *Universal British Directory of Trade, Commerce and Manufacture* (London: The Patentees, n.d., c.1795) 108; *The Staffordshire Pottery Directory* (Chester and Mort, Hanley, n.d., 1796) 32; and *The Staffordshire Pottery Directory* (Hanley: Allbut, 1802) map and key, No. 72.
10. Wedgwood MS 75/12828.
11. *Holden's Triennial Directory for 1805, 1806, 1807* (London, 1805) 251 to *History, Gazetteer and Directory of Staffordshire* (Sheffield: White, 1834) 560; A. Meigh *Manufacturers of Pottery in the Staffordshire Potteries ... 1807-1859 from the Rate Books* (privately, 1940) *passim*; Stafford Record Office: QRPL/5/23A-C, Land Tax.

12. *Staffordshire Advertiser*, 16 January 1813.
13. Meigh, op. cit., 264, 275.
14. *Staffordshire Advertiser*, 30 June 1860.
15. *Staffordshire Advertiser*, 7 July, 24 November 1860; 17 May 1862 *passim* to 27 June 1863.
16. *Staffordshire Advertiser*, 6 January 1821, 9 June 1827; Mankowitz and Haggar, op. cit., 145.
17. *Joseph Mayer of Liverpool 1803-1886* ed. M. Gibson and S.M. Wright, Occasional Papers (New series) XI (London: Society of Antiquaries, in association with The National Museums and Galleries on Merseyside, 1988).
18. Allbut, op. cit., map and key, No. 72.
19. Jewitt, op. cit., II, 339.
20. Meigh, op. cit., 264, 275.
21. *Royal National and Commercial Directory of ... Staffordshire for 1841* (Manchester: Pigot, 1841) 46.
22. *Staffordshire Advertiser*, 8 October 1864.
23. S. Shaw *History of the Staffordshire Potteries; and the Rise and Progress of the Manufacture of Pottery and Porcelain; with references to Genuine Specimens, and notices of Eminent Potters* (Hanley: privately, 1829, rep. Newton Abbot: David & Charles, 1970) 209.
24. G.E. Stringer *New Hall Porcelain* (London: Art Trade Press, 1949) 75.
25. Wedgwood MS 36/30938.
26. Wedgwood MS 31/5119.
27. Wedgwood MS WM 1566.
28. Wedgwood MS 36/27830; 75/12835-36.
29. Jewitt, op. cit., II, 301-02; *Staffordshire Advertiser*, 12 July 1828, Bagster's works for auction.
30. *Staffordshire Advertiser*, 27 June 1863.
31. Anon. *Personal recollections of the late Leonard James Abington* (Hanley: Allbut & Daniel, 1868) 11, 45.
32. *Staffordshire Advertiser*, 15 September 1860.
33. *New Commercial Directory for ... Staffordshire ... for 1828-9* (London: Pigot, 1828); *National Commercial Directory of Staffordshire 1830* (London: Pigot, 1830) 725.
34. *Staffordshire Advertiser*, 1 December 1860.
35. Ibid., 9 February 1861.

Minton

1. L.L. Jewitt *The Ceramic Art of Great Britain*, 2 vol. (London: Virtue, 1878) II, 185-212; G.A. Godden *Minton Pottery & Porcelain of the First Period 1793-1850* (London: Barrie & Jenkins, 1968; P. Atterbury and M. Batkin *The Dictionary of Minton* (Woodbridge: Antique Collectors' Club, 1990), esp. 9-22; P.R. Booth 'Herbert Minton, pottery manufacturer, entrepreneur and philanthropist 1793-1858', Keele University, unpublished History M.A. thesis; J. Jones *Minton: The First Two Hundred Years of Design and Production* (Shrewsbury: Swan Hill, 1993); R. Cumming 'Joseph Poulson 1749-1808: Bone China Pioneer: Minton & Poulson 1796-1808' in *Journal of the Northern Ceramic Society Vol. 12* (1995) 59-91.
2. A. Meigh *Manufacturers of Pottery in the Staffordshire Potteries ... 1807 to 1859 (inclusive) from the Rate Books* (privately, 1940) 33 *passim* to 97.
3. *Staffordshire Advertiser*, 4 January 1823.
4. Atterbury and Batkin, op. cit., 199.

Mist

1. J. Howarth 'Andrew Abbott and the Fleet Street Partnerships' in *Journal of the Northern Ceramic Society Vol. 13,* (1996) 75-117, 108.
2. Ibid., 108.
3. Ibid., 111.
4. Ibid., 81, 91, 96.
5. *International Genealogical Index*, London (1984).
6. Ibid.
7. B. Horn 'Ceramic Bills paid by Alexander, 4th Duke of Gordon' in *English Ceramic Circle Transactions Vol. 15* (1995) 435-39, 435.
8. Howarth, op. cit., 107, 113.
9. Ibid., 108.
10. Ibid., 113.

11. T.A. Lockett and G.A. Godden *Davenport China, Earthenware, Glass* (London: Barrie & Jenkins, 1989) 216.

12. Howarth, op. cit., 111.

13. H.A. Shannon 'Bricks - A Trade Index, 1785-1849' in *Essays in Economic History* ed. E.M. Carus-Wilson, 3 vol. (London: Arnold, 1962) III, 188-201, 191.

14. Howarth, op. cit., 111.

15. Ibid., 112; Lockett and Godden, op. cit., 23, 63.

16. R. and E. Hampson 'Pottery Manufacturers, 1800-1807' in *Northern Ceramic Society Newsletter No. 68* (1987) 28-30.

17. *Stonewares & Stone chinas of Northern England to 1851* ed. T.A. Lockett and P.A. Halfpenny (Stoke-on-Trent: City Museum and Art Gallery, 1982) 118, No. 229, pl. 207.

18. 'More Mist marked Pieces' in *Northern Ceramic Society Newsletter No. 88* December 1992, 13.

19. A. Hayden *Chats on English Earthenware* (London: Fisher Unwin, 1909) 269, 277.

20. G.E. Stringer 'Notes on Staffordshire Bas-Reliefs of the Eighteenth and Nineteenth Centuries' in *English Ceramic Circle Transactions Vol. 4 Part I* 1957, 2-6, plates 3, A and B; 5, G and J.

21. R. Hildyard 'Country Classical' in *Antique Collecting Vol. 32, No. 4,* September 1997, 12-17, 14, figures 1 centre, and 4, left and right.

22. R. Hampson 'Longton Potters 1700-1865' in *Journal of Ceramic History Volume 14* 1990, i-viii, 1-236, 47 and plate 24.

23. H. Blakey 'Turner-type Stonewares and James Mist' in *Northern Ceramic Society Newsletter No. 85* March 1992, 31-34; A. Thomas 'A few thoughts on Mist' in *Northern Ceramic Society Newsletter No. 87* September 1992, 21-23; and see note 18.

24. A. Smith *The Illustrated Guide to Liverpool Herculaneum Pottery 1796-1840* (London: Barrie & Jenkins, 1970) 41, figures 95 and 97.

25. G. Haggarty 'Newbigging Pottery, Musselburgh, East Lothian' in *Scottish Pottery 18th Historical Review 1996*, 15-38, 23, Fig. 24.

Myatt

1. Former St John's churchyard, Longton, monumental inscription: Richard Myatt buried 30 June 1796, aged 57.

2. R. Hampson 'Longton Potters 1700-1865' in *Journal of Ceramic History Volume 14* (1990) 127-28.

3. Ibid.

4. Ibid.

5. Ibid.

6. A. Meigh *Manufacturers of Pottery in the Staffordshire Potteries ... 1807 to 1859 (inclusive) from the Rate Books* (privately, 1940) 4 *passim* to 76.

7. Hampson, op. cit., 126-27.

8. Ibid., 127.

Neale

1. The standard work is D. Edwards *Neale Pottery and Porcelain: Its Predecessors and Successors 1763-1820* (London: Barrie & Jenkins, 1987). D. Edwards has also written on the basalt wares of Palmer, Neale and Wilsons in *Black Basalt: Wedgwood and Contemporary Manufacturers* (Woodbridge: Antique Collectors' Club, 1994). G. Godden wrote on 'James Neale's porcelains, c.1783-1790' in *Staffordshire Porcelain*, ed. G. Godden (London: Granada, 1983) 46-56; and more recently in G.A. Godden *Encyclopaedia of British Porcelain Manufacturers*, (London: Barrie & Jenkins, 1988) 554-57.

2. D. Barker & P. Halfpenny *Unearthing Staffordshire: Towards a new understanding of 18th century ceramics* (Stoke-on-Trent: City of Stoke-on-Trent Museum & Art Gallery, 1990) 17-18.

3. *Burslem Parish Register*, 3 vol. (Stafford: Staffordshire Parish Registers Society, 1913) I, 235: Marriages, 2 May 1750, Mr Humphrey Palmer and Mrs Ann Adams; I, 154, Christenings, 10 March 1714/15, Anne Adams, daughter of John and Mabell de Byrches Hd [of Birches Head].

4. P.W.L. Adams *A History of the Adams Family of North Staffordshire & of their Connection with the Development of the Potteries*, (London: St Catherine Press, 1914) 197. Adams stated that Anne Palmer's gravestone in Hanley Churchyard gave her date of death as 14 May 1752, aged 35, but this must be a mis-reading, as Palmer married again in 1751, see note 5.

5. Stafford Record Office: microfiche 1048/1/2, Sandon Parish Register, 1751, Weddings Oct 28 married Humphrey Palmer of Hanley Green and Mary Heath of Lane Delph in the Parish of Stoke-upon-Trent.

6. *Stoke-upon-Trent Parish Register*, 4 vol. (Stafford: Staffordshire Parish Registers Society, 1914-1927) IV, 841.

7. *The Selected Letters of Josiah Wedgwood*, ed. A. Finer and G. Savage (London: Cory, Adams & Mackay, 1965) 98.

8. Edwards (1987), op. cit., 23-24.

9. W. Mankowitz & R.G. Haggar *The Concise Encyclopedia of English Pottery and Porcelain*, (London: Deutsch, 1957) 268; *Bailey's Western & Midland Directory for 1783*, (London, 1783) 283-85.

10. *Bailey's British Directory for 1784*, (London: 1784) 391; Wedgwood MS 30/22808-22812, 11/2029; Edwards (1987), op. cit., 156, partnership dissolved 24 April 1792.

11. *Staffordshire Advertiser*, 22 June 1816.

12. *Limehouse Ware Revealed*, ed. D. Drakard (London: English Ceramic Circle, 1993) 3, 57.

13. P. Bemrose 'The Pomona Potworks, Newcastle, Staffs.' in *English Ceramic Circle Transactions Vol. 9, Part I*, (1973) 1-18, *passim.*

14. Edwards (1987), op. cit., 156.

15. *Staffordshire Advertiser*, 24 January, 7 February 1801.

16. Wedgwood MS 11/2078, printed bill-head 'David Wilson ... successor to Robert Wilson ... 4 April 1801'; *Holden's Triennial Directory for 1805, 1806, 1807*, (London, 1805) 252; *Holden's Triennial Directory for 1809, 1810, 1811*, (London, 1809) 370.

17. Newcastle-under-Lyme Reference Library: TAB/2, Hanley Tabernacle Congregational Chapel Register of Baptisms. John Wilson's baptism appears in this register, but is not dated. His age was given as 61 when he died in 1835, giving a birth year of *c.*1784.

18. Ibid., James Wilson, baptised 25 November 1788.

19. Ibid., David Wilson, born 29 September, baptised 4 November 1790.

20. *Staffordshire Advertiser*, 18 January 1817: 'Died Wednesday [15th] David Wilson, one of the sons of the late David Wilson Esq., of Hanley'.

21. Ibid., 10 September 1814; 'Died 6th September at Hanley, aged 25, James, son of David Wilson Esq. and a partner in D. Wilson & Sons'.

22. Ibid., 17 February 1816.

23. Ibid., 8 August 1807; also 16 March 1816 for a slander case, when John Wilson was said to have murdered his brother.

24. Wedgwood MS 10/7892A.

25. *Staffordshire Advertiser*, 16 March 1816.

26. Wedgwood MS 10/7892B.

27. *Staffordshire Advertiser*, 17 February 1816.

28. Ibid., 22 June 1816.

29. Ibid., 29 June 1816.

30. Ibid., 12 July 1817.

31. Ibid., 6 June 1818; also 23 August 1806, when John Hatherley of Fishwick, Devon married Martha, daughter of David Wilson at Hanley, 5 August 1806.

32. Ibid., 20 September 1817, 2 May, 9 May, 19 September, 7 November 1818.

33. Ibid., 6 November 1819.

34. Ibid., 18 April 1835: 'John Wilson ... aged 51, son of the late Mr Wilson, formerly an extensive manufacturer'.

35. *A History of the County of Stafford*, ed. J.G. Jenkins, multi-vol. (London: Oxford University Press, VIII, 165 and note 15.

36. Edwards (1987), op. cit., 43-44.

37. *Staffordshire Advertiser*, 8 March 1828.

38. Edwards (1987), op. cit., 44, 207.

39. Holden, 1805, op. cit. A. Meigh *Manufacturers of Pottery in the Staffordshire Potteries ... 1807-1859 from the Rate Books*, (privately, 1940) 12, 27; *Staffordshie Advertiser*, 24 December 1808, partnership dissolved.

40. Meigh, op. cit., 39 *passim* to 60; *Staffordshire Advertiser*, 11 May 1811.

41. *Staffordshire Advertiser*, 11 May 1811, Meigh, op. cit., 64 *passim* to 85.

42. Meigh, op. cit., 53 *passim* to 95.

43. *Staffordshire Advertiser*, 5 April 1817.

44. Ibid., 6 November 1819.

45. Meigh, op. cit., 95 passim to 137; Staffordshire Advertiser, 27 November, 9 December 1820, 3 March 1821.
46. Staffordshire Advertiser, 22 November 1828.
47. Ibid., 22 July 1816.
48. Ibid., 28 December 1805.
49. J. Turnbull 'Staffordshire Potters and Scottish Merchants' in Journal of the Northern Ceramic Society Volume 9, (1992) 105-22, passim.
50. G. Quail 'The later Period of the West Pans Pottery' in Northern Ceramic Society Newsletter No. 63, (September 1986) 9-21, 19.

Pratt

1. J. and G. Lewis Pratt Ware: English and Scottish relief decorated and underglaze coloured earthenware 1780-1840 (Woodbridge: Antique Collectors' Club, 1984) 13-21.
2. Ibid., 288-89.
3. Ibid., 289-91.
4. Staffordshire Record Office: Q/RPL/5/37A, Land Tax returns, Fenton Culvert, 1781-1815.
5. Staffordshire Advertiser, 9 February 1799: William Pratt, Lane Delph, manufacturer, died Friday sennight [seven-night, i.e. 1 February].
6. The Staffordshire Pottery Directory (Hanley: Allbut, 1802) map and key, No. 110.
7. See note 4.
8. Lewis, op. cit., 17.
9. Ibid., 21.
10. See note 4; D. Edwards Black Basalt: Wedgwood and Contemporary Manufacturers, (Woodbridge: Antique Collectors' Club, 1994) 222: partnership between Felix Pratt and William Coomer dissolved 11 November 1809.
11. A. Meigh Manufacturers of Pottery in the Staffordshire Potteries … 1807 to 1859 (inclusive) from the Rate Books (privately, 1940) 86, 90; Staffordshire Advertiser, 9 March 1816: potworks to be let, long unexpired lease, china or earthenware, apply to Felix Pratt, Lane Delph.
12. Staffordshire Advertiser: 26 June, 28 August 1813; 14 May 1814; 20 May 1815.
13. Staffordshire Advertiser, 9 March 1816.
14. Meigh, op. cit., 90.
15. Allbut, op. cit., No. 105.
16. Staffordshire Advertiser, 5 April 1806: partnership between William Hyatt and George Harrison, manufacturers of earthenware, dissolved 5 March 1806.
17. Meigh, op. cit., 1, 50; Staffordshire Advertiser, 22 March 1806: Josiah Byerley's intended partnership with George Harrison cancelled, Josiah Byerley in business alone at Fenton; 20 October 1810: unexpired lease of Josiah Byerley's potworks at Fenton, and his utensils, for auction; 19 June 1813: Josiah Byerley's creditors receive first dividend.
18. Meigh, op. cit., 54, 90.
19. Staffordshire General & Commercial Directory (Manchester: Parson and Bradshaw, 1818) 109.
20. Royal National and Commercial Directory … of … the Counties of … Stafford … (London: Pigot, 1841) 46.
21. A History of the County of Stafford ed. J.G. Jenkins, multi-vol. (London: Oxford University Press, 1963) viii, 220.
22. S. Andrews Crested China: The History of Heraldic Souvenir Ware (London: Springwood, 1980) 30; S. Levitt Pountneys: The Bristol Pottery at Fishponds 1905-1969 (Bristol: Redcliffe, 1990) 82, 94.
23. See note 21.
24. Staffordshire Advertiser, 8 December 1810.
25. Meigh, op. cit., 92; Staffordshire Advertiser, 4 August 1821: Sarah Weston left the partnership of Felix Pratt, Weston and Co., china manufacturers, Lane Delph on 27 July 1821, Felix Pratt, Thomas Hassall and Thomas Gerrard continued.
26. G.A. Godden Encyclopaedia of British Porcelain Manufacturers (London: Barrie & Jenkins, 1988) 611; Staffordshire Advertiser, 6 April 1833: died 29th [March] at Lane Delph, Thomas Gerrard, china manufacturer, aged 62.
27. Meigh, op. cit., 1, 92.
28. Holden's Triennial Directory for 1805, 1806, 1807 (London, 1805)

252; Holden's Triennial Directory for 1809, 1810, 1811 (London, 1809) 369.
29. Lewis, op. cit., 290.
30. Staffordshire Record Office: Q/RPL/5/38, Land Tax returns, Fenton Vivian, 1781-1831; Meigh, op. cit., 90, 92, 99.
31. Staffordshire Advertiser, 16 April 1836: List of members of the Chamber of Commerce for the Staffordshire Potteries.
32. Staffordshire Advertiser, 13 November 1847.
33. L.L. Jewitt The Ceramic Art of Great Britain … 2 vol. (London: Virtue, 1878) II, 410.
34. L.L. Jewitt The Ceramic Art of Great Britain new edition, revised (New York: Worthington, 1883, rep. Chicheley: Minet, 1971) 555.

Ridgway

1. G.A. Godden Ridgway Porcelains second edition (Woodbridge: Antique Collectors' Club, 1985) contains a very comprehensive account of the Ridgway potteries. A typescript in Hanley Reference Library: A. Shelley 'History of Ridgway' (1971) is also informative.
2. Staffordshire Advertiser, 4 June 1814.
3. Ibid., 19 July 1823.
4. Godden, op. cit., 205, 208: three years prior to partnership with Smith, who died in 1799 after five years' partnership.
5. Staffordshire Advertiser, 23 February 1799: William Smith, earthenware manufacturer and lay preacher died aged 34.
6. Godden, op. cit., 48, 208.
7. Staffordshire Advertiser, 27 October 1821.
8. Ibid., 31 August 1833.
9. Ibid., 9 April 1864.
10. J. Ward The Borough of Stoke-upon-Trent (London: Lewis, 1843, rep. Wakefield: S. R., 1969) 374 notes William Ridgway as being involved in six manufactories.
11. Staffordshire Advertiser, 28 October 1837.
12. J.G. Stradling 'Ridgway in America' in Northern Ceramic Society Newsletter No. 93 (March 1994) 10-11.
13. T.L. Markin 'The Bankruptcy of William Ridgway in 1848' in Journal of the Northern Ceramic Society Vol. 6 (1987) 119-25.
14. Staffordshire Advertiser, 22 April 1848.
15. P. Halfpenny 'Joseph Clementson: "a Potter Remarkable for Energy of Character"', in Northern Ceramic Society Journal Vol. 5 (1984) 177-206, 188.
16. Staffordshire Advertiser, 9 April 1864.
17. Ibid., 30 July 1864, 1 December 1866.
18. Godden, op. cit., 208.
19. Ibid., 48, 209.
20. Staffordshire Advertiser, 4 June 1814.
21. Ibid., 27 September 1856.
22. Ibid., 15 March 1823.
23. Ibid., 31 July 1858.
24. Ibid., 8 December 1860.
25. Godden, op. cit., 51.

Sheridan

1. R. Hampson 'Longton Potters 1700–1865' in Journal of Ceramic History Volume 14 (Stoke-on-Trent: City Museum & Art Gallery, 1990) 91–92, 147– 148; and D. Edwards Black Basalt: Wedgwood and Contemporary Manufacturers (Woodbridge: Antique Collectors' Club, 1994) 230, are the only published accounts of Sheridan.
2. A. Eatwell and A. Werner 'A London Staffordshire Warehouse – 1794–1825' in Journal of the Northern Ceramic Society Volume 8 (1991) 91–124, 100, 101, 102, 115, 123.
3. Edwards, op. cit. 230 has considered Wyllies' accounts with Sheridan in relation to basalt wares.

Shorthose

1. W. Mankowitz & R.G. Haggar The Concise Encyclopedia of Engish Pottery and Porcelain (London: Deutsch, 1957) 201.
2. Hanley Reference Library, EMT 20/Simpson/789: will of John Simpson, 20 December 1785; Staffordshire Advertiser, 31 March 1804.
3. Hanley Reference Library, EMT 13/805. The Heath families of both Burslem and Hanley are referred to in P.W.L. Adams A History of the Adams Family of North Staffordshire … (London: St

Catherine Press, 1914), and also in his *Notes on some North Staffordshire Families ...* (Tunstall: Eardley, 1930); but the relationships are not clear.

4. H. Blakey 'Sun Fire Insurance Polices from the Country Department Policy Registers' in *Northern Ceramic Society Journal Vol. 3, 1978-1979* (1979) 101-48, 104.

5. *The Univeral British Directory* (London: The Patentees, 1790-1798) (the Staffordshire section dated *c.*1795 by mention of the death of Josiah Wedgwood, 3 January 1795) 108; *The Staffordshire Pottery Directory ...* (Hanley: Chester and Mort, *c.*1796) 35.

6. Keele University Library: Wedgwood MSS 31/23290-91.

7. S. Shaw *History of the Staffordshire Potteries; and the Rise and Progress of the Manufacture of Pottery and Porcelain; with References to Genuine Specimens, and Notices of Eminent Potters* (Hanley: privately, 1829, reprinted Newton Abbot: David & Charles, 1970) 138.

8. *The Universal British Directory*, op. cit., 108.

9. *A View of the Staffordshire Potteries* (Burslem: T. Allbutt, 1800); *The Staffordshire Pottery Directory* (Hanley: Allbut (*sic*), 1802).

10. City Museum and Art Gallery, Stoke-on-Trent, Ceramics Department: Enoch Wood Scrapbook, 1 February 1797.

11. *Holden's Triennial Directory for 1805, 1806, 1807* (London, 1805) 252; *Holden's Triennial Directory for 1809, 1810, 1811* (London, 1809) 370.

12. R. Hirsch 'Dutch Decorated English Creamware' in *English Ceramic Circle Transactions Vol. 12 1986* (1986) 265-72, 270, plate 175a.

13. L. Whiter *Spode: A History of the Family, Factory and Wares from 1733 to 1833*, 2nd ed. (London: Barrie & Jenkins, 1978) 46-47.

14. Liverpool Central Library, 380 MD 48: 'Herculaneum Potteries Ledger 1806-1817', p.294.

15. T.A. Lockett 'Minton in 1810' in *Northern Ceramic Society Journal Vol. 4, 1980-81* (1981) 1-36, 31.

16. Ibid., 32.

17. *Staffordshire Advertiser*, 23 March 1811.

18. Hanley Reference Library, EMT 20/Simpson/789: will of John Simpson, 20 December 1785.

19. A. Meigh *Manufacturers of Pottery in the Staffordshire Potteries ... 1807 to 1859 (inclusive) from the Rate Books* (privately, 1940) 6 *passim* to 97.

20. *Staffordshire Advertiser* 30 September 1815, 24 February, 2 March 1816, 13 September 1817.

21. *Staffordshire Advertiser*, 16 August, 27 September 1823.

22. *Parson & Bradshaw's Staffordshire General and Commercial Directory* (Manchester, 1818); *Newcastle and Pottery Directory 1822-23* (Hanley: Allbut, 1822).

23. *Staffordshire Advertiser*, 22 January 1825, 2 January 1830, 17, 24 December 1831, 15 February, 21 March 1840.

24. *Staffordshire Advertiser*, 14 June 1828.

Sowter

1. See H. Lawrence *Yorkshire Pots and Potteries* (Newton Abbot: David & Charles, 1974) 114-16, for the most detailed account of this firm.

2. Ibid., 115-16.

3. A. and A. Cox 'Yorkshire Potteries: Some Personal Notes' in *Northern Ceramic Society Newsletter No. 106*, June 1997, 4-14, 11.

4. Dr G.A. Godden 'Observations on S & Co Marked Felspathic Stonewares' in *Northern Ceramic Society Newsletter No. 107* September 1997, 34-35.

Spode

1. The Spode Manuscripts are deposited at the University of Keele. L. Whiter *Spode: a History of the Family, Factory and Wares from 1733 to 1833* (London: Barrie & Jenkins, 1970) is the definitive work up to 1833, a classic ceramic history. R. Copeland *Spode & Copeland Marks, and other relevant Intelligence* (London: Studio Vista, 1993) includes much more information than its title suggests, for the entire period, 1733-1993, and gives the most recent bibliography. Two specialised works are R. Copeland *Spode's Willow Pattern and other designs after the Chinese* (London: Studio Vista, 1980) and D. Drakard & P. Holdway *Spode Printed Ware* (London: Longman, 1983). The Spode Society publishes *The Spode Society Review* and *The Spode Society Recorder*. P.F.C. Roden 'Josiah Spode (1733-1797) his formative influences and the various Potworks associated with him' in *Journal of the Northern Ceramic Society Volume 14*, (1997) 1-43.

2. Copeland (1993) op. cit., 9.

3. Whiter op. cit., 3.

4. Ibid., 4.

5. S. Shaw *History of the Staffordshire Potteries; and the Rise and Progress of the Manufacture of Pottery and Porcelain; with references to Genuine Specimens, and notices of Eminent Potters* (Hanley: privately, 1829; rep. Newton Abbot: David & Charles, 1970) 215.

6. Whiter op. cit., 5, 12.

7. Ibid., 6.

8. T. Cannon *Old Spode* (London: Werner Laurie, n.d.) 73.

9. Roden op. cit., 19-34.

10. Cannon op. cit., 69-82.

11. Roden op. cit., 19-20, and Whiter op. cit., 211, for an account dated 7-21 September 1771 from Spode and Tomlinson to Josiah and Thomas Wedgwood, for plates, soup and other dishes.

12. Whiter op. cit., 8.

13. Ibid., 12.

14. Ibid., 13.

15. Ibid., 24.

16. Information from P. Roden.

17. A. Meigh *Manufacturers of Pottery in the Staffordshire Potteries ... 1807-1859 from the Rate Books* (privately, 1940) 87, 91: Samuel Spode apparently ceased business between 24 April 1815 and 2 April 1816; *Staffordshire Advertiser*, 1 February 1817: Samuel Spode died 26 January 1817 aged 59.

18. *Staffordshire Advertiser* 21 July 1827: Josiah Spode II died 16 July 1827, aged 72.

19. Whiter op. cit., 76.

20. Whiter op. cit., 76; *Staffordshire Advertiser*, 10 October 1829: died 6 October 1829, aged 52.

21. Whiter, op. cit., 77.

22. Ibid., 209.

23. Ibid., 210.

24. Copeland (1993) op. cit., 27.

25. Ibid., 36.

26. *Tableware International*, October 1995, 11.

27. *The Staffordshire Pottery Directory* (Hanley: Allbut, 1802) map and key, No. 94.

28. Whiter op. cit., 12-13.

29. Ibid., 206.

30. Ibid., 243.

31. Ibid., 209.

32. Ibid., 209.

33. Ibid., 210.

34. Ibid., 16.

35. Ibid., 34.

36. Shaw op. cit., 215.

37. Copeland (1993) op. cit., 130.

38. Ibid., 132.

39. Whiter op. cit., 66-69.

Steel, Daniel

1. R.L. Hobson *Catalogue of the Collection of English Pottery in the ... British Museum* (London: Trustees of the British Museum, 1903) 267.

2. A. Hayden *Chats on English Earthenware* (London: T. Fisher Unwin, 1909, repr. 1912) 282.

3. G.A. Godden, *Encyclopaedia of British Pottery and Porcelain Marks* (London: Barrie & Jenkins, 1964), 595.

4. Wedgwood MS 28409-39, Commonplace Book, 27.

5. *Burslem Parish Registers*, 3 vol. (Stafford: Staffordshire Parish Registers Society, 1913) I, 258, 268; II, 281, 285, 368.

6. *The Staffordshire Pottery Directory* (Hanley: Chester and Mort, n.d, 1796) 41.

7. A. Eatwell and A. Werner, 'A London Staffordshire Warehouse - 1794-1825' in *Journal of the Northern Ceramic Society Vol. 8* (1991) 91-124, 100-01, Steele & Co.

8. Stafford Record Office, Q RPL/5/23 A: Land Tax.
9. *The Staffordshire Pottery Directory* (Hanley: J. Allbut and Son, 1802), map and key: No. 43, Daniel Steel.
10. W. Chaffers *Marks and Monograms on European and Oriental Pottery and Porcelain ...* rev. and ed. Frederick Litchfield, eighth edition (London: Reeves & Turner, 1897) 674.
11. L. Jewitt *The Ceramic Art of Great Britain from Pre-Historic Times down to the Present Day*, 2 vol. (London: Virtue, 1878) II, 279.
12. *Staffordshire Advertiser*, 10 February 1816, 10 May, 27 September 1817.
13. Stafford Record Office, Q RPL/5/23 B, Land Tax; *National Commercial Directory* (Manchester: Pigot, 1822), 477; *The Newcastle and Pottery Directory for 1822-23 ...* (Hanley: Allbut, n.d.), 51.
14. Stafford Record Office, Q RPL/5/23 B: Land Tax; *Staffordshire Advertiser*, 20 December 1828.
15. *New Commercial Directory for ... Staffordshire ... 1828-9*, (Manchester, Pigot, 1828), 726; *National Commercial Directory ... Staffordshire 1830-1*, (Manchester: Pigot, n.d.), 725.
16. Godden, op. cit., 595.
17. *Staffordshire General and Commercial Directory*, (Manchester: Parson & Bradshaw, 1818) 47, 128.
18. Stafford Record Office, Microfiche E 3571/1/23, Burslem Parish Registers, p.296.

Steele, Henry

1. *Staffordshire Advertiser*, 22 July 1837.
2. *Royal National and Commercial Directory ... Staffordshire*, (London: Pigot, 1841).
3. *Staffordshire Advertiser*, 22 June 1822.
4. *Burslem Parish Registers*, 3 vols. (Stafford: Staffordshire Parish Registers Society, 1913) II, 448.
5. G.A. Godden, *Encyclopaedia of British Pottery and Porcelain Marks*, (London: Barrie & Jenkins, 1964) 595.

Swansea

1. L.L. Jewitt *The Ceramic Art of Great Britain*, 2 vol. (London: Virtue, 1878) II, 435-44; W. Turner *The Ceramics of Swansea and Nantgarw* (London: Bemrose, 1897); E.M. Nance *The Pottery & Porcelain of Swansea & Nantgarw* (London: Batsford, 1942, rep. 1985); W.J. Grant-Davidson 'Early Swansea Pottery 1764-1810' in *English Ceramic Circle Transactions Vol. 7, Part 1* (1968) 59-82, plates 72-88; and R. Pugh *Welsh Pottery* (Bath: Towy, n.d., c.1995) 5-40.
2. H.L. Hallesy *The Glamorgan Pottery Swansea 1814-38* (Llandysul, Gomer, 1995).
3. Nance, op. cit., 8, 26.
4. Ibid., 8, 26, 34, 68, 89, 108, 139, 155, 192, 195.
5. Jewitt, op. cit., II, 436.
6. Nance, op. cit., 41.
7. Ibid., 66, plate XXIX.
8. Ibid., 66, plates XXX, XXXI.
9. Ibid., 66.

Swinton

1. H. de la Beche and T. Reeks *Museum of Practical Geology. Catalogue of Specimens illustrative of the Composition and Manufacture of British Pottery and Porcelain ...* London: Museum of Practical Geology, 1855) 165-67.
2. A. Cox and A. Cox *Rockingham Pottery and Porcelain 1745-1842* (London: Faber, 1983) is the most recent general monograph. Their bibliography lists many works on aspects of the subject, but attention is drawn to L. Jewitt, who wrote extensively on the factory in the *Art Journal 1865*, 348, and also in his *The Ceramic Art of Great Britain from Pre-Historic Times down to the Present Day*, 2 vol. (London: Virtue, 1878) I, 495-517; and to A.A. Eaglestone and T.A. Lockett *The Rockingham Pottery* new revised edition (Newton Abbot: David & Charles, 1973).
3. Cox and Cox, op. cit., 50.
4. D.G. Rice, *Rockingham Pottery and Porcelain*, (New York: Praeger Publishers, 1971), Pls.39-46. The cup (Rice's plate 39), in the Victoria and Albert Museum, is accession number 3176-1901.

Unfortunately, the costs for reproduction of this important piece and other objects from the V. & A. collection were prohibitive for the authors.

Taylor, George

1. *Bailey's British Directory for ... 1784* (London, 1784) II, 391. George Taylor does not appear in Directories for 1781 or 1783.
2. *Staffordshire Advertiser*, 24 June 1809: died 16 June, George Taylor, Hanley, manufacturer.
3. Hanley Reference Library, EMT 11/815C, will of George Taylor; R. Edmundson 'Staffordshire Potters insured with the Salop Fire Office 1780-1825' in *Journal of the Northern Ceramic Society Vol. 6, 1987* (1987) 92; *Staffordshire General and Commercial Directory* (Parson and Bradshaw, Manchester, 1818) 75.
4. *Staffordshire Advertiser*, 31 July 1819: partnership dissolved 7 July 1819.
5. A. Meigh *Manufacturers of Pottery in the Staffordshire Potteries ... 1807 to 1859 (inclusive) from the Rate Books* (privately, 1940) 252, 265, 280.
6. Hanley Reference Library, EMT 11/807, 17 September 1807.
7. *Staffordshire Advertiser*, 30 June 1815.
8. Hanley Reference Library, EMT 7/815C: bought out 25 February 1811.
9. Hanley Reference Library, EMT 11/844.
10. Hanley Reference Library, EMT 8/815.
11. *Newcastle and Pottery Directory 1822-23* (Allbut, Hanley, 1822) 87: George Taylor, potter, New Hall Street; George Taylor, warehouseman, Broad Street, Shelton.
12. Meigh, op. cit., 155 *passim* to 193; Edmundson, op. cit., 92.
13. Hanley Reference Library, EMT 7/844B.

Taylor, John

1. *The Staffordshire Pottery Directory* (Chester and Mort, Hanley, c.1796)
2. *Staffordshire Advertiser*, 26 May 1798.
3. H. Blakey 'Sun Fire Insurance Policies from the Country Department Policy Registers' in *Northern Ceramic Society Journal Vol. 3, 1978-1979*, 115, 120.
4. *Staffordshire Advertiser*, 16 January 1802.
5. Ibid., 14 April 1804.
6. Ibid., 19 May, 16 June, 20 October 1810; 2 February 1811.
7. Ibid., 22 March 1817.
8. Ibid., 1 November 1834: J. Stubbs ... declining business.
9. *Holden's Triennial Directory for 1809, 1810, 1811* (Holden, London, 1809).
10. *Newcastle and Pottery Directory 1822-23* (Allbut, Hanley, 1822).
11. *Staffordshire Advertiser*, 29 December 1810; 2 March 1811.
12. Ibid., 1 January 1814.
13. *London and Provincial New Commercial Directory 1822-23* (Pigot, London, 1822).
14. *Staffordshire Advertiser*, 8 March 1823.
15. Ibid., 28 June 1828.

Turner

1. B. Hillier *Master Potters of the Industrial Revolution: The Turners of Lane End* (London: Cory, Adams & Mackay, 1965) is the only monograph on Turners. R. Hampson 'Longton Potters 1700-1865' in *Journal of Ceramic History Vol. 14* (1990) 157-66 gives comprehensive information about the firms. D. Holgate and G. Godden 'The Turner porcelains, c.1786-c.1805' in *Staffordshire Porcelain* ed. G. Godden (London: Granada, 1983) 90-99, cover Turners' porcelain and Turner's Patent wares.
2. Brewood Church, Staffordshire: monumental inscription in churchyard: 'In memory of John Turner of Lane End who departed this life December 21st 1787, aged 49'.
3. Hillier op. cit., 3.
4. Spode MS 932, an agreement to sell the factory site.
5. N. Valpy 'Extracts from 18th Century London Newspapers and Additional Manuscripts, British Library' in *English Ceramic Circle Transactions Vol. 13, Part 1* (1987) 77-95, 92, an advertisement by Turner 16 May 1768.
6. *Baileys British Directory for 1784* (London: 1784) 393.

7. Wedgwood MS 49/29843.
8. S. Shaw *History of the Staffordshire Potteries; and the Rise and Progress of the Manufacture of Pottery and Porcelain; with references to Genuine Specimens, and notices of Eminent Potters* (Hanley: privately,1829; rep. Newton Abbot: David & Charles, 1970) 173.
9. Shaw op. cit., 201.
10. Hillier op. cit., 40-46. Arcanist: a carrier of the secret (or *arcanum*) of the materials and processes used in the manufacture of hard-paste porcelain. (J. Fleming and H. Honour, *The Penguin Dictionary of Decorative Arts* (Harmondsworth; Penguin Books, 1977) 32.
11. J. Howarth 'Andrew Abbott and the Fleet Street Partnerships' in *Journal of the Northern Ceramic Society, Vol. 13* (1996) 75-117, 81-91.
12. *Patents for Inventions. Abridgments of the Specifications relating to Pottery* (London: Commissioners of Patents, 1863) 17: A.D.1800, 9 January - No. 2367.
13. R.G. Haggar *Staffordshire Chimney Ornaments* (London: Phoenix House, 1955) 53.
14. *Staffordshire Advertiser*, 17 November 1804.
15. Ibid., 5 April 1806.
16. Ibid., 5 July 1806.
17. A. Meigh *Manufacturers of Pottery in the Staffordshire Potteries ... 1807-1859 from the Rate Books* (privately, 1940) 1 *passim* to 76.
18. L. Jewitt *The Ceramic Art of Great Britain from Pre-Historic Times down to the Present Day*, 2 vol. (London, Virtue, 1878) II, 186-87.
19. *Staffordshire Advertiser*, 17 September 1814.
20. Ibid., 12 August 1815.
21. Ibid., 3 July 1824.
22. Meigh op. cit., 157 *passim* to 250; *Staffordshire Advertiser* 10 October, 1829.
23. *Staffordshire Advertiser*, 11 July 1835.
24. P.F.C. Roden 'Josiah Spode (1733-1797) his formative influences and the various Potworks associated with him' in *Journal of the Northern Ceramic Society Volume 14*, (1997) 10.
25. Spode MS 932.
26. Ibid.
27. *The Staffordshire Pottery Directory* (Hanley: Allbut, 1802) map and key, No. 136.
28. William Salt Library, Stafford: D 1798/287; *Staffordshire Advertiser*, 12 February, 1803.
29. See note 17.
30. Allbut, op. cit., No. 117.
31. See note 22.
32. See note 19.
33. See note 5.
34. N. Valpy 'Extracts from 18th Century London Newspapers' in *English Ceramic Circle Transactions Vol. 12, Part 2* (1985) 161-88, 170: an advertisement by Turner, 6, 10 January 1774.
35. Hillier op. cit., 57.
36. See note 11.
37. See note 6.
38. See note 7.
39. Wedgwood MS 11/29501.
40. Hampson, op. cit., 160.
41. D. Hollens 'Some Researches into the Makers of Dry Bodies' in *English Ceramic Circle Transactions Vol. 11 Part 3* (1983) 222-29, 226.
42. Howarth, op. cit., 109-11.
43. Hillier op. cit., 69-70.
44. *Staffordshire Advertiser*, 13 June 1807. William Turner's 1807-12 works at Foley could be described as at 'Lane End'.
45. There is a basalt 'cane' teapot from the Mayer collection in the Liverpool Museum marked *Wedgwood & Bentley* with *three* pads on the base.

Twemlow

1. F.R. Twemlow *The Twemlows, their wives and their homes* (Wolverhampton: privately, 1910) chapter III.
2. Ibid., chapter IX.
3. Ibid.
4. *Letters of Josiah Wedgwood 1762 to 1770* ed. K.E. Farrar

(privately, 1903, repr. Manchester: Morten, n.d. *c.* 1973) 264.
5. Twemlow op. cit., chapter IX.
6. D. Edwards *Black Basalt: Wedgwood and Contemporary Manufacturers* (Woodbridge: Antique Collectors' Club, 1994) 253.
7. *Staffordshire Advertiser* 15 April, 29 July 1797, 28 April 1798.
8. H. Blakey 'Sun Fire Insurance Policies from the County Department Policy Registers' in *Northern Ceramic Society Journal Volume 3*, 1978–79, 106.
9. *Staffordshire Advertiser* 19 January 1799.

W(★★★)

1. *C.E. Schreiber Collection: Catalogue of English Porcelain, Earthenware, Enamels, &c., collected by Charles Schreiber, Esq., M.P., and The Lady Charlotte Elizabeth Schreiber, and presented to The South Kensington Museum in 1884* (London: South Kensington Museum, 1885) 136, Fig. 120.
2. B. Rackham *Victoria and Albert Museum Department of Ceramics: Catalogue of English Porcelain Earthenware Enamels and Glass collected by Charles Schreiber Esq. M.P. and The Lady Charlotte Elizabeth Schreiber and presented to the Museum in 1884* Volume II *Earthenware* (London: Board of Education, 1930) 64, 67, plate 49.
3. G.A. Godden *Encyclopaedia of British Porcelain Manufacturers* (London: Barrie & Jenkins, 1988) 743-47.
4. L.A. Compton with R. Meldrum 'W(★★★) Revived' in *Northern Ceramic Society Newsletter No. 103* September 1996, 30-39, 32.
5. D. Darlington 'W(★★★) - a Mark of Reference' in *Northern Ceramic Society Journal Vol. 4 1980-81* (1984) 113-25; *Staffordshire Porcelain* ed. G. Godden (London: Granada, 1983) 556-69; and see note 3.
6. J. Robinson et al., *William Billingsley (1758-1828)* (Lincoln: Usher Gallery, 1996) 35.
7. Godden, op. cit., 746.
8. Ibid., 744.
9. R. Hampson 'Longton Potters 1700-1865' in *Journal of Ceramic History Vol. 14* (1990) 1-232, 146, 142.
10. Hanley Reference Library: West of Trent Rate Book 4th August 1807, 70; A. Meigh *Manufacturers of Pottery in the Staffordshire Potteries ... for the years 1807 to 1859 (inclusive) from the Rate Books* (privately, 1940).
11. *Holden's Triennial Directory for 1809, 1810, 1811* (London, 1809).
12. R. Hampson 'North Staffordshire Potters in 1811' in *Northern Ceramic Society Newsletter No. 54* (June 1984) 33-37, 35.
13. Hanley Reference Library: Adams Papers, EMT 11/811.
14. *Staffordshire Advertiser*, 7 September 1816.
15. Ibid., 6 October 1821, 24 October 1835.
16. *The Staffordshire Pottery Directory* (Chester and Mort, Hanley, n.d., 1796); *Staffordshire Advertiser*, 22 September 1798.
17. *The Staffordshire Pottery Directory* (Allbut, Hanley, 1802) map and key, No. 45, see Appendix 1.
18. *Staffordshire Advertiser*, 8 May 1802.
19. Ibid., 2 October 1802.
20. Ibid., 29 December 1821.
21. *Holden's Triennial Directory for 1805, 1806, 1807* (London, 1805); *Holden's Triennial Directory for 1809, 1810, 1811* (London, 1809); *Staffordshire General and Commercial Directory* (Parson and Bradshaw, Manchester, 1818).
22. G.W. Rhead *British Pottery Marks* (London: Scott, Greenwood & Son, 1910) 253; G.A. Godden *Encyclopaedia of British Pottery and Porcelain Marks* (London: Barrie & Jenkins, 1964) 598.
23. Parson and Bradshaw, op. cit., 75.

Warburton

1. Wedgwood MS: 25/18263.
2. S. Shaw *History of the Staffordshire Potteries ... * (Hanley: privately, 1829; repr. Newton Abbot: David & Charles, 1970) 207.
3. *Bailey's Western & Midland Directory ... for ... 1783* (Birmingham: 1783); *Bailey's British Directory 1784*, multi-vol. (London: 1784) II; *The Staffordshire Pottery Directory* (Hanley: Chester and Mort, n.d., *c.*1796).
4. H. Blakey 'Fire Insurance and Ceramic History - including extracts from the Sun Fire Office Policy Registers: 1782-1793'

in *Journal of the Northern Ceramic Society Vol.10 1993* (1993) 161-97, 185.

5. *Staffordshire Advertiser*, 22 November 1800.

6. *Staffordshire Advertiser*, 17 November 1827, auction of John Warburton's utensils, etc., declining business.

7. D. Holgate *New Hall* (London: Faber, 1987)18-20.

8. *Staffordshire Advertiser*, 21 April 1832, auction of house previously John Warburton's and potworks at Cobridge, now occupied by William Cope.

9. Hanley Reference Library, SA MO 1.14(b): 24/25 December 1796; 25 August 1802.

10. R. Edmundson 'Staffordshire Potters insured with the Salop Fire Office 1780-1825' in *Journal of the Northern Ceramic Society Vol.6 1987* (1987) 81-93, 88.

11. *Staffordshire Advertiser*, 3 April 1802.

12. Ibid., 30 January 1813.

13. Ibid., 30 May 1818, died, Robert Blackwell; D. Edwards *Black Basalt: Wedgwood and Contemporary Manufacturers* (Woodbridge: Antique Collectors' Club, 1994) 261; *Newcastle and Pottery Directory 1822-23* (Hanley: Allbut, 1822) 56: Wood, Enoch jun. ... house Bleak Hill.

14. B. Woodcroft *Alphabetical Index of Patentees of Inventions ...* (1854, rep. New York: Kelly, 1969) 594, patent No. 3304, 13 February 1810.

15. Edwards, op. cit., 260.

16. P.W.L. Adams *A History of the Adams Family ...*(London: St Catherine Press, 1914) Add. & Corr., C, p.287-88.

17. *Staffordshire Advertiser*, 17 February 1855.

18. Edwards, op. cit., 205-07.

19. A. Mountford 'Thomas Whieldon's Manufactory at Fenton Vivian' in *English Ceramic Circle Transactions Vol.8 1972* (1972) 164-82, 166-67.

20. W. Mankowitz and R. Haggar *The Concise Encyclopedia of English Pottery and Porcelain* (London: Deutsch, 1957) 230-31.

21. Adams, op. cit., 137-38, 284.

22. E. Adams 'The Bow Insurances and related Matters' in *English Ceramic Circle Transactions Vol. 9 1973* (1973) 67-108, 75, 106.

23. Shaw, op. cit., 207; N.Valpy 'Extracts from 18th Century London Newspapers' in *English Ceramic Circle Transactions Vol. 12 1985* (1985) 161-88, 168.

24. *Bailey's Northern Directory 1781* (London: 1781); *Bailey's Western & Midland Directory ...for ... 1783* (Birmingham: 1783); L.H. Mero *Chronicle of Our Heritage: History of some Harrison, Harris and connected Families* (Utica, Ky, USA: privately, 1995) 80, 90, quoting Newcastle-under-Lyme Manor Court proceedings, 21 July 1788, where Joseph Warburton, potter, surrendered potworks etc., in Cliff Bank to John Harrison the younger.

25. T.A. Lockett 'Minton in 1810' in *Northern Ceramic Society Journal Vol. 4 1980-81* (1981) 1-36, 31: Quarries (tiles) bought from James Warburton, Cobridge; Directories 1818, 1822; *Staffordshire Advertiser* 29 December 1827, died Christmas Day at Hot Lane, James Warburton, common ware manufacturer; *National Commercial Directory for 1830-31* (London: Pigot, 1830): Warburton, Mary, coarse (ware), Hot Lane.

26. R.C. Bell *Tyneside Pottery* (London: Studio Vista, 1971) 113.

27. R. Morley 'The Enigma of the Leeds Pottery's Co-partnership Shares' in *Journal of the Northern Ceramic Society Vol. 6 1987* (1987) 23-48, 42-43.

28. R.G. Haggar *The Concise Encyclopedia of Continental Pottery and Porcelain* (London: Deutsch, 1960) 242.

Wedgwood & Co.

1. K. Niblett 'A Useful Partner - Thomas Wedgwood 1734-1788' in *Northern Ceramic Society Journal Vol. 5 1984*, 1-22, 1.

2. Wedgwood MS: 13/2427.

3. Wedgwood MSS: 13/2420-22.

4. City Museum and Art Gallery, Stoke-on-Trent: Enoch Wood's Scrapbook, Vol.II, 18 February 1826, letter from Ralph Wedgwood to Enoch Wood.

5. Wedgwood MS: W/M 1460.

6. Wedgwood MS: 50/29975.

7. J.C. Wedgwood *A History of the Wedgwood Family* (London: St

Catherine Press, 1908) 210. On page 216, J.C. Wedgwood acknowledged that J.G.E. Wedgwood, a descendant of Ralph Wedgwood, was particularly responsible for J.C.W.'s Chapter X on 'The Wedgwoods of London and Dumbarton', where this information first appeared, and it is assumed that J.G.E.W. was the source.

8. M. Holdaway 'The Wares of Ralph Wedgwood' in *English Ceramic Circle Transactions Vol.12, Part 3 1986*, 255-64, Plates 154-68, *passim*.

9. J.C. Wedgwood op. cit., 207; J.C. Wedgwood and J.G.E. Wedgwood *Wedgwood Pedigrees ...* (Kendal: Wilson, 1925) 135-36.

10. R. Reilly *Wedgwood* 2 vol. (London: Macmillan, 1989) I, 105.

11. Wedgwood MSS: 91/16704-32.

12. Wedgwood MSS: 14/13638, 91/16733.

13. Wedgwood MS: 39/28404.

14. H. Blakey 'Fire Insurance and Ceramic History - including extracts from the Sun Fire Office Policy Registers: 1782-1793' in *Journal of the Northern Ceramic Society Vol. 10 1993*, 161-97, 186.

15. Wedgwood MS: 14/13642.

16. N.Valpy 'Extracts from the Daily Advertiser and Additional Manuscripts, Department of Manuscripts, British Museum' in *English Ceramic Circle Transactions Vol. 14, Part 1 1990*, 106-17, 106.

17. R. Edmundson 'Staffordshire Potters insured with the Salop Fire Office 1780-1825' in *Journal of the Northern Ceramic Society Vol. 6 1987*, 81-93, 87.

18. H. Blakey 'Ralph Wedgwood: Decline and Bankruptcy in Staffordshire and Arrival in Yorkshire' in *Northern Ceramic Society Newsletter No. 53,* March 1984, 13-17, 13.

19. N.Valpy 'Extracts from the Daily Advertiser 1792-1795' in *English Ceramic Circle Transactions Vol. 4, Part 2 1991*, 228-34, 230.

20. H. Blakey 'Ralph Wedgwood's Steam Engine' in *Northern Ceramic Society Newsletter No. 73,* March 1989, 10-11, 10.

21. *Staffordshire Advertiser*, 29 April 1797; commission appointed 4 April 1797, ibid., 24 November 1804.

22. L. Jewitt *The Ceramic Art of Great Britain ...* 2 vol. (London: Virtue, 1878) I, 490.

23. *Staffordshire Advertiser*, 17 June 1797.

24. D. Edwards *Black Basalt: Wedgwood and Contemporary Manufacturers* (Woodbridge: Antique Collectors' Club, 1994) 262: auction sale notice for 17 May 1798.

25. Wedgwood MS: 56/31532.

26. H. Lawrence *Yorkshire Pots and Potteries* (Newton Abbot: David & Charles, 1974) 148.

27. Wedgwood MSS: 56/31411, 56/31415 and 56/31532, page 14.

28. *Staffordshire Advertiser*, 8 December 1804.

29. *Patents for Inventions: Abridgments of the Specifications relating to Pottery*, ed. B.Woodcroft (London: Commissioners for Patents, 1863) 14-15.

30. Wedgwood MSS: 36/27837, 56/31411-31415.

31. J.C. Wedgwood op. cit., 215.

Whitehaven

1. F. Sibson *The History of the West Cumberland Potteries* (Hong Kong: privately, 1991) 73, quoting *The Cumberland Pacquet*.

2. P.C.D. Brears *The English Country Pottery Its History and Techniques* (Newton Abbot: David & Charles, 1971) 172; Sibson, op. cit., *passim*.

3. Sibson, op. cit., 42, 82, 87.

Whitehead

1. Wedgwood MSS: 30/22572-99, 12/2289-93.

2. Public Record Office: DL30 507/26, will of C.C. Whitehead.

3. Wedgwood MSS: 12/2274-80.

4. S. Shaw *History of the Staffordshire Potteries; and the Rise and Progress of the Manufacture of Pottery and Porcelain; with References to Genuine Specimens, and Notices of Eminent Potters* (Hanley: for the author, 1829, rep. Newton Abbot: David & Charles, 1970) 44, 210.

5. Hanley Reference Library: EMT 8/790, 7/868D, 11/791B, 11/819B & C.

6. Public Record Office: DL 507/21, 12 May 1776.

7. Wedgwood MSS: 12/2281-88.

8. Wedgwood MSS: 12/2269-73.
9. *Staffordshire Advertiser*, 30 April 1803, 15 September 1804.
10. A. Meigh *Manufacturers of Pottery in the Staffordshire Potteries ... 1807 to 1859 (inclusive) from the Rate Books* (privately, 1940) 95, 96, 106, 109; *Staffordshire General and Commercial Directory* (Manchester: Parson and Bradshaw, 1818) 77: Whitehead, Christopher (executors of) earthenware manufacturers, Broad Street, Shelton.
11. *Staffordshire Advertiser*, 10 January 1818.
12. Wedgwood MS: 30/22596.
13. R. Edmundson 'Staffordshire Potters insured with the Salop Fire Office 1780-1825' in *Journal of the Northern Ceramic Society Vol. 6* (1987) 81-93, 87.
14. G.A. Godden *Encyclopaedia of British Porcelain Manufacturers* (London: Barrie & Jenkins, 1988) 765.
15. *James and Charles Whitehead manufacturers Hanley Staffordshire* int. R. Haggar (Bletchley: Drakard, n.d., *c.*1973).
16. *Staffordshire Advertiser*, 21 April 1810.

Wolfe
1. T. Markin has written extensively on Thomas Wolfe and his enterprises in *Northern Ceramic Society Newsletters 48, 52, 55, 58* and *63*; and in *Journal of the Northern Ceramic Society Vols. 7, 9* and *11*.
2. *Bailey's British Directory for 1784: Vol. II, The Western Directory* (London: 1784) 392.
3. *The Staffordshire Pottery Directory* (Hanley: Allbut, 1802) map and key, Nos. 101 and 102 (Appendix 1).
4. T.A. Lockett 'Early Davenport Wares – Recent Discoveries' in *English Ceramic Circle Vol. 12*, 139-55, 139.
5. B. Watney 'Four Groups of Porcelain Possibly Liverpool, Parts 3 and 4' in *English Ceramic Circle Transactions Vol. 5*, 42-52, 51.
6. Ibid., 50.
7. J. Ward *The Borough of Stoke-upon-Trent ...* (London: Lewis, 1843, rep. East Ardsley: SR Publishers, 1969) 502; A. Smith *The Illustrated Guide to Liverpool Herculaneum Pottery 1796-1840* (London: Barrie & Jenkins, 1970) 96.
8. T. Markin 'Procurement of Raw Materials by the Spode-Wolfe Partnerships' in *Journal of the Northern Ceramic Society Vol. 11* 1994, 1-18, 1, 9.
9. Allbut, op. cit., No. 102.
10. *Holden's Triennial Directory for 1805, 1806, 1807* (London: 1805) 252.
11. *Staffordshire Advertiser*, 6 November 1813.
12. T. Markin 'Thomas Wolfe and his Associates Part II' in *Northern Ceramic Society Newsletter No. 55* 1984, 15-22, 16-19.
13. *Staffordshire Advertiser*, 24 May 1817.
14. Markin, op. cit., 19.
15. *Staffordshire Advertiser*, 24 October 1818.
16. Ibid., 20 July 1819.
17. Ibid., 29 March 1823.
18. P.W.L. Adams *A History of the Adams Family of North Staffordshire ...* (London: St Catherine Press, 1914) supplement III, 6.
19. *Staffordshire Advertiser*, 7 March 1857.

Wood
1. F. Falkner *The Wood Family of Burslem* (London: Chapman & Hall, 1912, repr. East Ardsley: EP Publishing, 1972); R.G. Haggar *Staffordshire Chimney Ornaments* (London: Phoenix, 1955) 31-40, 63-69; G.A. Godden *Encyclopaedia of British Porcelain Manufacturers* (London: Barrie & Jenkins, 1988) 787-93; P. Halfpenny *English Earthenware Figures 1740-1840* (Woodbridge: Antique Collectors' Club, 1991) 58-95; M.F. Goodby 'The Lost Collection of Enoch Wood' in *Journal of the Northern Ceramic Society Vol. 9* 1992, 123-51.
2. *Burslem Parish Registers*, 3 vol. (Stafford: Staffordshire Parish Registers Society, 1913) I, 264.
3. Falkner op. cit., 34, 39, 44.
4. Ibid., 40-43; 'A Miscellany of Pieces' in *English Ceramic Circle Transactions Vol. 8, Part I* (1971) 17 and Plate 15a.
5. Halfpenny op. cit., 71.
6. Wedgwood MS: WM 1459.

7. City Museum and Art Gallery, Stoke-on-Trent, Ceramics Department: Sales Ledger, John Wood of Brownhills, 1783-1787, p.34. The item is dated 'Nov' although it is interpolated between entries for 20 and 19 (*sic*) September 1783.
8. J.E. Norton *Guide to the National and Provincial Directories of England and Wales, excluding London, published before 1856* (London: Royal Historical Society, 1950) 30-31.
9. W. Mankowitz & R.G. Haggar *The Concise Encyclopedia of English Pottery and Porcelain* (London: Deutsch, 1957) 250.
10. Wedgwood MSS: WM 1459, 12/11496.
11. Wedgwood MS: 12/11497.
12. Staffordshire Record Office: Q RPL/5/23A, Land Tax records for Burslem, 1781-1809.
13. Falkner, op. cit., 42, quoting Enoch Wood's memorandum.
14. S. Shaw *History of the Staffordshire Potteries ...* (Hanley: privately, 1829, rep. Newton Abbot: David & Charles, 1970) 223.
15. Halfpenny, op. cit., 82.
16. *Staffordshire Advertiser*, 18 July, 5 September 1801, 6 November 1802.
17. Shaw, op. cit., 30; J. Ward *The Borough of Stoke-upon-Trent ...* (London: Lewis, 1843, repr. East Ardsley: SR Publishers, 1969) 259.
18. City Museum and Art Gallery, Stoke-on-Trent, Ceramics Department: Enoch Wood Scrapbook, Vol. I, memo. on plan; Wedgwood MSS: 96/17838, 12/2249, 28/20504.
19. Wedgwood MSS: 28/20500, 12/2238.
20. *A History of the County of Stafford* ed. J.G. Jenkins multi-vol. (London: Oxford University Press) VIII (1963) 112, 135.
21. H. Blakey 'Fire Insurance and Ceramic History – including extracts from the Sun Fire Office Policy Registers: 1782-1793' in *Journal of the Northern Ceramic Society Vol. 10* 1993, 161-97, 188.
22. Blakey, op. cit., 193.
23. Wedgwood MS: 28/20506.
24. Wedgwood MSS: 10/2348, 12/2243, 28/20508-10, 20576.
25. Ward, op. cit., 259.
26. Wedgwood MSS: 12/2328-33, 28/20688-90.
27. Falkner, op. cit., 61, plate XXXIX, illus. No. 128.
28. Cheshire Record Office: DCN 7, box 31, indenture of sale 18/19 May 1818.
29. Wedgwood MS: 12/2252.
30. H. Blakey 'Sun Fire Insurance Policies from the Country Department Policy Registers' in *Northern Ceramic Society Journal Vol. 3*, 1978-1979, 101-48, 119.
31. *Staffordshire Advertiser*, 30 November 1799.
32. *Holden's Triennial Directory for 1805, 1806, 1807* (Holden, London, 1805).
33. *A History of the County of Stafford* ed. J.G. Jenkins multi-vol (London: Oxford University Press) VIII (1963) 108; Ward, op. cit., 260.
34. Falkner, op. cit., 76.
35. Ibid.
36. Cheshire Record Office: DCN 7, box 30, draft agreement of co-partnership, 1841.
37. Wedgwood MS: 28/20526.
38. D. Edwards *Black Basalt: Wedgwood and Contemporary Manufacturers* (Woodbridge: Antique Collectors' Club, 1994) 271.
39. British Sessional Papers 1833 Vol. XX, House of Commons, Factories Inquiry Commissioners, First Report, B2, 13.
40. Wedgwood MSS: 33/25219-77.
41. Falkner, op. cit., 76, states 1818-1835, but *Staffordshire Advertiser*, 29 December 1821 shows still owned then by Breeze, and lately occupied by W. Stanley.
42. Ward, op. cit., 260.
43. See note 36.
44. *Staffordshire Advertiser*, 22 August 1840.
45. Ibid., 16 August 1845.
46. Ibid., 13 December 1845.
47. Ibid., 14 February, 7 March, 25 April, 2, 30 May, 29 August, 13 September 1846; 30 March, 29 June, 9 November 1850.
48. Ibid., 5 July 1851; W.P. Jervis *Rough Notes on Pottery* (Newark, New Jersey: privately, 1896) 27-28.
49. *Staffordshire Advertiser*, 13 March, 21 August 1852.
50. Ibid., 19 June 1852.

CHAPTER IX
SOME CONTINENTAL MANUFACTURERS

Nyon, Switzerland

1. Hilde Bobbink-de Wilde, *Porcelaines De Nyon* (Geneva: Christian Braillard Publisher (n.d.).

S & G

1. W.B. Honey 'Fallacies and Mistaken Attributions in English Ceramic Studies' in *English Ceramic Circle Transactions No. 10, Vol. 2* (1948) 240-47, 245.
2. L. Jewitt *The Ceramic Art of Great Britain,* 2 vol. (London: Virtue, 1878) I, 161-62.
3. [C.E. Schreiber] *Schreiber Collection. Catalogue of English Porcelain, Earthenware, Enamels, &c., collected by Charles Schreiber, Esq., M.P., and The Lady Charlotte Elizabeth Schreiber, and presented to The South Kensington Museum in 1884* (London: Eyre and Spottiswood, 1885) 133, 135.
4. B. Rackham *Catalogue of English Porcelain Earthenware Enamels and Glass collected by Charles Schreiber Esq. M.P. and The Lady Charlotte Elizabeth Schreiber and presented to the Museum in 1884,* 3 vols. (London: Victoria and Albert Museum, 1930) II, 112.
5. H. Clay 'Isleworth Pottery' in *The Burlington Magazine for Connoisseurs Vol. xlix* July-December 1926, 83-85.
6. W.B. Honey *European Ceramic Art from the end of the Middle Ages to about 1815* (London: Faber, 1952) 79, referring to G.E. Pazaurek *Steingut: Formgebung und Geschichte* (Stuttgart, 1927).
7. G.A. Godden *Godden's Guide to European Porcelain* (London: Barrie & Jenkins, 1993) 261, 269, 319.

Sarreguemines

1. Information about this manufacturer is derived from J. Kybalová *European Creamware* (London: Hamlyn, 1989) 83, 87, 89; E. Cameron *Encyclopedia of Pottery & Porcelain, The 19th & 20th Centuries* (London: Faber, 1986) 102; the Musée de Sarreguemines; and A.-M. Marien- Dugardin, *Faiences Fines* (Bruxelles: Musées Royaux D'Art et D'Histoires, 1961) 58, 59.
2. Cameron, op. cit., 294.
3. R. Reilly *Wedgwood* 2 vol. (London: Macmillan, 1989) II, 78.

Sèvres

1. This summary is from R.G. Haggar *The Concise Encyclopedia of Continental Pottery and Porcelain* (London: Deutsch, 1960); *The History of Porcelain* ed. P. Atterbury (London: Orbis,1982); E. Svend and G. de Bellaigue *Sèvres Porcelain: Vincennes and Sèvres 1740-1800* (London: Faber, 1987); and G.A. Godden *Godden's Guide to European Porcelain* (London: Barrie & Jenkins, 1993).
2. Aileen Dawson, *French Porcelain: A Catalogue of the British Museum Collection* (London: British Museum Press, 1994), 191.

APPENDIX 2
TERMINOLOGY

1. T. Lakin *Potting, Enamelling and Glass Staining. The Valuable Receipts of the late Mr Thomas Lakin ...* (Leeds: privately, 1824) Index, section I.
2. *Pigot & Co's New Commercial Directory for ... Staffordshire ... for 1828-9* (London: Pigot, 1828); *Pigot's National Commercial Directory of Staffordshire 1830* (London: Pigot, 1830).
3. *Staffordshire Advertiser,* 1 December 1860.
4. S. Shaw *History of the Staffordshire Potteries ...* (Hanley: privately, 1829, repr. Newton Abbot: David & Charles, 1970) 122, 160; *The Chemistry of ... Porcelain, Glass and Pottery* (London: Lewis, 1837, repr. London: Scott, Greenwood, 1900) 458.
5. Shaw, 1837, op. cit., 458.
6. Ibid., 462-63.
7. A.R. Mountford 'Documents relating to English ceramics of the 18th & 19th centuries' in *Journal of Ceramic History No. 8* (1975) 3-41, 11.
8. Ibid.
9. 'A Manufacturer [C. Simpson]' *The Ruin of Potters, and the Way to avoid it ...* (Lane-End: privately, 1804).
10. G.L. Miller 'George M. Coates, Pottery Merchant of Philadelphia, 1817-1831' in *Winterthur Portfolio 19,* 37-49, 42-43.
11. Flintshire Record Office, D/HC/C/47.
12. W.H. Warburton *The History of Trade Union Organisation in the North Staffordshire Potteries* (London, Allen & Unwin, 1931) 29-32.
13. *Staffordshire Advertiser,* 2 April, 5 November 1825, 11 March 1826.
14. *The Selected Letters of Josiah Wedgwood* ed. A. Finer and G. Savage (London: Cory, Adams & Mackay, 1965) 231, 236.
15. *Staffordshire Advertiser,* 13 June 1807.
16. R. Pomfret 'John and Richard Riley China & Earthenware Manufacturers' in *Journal of Ceramic History Volume 13* (1988) 'Page 45'.
17. A. Cox and A. Cox *Rockingham Pottery and Porcelain 1745-1842* (London: Faber, 1983) 246-48.
18. Shaw, 1829, op. cit., 225-26.
19. *The Popular Encyclopedia* multi-vol. (Glasgow: Blackie) II, Part I (1836) 192.
20. H. de la Beche and T. Reeks *Catalogue of Specimens in the Museum of Practical Geology ... of British Pottery and Porcelain ...* 2nd ed. (London: HMSO, 1871) 192.
21. E.g. *Stonewares & Stone chinas of Northern England to 1851* ed. T.A. Lockett and P.A. Halfpenny (City Museum and Art Gallery, Stoke-on-Trent, 1982) *passim.*
22. *Staffordshire Advertiser,* 13 June 1807.

Index

><+◆>-O-<◆+><

Numbers in **bold** type refer to pages for illustrations or captions